TORN ASUNDER

The David J. Weber Series in the New Borderlands History

Andrew R. Graybill and Benjamin H. Johnson, editors

EDITORIAL BOARD

Juliana Barr
Sarah Carter
Maurice Crandall
Kelly Lytle Hernández
Cynthia Radding
Samuel Truett

The study of borderlands—places where different peoples meet and no one polity reigns supreme—is undergoing a renaissance. The David J. Weber Series in the New Borderlands History publishes works from both established and emerging scholars that examine borderlands from the precontact era to the present. The series explores contested boundaries and the intercultural dynamics surrounding them and includes projects covering a wide range of time and space within North America and beyond, including both Atlantic and Pacific worlds.

Published with support provided by the William P. Clements Center for Southwest Studies at Southern Methodist University in Dallas, Texas.

A complete list of books published in the David J. Weber Series in the New Borderlands History is available at https://uncpress.org/series/david-j-weber-series-in-the-new-borderlands-history.

TORN ASUNDER

REPUBLICAN CRISES AND CIVIL WARS —— IN THE —— UNITED STATES AND MEXICO, 1848–1867

Erika Pani

THE UNIVERSITY OF NORTH CAROLINA PRESS
CHAPEL HILL

© 2025 The University of North Carolina Press
All rights reserved

Designed by April Leidig
Set in Warnock by Copperline Book Services, Inc.

Manufactured in the United States of America

Cover art: *Left: El requiebro* by José Agustín Arrieta, c. 1850. Courtesy of Wikimedia Commons. *Right:* Detail from *Battle of Cold Harbor* by Kurz and Allison, c. 1888. Courtesy of the Library of Congress.

Library of Congress Cataloging-in-Publication Data
Names: Pani, Erika, author.
Title: Torn asunder : Republican crises and civil wars in the United States and Mexico, 1848–1867 / Erika Pani.
Other titles: David J. Weber series in the new borderlands history.
Description: Chapel Hill : The University of North Carolina Press, [2025] | Series: The David J. Weber series in the new borderlands history | Includes bibliographical references and index.
Identifiers: LCCN 2025030749 | ISBN 9781469689074 (cloth ; alk. paper) | ISBN 9781469689081 (paperback ; alk. paper) | ISBN 9781469689098 (epub) | ISBN 9781469689104 (pdf)
Subjects: LCSH: United States—Politics and government—1845–1861. | United States—History—Civil War, 1861–1865. | Mexico—Politics and government—1821–1861. | Mexico—History—European intervention, 1861–1867. | United States—Relations—Mexico. | Mexico—Relations—United States. | BISAC: HISTORY / United States / 19th Century | HISTORY / United States / Civil War Period (1850–1877)
Classification: LCC E415.7 .P36 2025
LC record available at https://lccn.loc.gov/2025030749

For product safety concerns under the European Union's General Product Safety Regulation (EU GPSR), please contact gpsr@mare-nostrum.co.uk or write to the University of North Carolina Press and Mare Nostrum Group B.V., Mauritskade 21D, 1091 GC Amsterdam, The Netherlands.

To my brother Sebastián (1978–2019).

For courage, large-heartedness, and laughs.

CONTENTS

List of Illustrations ix

Acknowledgments xi

Introduction 1

PART ONE
Republics Break Down

CHAPTER ONE
1848:
Continental Crisis 19

CHAPTER TWO
Seismic Hazards:
The Coming of Civil War 45

PART TWO
In the Laboratory of Politics

CHAPTER THREE
Revolutionary Reaction:
Confederate America and Conservative Mexico 75

CHAPTER FOUR
Radical Chemistry:
The US Union and Mexico's Constitutional Republic 103

PART THREE
To Win the War

CHAPTER FIVE
The Righteousness of Our Cause 131

CHAPTER SIX
Men and Money 171

PART FOUR
Putting the Republic Back Together Again

CHAPTER SEVEN
From War to Normalization:
North America Reconfigured 207

Epilogue.
The Republic, Restored and Reconstructed 231

Notes 239

Bibliography 289

Index 331

ILLUSTRATIONS

Diego Rivera, *Civil War* panel, *Portrait of America*, 1933 xiv

José Clemente Orozco, *La Reforma y la caída del Imperio*, 1948 2

Seal of the Confederate States of America, 1862 78

Crest of the Mexican Second Empire, 1865 79

Brownsville, 1863 159

Battle of Pea Ridge, 1866 169

Zacapoaxtlas on parade, 1962 170

José Agustín Arrieta, *El requiebro*, c. 1850 189

Casimiro Castro, *Chinacos during the Reform War*, 1855 190

Cartoon, Philip Sheridan crosses the Río Grande, 1865 225

Cartoon, Uncle Sam intimidates Napoléon III and Maximilian, c. 1865 227

Jefferson Davis released from prison, 1869 235

Maximilian's cadaver, 1867 236

ACKNOWLEDGMENTS

IT TOOK ME A VERY LONG TIME to write "the North American book." I incurred a correspondingly extensive list of debts along the way. I can only acknowledge them here; settling them would prove impossible. My thinking about how—and why—to reconstruct and interpret the past has profited immensely from sometimes decades-long conversations with José Antonio Aguilar, Cath Andrews, Luis Barrón, Roberto Breña, Jordi Canal, Elisa Cárdenas, Brian Connaughton, Romana Falcón, Will Fowler, Fausta Gantús, Daniela Gleizer, Aurora Gómez Galvarriato, Gerardo Gurza, Clara E. Lida, Andrés Lira, Soledad Loaeza, María Dolores Lorenzo, Cecilia Noriega, Carlos Marichal, Óscar Mazín, Jean Meyer, Pablo Mijangos, Marco Palacios, Pablo Piccato, Antonia Pi-Suñer, Alicia Salmerón, José Antonio Serrano, Paolo Riguzzi, Ariel Rodríguez Kuri, Beatriz Rojas, Rafael Rojas, Valeria Sánchez Michel, Rebecca Scott, Jay Sexton, Anne Staples, Regina Tapia, Mauricio Tenorio, Marcela Terrazas, Josefina Z. Vázquez, Pablo Yankelevich, Cecilia Zuleta, and the sorely missed Enrique Florescano, Bernardo García Martínez, Nicole Giron, Pilar Gonzalbo, Charles Hale and Juan Pedro Viqueira.

I am very grateful to the colleagues who, as I embarked on writing about what I did not know enough about, brought me into illuminating discussions that helped me find my way through convoluted historical processes and the historiographical discussions they have engendered: Don Doyle in Columbia; Frank Towers and Elliott West in Calgary and Banff; Brodie Fischer, Mariana Flores, Emilio Kourí, and Mauricio Tenorio in Chicago; Jordi Canal and Diana Perea in Culiacán; Ed Countryman in Dallas; Patrick Kelly in San Antonio; Emmanuelle Pérez Tisserant and Sonia Rose in Toulouse; Maddalena Burelli and David Carbajal in Guadalajara; Rebecca Scott in Ann Arbor; Adam Smith and Mark Power Smith in Oxford; Matthew Butler, Jorge Cañizares-Esguerra, and Eddie Wright-Ríos in Austin; José Cázares in Acatlán; José Ramón Cossío, Rafael Estrada Michel, Ariel Rodríguez Kuri, and Ana Rosa Suárez Argüello in Mexico City; and Nicolas Barreyre, Nathan Perl-Rosenthal, and Clément Thibaud in a virtual space created between Los Angeles and Paris.

I could not have written this book without the generosity of the colleagues who graciously read my rambling manuscript closely, critiqued its form and content, and coaxed it along: Elisa Cárdenas, Ed Countryman, Greg Downs, Will Fowler, Ben Johnson, Patrick Kelly, Pablo Mijangos, Paolo Riguzzi, Héctor Strobel, and Juan Pedro Viqueira. I am especially grateful to Héctor for sharing his knowledge and fascinating collection of period illustrations. I am beholden to Yolanda Becerra Grajales, Bryan Alan Hernández, Angélica Mendoza, and Guadalupe Sánchez Bautista for their able research assistance, and to Laura Villanueva for her professionalism and efficacy in securing the book's illustrations. At UNC Press, Andrew Graybill and Ben Johnson, the series editors, Debbie Gershenowitz, Charles Grench, Cate Hodorowicz, and the members of their team have been extraordinarily patient, understanding, and helpful.

Historians often describe the work they do as a solitary endeavor, even as we write on the work of so many others. It is, nevertheless, those who walk with us that make it possible and give it meaning. This book was written during a period made dark and harrowing by my brother's death. It coincided with shifts in the ways we think and talk about politics, exacerbated by a pandemic, that seemed to erode the possibilities of persuasive reason and of building better lives together, if slowly and laboriously. Now that the book is done, I find cause for subdued optimism in the recovery of North America's shattered republics by way of republicans' resilience and inventiveness. But it was the kindness and support of colleagues, friends, and family that kept me together. It is a tremendous privilege to be part of El Colegio de México's Centro de Estudios Históricos. I have benefited from El Colegio's remarkably effective administration, learned much from its exceptional students, and drawn from my colleagues' wisdom and generosity. I was lucky to grow up with an amazing group of women; I am doubly blessed that they surround me still. Last and most, I owe everything to my family: my parents, brothers, in-laws, nieces and nephews, aunts and cousins, and, especially, to Pablo, Íñigo, and Bernardo. They are the water I swim in.

Mexico City, October 2024

TORN ASUNDER

Diego Rivera, *Civil War* (destroyed), panel in the series *Portrait of America*, ca. 1933. Photographer unknown. International Ladies Garment Workers Union Photographs Collection, Kheel Center, Cornell University.

INTRODUCTION

IN 1933, when his project for Rockefeller Center was censored and canceled, Mexican muralist Diego Rivera took the money he was paid and painted a *Portrait of America* on twenty-one portable panels for the New Workers' School in New York City. He described his history-in-pictures of the United States, from "Colonial America" to "Proletarian Unity," as "the best" he had "ever painted . . . the most correct in historical dialectic, the richest in materialistic synthesis." Fellow traveler Bertram Wolfe declared this series to be a "truer portrait" than anything written by "orthodox . . . , academic" historians.[1]

Rivera's depiction of the US Civil War shows a befuddled Abraham Lincoln—whom he chastises as a "pettifogging" lawyer—flanked by two generals who look equally confused. The president holds the Emancipation Proclamation, a symbol of his important—if, in Rivera's opinion, unintentional—"objective historical role" in the abolition of slavery. The real hero in this picture is the martyred John Brown, whose ill-fated raid on the armory at Harpers Ferry set off the decisive battle in the historic struggle for freedom. The Confederate adversary is almost invisible: soldiers in gray crowd the left side of the panel, the embodiment of an obsolete "social system," destined for the ash heap of history. The real enemy stands at the forefront, to the right: it is "J. P. Morgan the First," the capitalist, surrounded by malfunctioning rifles, "his right hand on a money bag" as his left reaches into the next panel, where his gold subsidizes those intent on derailing Reconstruction.[2]

To Mexicans, whose collective imagination is filled with the vivid imagery painted by the *muralistas*, these frescoes seem both familiar and unsettling. When they think of the nation's past, it is the pictures painted by Rivera, José Clemente Orozco, and David Alfaro Siqueiros on the massive walls of public buildings and replicated ad nauseum in schoolbooks that come to mind. The muralists' rendition of Mexico's history is imposing, colorful, dramatic, and flat. Their version of the intense period contemporaneous to the US Civil War, when first the Reform War (1858–60) and then the struggle against the French Intervention (1861–67) tore the country apart, has none of the unorthodox, provocative elements of Rivera's *Portrait* of the next-door neighbor. Instead, they echo the same conventional, nationalist moral tale that was celebrated, disseminated, and taught by the Liberal and then the Revolutionary state.

José Clemente Orozco, *La Reforma y la caída del Imperio* (The Reforma and the Fall of the Empire), 1948. Reproduction courtesy of the Instituto Nacional de Antropología e Historia, Secretaría de Cultura. © 2024 José Clemente Orozco/SOMAAP/México.

Save some cameo appearances by Karl Marx or Vladimir Lenin, a predictable cast of great, dead men engages in a timeless struggle pitching good against evil. You can tell heroes from villains by the way they look and dress, even by where they stand: cruel soldiers, mean capitalists, and corrupt priests are quashed by virtuous Liberal lawyers who both lead and embody the people.[3] In contrast, Rivera's graphic biography of the New World's "supercapitalist country," taken on by an inside outsider, steps away from a nationalist, didactic, sanctimonious, inexorable historical narrative.[4] It is not necessarily a more accurate version of the past, but it is certainly more intricate, more ambivalent, less predictable, . . . and more interesting.

IN WRITING THIS BOOK, I wanted to do what Rivera's *Portrait of America* does, not for its materialist accuracy or its unorthodox content but in its effects: the way it unsettles the nationalist, exceptionalist, self-referential narratives of the two nations depicted and how it jostles our notion of time and space in the past. Bernardo García reminded us that geography is not the stationary "framework" in which history takes place but an actor on its stage. Time and space are the stuff of history: their contours, shape, and content are made and unmade by human action, by what people create, the relationships they establish, the structures they set up.[5] As historians trying to make sense of the past, we account for, grapple with, challenge, and maneuver around conventional boundaries. This book examines two well-known, dramatic processes of national division, violence, emancipation, and national consolidation—depicted by Rivera on both sides of the border—but plays with and refashions their scale, confines, and driving narrative. It tells the story of North America's concurrent mid-century wars as part of the same story, a story of synchronicity, connections, and reciprocal effects that also coincides with historical processes that were transnational, continental, and global.

The North American civil wars were part of a dramatic global upheaval that included the 1848 European revolutions, the Tai Ping Rebellion in China (1850–64), the Paraguayans' Great War (1864–70), the unifications of Italy (1861–71) and Germany (1866–71), the beginning of the Ten Years War in Cuba (1868–78), and the Meiji Restoration in Japan (1868–89). Contemporaries read the complicated developments that subverted North American politics between 1848 and 1867 as expressions of a global clash between revolution and counterrevolution, the struggle between the past and the future, a battle between good and evil.[6] Confrontation convulsed and connected the Old and New Worlds, as ideals and combatants crisscrossed the Atlantic to fight each other's battles.

Thus, frustrated German revolutionaries in exile became abolitionists and devoted Union officers. Defeated Carlistas who defended the most traditional incarnation of monarchy in Spain sailed over to join Confederate and Conservative armies. Karl Marx praised Abraham Lincoln; French literary giant Victor Hugo eulogized John Brown and Mexico's president Benito Juárez, as well as the "brave men of Puebla" who defeated Napoléon III's troops on May 5, 1862.[7] A compelling, legible image of a world divided, inspired, and sustained real and symbolic alliances. But despite its resonance, this picture can be misleading: it is difficult to trace and evaluate, in Mexico and the United States, the impact of these sympathies and combinations on war on the ground and even on the belligerents' diplomacy.[8] Perhaps more significant, this picture flattens perceptions and experience: rigid opposition, tinged with a moral vision, cannot render the complexity of the responses to a crisis that did not lend itself to binary politics.

If the global perspective is suggestive but illusive, reading the US and Mexican mid-century wars within a continental frame throws light on the contrived nature of national boundaries, on how they can be both contingent and compelling. It destabilizes the political and cultural landscapes that we construe as compartmentalized and static so that we can map out—and inevitably simplify—reality. Bringing together the momentous processes that remade two nations during the 1850s and 1860s reveals the historicity of political morphology. It shows how, during two turbulent decades, nation-builders challenged, reimagined, and refashioned the state, the foundations of political community, and the republican polities established on the landmass that separates the Atlantic and Pacific Oceans. As the continent that sixteenth-century Europeans conceived as a New World became a site for vigorous, often violent political and institutional innovation, transformative turmoil conceptually split it in two: two Americas, North and South.

Caught between the dissolution of the Atlantic empires and a second globalization that reorganized continents into metropolitan centers and colonial peripheries, the New World came to be seen as two connected but separate entities: one America deemed "Latin," the other not; one inhabited by wily, nimble, modern Protestant foxes, the other by staid, backward, Catholic hedgehogs; one almost effortlessly and competently modern, the other remained mired in backwardness and stagnation; one would embody spiritual Ariel, the other Caliban the materialist, the sprite's victimizer.[9] The construction of this illusion of radical difference between the two Americas is part of the story I want to tell. It has proved surprisingly resilient, even as poetic license allows the border that separates them to shift from the river that changes its name when you cross it—the Rio Grande becoming the Río Bravo—to the Panama Canal. These striking, essentialist images inscribe the continent's history onto narrow, simplistic, often circular plots, rooted in irreconcilable difference.

I hope to chip away at this conceptual wall of difference and estrangement. This book brings the two Americas together where they meet geographically and where what we think of as "civilizational" disparities loom the starkest: Mexico and the United States. As it chronicles the troubles that befell both republics at mid-century, this book shifts perspectives and broadens our scope of vision to reveal parallel trajectories, shared developments, common influences, and convoluted connections. This narrative not only allows for comparison and contrast but also uncovers the implausible common ground on which stood, at a critical juncture, both the world's first modern republic, considered by liberal, democratic, and republican optimists to be a wild success—until it fell apart at mid-century—and its late-in-coming, not-quite-there-yet neighbor.[10]

This is, then, a story of North America transformed. It begins with the end of the US-Mexico War in 1848 and concludes in 1867, when republican government in Mexico was restored, after almost ten years of intermittent violence. It tells of major geopolitical changes—as Mexico lost half its territory to the United States—of republican crises and civil war, of radical political experimentation, and of national and continental reconfiguration, as political dissolution and violence impacted foreign policies and international relations. During the 1850s and 1860s, north of the Suchiate River, political structures shifted, morphed, and sometimes broke down. They were rebuilt to configure what Charles Maier has described as "territoriality," a central feature of a "modern" world. North America's loose confederal arrangements—including those of British North America—gave way to more centralized political systems, endowed with greater military capacities and supported by increasingly diverse elites who came together to push for building up the legal and physical infrastructure needed to access an increasingly industrialized and globalized economy. Each of the continent's three nations became "a bounded geographical space" that provided "a basis for material resources, political power and common allegiance."[11]

Canada, the United States, and Mexico have memorialized this turbulent process as a watershed moment, heroic and inexorable, in their patriotic histories. During the decades that followed the territorial adjustment that turned the United States into a continental power, painful but salutary trials allowed each North American nation to destroy what was holding it back: each settled into its "natural" boundaries and fulfilled its providential destiny. The Canadian Confederation united two nations, secured self-government, and preserved the bonds of empire; its creation was held up as the product of rational discussion, adherence to the rule of law, loyalty to the Crown, and British pride. The Civil War, the bloodiest, most harrowing conflict to date in the history of the United States, purged the nation "conceived in liberty" of its original sin—slavery—and preserved "the government of the people, by the people, for the people."[12] Mexico's "great national decade" (1857–67) saw the ideals of freedom, national sovereignty, and patriotism triumph over the legacies of colonial domination, the unfair and obsolete pretensions of the Catholic Church, the reactionary chimeras of treasonous Conservatives, and the imperialist ambitions of the French.

These nationalist, optimistic narratives are persuasive: key historical processes drew the rough outline and basic assumptions that we live with today, in terms of national borders, political and economic regimes, and the nations' foundational myths. Patriotic history offers a satisfying explanation of the way things turned out and makes a convincing case for why this is a good thing. Nevertheless, I wanted to tell the messier story and track the historical developments, marked by contingency, conflict, and unanticipated consequences, that traversed North America, spilling over self-contained and complacent national biographies, belying the idea of unavoidable fates for either the Land of Manifest Destiny or its neighbor to the south.

Within this more expansive geography, the decades that followed the US-Mexico War witnessed the strain, erosion, and breakdown of the political arrangements that crystallized after independence, when most Americans—North and South—embraced a novel regime: that of the representative, popular republic. Between 1776 and 1833, New World colonists who had claimed to be the Crown's "most loyal subjects" made war on its men and institutions. They not only brought down the Atlantic empires; from Acadia to Patagonia, in societies marked by ethnic diversity, glaring economic inequality, and slavery, the new nations' founders walked away from divine right, "ancient constitutions," and the hierarchies of "well-ordered" polities. Clutching their Montesquieu and nervously glancing at Rousseau, they established kingless states under the authority of a people whose members were conceived as free and equal, each entitled to "as much of the common sovereignty as another."¹³

Given the boldness and scale of the American republican experiment, it is surprising that historians have not made more of it. With some exceptions, when we write about the nineteenth century in the United States and Mexico, the republic serves as the setting of politics, not an object of study.¹⁴ As the backdrop for public life, it is frequently mentioned but rarely examined. Unlike the nation, whose "imagined" and constructed qualities historians have assumed and capitalized on, or, in the Mexican case, liberalism, whose triumph and degradation have guided the interpretation of the century's turbulent politics, we have, with notable exceptions, naturalized the republic, rendered it timeless and stable, when it is everything but: engendered and regulated by popular will, inconstant by definition, its politics unmoored from the transcendent, the traditional and the conventional because locked in the here and now, the shape of the republic, as a regime and a polity, remained—remains?—contingent and uncertain.¹⁵

As revolution swept away the ancien régime's ideological scaffolding, the rallying cries of revolution—freedom, equality, constitution, rights—became powerful "contested truths," the unavoidable bywords of politics.¹⁶ Radical, abstract ideals supposedly transformed stratified societies and corporate, composite polities into a consolidated sovereign people, but they did not destroy the concrete realities of exclusion and inequality, exploitation and unfree labor and patriarchy. They nevertheless provided the language to call them into question and challenge given authority. Republican statesmen had to work out the undefined, unpredictable new sovereign's territorial, institutional, and normative expressions. They debated who "the people" were, fought over the locus of sovereignty (Was it the "free and independent" states? The "sovereign nation"? The free, rights-bearing individual?) and drafted constitutions to set down basic rules for the political game. They tried to figure out what to do with God in a world where God has still ubiquitous but no longer immanent. While a "wall of separation" was sometimes reluctantly raised between church and state in the religiously diverse northern republic, the constitutions of Catholic Spanish America, including Mexico's, mandated—albeit in the face of incidental, if growing, dissent—religious exclusivity.¹⁷

Since the sovereign's voice had to undergird stable institutions and be translated into law and policies, elections, representative government, and constant appeals to public opinion were the inevitable, if sometimes unsettling, features of republican politics. Contingent political legitimacy crystallized into a politics of "arms, votes, and voices," which in the United States was stabilized and disciplined by constitutional consensus and party politics, but which proved more disruptive—but no less republican—in the former Spanish possessions, beset by economic woes and disjointed geographies.¹⁸ Throughout the continent, former colonists reached for republican legitimacy and systems of government when the logic of empire and monarchy became inoperative, but their animating principles remained contentious, unsettled, and corrosive well beyond the founding: they made for shifting borders, fluctuating loyalties, and a raucous public sphere.[19] To make sense of modern politics and deal with its many conundrums, the architects of new nations wrestled with, reinterpreted, and refashioned liberalism, federalism, and democracy. Conscious that state- and nation-building were a transnational endeavor, they looked over borders for models to follow, dangers to avoid, and signs of what was coming.

Politicians' efforts to prescribe, tame, and stabilize the republic spawned cycles of political invention, reconstruction, and attrition. This is the unstable common ground on which stood both Mexico and the United States, despite significantly different legacies, contexts, and experiences. The crises that sundered the two nations at mid-century were, on the one hand, the product of unresolved confrontations over the republic's character, its nature and implications, and, on the other, of the failure of republican politics, which, in the wake of war and geopolitical reconfiguration, were unable to defuse confrontations, bridge gaps, and reconcile conflicting visions. In two very different settings, polarization, division, and fratricidal violence were brought about by, to echo James Madison, republican ills and the exhaustion of republican remedies.[20]

The fatal mid-century predicaments of Mexico and the United States are part of a crucial process in North American history, as the continent's three countries moved away from decentralized schemes of governance and set up more integrated nation-states, if without abandoning the principles and procedures of federalism. These developments also comprise a privileged point of access from which to probe the inner workings of republican machineries and account for their spark plugs and glitches. Paradoxically perhaps, the conspicuous dissimilarity between the two nations' republican experience makes their shared trials a more fertile field for observation. The vigorous, prosperous northern model republic, which had escaped the corrosive cycle of political instability that ailed its southern sisters, was nevertheless dragged—along with its next-door neighbor—into the maelstrom of irreconcilable politics during the 1850s and in 1861 into the calamity of civil war. That national disaster befell both the United States and Mexico suggests that it was not due to the latter's disarray, slovenliness, and incompetence. Identifying the causes of republican breakdown and tracing its development in such different contexts should throw light on the dynamic but fragile regime that is the republic.

Few expect a history of the "distant neighbors" to be more than a chronicle of stark contrasts and unsurmountable difference; however, the challenges they faced at mid-century reveal that they shared similar problems, exacerbated by the consequences of the war in which they fought each other. On both sides of the new border, statesmen engaged in parallel, increasingly desperate, searches for solutions and compromise. None could ward off disaster. Moreover, the outbreak of the US Civil War affected no other country more than it did its neighbor to the south, as it enabled the last armed European intervention in Mexican territory. These similarities and connections have been obscured by nationalist historiographies and the persistent othering of the nation across the border.[21] By focusing on republican afflictions and on how citizens of Mexico, the United States, and the Confederacy fought over this polity, tried to turn it on its head, tear it down, and put it back together again, this book will hopefully throw light on the republic's fragilities, its quandaries and its resilience.

HOW DO WE ACCESS these worlds, as they fell apart and were transformed? The word *politics*, wrote French poet Paul Valéry, has two meanings: "The conquest and preservation of power and the organization of the city. The first meaning is very precise; the latter is not. Yet the latter perpetually serves to disguise the former."[22] The political realm is engendered, then, by productive tension between the unvarnished quest for power and its need for legitimacy, since it is, in Pierre Rosanvallon's words, "the symbolic matrix" where collective experience coalesces and the stage on which it is represented, where the real and the ideals of living together are tied into knots. I seek not to untangle them but to understand how historical actors formulated and tried to solve these problems.[23] Furthermore, the modern republic—as an ideal, a polity, and a regime—is built with words: it is instituted by a written constitution; the rights of man and citizen are boldly proclaimed in bills of rights; the sovereign people speak through elections, petitions, the press, congressional deliberations, the law, . . . and the occasional insurrection. In both the United States and Mexico, politicians wrote and published, harangued crowds, organized to conquer power, debated fellow legislators, drafted laws, amended or redrafted constitutions, and implemented policy.

To access the radicalization and polarization that fractured North America's republican edifices and unleashed civil war, then, I will use the words uttered by politicians and focus particularly on legislation. Language is never transparent—and some would say that that of politicians is particularly unreliable. It nevertheless clues us into speakers' intentions, their aspirations and fears. Political discourse is deployed strategically in the struggle for power; it is used to convince, entice, rally, incite, and frighten; it codifies what the state does through law, policy, and judicial adjudication: it builds and animates, alters, and shapes the republic.

There is also an intuitive, practical, perhaps ingenuous reason for focusing on legislation. America's newborn nations were instituted as communities of law; statutes are supposed to reflect the will of the sovereign people, even as they inevitably fall short. Laws, then, provide a—certainly imperfect—shortcut to survey the life of two republics. To rely on legislation—the product of inevitably grubby politics—to scrutinize such complicated, multidimensional, transnational processes might seem naive, especially when surveying a period in which legal structures and norms were severely strained by crisis and war. Marxists would contend that, even in ordinary times, the law is "nothing more than a mystifying and pompous way in which class power is registered and executed." It reflects nothing but "ruling-class hypocrisy."[24]

It is nevertheless precisely because laws are, in E. P. Thompson's words, the contested "institutionalized procedures" of a divided "ruling class," because they are meant to "serve as instruments for mediation, legitimation and implementation" between governors and governed, that they allow us to open a window on the turbulent developments they meant to direct and control.[25] Congressional deliberation—rambling, technical, or passionate—political posturing and manipulation, and even the much-maligned bargaining that turns horses into camels in committee, are structured by the grammar of political culture: they sketch out the shape of politics and its evolution. On the practical side, in the face of a plethora of sources, located in different countries, laws and the debates that produced them, their context of enunciation and their execution on uneven ground, comprise coherent, comparable objects that allow us to demarcate and scrutinize the extensive, congested, variegated phenomena that shaped politics during two very complicated decades in two countries split by political strife.

BECAUSE OF THIS STORY'S extension and complexity, this book could only be written thanks to the broad, diverse, wide-ranging contributions made by generations of historians. It nevertheless stands on uneven historiographic ground. Although both of these wars have been consecrated as key episodes in the nationalist chronicles of Mexico and the United States, historians have approached them differently. The US Civil War is still exceptionally popular, among both academics and a broader public. Over 50,000 books have been published—almost one for every day since Appomattox—addressing every aspect of the conflagration.[26] Ken Burns's 1990 nine-episode series on the war is the most-watched program to air on PBS. Conversely, in Mexico, as Will Fowler recently noted, the Reform War has barely piqued the interest of historians since the early twentieth century, perhaps because of the dismay that fratricidal conflict inspires, or because it has been overshadowed by the more appealing tale of heroic victory against a foreign invader only a few years later. There are plenty of academic and popular histories, as well as novels, short stories, plays, and soap operas set during the Second Empire, depicted as exotic and ridiculous, and mostly focused on the imperial couple's tragic fate. Much of this literature is repetitive, sensationalist, and derivative.[27]

In recent years, historians of Mexico have avoided the well-worn, melodramatic tales of heroism, sacrifice, and treason to normalize the study of politics during the nineteenth century's central decades. They have assessed the substance and practical implementation of the 1857 constitution and pondered the reach and limitations of imperial policy.²⁸ US historians have written about the variegated, pervasive, at times inconspicuous, at others dramatic endeavors of enslaved people and free Blacks, which were crucial to the destruction of the system of bondage.²⁹ They have insisted on the importance of the Civil War and the changes it wrought as the republic's second founding.³⁰ In recent years, they have also broadened the geography of war, which has taken a regional, international, even global, turn, attentive to the Civil War's transnational dimensions and impact beyond US borders.³¹ My research, which centers on political fracture and experimentation, builds on the latter's insights as it tries to dissect how a major geopolitical shift, polarization, and war engendered a political quagmire, unprecedented violence, and audacious regime innovation.

This is not a continental history of Mexico or of the United States, made more complex, robust, and engaging by its being set in a broader framework. It is the entangled account of two bordering republics in crisis and war. As such, it will probably make Americanists and Mexicanists equally unhappy. Of necessity, its line of argument will shift back and forth between the congressional halls, government buildings, and courts of law of Washington and Mexico City, Richmond, Veracruz, and Paso del Norte; it involves presidents, lawmakers, judges, politicians, diplomats, journalists, and members of the clergy and of the armed forces. It is a convoluted read that unsettles tales of exceptionalism by revealing the history shared by two republics we imagine as radically different. Unexpected coincidences in the midst of disparity make it easier to identify and isolate a historical process's relevant variables.

Recognizing parallels, similarities, connections, and differences allows us to hypothesize about how and why the unavoidable problems of building a life together through politics appear, at particular junctures, unsurmountable, when the effort's give-and-take becomes impossible; about what it takes for governments to fight bloody, drawn-out wars; why some win and others lose. This book hopes to throw light on the clashing political projects that account for the deep fractures in North America's republican edifice in the mid-nineteenth century. It describes the efforts of those who strove to keep the republic from falling apart and of those who wanted to remodel it, even tear it down and replace it. It explores how war tested, warped, and transformed these visions, the societies that engendered them, and the relationships between neighboring nations. It is an invitation to think critically about the strengths, weaknesses, and challenges of a form of government that we need to understand in order to uphold.

THE STORY OF republican crisis in North America begins with a war that moved the continent's boundary lines, and disturbed and disorganized both victor and vanquished. In the decades that followed the US-Mexico War, republicans on both sides of the new border saw their polities shatter and collapse. The story ends when the life-threatening conflagrations that this engendered wound down. The exhilarating victory and traumatic defeat of 1848 were interpreted—by observers then and historians afterward—as the predictable product of the two contenders' profoundly different characters and histories.[32] The democratic, capitalist, Anglo-Saxon northern giant could run over its unstable, backward, impoverished, priest-ridden, mongrel, not really republican southern neighbor. On both sides of the border, however, the conflicts' features spoke to the energy of republican politics, and to its foibles.

As we shall see in chapter 1, democratic politics strained and tested republican governments even before hostilities broke out in 1846. In Mexico, popular reaction to centralizing reform in 1835–36 unleashed widespread opposition. In Texas, whose population was overwhelmingly comprised of immigrants from the United States whose fortunes were tied to the Mississippi Valley's cotton economy, resistance grew into a secessionist movement that the national government was unwilling to accept but unable to suppress.[33] In the United States, the debates surrounding Texas's annexation revealed wildly divergent visions of what the republic should be. Its incorporation as the Union's twenty-eighth state and the triumph, in 1844, of dark-horse expansionist candidate James K. Polk over "the Great Compromiser," Whig Henry Clay, made international conflict inevitable, as the Mexican government—undermined by federalist defiance and some politicians' brief flirtation with monarchy in 1846—refused to traffic with the people's patrimony and sell land to the United States. Mobilization was relatively successful in both nations-at-war, as local governments and citizens made theirs the nation's plight.[34] But the war and its aftermath undermined faith in the republican system, as they revealed the instabilities of allegiance, the ingrained impermanence of the republic's artificial territorial expression, federalism's potential for antagonism and the vulnerability of democracy to dissolution.

Fractious politics followed in the wake of what Ulysses S. Grant labeled a most "wicked war." Chapter 2 follows a politics that grew increasingly frenzied, emotional, and uncompromising, and eroded the common ground that had sustained them. It describes the dismantling of mechanisms that had contained and defused—but not resolved—the young republics' most pernicious problems: in the United States, the tensions that riddled a government that was, in Abraham Lincoln's words, "half slave and half free"; to the south, the increasingly hostile relations between church and state, given the former institution's oversized social, cultural, economic, and political influence in the face of the state's weakness, coupled with the growing intransigence of the ecclesiastical establishment and its censure of all that was "modern," "liberal," and "democratic." Within twelve years of the end of armed conflict between neighbors, war once again set them both on fire.

In Mexico, the disgraceful failure of national defense and the loss of half of the nation's territory pushed politicians into increasingly disenchanted, obturate, and desperate efforts to build a regime strong and stable enough to withstand rebellion within and aggression from without. They reached for novel partisan organization, legislative and administrative innovation, constitutional reform, and dictatorial rule, all to no avail: the federal republic (1847–53) was replaced by a Conservative, centralizing dictatorship (1853–55), which was overthrown by a Liberal revolution. A groundbreaking constitution, crafted throughout 1856 and enacted in February 1857, sought to strengthen the state and secularize the nation so that it could be modernized. Its proclamation spawned not consent but unmanageable conflict.[35]

In the United States, efforts to incorporate the conquered territories into the Union introduced the intractable issue of slavery into national debate, where it fanned growing polarization, legislative paralysis, and party decomposition. Neither electoral politics, compromise legislation, nor judicial review were able to channel or deflect conflict.[36] By the end of the 1850s, the common ground that made the negotiations of routine politics possible disappeared. As vital disagreements became impossible to process, they tore the North American republics apart and opened the door to the continuation of politics by other—frantic—means. In Mexico, civil war erupted over transformative fundamental law: rallying to the defense of religion and the legal privileges of officers and clergy, Conservatives took up arms to put an end to what they perceived as an extremely dangerous constitutional exercise and set up a military dictatorship in Mexico City. Most Liberals rallied around Chief Justice and constitutional interim president Benito Juárez to defend the embattled constitution. The country split in two.

In the midst of bloody, indecisive war, the Juárez administration deepened reform: it nationalized ecclesiastical wealth, established the independence of church and state, and tried to recast Mexico's relationship with its neighbor to the north. Its improvised armies drew their strength from the still functional economies of the North and West, while the nation's more densely populated, urbanized central highlands were devastated by war. In December 1860, Liberal forces defeated the impoverished, worn-out Conservative army. The Juárez government returned to Mexico City and reestablished constitutional rule but failed to bring about peace: Liberals bickered, Conservative guerrillas ran roughshod over the countryside and conspirators courted foreign intervention to unseat the "demagogues."

In the United States, bickering over the status of slavery in the Mexican Cession revealed a rift so deep that it could not be mended. The Compromise of 1850, the popular sovereignty solution, and the Supreme Court's egregious 1857 *Dred Scott* decision only exacerbated confrontation. The 1860 electoral victory of a candidate whose party was committed to "free labor, free men," and free soil in the Western territories drove seven slave states to secede. By February 1861, they had confederated into a new nation, founded on white supremacy and the rightfulness of slavery. When the Charleston militia fired on Fort Sumter in April 1861, President Lincoln called on 75,000 volunteers to put down the Southern rebellion. Four more states joined the Confederacy as it went to war to preserve its independence. The resulting conflict, described by many as a harbinger of modern, "total" war, was protracted and bloody. It lasted for four years, mobilized over 3 million men, and cost the lives of approximately 620,000 men. It touched the life of practically every family in the divided country, warped family, labor, and social relations, and transformed production, politics, and the economy.[37] In 1862, the North's defense of the Union became a fight to destroy slavery. Three years later, the end of the war confirmed the emancipation of 4 million enslaved men, women, and children.

Beyond US borders, the outbreak of this decapacitating conflict resurrected the possibilities of European expansionism in the Americas. The Civil War turned Napoléon III's pipe dream of restoring France's presence in the New World into a feasible—if risky—venture. The emperor heeded Mexican Conservatives' call for help and, in early 1862, British, French, and Spanish troops disembarked in Veracruz, alleging the nonpayment of debts as a legitimate cause for military intervention. Foreign invasion intersected with domestic strife. French bayonets eventually helped set up a monarchical regime with the Austrian emperor's younger brother, Maximilian von Hapsburg, at the helm. It was a radical departure from Mexico's republican tradition which, since the fall of Agustín de Iturbide's imperial government (1822–23), had made talk of monarchy both threatening and ridiculous.[38]

Nevertheless, far from ensuring peace, order, and the rule of law, Mexico's Second Empire fanned the flames of fratricidal conflict and republican resistance. Another devastating wave of violence swept over the country, taking the lives of at least 30,000 Mexicans. Once the US war ended and Prussian territorial ambitions grew more ominous, Louis Napoléon's cost-benefit analysis drove him to put an end to the Mexican adventure. With the French Army gone, the empire crumbled. In June 1867, the emperor and two of his Mexican generals were court-martialed and shot on a wind-swept hill outside Querétaro. Throughout the Atlantic world, the provocative image of his execution, refashioned by Édouard Manet, inspired horror and pity in some, enthusiasm in others. On this side of the ocean and on both sides of the Río Bravo, republican victory determined the nations' shattered and reconstituted image of themselves and their future.

Chapters 3 and 4 take us into the laboratory in which Liberales and Conservadores, Confederates and Unionists, *republicanos* and *imperialistas* tried to cobble together a new political order that would allow them to reassess, resolve, or destroy the difficulties that had torn the nations apart. We will explore their high-stakes, trial-and-error attempts at state- and nation-building, the political visions, aspirations, anxieties, and actions of the men who, as nation and state fell apart, tried to reestablish order, restructure societies, and build machines for governing ... and waging war. These politicians followed no set of instructions: they drew on eclectic intellectual traditions, pragmatically changed directions out of convenience or because of extenuating circumstances. All experimented boldly.

The first of these two chapters tells of the reactionaries who, as they strove to preserve what they conceived of as the natural order of things, took it upon themselves to revolutionize North America's political landscape: Southern secessionists created a nation from scratch. In Mexico, the enemies of the 1857 constitution first tinkered with military dictatorship and then, hard-pressed by defeat, restored a monarchist regime, sponsored by foreign invaders, at a moment when their fears of US interference were mitigated by the convenient stranglehold that civil war had placed on the northern colossus. The next chapter focuses on the Union and Mexico's Liberal governments. Their defense of the popular, federal republic would make it over into something new: slavery was abolished and the Catholic foundations of the Mexican polity dismantled; on both sides of the border, the relationship between citizen, state, and nation was remade.

Sweeping change was the product of not only audacious political imagination but also compelling action, brought forth by violent, persistent conflict. Chapters 5 and 6 examine how the urgency of war massively increased the pressure on the governments it swept into violent confrontation, how it distorted—and sometimes destroyed—the mechanics of limited, democratic governance and radicalized political ambition. The desperate need of governments at war for resources, both immaterial (patriotism, loyalty, law, Providence) and material (men, guns, and money) stimulated incendiary public rhetoric, far-reaching, intrusive, sometimes constitutionally dubious legislation, unorthodox financial schemes, and subversive diplomacy. Efforts to legislate membership, beliefs, and feelings were perceived as deeply disturbing but probably had limited impact and were sometimes counterproductive. A government's ability to mobilize men and marshal firepower and economic assets, consistently and over an extended period, made the difference between winning or losing these long, harrowing wars.

The final chapter analyzes how crisis and war remade the relationship between neighboring republics within a continental framework. As strife scrambled international relations, it raised the stakes of foreign policy. Statesmen and diplomats probed the possibilities of breaking with hallowed tradition and practices—like the diplomatic recognition of de facto governments—and of seeking out alliances grounded in ideology. Others clung instead to the guardrails of the laws of war and nations, sometimes creatively reinterpreted. The latter were eventually more successful. When peace finally came to North America, it did not bring with it a special relationship between the two neighbors that enthusiastic republicans had foretold, sustained by commercial interests, Pan-American solidarity, and republican sympathies. The logic of markets and investment, of technological innovation and a growing, integrated infrastructure would join the two nations' economies together, but only during the century's last decades.

Harrowing, exhausting struggles nevertheless transformed relations between the United States and Mexico: by removing territorial expansion from the US agenda, they decompressed and standardized dealings between the two neighbors. War, continental crisis, and the ephemeral but disturbing revival of Old World expansionism in the New also spurred constitutional renewal throughout the region—conspicuously in British North America—and pushed statesmen further south to rethink the purposes of government and the place of "Latin America" in a "concert of nations" structured by an imbalance of power. A tilt in the continental order of things signaled the end of this story.

PART ONE

REPUBLICS BREAK DOWN

CHAPTER ONE

1848

Continental Crisis

ON FEBRUARY 22, 1848, exalted Parisian revolutionaries brought down the constitutional government of Louis-Philippe, the "citizen king," and established a republic. An insurrectionary wave swept over Europe, from the Channel to the borders of the Russian Empire. Revolution hailed democracy and consecrated nation and nationalism; a *Communist Manifesto* promised utopia to "working men of all countries" who had "nothing to lose but their chains."[1] Reaction soon put an end to the "Springtime of the Peoples": by the end of 1852 a Bonaparte sat on an imperial throne in France, the emperor of Austria-Hungary doubled down on absolutist rule, the pope returned to Rome, and unification would come to Germany, decades later and only through war. There would be, as Jürgen Osterhammel has written, no global "second age of revolution," only a "great turbulence" at mid-century.[2] On the other side of the Atlantic, however, revolutionary change had taken place, less than a month before the barricades went up in the streets of Paris. It was the product not of popular commotion but of lackluster, painful diplomatic negotiations on the outskirts of Mexico City.

On February 2, 1848, in the shadow of the nation's most hallowed shrine, government commissioners put an end to the US-Mexico War by signing a treaty of "Peace, Friendship, Limits and Settlement." Mexico lost half of its territory; the United States became a continental power, an "ocean-bound republic" with a long and long-coveted Pacific coastline.[3] The war tested the two national states' capacity for mobilizing people and resources. At the outbreak of war, the US regular army had 5,500 men in uniform and had to be greatly expanded for war. Its larger contingent came from the volunteer militias recruited in the states: over 50,000 men enthusiastically responded to President Polk's call to avenge the national honor and conquer vast tracts of land. In the end, approximately 59,000 volunteers and 31,000 regulars served in the war against Mexico.[4] In the early 1840s, the Mexican standing army was larger, with over 20,000 enlisted men and an overgrown, fractious officer corps, prone to political meddling. Its soldiers were often forcibly recruited, inadequately trained and equipped, poorly and inconsistently paid and geographically dispersed. In response to the US invasion, federal authorities, who had only come to power in August 1846 through armed insurrection, scrambled to set up a new model for the nation's defense, one that responded to both local and regional sensibilities and to the needs of national defense: a National Guard, made up of citizens, locally recruited, commanded by elected officers, who could be called upon by the president to defend the fatherland and the republic.[5]

When seen through a lens that naturalizes nation-states as both essential and eternal, the outcome of the US-Mexico War is often held up as the predictable result of different roads taken on the way to nation-making: in hindsight and until recently, US victory was cast as the natural outgrowth of Manifest Destiny, Anglo-Saxon gumption, and democratic ferment. Conversely, generations of Mexicans—politicians, scholars, and run-of-the-mill citizens—have agonized over the reasons for Mexico's dismal failure, and often pointed to government weakness and a lack of national unity and willingness to sacrifice.[6] Yet despite their shortcomings, Mexican armed forces mounted fierce—if not particularly successful—resistance: under dire circumstances, and without the support of many state governors, President Antonio López de Santa Anna managed to field 20,000 troops to face Zachary Taylor's advances in the North. In the wake of defeat, he organized an 8,000-man army to stop Winfield Scott's march from Veracruz.[7] Both governments made significant efforts to channel love of country into military action and transformed citizens into soldiers.[8] At mid-century, patriotism did not set the neighboring nations apart.

The ability to secure financial resources did make a difference, however. As the US armed forces grew to three times their original size between 1846 and 1848, $74.6 million dollars were added to government expenditures: public debt rose from $15.5 million in 1846 to $63 million in 1849. To cover these expenses, the Polk administration did not raise taxes but floated three loans that amounted to a little over $49 million, at 6 percent interest. Bonds were placed, effortlessly, and then covered with similar ease, in the healthy economic and fiscal environment that followed the war. In contrast, the Mexican government faced invasion with a nearly empty treasury, a very narrow range of action for raising revenue and a drab track record in debt markets, both foreign and domestic. Everything it did to finance the war—canceling payments on the public debt, slashing the salaries of bureaucrats, levying forced loans and army requisitions, and commandeering church property to guarantee public credit—alienated broad sectors of the population: creditors, government employees, the moneyed elite, the clergy, and even some of Mexico City's National Guard battalions, who, in the midst of foreign invasion, revolted against the government's perceived aggressions against religion. Its efforts also came painfully short of what was needed. Things barely looked up once the war was over: despite the ephemeral breather provided by the $15 million war indemnity funds, the Mexican government remained dangerously insolvent into the 1860s.[9]

The year 1848 was a momentous one in North America. The US invasion of Mexico dashed the hopes of independence ushering in a Jeffersonian age of "peace, commerce and honest friendship" among New World nations.[10] The imperial rivalries and dynastic rationalities of war and peace had become inoperative, but the new "American order" did not warrant peace and harmony. In this convoluted context, the actions and reactions of soldiers, diplomats, politicians, local authorities, and men and women on the ground allow us to open a window on the ways they imagined the nation, conceived patriotic duty, and construed allegiance and belonging. Fighting the war, negotiating the peace, and settling issues of responsibility, retribution, and accountability challenged the efficacy of the state, strained the principles and mechanisms of federalism, and put citizens' sense of loyalty and obligation to the test. This chapter will show how it jumbled convictions, warped relationships, and revealed cracks in the republican edifice.

North America's federal republics had to digest new territorial and demographic realities, allocate the spoils of victory or the cost of defeat, and translate the outcome of war into legislation. Politicians struggled as the abstractions of republican legitimacy—a sovereign people, sovereign states, sovereign citizens—crystallized into increasingly contentious incarnations, including, in Mexico, peasant rebellions labeled "caste wars" and, in the United States, reckoning with Rhode Island's tussle over suffrage. As the stakes of politics rose, the stage on which they played out grew narrower and more unstable. If revolution in the Old World had been quashed, it had fired imaginations and provided those who wanted radical change in the Atlantic world with impassioned words, inspiring images and willing foot soldiers. The year of turmoil stoked hopes and fears, scrambled the certainties of the past, and warned of trouble in the future.

State and Nation in the Cauldron of War and Peace

The Mexican War was a land grab dressed up as the defense of national honor: President Polk provoked Mexico into a military scuffle in the disputed territory between the Bravo and Nueces Rivers, and then condemned the republic to the south as a wanton aggressor. The president asked Congress for a declaration of war to right the many "grievous wrongs perpetrated by Mexico ... throughout a long period of years." Only fourteen US congressmen voted against the invasion of their southern neighbor.[11] The breakdown of relations between Washington and Mexico City had its origin in—at least—a decade of domestic controversy, which came to a head in Texas. In Mexico, after several unsuccessful attempts at constitutional reform to repair what many saw as the federal government's fatal weakness, Congress, bolstered by a series of local insurrections against federal policy in 1834 and 1835, drafted a new, centralist constitution that curtailed the prerogatives of state governments.[12] Amid a wave of protest and resistance in states that would no longer be sovereign, none had greater consequences than those of Texas's "recent settlers and citizens by adoption," who, by hook or by crook, had managed to circumvent Mexico City's efforts to restrict immigration and abolish slavery. What began as a call for the defense of liberty and the 1824 constitution, performed in the distinctive key of Mexican political culture, ended with a declaration of independence, signed at Washington-on-the-Brazos and drafted in the language of 1776.[13]

US support and recognition of rebellious Texans in 1835–36, and annexation in 1845, were seen by Mexican authorities and public opinion as part of a sinister plot, concocted to fulfill the long-held US objective of taking Mexico's territory. History is rarely that consistent and clear cut. Anglo immigration into Texas, the hybrid, multivalent politics of Anglo Texans, Texas independence, the Republic of Texas's resilience and, finally, annexation, were not stepping stones in the preset, seamless progression of an expansive people, genetically and providentially destined to become a continental republic. Contentious processes, involving the interests and aspirations of multiple actors—including the Indigenous nations who did not recognize either republics' authority and often held control on the ground—shaped by diverse, sometimes clashing visions of what the republic should be and what needed to be done to keep it, shaped the processes of secession, nation-building, and joining the Union.[14] In Thomas Hietala's words, it was not Manifest Destiny that drove Texas annexation but profoundly controversial "Manifest Design." Anxious politicians who believed that territorial expansion and increased commercial activity would neutralize the threats that slavery and industrialization posed to the republic, North and South, came together to promote the unprecedented acquisition of land: almost 800 million acres between 1845 and 1848.[15] The Republic of Mexico was the main casualty of these developments.

System Fail: Shattered Beliefs, Contested Mechanisms

Given the notorious weakness of the Mexican government, Polk thought the war would be short and US victory swift. Nevertheless, the Army of the West's efficient occupation of New Mexico and California and Zachary Taylor's victories over the chronically underfed and shoddily armed Mexican troops in the northeastern theater were not enough to force the beleaguered Mexican government to sue for peace.[16] Under the command of Winfield Scott, US troops marched from the Gulf of Mexico to Mexico City and, after a short truce in September 1847, occupied the nation's capital.

Polk demanded peace come by treaty. Some veteran politicians questioned his decision to pursue the war by taking it into the heart of Mexico, even as the army had already secured the territories that the United States wanted. Senator John C. Calhoun argued that, by insisting on "peace with honor," the government would waste lives, time, and money. It also placed ending of the war "out of the hands" of the United States and into Mexico's.[17] The president wanted a treaty not only to confirm the extensive US territorial gains but also to also acknowledge the legitimacy of its claims, formally, on paper. For Mexico, resounding military defeat meant only humiliation and territorial loss, but diplomatic negotiations offered a—rather narrow—opportunity to try to limit the damage, protect the rights of the Mexicans who would remain "on the other side," get compensated for the war's injustice, and, if possible, claim the moral high ground.

In August 1847, with Scott's army camped on the outskirts of Mexico City, peace negotiations failed as Mexican commissioners pressed for a miscellaneous list of demands that included a demand for an explanation in writing for why the United States had waged an unjust, unchristian, unrepublican war on its neighbor, a refusal to recognize the Rio Grande as the national border—which would have legitimized Polk's strategy of provocation—and an effort to limit territorial loss to the "ungrateful" province of Texas.[18] These exertions came to naught: negotiations broke down, the truce ended, and Scott's army moved on Mexico City. In early 1848, however, pressing circumstances pushed both parties toward an understanding: occupation lay great stress on Mexico's insolvent, divided government, while the Polk administration bristled at the political strife fanned by the apparent inefficacy of its envoy, Nicholas Trist, in his pursuit of negotiated peace.

In Washington, Polk faced calls for the conquest of "all of Mexico," on the one hand, and growing opposition to the war, on the other. In February, negotiators signed a formal legal instrument that sanctioned the transformation of Mexico's Far North into the US Southwest. Mexico accepted Texas's secession and annexation, and relinquished the territories of California and New Mexico, as well as parts of Tamaulipas, Sonora, Durango, Chihuahua, and Coahuila. It lost 525,000 square miles, over half of its territory, and over 100,000 of its citizens were placed under the enemy's jurisdiction. The Treaty of Guadalupe Hidalgo unleashed furious reactions that stemmed from patriotic indignation and political antagonism, but also from different conceptions of what political authority could and should do. Its critics condemned it publicly, as "costly, inconvenient, and degrading."[19] They censured the politically moderate government for agreeing to an immoral and hence illegal settlement to the war. The government—the people's representative, and consequently, their servant—could not give up the nation's territory or abandon its inhabitants, as if they were slaves, or "herds of sheep." As a Mexican politician sarcastically pointed out, alluding to the three-fifths clause, only in the US constitution were men "assigned numerals." Mexican authorities could not traffic "contemptibly with the creatures of God."[20]

Some of the criticism was more technical and sophisticated. The more radical federalists claimed that negotiations were unconstitutional, and that the treaty belied democracy and federalism. They argued—deceptively—that the 1847 constitutional Reform Act, which had restored federalism in the midst of war, denied the central government the power to reorganize the national territory.[21] No federal authority could transfer "even a hand-span of land belonging to a state" to a foreign power."[22] The transcendental decision of territorial cession could not be left to a handful of bureaucrats. The *moderados* who sat in the war government could not understand this, because they had been brought up under "the despotism of the colonial government." They read their constitutional attributions "literally," instead of channeling "the spirit of our institutions."[23]

Angry advocates of states' rights argued that the proposed treaty breached the federal pact. The people of the different states had banded together in order to profit from "the benefits of Union" while maintaining their "natural and preexisting independence." As prominent jurist Mariano Otero noted, it was "very obvious" that the states constituted the nation: it did not exist above them. Yet state governments had been excluded from life or death negotiations, segregated from national "communion," and turned over to a foreign power.[24] Acknowledging the legitimacy of the peace negotiations meant recognizing the "central power's" despotic right to sell states off "against their will."[25] Until the sovereign states' approval could be ascertained, the terms offered by the US envoy had to be rejected. Instead, the commissioners had signed the treaty over the cries of the Mexican opposition and without subduing what seemed to be the Polk government's insatiable appetite for land.

A few months later, the text of the treaty, amended by the US Senate, was introduced into the Mexican Congress for ratification. Amendments were cast by Washington as minor modifications, revisions of form rather than substance. US legislators had simply sought to adjust the expansive language of the Mexican negotiators to that of previous treaties. The southern republic's mediators had been especially concerned with protecting the religious rights of their soon-to-be former compatriots: freedom of religion, the protection of church property, and the free communication between the faithful and the episcopal see, which for New Mexicans was in Durango. The US government argued that the protection of the "invaluable blessings" of liberty and property needed no treaty stipulations, since "the very nature and character of our institutions" was their shield. The treaty was also amended so that admission to "all the rights and privileges of U.S. citizenship" would take place "at the proper time, to be judged by Congress," and not, as had been initially stipulated, "as soon as possible."[26]

Peace negotiations, like the bilateral relationship during much the nineteenth century, were marked by a silent but unyielding presence: that of the Indian nations who, as Brian DeLay has shown, profoundly affected perception and policy in the borderlands and wielded effective power over much of the land that was to change hands. The Indian nations did not sit at the negotiating table. Their exclusion as legitimate political actors, as objects and not parties to the treaty, despite their obvious weight in the region, spoke to the rigidities underpinning the nation-state as it revealed the flimsiness of its pretensions to territorial sovereignty.[27] The possibility of effective US protection against the "savage tribes" was pushed as an incentive for the Mexican Senate's ratification. Washington's commitment to "forcibly restraining" Indian incursions into Mexican territory was one of the few advantages secured by the defeated nation's commissioners.[28]

In the amended version of the treaty, the US government maintained this pledge on paper but, "for humanity's sake," refused to stop providing arms and ammunition to Indian nations, since they lived by the hunt. It would soon prove to be both unwilling to enact its obligations and unable to do so, and would forswear them only five years later, as part of the agreements contained in the Gadsden Purchase.[29] The Senate also struck out Article X, which had established Washington's blanket commitment to upholding Spanish and Mexican land grants in Texas. In the words of Secretary of State James Buchanan, it was "the glory" of the United States that "no human power" existed that would allow for depriving individuals—such as those who in good faith had acquired land in Texas—of their property to transfer it to another.[30]

As Congress debated ratification in Mexico's wartime capital of Querétaro, eleven radical Liberal lawmakers—known as *puros*—attempted one last, desperate move. Under Article 23 of the Reform Act, a groundbreaking mechanism giving state legislatures the authority to determine a statute's constitutionality, they called on the Supreme Court to intervene, and send the treaty to the states for their approval before it could be accepted. They were unconcerned with the fact that some of the procedures prescribed by the treaty—such as preparations for the US armies' evacuation—had already been put into effect. Actions, they argued, were in this case less important than words. The fact that the treaty impinged on Mexican fundamental law, and that it violated the nation's rights, had to be clearly enunciated, so as to safeguard Mexico's right to insist, eventually and under less dire circumstances, that the nefarious—and hence illegitimate—agreement be reversed.[31]

The Court denied the puro senators' request: the same constitution they appealed to recognized "in the most positive and explicit manner" the federal government's "undoubtable supremacy" in all matters related to foreign affairs. The justices also emphasized that, beyond legal considerations, necessity was, in politics, conclusive. To revisit something that had been settled by overbearing violence went against every "healthy principle" and would spawn "incalculable evils."[32] No one could argue that the peace treaty was a good thing, but there was no better alternative: it was impossible to keep up the fight. A new border had been drawn "by the sword"; military occupation turned the conqueror into a "de facto sovereign." The puros' conception of the nation as a voluntary association of citizens committed to fighting for a fatherland founded on civic obligation imploded in the face of harsh reality. For all the acts of bravery and sacrifice, neither the states nor the people had managed to sustain the war. The advocates for peace-by-treaty insisted that the government was not mistaken when it claimed that public opinion craved an end to war: it had refused to keep up the fight.[33]

The treaty's detractors disagreed: there could be no greater evil than that which would befall the country from the peace mandated by these terms. They implied the destruction of the sovereign rights of states, the loss of extensive tracts of territory to which Mexico held "undisputed" title, and the selling of its inhabitants to the enemy.[34] Nothing but a "mathematical line" now separated Mexicans from a country whose intentions, character, and capacities were now clear. In ten or fifteen years the nation would disappear under the might of the arrogant, racist, expansive northern republic.[35]

Radical legislators called for principled resistance and painted an apocalyptic picture of what ill-gotten peace held in store. Their adversaries put forth a discourse of resignation and a vision of the nation's future that was both more disenchanted and less pessimistic. To soften the blow of inevitable defeat, negotiators desperately reached for two sets of arguments: the real possibility that the war's outcome could have been much worse and their adherence to the law of nations. They claimed to have guaranteed, to the best of their abilities, the protection, property, and prerogatives of the Mexican citizens who would come under US jurisdiction if they chose to stay put. They had not sold, nor had the US government bought, either land or people: territories had been lost in war—as had happened, time and time again, throughout history—and the Mexican government received 15 million pesos to minimally offset the "calamities" of an unjust invasion.[36]

To deny the executive's authority to negotiate, agree to territorial cessions, and obtain an indemnity was to "dispute its right to diminish the nation's devastation."[37] While the treaty's detractors condemned international law as nothing but "sarcasm," meant to paper over the bullying of the stronger party, their opponents quoted profusely from the law of nations.[38] They insisted on the executive's exclusive constitutional authority, endorsed by distinguished authors like Emer de Vattel, to negotiate with foreign powers and to make peace. Their reliance on the language of natural law, which stressed "the Prince's legitimate powers" to conduct the nation's business, in some ways marred their arguments by giving them an aristocratic, reactionary edge.

Nonetheless, their vision of the defeated nation's future was less dire than their rivals'. The difficult lessons of defeat would allow Mexico to get rid of its "old vices" and heal the divisions that had plagued it since independence.[39] Some thought—and time would prove them right, if only partially and momentarily—that expansion would not turn the United States into a more threatening neighbor. Now oversized, the "great nation" of the north would eventually split in two; the part that bordered on Mexico would not be populated by restless and hostile Anglo-Saxons but by a mixed race, "much less terrible" to its neighbor, which could even become a hybrid, "useful barrier," keeping Anglo and Spanish Americans apart. Somewhat paradoxically, they also argued that this new geography brought about the "incalculable advantage" of bringing the two neighbors closer: Mexico's northern states' would now border on a "civilized nation," instead of on a "desert" populated by "barbaric" tribes.[40]

Those disparaging the peace agreement relied on a vision of political community that was perhaps more complex, more modern, and more democratic than that of their rivals. To them, the nation was engendered by a voluntary pact, in which the exercise of sovereignty was always contingent and limited. Their antagonists conceived of the nation as an organic—and inert—whole. During an international conflict, only the president could enunciate its position: they deemed the nation's sovereignty to be greater than that of its parts. Its practically unconditional delegation enabled the federal government to amputate part of the nation's territory and dispose of some of its population, in order to save the rest. This stark contrast did not flatter the government's position. Nonetheless, Congress apparently found it convincing enough. Censure of the treaty, some senators claimed, belonged "in the scholastic arena." Faultfinders added "new subtleties" to the debate, while "reason and public interest" lay shipwrecked. The war was lost, and the treaty's critics could not expect, now, to win it with arguments.[41] Despite loud and ostentatious cries of illegality and danger, the Senate ratified the treaty on May 30, 1848, 33 votes to 4.[42]

On the other side of the new border, formalizing the peace could only be easier. The victors' burden would consist of administering military success and the vast expanses of the "Mexican Cession." Many legislators had exulted in the uninterrupted victories of the US Army, made up mostly of volunteers. Success on the battlefield soundly refuted the European "anti-republican croakers" who had derided the "pattern republic's" military capacities—as had Mexican lawmakers, even with defeat staring them in the face.[43] The United States had become a power to contend with.[44] But despite these military achievements, the war lasted longer than expected. Polk had to petition Congress for more money and the recruitment of additional troops, spurring discussions over the war's legitimacy, the way it was being fought, and the nature and desirability of its objectives.

These debates revealed problems and confrontations running through a society that only apparently marched in unison to the beat of Manifest Destiny. Although fueled by partisan and regional rivalries, the confrontations that arose with the war crossed over party and section. The waning Whigs were—predictably—scandalized by the war's immorality, but the most corrosive denunciations of the conflict came from the ranks of the president's own party. Senators John P. Hale, of New Hampshire—who would soon join the Free Soil Party—and South Carolina's celebrated John C. Calhoun led the charge against the war's progress and its foreseeably dire consequences: actions that were "unadvised, unconstitutional and illegal," even if militarily successful, would not contribute to the national honor.[45] The war—and its costs—worried the people's representatives; the social and political impact of its outcome troubled them more. As early as August 1846, a Democrat, David Wilmot of Pennsylvania, put forth a proposal to condition additional war funds on slavery's being outlawed in the new territories.

President Polk justified his decision to pursue the conflict and occupy Veracruz, Mexico's main port, and then Mexico City, by emphasizing the need to secure both "indemnity for past wrongs and security for the future." As a rallying cry, this was cryptic enough to allow each legislator to imagine a different outcome, attuned to his political inclinations, imperialist ambitions, and state of mind. Some thought the new borderline should be drawn at the Rio Grande, others thought it should be pushed over 440 miles south, to San Luis Potosí. A few even claimed "all of Mexico." Advocates for greater expansion argued that it would signal the broadening of liberty in the Americas: like a "new Rome," the United States would provide for the "ultimate diffusion and perpetuity of the great principles of civil and religious liberty." Mexico would be "Americanized" in the "noble nursery" of state sovereignty and free trade. Mexico's democrats, the puros, the "bone and sinew of the country, the most intelligent, virtuous and orderly people"—who, according to one enthusiastic speaker, numbered about 2 million—had recognized US soldiers as their "deliverers" and would man a solid, stable, authentically republican regime under US tutelage.[46]

It was unclear, in this optimistic vision, what would become of the mixed-race peon "slaves," the "docile and obedient" Indians whom no "man of sound practical intelligence" would entrust with "the rights of American citizenship," but whom Mexican law recognized as full-fledged members of the political community.[47] Advocates of annexation avoided specifics. The dangers of assimilating a mongrel population into the US polity worried many legislators, less concerned with the war's immorality than with the plausible effects of conquest on their own republic. "Nations conquered and held," John C. Calhoun preached somberly, retaliated by destroying the liberty of their conquerors, "through the corrupting effect of extended patronage and irresponsible government." More ominous still was the inevitable perversion of free institutions if unfit Indians, mestizos, and mulattoes were brought into the body politic of what was meant to be "a white man's government."[48] But at the heart of these anxieties lay not Mexico's deeply foreign nature, or its lack of democratic potential. The most destabilizing issue was domestic; it touched upon a distinctive feature of the northern republic, slavery, and its possible expansion into newly acquired territories.

Except for the more radical abolitionists, who rejected the constitution as a "covenant with death" for its sanction of slavery, most inhabitants of the United States, and the politicians who represented them, were convinced that human bondage was a "municipal" institution: Congress could not regulate it where it already existed. Throughout the 1830s, most lawmakers agreed to disagree on slavery and avoided debating the issue, even when pressed by constituents.[49] Nevertheless, the possibility that unfree labor could extend into—and pollute—this new promised land, strengthen the hand of the southern "slaveocracy," and limit the opportunities available to free men put this intractable issue at the center of congressional debate. Slavery was no longer—if it had ever been—a "mere abstraction" for the republic. The interests of slaveholders had been "an element of political power in the formation of the Constitution," and they were directly responsible for inciting an expensive "foreign and aggressive war." In the words of Senator Hale, US taxpayers had a right to ask their representatives to give this matter a "fair hearing."[50]

Debates about the war and its aftermath disrupted the already fractious, unstable site occupied by the South's peculiar institution within the US political system. Confrontations between those who believed that slavery should be kept out of the conquered territories and those who defended the right of the slaveholding South to share in the spoils of victory would soon turn on rights defended as absolute. Citizens, argued Hale, should not be paying for a war meant to reinforce an institution they detested. Conversely, Congressman Henry Hilliard of Alabama claimed that Northerners sought to monopolize, "for their exclusive benefit," territorial gains that had cost the blood and treasure of the whole nation.[51] This confrontation soon became a scuffle about who—the federal government or state legislators—had a right to determine the fate of conquered land. According to Hilliard, the doctrine that Congress should legislate for the territories "for their good alone" had "a certain charm about it" but was "wholly erroneous." It could be true only if the US government were a monarchy. The war had been fought and won by "the people of the several states": all states should enjoy its rewards. Congress was only the people's "agent."[52]

The irruption of slavery onto legislative debate acquired a menacing tone almost immediately. According to Louisiana's Isaac Moore, strident condemnation of slavery was not only misguided—since the institution was "the greatest blessing God Almighty himself could have ordained"—but served only to irritate and alienate the Southern states. All the "talking, preaching and writing" would never "induce men with common sense to surrender their property." It would strain the bonds of Union, for it rendered "the tenure with which we hold property so unstable" that the advantages of belonging to the Union would "cease to be of value."[53] As Elizabeth Varon has written, talk of "disunion"—the "most provocative and potent word in the American political vocabulary"—was used to conjure up the dangers that threatened a fragile republic. But in the run-up to the Civil War, the threat of secession became a program for Southern independence that seeped into Southern political discourse and became commonplace on the floor of Congress.[54]

Slippery Allegiances

What do the US-Mexico War and its consequences tell us about how the national community was conceived and citizenship imagined in the North American republics? How did fighting the war and striving for peace alter lived realities, warp convictions, and refashion key political categories? Descriptions of the conflict often dwell on contrast: civilization versus barbarism; backwardness versus progress; masculine strength versus feminine weakness. Like the civil wars that would later plague its contenders, however, the US-Mexico War revealed the convoluted, contradictory nature of the two countries' shared insurgent heritage. Revolution had wrought the transformation of subjects into citizens, collectively holding title to sovereignty and duty-bound to defend their nation. Cries of revolution, expatriation, and secession, clothed in the language of liberty, had rattled the structures of young nations since independence.

Thus, devoted US citizens left the United States behind to colonize Texas, or moved further west to build new Zions. When a centralizing constitution was proclaimed in Mexico City in 1836, Texans, Californios, and Yucatecans declared themselves independent of a national government that had failed to either protect them or uphold the commitment of state autonomy.[55] Armed conflict had strained already unstable relationships. If the prescriptions of patriotism and natural law in times of war were clear enough on paper, things on the ground were, as they usually are, much messier, as flesh-and-bone citizens found these ideal constructions unconvincing and inconvenient.

Some US soldiers deserted and sometimes joined Mexican irregular forces. Over a hundred recruits, most of them foreign-born and recently immigrated, formed the "San Patricio Battalion" to fight on the Mexican side. Their defection had material, psychological, and ideological incentives. Many—but not all—of these men were Irish and Catholic. The Mexican Army, whose propaganda hailed the bonds of "holy religion" and "love of liberty" it shared with the often-abused regular soldiers, offered bounties of money and land to actively recruit US troops. When Mexican forces were defeated at Churubusco in August 1847, the San Patricios were put on trial. Most understandably ascribed their switching sides on alcohol or coercion, not principle. They were punished with severity regardless, as prescribed by the US Army's *Articles of War* and to the dismay of Mexican observers.[56]

The grimmer situation faced by the southern republic heightened tensions and ambiguities. Mexican merchants served as suppliers, informers, and interpreters to the assailants.[57] Some of Mexico's state governors put off sending troops to the front lest their territory be left defenseless. When the federal government, in dire need of funds, ordered the Catholic Church's real estate serve to warrant government bonds, it met with the bishops' intransigent refusal and the rebellion of some of Mexico City's National Guard battalions who perceived anticlerical policies as anathema to the Mexican nation.[58] In September 1847, efforts to negotiate peace failed, and Winfield Scott's troops marched into Mexico City. The city witnessed both fierce popular resistance—harshly suppressed by the occupying army—and accommodation, as notions of patriotism, self-preservation, and duty became malleable and circumstantial. Occupation was seen, by some, as an opportunity.[59]

As "the army of a republic occupied the territory of another," Mexico's government, manned by moderate Liberals, abandoned the capital and declared the constitutional order null and void, since it had been "ripped apart by the enemy's sword." The Mexico City puro politicians disagreed: the city needed a working, legitimate government that would guarantee its tranquility and welfare. With the approval of US military authorities and against the federal government's express prohibition, they called for, organized, and won elections to renew the municipal council. Moreover, during the occupation, the capital's *ayuntamiento* was liberated from the routine interventions of federal authority and enjoyed an unprecedented degree of autonomy in the handling of its business.[60]

In 1850, Francisco Suárez Iriarte, who had presided over the municipal council during most of the occupation, was brought to trial on treason charges for what he described as putting "himself decidedly between the enemy and his compatriots," his defense of the city's prerogatives, and his "excessive enthusiasm" for "the rights of humanity." The federal government condemned Suárez Iriarte and other councilmen's wartime actions as the most "treacherous machinations against the country's nationality." At the heart of the confrontation lay different conceptions of loyalty. The prosecution was most incensed by the ayuntamiento's collaboration with the enemy in arraigning the "deserters and turncoats" who had fled the US Army and joined Mexican guerrillas. These men, prosecutors argued, had—like the San Patricios—chosen what was right over a contractual obligation in an unjust war. They had been savagely punished for it. Suárez Iriarte disagreed: deserters deserved little sympathy for violating the oath they had taken when inducted into the US Army and shirking their responsibilities.

More important, argued don Francisco, these renegade guerrillas had hurt Mexicans. Municipal authorities had acted against these "destructive adventurers" to protect "our brethren, who, on top of all the evils suffered as the inevitable consequences of war," had been injured by these "hordes of bandits ... wild men, with no knowledge or respect for the law of nations," bent on destroying the lives and property of a peaceful population.[61] The former mayor insisted that his duty lay in upholding the rule of law and promoting the welfare of his constituents, not the abstractions of Justice and Nation bandied about, sanctimoniously and—years—after the fact, by a cowardly government that had abandoned the capital.

Nowhere were issues of national loyalty and political allegiance more ambiguous than in the conquered territories of the faraway North. Citizenship, as a central category of modern politics, channels and fashions the relationship between government and governed. Rarely is it a fixed and transparent object. When the war was over, for all the treaty's stipulations meant to protect the "Mexicans now established in territories formerly belonging to Mexico," their legal status, the nature of citizenship, and the prerogatives and obligations associated with membership, had to be worked out on the ground, sometimes following a binary friend/enemy logic, and at other times that of local political disputes and economic rivalries.[62] On both sides of the border, determining membership in the republic remained a profoundly contentious issue. It could make the political personal and fan the flames of discord.

Both interested actors and later historians have remarked on the relatively bloodless nature of US occupation in New Mexico and California. Uncertainty and expectation, rather than open hostility, greeted the invading US troops. Local wait-and-see attitudes were not surprising: throughout the first decades of independence, great physical distances, inefficient national governance, the transnational mingling of commercial and entrepreneurial interests on site, and the projection of national politics onto local disputes had made for ambivalent, fluctuating relationships between regions and nation.[63] Faced with the challenges of establishing political dominion over a society with whom they were at war, US authorities opted to both threaten and cajole.

Stephen Kearny, commander of the Army of the West, told the inhabitants of New Mexico that it would be "folly or madness" to resist the overwhelming might of his army.[64] He marched into the territory untrammeled—since Manuel Armijo, the territory's governor, had gone south to ask the Mexican government for arms and funds for the resistance—absolved Nuevomexicanos of their allegiance to Mexico and offered to protect them from hostile Indians, establish a republican form of government, and transform them into US citizens. Acting governor Juan Bautista Vigil called for acceptance of the new order of things in the traditional language of political subjection: the territory's inhabitants could not "determine the boundaries of the nation" but only "obey the established authorities"—whoever effectively wielded power—no matter what their "private opinions" were.[65] Kearny administered oaths of allegiance to the sitting authorities: some of the territory's *alcaldes* (mayors) pledged their loyalty to US military authorities in the name of the people they governed, as was mandated by Hispanic tradition. Thus, according to one observer, "the province was Americanized."[66]

In California, Monterey was occupied without major incident, but to the south, the population took up arms. In December 1846, a group of Californios, under the command of Andrés Pico, the governor's brother, defeated US forces at San Pascual. A month later, after Mexican troops were defeated at San Gabriel and La Mesa, the Treaty of Cahuenga put an end to hostilities. The terms of agreement required the Californios to "deliver up their artillery and public arms . . . return peaceably to their homes, [conform] to the laws and regulations of the United States," and not take up arms again but contribute instead to "placing the country in a state of peace and tranquility." Californios would not be required to swear an oath of allegiance until the war with Mexico was over, but the occupying authorities would grant them "equal rights and privileges" as were "enjoyed by the citizens of the United States of North America."[67]

In New Mexico, despite its apparently auspicious beginnings, the transition to US rule was not smooth. Rebellion broke out in January 1847 and spread north: Charles Bent, the governor named by Kearny, was murdered, and the rebels—Nuevomexicanos and Pueblo Indians—took refuge in the Sangre de Cristo Mountains until they were defeated in bloody battle at Taos in February 1847. The Mexican government hailed the Taos rebels as Mexican patriots, as did some US journalists.[68] New Mexican authorities—old and new—had a harder time parsing out the nature of the insurgency. Dent's successor, Donaciano Vigil, claimed the rebellion had no political content: it was nothing but a "war" between "the rabble and honest, decent men." This did not reassure US authorities, who insisted justice be served swiftly and the rebels punished.[69]

Pablo Montoya, identified as one of the leaders of the insurrection, was captured, summarily judged ,and put to death. Seventy-five-year-old Antonio María Trujillo, the member of an influential family, was accused of having "disrespected his allegiance" and "maliciously, wickedly and traitorously levied war against the United States." He also was sentenced to death. For all the officers' promises of assimilation and recognition of rights, the idea that the New Mexican rabble-rousers had become US citizens by virtue of military occupation troubled many, and did not sit well with the federal government. As Secretary of War William Marcy wrote to Col. Sterling Price, New Mexico's military commander, the territory had not become, "by the mere act of conquest," permanently attached to the United States, nor had its residents been automatically transformed into US citizens: they owed obedience to the conquerors and their laws, they could be prosecuted for common law offenses, such as theft and murder. But they were not—they could not be—automatically recognized as part of a republican community in which membership was allegedly founded on volitional allegiance, another seductive but equivocal political fiction. Occupation did not turn enemies into citizens. The rebels' actions were expressions of defiance; they could not, in "proper legal terms," be described as treason.

Consequently, when three other "prominent persons in the late rebellion"—described as "divers other false traitors"—came before the US district court, they were not charged with this heinous crime but with murder, a less substantial felony. This must have provided little solace to the indicted, since it also carried a death sentence.[70] Twenty-four other prisoners were discharged for lack of evidence but also because in taking up arms against the US occupation they had acted as was expected of spineless Mexicans, "under the influence and deceived by ... men who had always exerted tyrannical control over them."[71] Peace, and the establishment of US jurisdiction in what had been Mexico's distant northern frontier did not resolve the thorny issues of allegiance and membership. The Treaty of Guadalupe Hidalgo established the groundwork for Mexicans' becoming US citizens, if this was their wish. Most historians have rightfully insisted on the peace treaty's "legacy of conflict" and betrayal, and the Hispanic population's bitter experience of dispossession and marginalization.[72] Conflict, Anglo immigration, economic transformation, and displacement prompted some to leave their homes, and try to recreate family and community on the Mexican side of the new border.[73] Most former Mexicans, nevertheless, stood their ground, and some—usually those with enough resources, wherewithal, and connections—sought to bolster their aspirations by performing their rights as citizens.

In the conquered territories, establishing and adjudicating their rights and status became a protracted, contentious, open-ended process shaped by the interplay between diplomatic negotiations, legislation, local power wrangling, and judicial arbitration.[74] After 1848, the longtime settlers of Mexico's lost territories confronted very different circumstances. Californios faced a massive immigration and the overheated, cut-throat economy brought on by the gold rush, while New Mexico remained a relatively isolated, poor, and sparsely populated territory, which would stay under the purview of federal authority for decades. Both Californios and Nuevomexicanos participated in setting the ground rules for governance in the wake of peace, if the latter in higher numbers and with greater staying power.[75] Thus, the members of the Nuevomexicano elite who dominated the territorial convention in 1850 managed to preserve certain hierarchies and labor and mining legislation that was favorable to them. Territorialization bolstered their intermittent campaign against the Navajo and fostered a political arrangement that partially buffered them from unruly state party politics that in both Texas and California were soon dominated by Anglo settlers.[76] When Nuevomexicano politicians did seek to obtain statehood, they were denied until 1912.[77]

Conversely, the few Californios who contributed to drafting California's constitution had to confront a pugnacious majority that asserted its right to legislate "for the great American population" that had come into the region dreaming of gold, not "for the native Californians."[78] They could not block the incorporation of California as a state, nor did they manage to create a federal territory in the south, as some had hoped to.[79] They were, for instance, powerless against the nativist impulses of recent arrivals who used the law to exclude "foreigners"—Mexicans, Chinese, Chileans, Irish—from the mining bonanza.[80] Nonetheless, in both the new state and the old territory, members of the Mexican elite were able to establish legal safeguards for their political rights.

California and New Mexico both restricted the right to vote, as did most other US states at the time, to "free white males." An amendment to introduce this restriction into the plan for territorial government was sanctioned unanimously by the Nuevomexicano delegates.[81] The Californios had a more difficult time: they faced assertive politicians intent on carving out greater clout for the recent immigrants riding the wave of western expansion.[82] These men tried to forbid the immigration of free Blacks into the state, and tried to exclude Indians from the elective franchise. Chafing against the constraints imposed by the peace treaty, some delegates denied the "monstrous doctrine" that the treaty-making power could nullify the constitution and make every US citizen a voter.[83] They nevertheless met opposition from former Mexican members of the constitutional convention who also had political experience.[84]

Pablo de la Guerra, for example, scion of a prominent Santa Barbara family, pushed away from the dead-end discussions on the treaty's possible interpretations and the uncertain status of Indians within the Mexican polity. He did not object to the insertion of the word "white" into the article determining the right of suffrage, as long as the word's "true signification" was "perfectly understood" to include men who, like himself and other "citizens of California," had "received from nature a very dark skin." De la Guerra also contended that denying Indians the vote would be fundamentally unfair, given that so many paid taxes: it would be unrepublican to deprive them of "equal privilege" when they bore an "equal burden."[85] Exclusion of the "African race," he argued, was nonetheless "correct and satisfactory."[86] Both Californios and Nuevomexicanos would assert their whiteness, and strove to make sure that it was acknowledged in a "white man's republic."

The outlines and content of citizenship in the conquered territories remained blurry and contentious for years after the peace was signed. The issue proved to be especially slippery in the case of Native Americans, whose status under Mexican law was questioned repeatedly. The alleged persistence of Mexican citizenship was deployed strategically in struggles over political authority, civil and criminal trials, and disputes involving access to resources—such as Indian land and labor. It also was used as a legal stratagem for disarming or paralyzing a political or economic rival, or to keep an actor—and his or her goods—in the open market. Former Mexicans from all walks of life were affected by these usually hit-or-miss efforts to disempower them.

In the disputatious arena of adversarial justice, some litigators argued that former Mexicans could not have become US citizens. In 1870, Pablo de la Guerra, former member of the California constitutional convention, state senator, and lieutenant governor (1861–62), was elected district judge. His election was declared invalid in court, where it was alleged that he was not a US citizen. Litigators asserted that treaty stipulations could not warrant such a transformation, since the treaty-making power was "incompetent to naturalize." Nor could the acquisition of US citizenship reasonably depend on the will of those who desired it. The US Senate had rightly stipulated that the admission into the Union of those Mexicans who had decided not to "preserve the character of citizens of the Mexican Republic" would take place "at the proper time (to be judged of by the Congress of the United States)." Congress had taken no steps to regulate their incorporation into the national community: former Mexicans had not become US citizens, even if, like de la Guerra, they had acted as such for decades.[87]

Furthermore, even if the Treaty of Guadalupe Hidalgo had given the inhabitants of the conquered territories the "full and perfect" right to choose between US and Mexican citizenship, no legislation had been enacted to prescribe the ways such a choice was to be made and registered. It thus could not be ascertained.[88] Judges consistently pushed back against these arguments: the "sanctity and inviolability" of a lawful agreement between nations could not be questioned—even if the other party was a "weak, ill-governed and distracted" country such as Mexico. The treaty was intended "to operate directly, and of itself to fix the status" of the inhabitants of the territories acquired in 1848. This did not "admit of a doubt."[89]

In cases affecting Native Americans, and their right to "take, hold and convey" real property (*Ritchie*) or to remain beyond the purview of the Bureau of Indian Affairs (*Lucero*), the California and New Mexico courts insisted on the historical argument that Indians had been considered citizens by the Mexican government. They argued that Mexican Indians were different—settled, "civilized, peaceful and kind"—from those that US imagination had construed in order to attack, dispossess, and displace them. They waxed lyrical about the heroism with which the "aboriginal" population had fought for independence against Spain, the moral solvency and personal merits of particular "civilized Indians"—despite the "race's" degraded condition and ignorance—and the distance that separated them from nomadic Indian nations that struck terror into settled populations in the territory. They praised their productivity as farmers.[90] The intent of these rulings seems to have been to except these "civilized" Indians from federal norms and mechanisms that were supposed to protect them as members of "domestic dependent nations." For decades after the conquered territories had become a part of the United States, the membership of its formerly Mexican inhabitants remained ambiguous and contentious. In the 1860s, civil war would put this nebulous citizenship to the test.

In the Mirror of Democracy: Testing the Limits of the Republic

The US-Mexico War revealed the republics' glitches, tensions, and fractures. The year the war ended would also confront the formerly belligerent nations with a series of events, both international and domestic, that compelled them to test the meaning and limits of the republic. Even as it imploded, Europe's "Springtime of the Peoples"—startling and overwhelming but ephemeral—forced Americans to, as Tim Roberts has written, take stock of their own democratic experiments.[91] Although no revolutionary transatlantic wave swept over the Old and New Worlds as it had half a century before, the 1848 upheavals electrified democratic, reformist groups in the Americas, expanding the language of politics by popularizing words like *proletarian* and *communism*. They fueled impassioned debates on the nature of property and labor, as both the United States and Mexico faced new developments in matters that had been contentious for some time (the Yucatán question, the eccentric trajectory of voting rights in Rhode Island), forcing their statesmen to probe and try to pin down some of the most contentious issues of democratic life.[92] The nature of their response to these challenges—unfinished and unstable by definition—sketched out the pitfalls and dead ends that would drag North America into civil war.

The 1848 revolutions offered nation-builders in the Americas "a glimpse of the future" and provided them with both a model and a warning.[93] The most liberal voices in the Mexico City press, who had celebrated the fall of France's July Monarchy in February, described the workers' taking to the barricades during the bloody days of June with increasing unease. In the United States, the European uprisings in the name of liberty and nation were hailed as the—somewhat belated—triumph of "American principles" across the sea. Some, nevertheless, felt obliged to emphasize the distance between the venerable, focused, and respectable American Revolution and these European commotions. Former US minister to Vienna William Stiles, a Georgia Democrat, pointed out that the colonists had fought not for "human rights" but for the right to local self-government.[94] Applauded or rejected, Europe's 1848 was seen as a point of no return. In the words of minister Luis de la Rosa, in the wake of "France's astounding revolution," it was now "not only impossible, but ridiculous" to defend the possibility of monarchy in the New World.[95]

Europe's revolutionary experience, imbued with the aspirations of nationalism and democracy, became a prism through which to make sense of American reality. In Yucatán, Mexico's southeastern peninsula, like in Texas before its independence in 1836, politicians challenged the national and republican order, not by subverting its tenets but by appropriating them. As it sought to preserve the commercial and fiscal privileges it had held since the late colonial period, the consistently quarrelsome Yucatecan elite had, from the 1830s on, maneuvered to safeguard the state government's autonomy against the encroachment of national authorities. Amid growing unrest, Yucatán's House of Representatives voted for independence in October 1841, readied itself to resist national mandates, and called on the rebel Texans for support.[96] Mexico City outlawed Yucatecan shipping to Mexican ports and, in August 1842, sent troops into the peninsula. Intense negotiations resulted in a brief reconciliation in the summer of 1843. Relations remained nonetheless antagonistic. When war with the United States broke out, peninsular authorities announced their neutrality.[97]

In the eyes of the national government, the schemes and actions of the Yucatecans were rebellious and treasonous. They were, however, perfectly congruent with liberal political economy and the principles of popular sovereignty. In the words of Yucatán's autonomists, the central government—Mexico's "oligarchs"—had "scandalously destroyed" the pact of confederation which Yucatán had voluntarily joined in 1824. It had imposed "ill-calculated tariffs" on the southeastern state, established "monstrous patterns of confiscation" and infringed upon Yucatán's sovereign rights to profit from its active Caribbean trade and protect its men from forced conscription. When a people "had enough resources to sustain itself with dignity," justice and natural law prescribed by that it should be independent and enjoy the same rights as "other civilized populations."[98]

Optimism and self-assuredness collapsed, not in the face of national opposition but when violent Indigenous rebellion broke out in mid-1847. Armed and mobilized during the tempestuous previous decade, when Mérida and Campeche political elites fought over preeminence in the state's government, Maya insurgents now called for the death of all "Spaniards" and the end of their dominion. They established an autonomous government in the eastern frontier region of the peninsula. In the rebel capital of Chan Santa Cruz, in present-day Quintana Roo, the insurgent Cruzo'ob, guided by the injunctions of a "Talking Cross," traded with British Honduras to obtain arms and ammunition and would only be put down in the early twentieth century. As rebellion grew, the beleaguered peninsular government begged for military intervention and entreated first the United States, and then Spain and Great Britain, to act against the rebels for "humanitarian reasons." In desperation, they offered up control over Yucatán's government in exchange for someone—anyone—saving them from "the Barbarian."[99]

Events in Yucatán were read with different levels of urgency and ideological congruence. Mexican legislators did not dwell on the fact that Yucatán's call for independence, founded on the people's will and their capacity to stand alone, echoed those of Mexico's own heroic struggle against Spain. Yucatecan autonomists described the national government's insistence on union and uniformity as nothing but despotism and greed. Maya insurrection shook them to the core and turned their old arguments upside down: destruction, not strength, originated from within. A large fraction of the people, whose resolve and genius they had so recently hailed as pillars of an independent Yucatán, they now feared as savages. Salvation could only come from without.

In 1841, advocates of independence had proudly told the world that "the number of inhabitants" was the basis of a state's strength, and that all 600,000 Yucatecans would "unanimously" and punctually pay their taxes and defend their "sovereignty and liberty," without need of any "foreign assistance." Six years later, the Yucatecan elite decried popular military mobilization as barbarous, indiscriminate violence intent on eliminating all whites, despite the fact that numerous Maya communities—the *pacíficos*—did not enter the fray, while a good number of white *vecinos*—the respectable family men, often property owners, who were considered citizens—did.[100] Most of the fascinating histories of Yucatán's "Caste War" have not highlighted this dramatic volte-face, perhaps because they have focused on the Caste War's characteristics as an Indian insurrection and analyzed the insurgency's long-standing, deep-rooted motivations. They have traced the insurgency's origins either to economic grievances—the erosion of communal land tenure and the modernization of agriculture, chiefly with the beginnings of the large-scale production of henequen and the exploitation of Indian laborers by powerful plantation owners—or to the struggle to preserve a Mayan identity, grounded in Indigenous religiosity and millenarian enthusiasm.[101]

Contemporary observers were perhaps more attuned to the weight of politics in both igniting and sustaining the conflict, even as they tried to construe it as nothing but an explosion of savage violence, devoid of the logic and legitimacy of revolution, civil war, or political insurrection. In 1848, Justo Sierra O'Reilly, the peninsular government's envoy to Washington, described the rebellion as a "social war" but also argued that the Yucatecans had only themselves to blame for their misfortune: in their "absurd politics," they had given the Maya "rights they do not understand, and possibly never will, given [their] brutal stupidity."[102] The judgment of this distinguished politician, diplomat, and man of letters was warped by racism and fear, but there was some truth to it. The rebels' resentment and violence—rhetorical and physical—against the "whites" were a reality. The alternative, militarized, theocratic frontier society they built, in which deities spoke to the faithful, meant to restore an idealized, precontact golden age. The insurrection was, nevertheless, as much the product of social disruption and economic distress, of identities suppressed and history denied than an offshoot of republican politics.[103] Thus, the letters and declarations of rebel leaders such as Jacinto Pat and Cecilio Chi expound on grievances that were not to be suffered by the free citizens of a republic: excessive taxes—including the irritating excises on distilled liquor and fees paid for the religious services of the Catholic clergy—the unequal treatment of Indians and efforts to take their guns away.[104] Sierra was right about rebellion stemming from what he now depicted as the poisonous tenets of modern politics but mistaken that the Maya misconstrued them. They understood them only too well.

The Maya insurgency was never merely a local conflict: it was sustained by trade with British Honduras and Yucatecan politicians, in their increasingly distressed appeals for foreign intervention, turned it into an issue of concern for foreign powers. In the United States, President Polk requested that Congress consider offering immediate relief to those suffering from a "war of extermination against the white race."[105] US lawmakers could afford a more dispassionate and critical analysis. If action was taken, they surmised, it had to respond to the US national interest and fall in line with its traditions, values, and foreign policy "doctrines." Some senators suggested that, after nearly three years of war against Mexico, it would be unwise to intervene in a region that was, at least nominally, under the jurisdiction of the country with whom peace was yet to be finalized. But neighborly relations were not their main concern. Apprehension about great power diplomacy and a concern over the geopolitics of slavery pushed some senators to call for the application of the "Monroe Doctrine," and prevent the establishment of a European beachhead on the American mainland. A cantankerous John C. Calhoun—who, as James Monroe's secretary of war, claimed to have been present at the creation—denied that Monroe's 1823 message had meant to articulate the nation's basic foreign policy objectives, once and forever. It was a response to specific circumstances and did not preclude careful cost-benefit assessments for every case, "to be decided on its own merit."[106] He saw nothing in the prospect of intervening in Yucatán that would benefit the Union.

Other lawmakers wanted Congress's decision to turn on principle: the republican values of the United States and being on the right side of history—which, in 1848, apparently meant being attuned to what was going on in France. Thus Ohio Whig Joseph M. Root wondered, tongue-in-cheek, how "any gentleman meant seriously to take the position that it was our duty as a nation of republicans, to take part with the aristocrats of Yucatán against *the democracy*?" The Maya were fighting their colonizers, they were defending their rights, they *were* the people of Yucatán, its "wool hats and check shirts." Their savage, unchristian war methods and lack of respect for other people's property were distasteful, but comparable to those of the working-class *blouses* in France. If the United States had "shown [its] sympathy" toward the blouses and congratulated them, it could not intervene in "a Mexican province" on behalf of the aristocratic party in what should be read as a revolution.[107]

Others, like Texas senator Sam Houston, argued that democracy could not be reduced to a matter of numbers. The Indians of Yucatán were, doubtless, a majority. But the United States should "interpose in favor of the whites," who bore upon them the "impression of civilization and brotherhood" with the whites of his nation. "Every Texian" sympathized with Yucatán's misfortunes: they, too, had been the victims of Indian aggression and Mexican tyranny. Houston argued that the Yucatecan crisis had no precedent, and no historical script could be marshaled as a response. Congress's policies should be guided by "the proud sentiment" of revolutionary patriots. Monroe's statement was not an "idle gasconade" but an "axiom of government." The United States had to answer the call of a "feeble, defenseless, oppressed" minority that was being "hunted down by barbarians," not only to keep Great Britain—and her hypocritical abolition politics—out of the American continent but also to "decide in favor of *civilization* or *barbarism.*"[108] In the end, what politicians alternatively called Monroe's "doctrine" or "declaration" was not put into effect. The Mexican government intervened in Yucatán, its firepower financed, in part, by the war indemnity it had received from the US government. Its pacification efforts rolled back the Maya rebellion and circumscribed the territory it controlled. They also shut down the Yucatecan autonomist experiment.

The Maya uprising in Yucatán left a deep imprint in the imagination of Mexicans, but it was far from a unique occurrence. Invasion, armed conflict, and occupation had fanned the flames of discord in the Mexican countryside, which was already riddled with agrarian conflict. In the nation's central valleys, in the Pacific's Great Nayar region, and in the Sierra Gorda, the "extreme situations" engendered by war both increased the suffering of numerous peasant communities and opened a window of opportunity. During the next decade, mobilized pueblos voiced their grievances and forcefully acted to warrant municipal autonomy and community control of land, water, and religious ritual.[109] These uprisings were labeled—both out of fear and because it was a mobilizing concept—as "caste wars." This label construed Indian rebels as profoundly alien—savage, primitive, cruel, and unredeemable—and justified their violent, intransigent repression when in fact, it was Indigenous communities' drawing upon the grammar of republicanism and their intervention in politics that unraveled the social controls of non-Indigenous authorities.[110]

The outbreak of "caste wars" in Mexico coincided, in the United States, with the culmination of a protracted debate, sparked by "Dorr's War" in Rhode Island, which despite its very different expressions, turned on similar, momentous issues: determining who "the people" were and what they could do in their sovereign capacity. With its decision in *Luther v. Borden*, the US Supreme Court drew the curtain on a heated conversation that had probed the meaning and possibilities of the republic since 1842. Rhode Island had not, unlike most other former colonies, drafted a constitution when it became an independent state. By 1840, its slightly modified colonial charter preserved a freehold requirement for voting which had survived the democratizing wave of suffrage liberalization of the earlier decade. In a context of significant urbanization and industrialization, this provision kept many of the state's adult males disenfranchised. In 1842, in the face of opposition from the political establishment, a movement to extend suffrage to working men summoned a people's convention, drafted a new constitution, and called for the election of a new government. Lawyer Thomas Dorr was elected governor under the "People's Charter" and attempted to assert his authority through force of arms in a failed insurrection known as Dorr's War.[111]

Armed rebellion was swiftly put down, but the debates surrounding the contentious issues endured. As those who had challenged the system were charged with federal crimes, debate spilled over state borders and drew in influential political players: Justice Joseph Story, President John Tyler, and leading politicians such as Whig Daniel Webster and Democrat Benjamin Hallet all had something to say. Even in 1848, when arguments were presented before the Supreme Court on whether the plaintiff's house—that of Martin Luther, one of Dorr's lieutenants—had been illegally broken into and searched, both sides agreed that the issue went beyond the Rhode Island government's alleged violation of the Fourth Amendment, and even the heated—and confusing—dispute over the controversial charging of Dorr with treason.[112] The Court's decision, it was argued, was to reveal "the true principles" of the—clearly superior—"American system of public liberty," to determine whether they were available to the people "in practice." The justices' decision would prove if popular sovereignty was "a living principle or a theory, always restrained . . . by the will of the law-making power."[113]

In determining the legitimacy of the Rhode Island rebels' claims, most observers and all judicial authorities recognized the people's sovereignty but asserted that their right to act "out-of-doors," and beyond what was explicitly established by law, was restricted. The advocates for the Rhode Island democrats put up a vigorous defense. They argued that, as their opponents admitted, the state's colonial charter had excluded a great number of deserving citizens from voting. They contended that restricted sovereignty was no sovereignty at all: "no statute of limitations" could be placed on the people if it condemned them to suffer the wrongs, injustices, and inequalities with which one generation might bind another. The men who had drafted the "people's constitution" had relied, prudently and judiciously, on the "sacred right of revolution": they could not be "hanged for treason" because they had failed. The "true doctrine of American liberties" was that the people's sovereignty meant "a majority can alter or change their fundamental laws at pleasure."[114]

Dorr's prosecutors found these arguments unconvincing, as would, eventually, the Supreme Court. "Tumultuous assemblies" in which "the timid were terrified," the prudent alarmed, and society disturbed, could not "call themselves the people."[115] They produced nothing but "anarchy," a "tumultuary, tempestuous, violent, stormy liberty . . . a sort of South American liberty . . . supported by arms to-day, crushed by arms tomorrow." The rule of law was itself the product of the will of the people, in its most mature, time-tested, cumulative version. Unlike its neighbors to the south, US republican citizens resorted to law to limit themselves, by setting "boundaries to their own power," and preserving institutions from the "sudden impulses of the majority." They prescribed the rules of the political game, and set up "THE STATE," which exercised sovereignty as "an organized government, representing the collected will of the people."[116] The sovereign people had to stick to well-established channels for action. Conversely, the Rhode Island revolutionaries postulated that power was "in the greater number" and had acted by themselves and apart from "the lesser number," and according to rules they had arbitrarily established. If the people abandoned stable, regulated "modes of exercising this power," they would end up with a government not of law but of "brute force, of military power," in which "the weak would become victims of the strong."[117]

In the end, the Supreme Court claimed that it had no authority to decide on what was undeniably a political question: the constitution provided for the Union's guarantee of "a republican form of government" and protection from foreign invasion and against domestic violence to every state. Consequently, the responsibility for determining when federal action was required could rest only with Congress. If it were not so, the legitimacy of a government's actions could "always remain unsettled and open to dispute," subject to judicial processes, jury trials, and their verdicts. The security and authority of the state could not, argued Chief Justice Taney, "rest on such unstable foundations."[118] Dorrite hopes were dashed as the nation's highest tribunal refused to say what popular sovereignty was.[119] But although the rebellion was suffocated and its principles maligned, its main objective was accomplished: Rhode Island's conservative assembly drafted a constitution that extended suffrage to most native-born adult men. Nonetheless, the legitimacy of the people's prerogative to intervene in public affairs, demand respect for their rights, and stand against established authority outside of the channels prescribed by law was flatly—if not congruently—denied.

THE YEAR 1848 was momentous. The outcome of the US-Mexico War transformed the continent and unsettled politics for both victor and vanquished. Fighting the war and settling the peace revealed the tensions that riddled federalism, antagonized the different powers, and provoked profound political disagreements. Complex historical processes fed into this turbulence. In the United States, Dorr's War, Rhode Island's movement for suffrage reform, came to an end not with the bang of popular triumph but with the whimper of a judicial resolution that, in a democratic republic, delegitimized the mobilization of the people "out-of-doors." In Mexico, the uprising of citizens who belonged to peasant communities on the Yucatán Peninsula, in Querétaro's Sierra Gorda, and the western Sierra Madre were decried as atavistic, terrifying, and unmanageable "caste wars." These disruptions engendered contradictory visions of what the republic should be, articulated by the contentious and polysemic fictions that underpinned its political legitimacy. Turmoil revealed that the maelstrom of popular politics could upend hierarchies—of race, money, and power—and dissolve an order allegedly grounded in the popular will. In both Mexico and the United States, 1848 exposed the republic's weaknesses and contradictions in the republican edifice. It made men in politics painfully aware of the slippery, unstable nature of its ideological foundations and the potentially dangerous practical consequences. Fault lines seemed deeper in the southern republic but would prove just as destabilizing in the one to the north. They would grow wider in the years to follow. Collapse was probably not inevitable, but, as we shall see in the next chapter, neither grounding open-ended disputes in unyielding moral truth nor the search for a consensus that became increasingly difficult to secure nor trusting the tethering mechanisms that had underpinned postrevolutionary politics neutralized growing conflicts. The stress on republican structures would become unbearable.

CHAPTER TWO

SEISMIC HAZARDS
The Coming of Civil War

IN THE WAKE OF THE US-MEXICO WAR, the territorial, social, and political upheaval it wrought raised the stakes of republican politics. In Mexico, territories lost embodied the failures of the state. In the United States, land conquered became a source of political strife, as corrosive disputes over the federal jurisdiction of slavery were no longer fought over "mere abstraction," but the tangible spoils of war.[1] Mexican politicians became convinced that their country had to change dramatically or face extinction. Their visions of government and political community grew increasingly apart. In the United States, corrosive discussions over slavery's expansion into the Mexican Cession deteriorated into arguments over states' and citizen's rights and the constitution's capacity to protect them, which fed sectional estrangement.[2] At decade's end, in both republics, confrontation gave way to civil war.

None of the thorny issues that obfuscated politics during the 1850s were new: the contentious politics of federalism—confrontations over public revenue, membership in the polity, and military recruitment—had tugged at the boundaries of powers conceived as delegated or concurrent. Even on the floor of Congress, political rivals traded insults and threats in quarrels that sometimes turned violent.[3] In the United States, slavery—increasingly profitable as it became more dynamically enmeshed in the circuits of global industry and commerce—had been a source of alarm, concern, and conflict since the founding.[4] In Mexico, struggles over the Catholic Church's authority, its leadership, resources, and jurisdiction had been equally pervasive and controversial.[5]

On both sides of the border drawn in 1848, politicians tried to settle these conflicts, but the principles they hailed and the schemes they enacted only tightened and tangled the strings of national politics until only the sword could cut the Gordian knot. Controversies surrounding slavery in the United States and the church in Mexico drew the fault lines along which the republican polity would crumble. They nonetheless do not explain the timing or manner of the nation's collapse. War was not only the product of what William Seward called the "irrepressible conflict," of what Mexican Liberals saw as the open wounds inflicted by colonial domination, or of their attacks on the political and religious traditions that their Conservative compatriots believed held the nation precariously together. The war came when the mechanisms that for decades had contained or defused confrontation wore down, tripped up, or failed. These devices were designed to temper the complex, contentious regime that was the modern republic, whose vulnerability—obvious or well-hidden—was an inescapable feature of its man-made, transient legitimacy and of its resting on the people's will.

Two of the instruments meant to institutionalize politics were especially conspicuous throughout a continent trying to domesticate revolutionary politics: constitutions and political representation. The latter allowed for the delegation of the people's power to a smaller group of—one could surmise, better qualified—elected citizens who would give voice to the nation.[6] The former was the belief that a higher, more enduring general law should structure and allocate political power, define its reach, and protect the rights of the governed.[7] By explicitly drawing the shape of the playing field and setting down basic, consensual rules, the written constitutions of the postindependence period were meant to ground and steady politics.

Throughout the first half of the nineteenth century, the stabilizing effect of constitutional rule and electoral politics was doubtless more effective in the United States than in the rest of the continent.[8] Within a framework of delegated powers, constitutionality was recognized as the ultimate test for law's validity, even in the midst of vigorous debates over the practical meaning of fundamental law and contentious efforts to determine the reach of authority—federal, state, or local; executive, legislative, and judiciary—within a federal framework grounded in the separation of powers.[9] After an early rush to amend it (1789–1804), the US constitution stood, unaltered, as the nation's population grew, its economy was transformed, and its landmass multiplied by three. As Alison LaCroix has pointed out, "jurisdictional multiplicity" was characteristic of the first half of the nineteenth century. Nonetheless, the ways arguments about the nature of the Union "eddied, collided, sometimes coalesced" in courtrooms across the United States and the Supreme Court's bold assertion that the judiciary was charged with saying what the law was, paired with the knowledge that its members could not enforce it, and its circumscribed decisions during the first half of the nineteenth century tentatively and progressively set up the groundwork for judicial review as a method for settling constitutional controversies.[10]

Fundamental law withstood the challenges of redrawing congressional policy on western expansion in 1820 with the Missouri Compromise and the threat of nullification in the 1830s. States broadened suffrage rights to include practically all white males, without any major disturbances—Rhode Island was, as we have seen, an exception—even as exclusion hardened on the basis of race and gender. Regular elections manned positions at the different levels of governments.

A noisy, rowdy—if ideologically rather monochromatic—political culture celebrated citizens' freedom and equality over the disparities of money, education, and influence. Rambunctious campaigns and elections, animated by alcohol, male bonding, and the exchange of promises, money, and favors, were followed by a collective—and soothing—"turning away from politics" once ballots were counted.[11]

The same could not be said about the rest of the Americas, even as the newly independent republics faced similar challenges: how to set up the practices and institutions that would articulate the people's will; bringing—and keeping—together different political communities, authorities and distinct, but sometimes overlapping, territorial jurisdictions. In the decades that followed independence, economic stagnation and political instability impaired most of the New World's republican governments. In Mexico, regular elections and the language of liberty and democracy were also the staple of raucous popular politics. Throughout the first half of the nineteenth century, efforts were made to limit access to polls on the basis of income and literacy, but they were never successful for long. Politicians—who would call them to the ballot box, the public square, or the defense of revolution—agreed that all "good" men—decent neighbors, upstanding patriarchs—should have the right to vote. Different stages for voting, however, were set up to reflect the "beneficial" hierarchies that structured society and construe a more enlightened version of public opinion.[12] All men who "made their living honestly" were citizens and had a right to partake in public life; but not all could decide who should lead the republic.

Mexican elections routinely activated systems of solidarity, ideological coincidence, communal ethos, clientelism, dependence, and subordination. These networks mobilized voters and disciplined electoral colleges.[13] Frequent, regular elections fostered the creation of a small, experienced national elite of legislators, but they did not bring about permanent political associations, openly organized to conquer and exercise power.[14] Regular elections did not ensure the peaceful transfer of power at the highest levels of the national government.[15] Between 1821 and 1855, the Mexican executive changed hands over fifty times, as a result not of suffrage but of armed uprisings and negotiations behind closed doors. In 1824, Guadalupe Victoria, a hero of the Insurgency against Spain, was elected president; only in 1852 did an election once again settle the presidential succession, when another general, Mariano Arista, won a majority of votes in an open, competitive election whose results were uncontested.[16]

Like elections, constitutionalism took root in Mexican politics, but it bore bewildering fruit. Throughout decades of "stumbling," a national constitution was hailed as essential, but its different iterations were repeatedly found ineffective, unsatisfactory, and deleterious to the nation's welfare.[17] Between 1823 and 1853, constitutional conventions discussed eight different fundamental laws. In the aftermath of armed conflict, these assemblies opened the door for reconciliation and tried to work out previous constitutional glitches and lay the foundations of a stable national pact.[18] Nonetheless, until 1867, no constitution could reliably and durably settle disputes between the different territories' authorities or the disagreements between civil, military, and religious authorities that all claimed to speak for the sovereign people. Pronunciamientos—armed uprisings against the existing order, often alleging that government had betrayed the people or violated the nation's "true" constitution—were prevalent and quickly became "the way of doing politics in nineteenth-century Mexico."[19]

These insurrections, usually characterized by contained, ritualized violence, hailed the principles of constitutionalism. Recognized as a legitimate—if distressing—expression of the people's voice, this device for mobilization and "forceful negotiations" was used to settle local disputes, bring down governments, and establish a new order of things. Only exceptionally (1841, 1846, 1853) did *pronunciados* resort to—allegedly provisional—dictatorial rule. The explicit goal of these movements, when they grew to a national scale, was the promulgation of a new fundamental law that would "definitely constitute the nation" by striking the right balance between order and liberty, which would allow it to preserve collective and individual rights and uphold efficient government.[20]

For all their failings and the conflicts they stirred but could not resolve, Mexico's constitutions, both federal and centralist, preserved the basics of republican politics: popular sovereignty, the division of powers, the concurrence of different territorial authorities, representative government and the republic's territorial integrity—the Texan secession excepted—while the Federal Republic of Central America, Gran Colombia, and the United Provinces of the Río de la Plata splintered and warred. There was, then, logic to the madness of Mexico's turbulent republican politics: it turned on the belief that the turmoil could, eventually, be tamed through constitutional and political engineering. This fragile rationale was not able to withstand the storm unleashed by dreadful defeat in war. But the squalls of republican politics would also overwhelm the triumphant republic, the exceptional sturdiness of its constitution notwithstanding. By the late 1850s, North America's republics spiraled into uncontrollable violence, less because of accumulating tensions than as a result of the breakdown of the mechanisms that had previously processed them.

The Blight of Political Parties

In their frustrating search for republican stability during the first half of the nineteenth century, Spanish American politicians looked to the United States in envious awe. Alone among those it briefly considered its "sister republics," the "northern colossus" disproved the postulates of venerable political philosophy: it seemed to have cheated fate and escaped the dangers of tumult, tyranny, and faction.[21] Its southern neighbors were impressed by its size, power, and astounding "material progress"—marred, some asserted, by the persistence of slavery. The political stability of the United States and its constitutional consistency—tussles over its interpretation, although frequent and contentious, remained confined to legislative assemblies, courtrooms and the pages of newspapers—fed the aspirations of politicians in the rest of the Americas. When reflecting on the reasons for the exceptional US success, these politicians listed rivers and canals; size and arrogance; Anglo-Saxon vigor or Protestant literacy; widespread land ownership; the presence of a large, energetic middle class; a stable fundamental law; the effective division of powers; and respect for the "true" principles of federalism and democracy.[22]

There was, nevertheless, one feature of US representative politics that only sporadically drew the attention of publicists to the south, despite its importance to and yet, often, absence from their own political repertoire: the existence of operational, relatively stable national political parties. In "Dismantling the Party System," Rachel A. Shelden and Erik B. Alexander have shown how the two-party-system model that historians have relied on to interpret nineteenth-century US politics has artificially simplified, systematized, and immobilized the fluidity, diversity, and responsiveness of political organizations in the nineteenth century; obscured the proliferation of parties at the local, state, and even national level; and concealed the importance of ideology in their making and unmaking.[23] Releasing the past from this projection of the way US politics were understood in the mid-twentieth century brings to the fore the multiple political dimensions, spaces, and actors that activated formal and informal politics a hundred years ago.

Shelden and Alexander's essay opens up exciting possibilities and allows for new answers to important questions.[24] Comparing the teeming US landscape of political organization with that of Mexico reveals political effervescence as a characteristic of New World republics. It also suggests that in the United States, party structures—perhaps not stable or far-reaching enough to be described as a "system"—served as a mechanism that disciplined, channeled, and defused political conflict. Mexican politicians, like their US colleagues, relied on "political networks, newspaper editors and friendly ... election laws" in their struggles for power.[25] Relevant issues, the stakes of politics, and the dynamics of opposition molded partisan organizations and were, as in the neighboring northern republic, more often than not determined locally: in Oaxaca in the 1820s, aristocratic "Oils" confronted the "popular party" of the "Vinegars," while family clans—Urreistas, Gandaristas, Pesqueristas—faced off in Sonora at mid-century.[26]

But if elections compelled organization on both sides of the border, they did not legitimize political opposition in nineteenth-century Mexico, where a monolithic vision of the people prevailed, and the general interest and the common good were conceived as absolute, unalterable, and transparent. There was consequently no need for parties: these permanent political associations could only be moved by ambition and selfish interests, not distinct—but equally legitimate—visions of law, society, state, and nation. Political opponents were thought of not as rivals but as enemies of the common good.[27] Conversely, in the United States, for all the persistence of "antiparty" rhetoric, setting up partisan organizations was considered necessary, legitimate, and healthy, and parties were exceptionally effective on the field. As future New York governor William L. Marcy wrote to fellow Democrat and committed partisan editor Azariah C. Flagg in 1830, "When party is strong almost anything that is done is right."[28]

If parties are, in Salmon P. Chase's words, bodies "of citizens, acting together politically, in good faith, on common principles, for a common object," the moral quality with which they were endowed in the nineteenth century determined what their explicit common objects could be.[29] Because in Mexico parties were an unwanted necessity, there were few incentives for Mexico's loose, often ephemeral political coalitions to try to go beyond winning elections and take on an assertive partisan role in the public sphere. This is why most Mexican politicians identified as "Liberal" before the US-Mexico War. In the United States, however, by the late 1820s, Democrats and Whigs had set up large, fairly stable networks that could weave together local and national politics, engender identities, defend certain issues, recruit impressive numbers of voters, and exercise the power of government.[30]

At mid-century, the republic's North American ordeal was accompanied and aggravated by deep transformations of the ways political organization was understood and undertaken. In the United States, the collapse of what historians have called the "second party system" was both cause and symptom of national crisis. In Mexico, the nation's somber predicaments somewhat surprisingly led some of its politicians to believe that a remedy could be found in the creation of a party system. The dire straits that pushed these political entrepreneurs to call for open partisanship and the organization of stable, competing political coalitions would also warrant their failure.

A Waning Party System . . .

In 1858, Stephen A. Douglas deplored the transformation of the US political scene: "Prior to 1854 this country was divided into two great political parties, known as the Whig and Democratic parties. Both were national and patriotic, advocating principles that were universal in their application. An old-line Whig could proclaim his principles in Louisiana and Massachusetts alike. Whig principles had no boundary sectional lines . . . but applied and were proclaimed wherever the Constitution ruled or the American flag waved over the American soil."[31]

This was clearly an idealized picture of the political scene on which the Illinois

Democrat had cut his teeth. But the two-party scheme that had come together out of Whig opposition to Jacksonian Democracy had complemented the consolidation, growth, and transformation of the young nation. Its mechanics stabilized political competition for over two decades. By extending bipartisan politics throughout the nation and both mobilizing and disciplining voters, legislators, and public opinion, it allowed for steering legislation and governance and uneventful rotations in power, even in the midst of war, momentous social transformation, and the rise of third parties.

Douglas mourned the fracture of a—certainly fragile—bipartisan consensus, based on legislators' agreeing to disagree on the most divisive, morally charged issue they faced: slavery. During the decade that followed the war this brittle arrangement became untenable. After the ratification of the Treaty of Guadalupe Hidalgo, administering the spoils of war implied establishing the conquering nation's laws and jurisdiction over new territories and assimilating a foreign population entitled to status and rights by treaty. It also meant dealing with domestic dissention over the status of slavery in the new territories. In response to the intricate challenges set—and, at first instance, the admittance of gold rush California into the Union as a free state, aggressively pushed forth by the territory's military government—politicians did what politicians do: they resorted to their rhetorical skills in order to convince, manipulate, and seduce; they jockeyed for advantage in Congress and on the electoral field; they derided and threatened their political rivals as they tried to negotiate and narrow the distance between competing visions. In the 1850s, this involved keeping one's own troops in line while reaching across the aisle, but also assuaging increasingly divided constituencies.

In the wake of war and destabilizing victory, legislators, military and civil officials, and judges sought to rebuild harmony. The architects of the Compromise of 1850, of the Kansas-Nebraska Act in 1854, and of the Supreme Court's 1857 *Dred Scott* decision all tried to put an end to the "excitement" triggered by the "great question of slavery" and to the legislative paralysis and increasing animosity it generated. No reliable constitutional, legal, or judicial compass guided the protagonists of these increasingly fractious politics. Instead of producing the "final settlement" they aspired to, their efforts contributed to the growing divergence that eventually became secession and war.[32]

By the end of the decade, the system cracked under the pressure of rising stakes and internal party divisions. California's entering the Union broke the parity between free and slave states in the Senate and "unsettled the question of slavery in all the territory."[33] Lawmakers turned to a strategy that both abrogated and echoed what had been hailed as one of the great accomplishments of US statesmanship: the Missouri Compromise. The "difficulties" entailed by the South's weakness in the Senate were to be balanced by a stricter Fugitive Slave Law, which Southerners had been lobbying for since the early 1840s.[34] In Washington, DC, the slave trade was abolished, but the institution itself was preserved. Nonetheless, unlike its forerunner—under which, as one legislator put it, the United States had lived "quietly and peacefully" for thirty years—the 1850 settlement was inconclusive and riddled by conflict.[35]

The Compromise of 1850 was an unstable and ultimately unsatisfactory solution; the product of party negotiations that were unable to deliver what they had before: an agreement across party and sectional lines—often enabled by Northern legislators' support for Southern positions on the crucial issue of slavery, for the sake of "comity" and party loyalty.[36] Legislative compromises between unequal parties are difficult to assemble and hard to maintain. Many lawmakers rejected compromise outright. They argued that it was premised on the principle "that disputing parties" would not get "all that they were contending for."[37] John P. Hale, who between the US-Mexico War and the civil wars was successively a member of the Democratic, Liberty, Free Soil, Opposition, and Republican parties, worried that the success of the piecemeal settlement depended on either the good faith or the discipline of its executors—their willingness to "stick" to these agreements, which might not extend to a politician's constituency, or to his successor.[38]

Party discipline—indeed, party cohesion—had been upheld in debates over issues vital to the republic: the Commerce Clause, territorial expansion, tariffs, banking, infrastructure. These confrontations were vested with constitutional import but not perceived as eschatological matters of conscience. It would, however, prove difficult—eventually impossible—to maintain partisan unity and restraint in a context of increasing anxiety, as lawmakers from both parties and on both sides of the slavery question resisted what they saw as flouting "the standards of the laws of God" and conceived concessions as "compromising with wrong."[39]

Former New York governor William H. Seward decried "legislative compromises" as "radically wrong and essentially vicious." When not "a cheat," a "delusion," or a "snare," these allegedly pragmatic resolutions meant surrendering "the exercise of judgment and conscience" and the right "to reconsider in the future the decisions of the present."[40] If the vast territories taken from Mexico were to become the Promised Land for free, white, hardworking citizens, they had to be preserved from the corrupting presence of slavery. Acquiescing to "temporary expedients" on the issue would effectively "nationalize" slavery and "Africanize the whole Territory."[41] Antislavery advocates were willing to allow nature and demography to take their course and eventually see the growing "intelligent and industrious yeomanry" of the North trounce the South's "untitled aristocracy" at the ballot box.[42] Conversely, delegates from the slave states argued that property—in slaves as in anything else—was a "sacred right" which no "human power"—of either voters or lawmakers—could restrict or impair.[43]

Mississippi's Jefferson Davis was a committed defender of both Southern rights and the morality of slavery, but he considered that the latter should be kept out of legislative debate. He called for prudence and continuity. It would be far better, he claimed, to preserve an agreement that had served the Union well than to devise—and perpetually debate—new policies. If the people of one section were to "keep discussing the affairs of the other," he prophesized darkly, there would be no end to vexatious controversies, and the Union would be placed "on the verge of civil war."[44] He sought to ground compromise in something more solid than comity: the nation's honor and respect for its international commitments. The future president of the Confederacy insisted that California's entering the Union as a free state violated the terms of the Treaty of Guadalupe Hidalgo. The United States had solemnly pledged to protect Mexicans and Indians in the conquered territories. The hasty establishment of state governments would expose these populations to "reckless" legislation "by those who [had] opposite interests and no sympathy" for them. He nevertheless rejected the "doctrine of noninterference," which held that slavery could not be reestablished where it had been abolished.[45]

Providentially, Davis argued, preserving the Missouri Compromise and simply extending the Mason-Dixon line to the Pacific would enable the federal government to uphold its treaty obligations. South of the line, two territorial governments could be established in what had been Alta California, breaking up a territorial entity so extensive that it harbored dangerous "imperial" tendencies. Other politicians contended that the 1820 Compromise had lived out its usefulness. Its arbitrarily drawn "mathematical line" irritated both defenders and detractors of slavery's extension. Even Henry Clay, who, as speaker, had shepherded this milestone piece of legislation through the House, called for its abrogation. He asked his colleagues for "concession and forbearance," or at least realism and a sense of proportion, when making decisions for the newly acquired territories: those condemning slavery acted on "sentiment [and] sentiment alone," while the slave states' claims involved "property, the social fabric, life, and all that [made] life desirable and happy."[46]

The Whigs' "Great Compromiser" opposed slavery's expansion but considered its existence "a fact," as inescapable as that of slaves not being able to remain in the republic "except as slaves." He deemed political antislavery divisive, noisy, self-righteous . . . and unnecessary. The "laws of nature, climate and soil"—the true "laws of God"—would keep slaves out of the conquered territories, just as Northern yeomen had refused to "compete with Southern slaves for the privilege of making rice, sugar, cotton, tobacco" in the appropriate climes.[47] Fundamental fairness required that the slave states not be excluded from territories acquired with their blood and treasure. Common sense dictated sisterly condescension to the Northern states: it would be cheap and harmless.

Comity and forbearance were not forthcoming. The precariousness of the 1850s deal reflected how difficult it was to hobble together. Although branded "an amicable arrangement of all questions in controversy," it was neither cordial, thorough, nor enduring.[48] As Stephen Maizlish has shown, during the nine months it took to negotiate, the language of diatribe and condemnation wracked Congress, as the advocates of compromise sought to construct voting coalitions large and stable enough to carry it. Congress could not agree on an omnibus bill. The "endless balloting" on the legislative package's separate measures proved a "brilliant stratagem": it allowed members of fractured parties to vote for the items they wanted, without actually having to concede on either interest or principle. Coalitions would come together and fall apart as soon as votes were cast. They did not reflect consensus. The 1850 statutes forestalled Southern secession, but terms of governance in the acquired territories had to be painfully reformulated only three years later. The Compromise of 1850 was, in many ways, not a compromise at all.[49]

The enactment of its terms raised tensions within and without the halls of government. In 1854, debates surrounding the Kansas-Nebraska Act revealed the deep chasms splintering the US political class. Its untidy, violent implementation on the ground led to gross manipulation of the state-making process to force the admission of Kansas into the Union as a slave state. Dismay over "Bleeding Kansas" fractured the Democratic Party and an "almost murderous feeling" rippled through Congress, erupting in the violent caning of Massachusetts radical senator Charles Sumner.[50] Incensed public reaction to highly symbolic and emotionally charged events, such as the return to slavery of fugitive Anthony Burns in Boston, or John Brown's raid, trial, and execution, expressed the outrage that legal resolutions, painstakingly brokered by politicians, provoked among ordinary citizens. Their indignation spoke to the inability of the "two great political parties" to process and respond to the concerns that most distressed their voters.

In the midst of growing anxiety and confrontation, politicians who for a decade had tried to come up with practical solutions to intractable problems blamed their colleagues' intransigence on party politics: the "political tornado of fanaticism" spawned by "fire-eaters" and abolitionist "agitators" who mixed up politics and religion, opinion and dogma.[51] They railed against a "party war over mere party questions" that threatened the "life of the great people" and jeopardized "the Constitution and the Union."[52] Party men were censured for both their dogmatism and their excessive pragmatism, for their willingness to pander to their electorate and their being deaf to and distant from their constituents. The resentment of the disappointed energized an alternative: the newborn Republican Party, which committed to opposing the expansion of slavery as a conservative strategy, meant to save the republic.[53]

When in 1858 Stephen Douglas condemned rival Whigs for their double-talk north and south, he could have been reminded about the mote and beam. Twelve years earlier, it had been a Democrat who had introduced a proviso that made funding for the army contingent on outlawing slavery in the conquered territories.[54] In the next ten years, the party of Jackson was riven by growing distrust. In 1860, the obduracy of Douglas's Southern brethren and their embrace of an extreme version of slaveholders' rights kept him from being the presidential candidate of a unified Democratic Party.

Rather than unprincipled partisanship or the involvement in politics of men inaccurately described by old hands as lacking in "years, responsibilities and restraint," it was the practical impossibility of Whigs and Democrats' putting "their own divided houses" in order that explained their crumbling membership.[55] They could not take a united and categorical stand on the issue of slavery within or broker stable agreements without. The freshly minted association of "Republicans" was reviled as "organized sectionalism" or hailed as free from "party shackles and party names." But Republicans—mostly former Whigs and Democrats who, in some cases, had perhaps also been active in one or several third parties—differed from their former comrades-in-arms only in their refusal to budge on the issue of slavery's expansion.[56] Party strife—fierce but stabilized and contained by the mutual recognition of legitimacy—was displaced by the sharper, messier divisions of section and ideology, as two "hostile geographical parties" confronted each other.[57]

THE COLLAPSE OF THE SECOND PARTY SYSTEM gave birth to the Republicans, doomed the Whig Party to irrelevance and shattered that of the Democrats. In April 1860, delegates meeting at the party's national convention in Charleston bickered over members' credentials and their right to vote "their conscience" if not specifically instructed to vote as a unit in their state delegations. They broke with the precedent of allowing Southern Democrats to write the party platform, while Northerners proposed the candidates. In the midst of these discrepancies over form, little could be agreed upon in substance. Northerners stuck to their view that popular sovereignty enabled territorial legislatures to outlaw slavery, while Southerners, encouraged by the Supreme Court's extreme 1857 *Dred Scott* decision, insisted on it being enshrined as party policy. In the end, Northerners voted down the Committee of Resolutions' majority report, authored by their Southern brethren.

Democrats' shared aspirations and objectives—the 1856 Cincinnati platform, the construction of a transcontinental railroad, the acquisition of Cuba, equal protection for natural-born and naturalized citizens, condemnation of personal liberty laws as subversive, unconstitutional and "revolutionary"—were not enough to heal the rift between delegates. After fifty-seven voting rounds, Douglas, the most successful contender for the party's nomination, was still 100 votes shy of the two-thirds supermajority of 252 votes required. The convention adjourned. When it reconvened in Baltimore in June, the Illinois statesman won the nomination, in the absence of most Southern delegates. while John C. Breckenridge of Kentucky became the candidate of a Southern Democratic party. Discontented defectors had already met in May to seek an alternative to disaster. Rallying around the flag of "Constitutional Union," they nominated Tennessee's John Bell.

In 1860, the deterioration of the party system gave way to one of the most dysfunctional—and certainly one of the most consequential—elections in US history. With the Whigs gone and the Democrats in disarray, a four-way election made the Republican candidate, Abraham Lincoln, president with 38.8 percent of the popular vote, with none cast in the Deep South. The erosion of political organization—what William Seward, as consummate a party animal as Douglas, described as the "agony of distracted parties"—weakened their ability to restrain, rationalize, and make politics predictable.[58] Political opposition drew the lines of war.

... Another Stillborn

The war against the United States spelled tragic loss for Mexico: half of its territory was gone, along with the—surprisingly naive—hope that right, not might, would determine relations between the New World republics. The war's outcome also fractured the fragile consensus that had sustained republican politics since independence, albeit tenuously. In the aftermath of disastrous defeat, experienced politicians who had grown increasingly skeptical of elections, popular politics, and federalism, clustered around Lucas Alamán, a prominent but controversial statesman, historian, and journalist, and embarked on a fierce, systematic critique of "the situation." From the pages of their "independent newspaper," *El Universal*, they called for profound changes to put an end to "the terrible anxiety" stirred by the expectations generated by an idealized system of government whose benefits never materialized.[59]

On September 16, the anniversary of the nation's founding, they harshly condemned the popular rebellion that had sparked the war for independence as ill-timed, wrong-headed, and destructive.[60] By tearing down a heroic foundational myth, these opposition politicians hoped to change Mexicans' interpretation of the past so they could imagine a different future. But they wanted more: they sought to dismantle the premises of modern republicanism. It was its poisonous political fictions, they argued, that had locked the nation in a spiral of disorder and violence. As "friends of progress," they nonetheless rejected the dominant Liberal political culture and, for the first time in Mexican politics, raised the flag of Conservatism. Their political foes, they contended, had stripped the nation of its "nationality, virtues, wealth, valor, strength, hopes" and declared their commitment to preserve (*conservar*) "what weak life" still animated the "poor society" that had been "fatally wounded" by the Liberals, the party of so-called progress.[61]

With pens that dripped with cynicism and corrosive irony, Mexico's Conservatives sought to expose the guiding principles of nineteenth-century politics not only as incongruent, corrupt, and dangerous but also as irrational, even ridiculous.[62] "Popular sovereignty" was a logical impossibility, an oxymoron: there could be no over if there was no under; if all ruled, none would obey.[63] If its semantic inconsistencies were somewhat amusing, popular sovereignty was, as a principle, "monstrous." It dissolved public authority, to the point of governments' being unable to fulfill their most essential duty: they were unable to keep the peace by "guarding and restraining individual rights, with equal force" and secure justice by warranting to each their due. If the principle of popular sovereignty was adopted to its full extent, everything "was, would be and would stay forever subject ... to the desires of the greatest number ... , those who know nothing, have nothing, respect nothing; and who, for these very reasons, assume everything, demand everything, destroy and obliterate everything."[64]

The Conservatives also turned their batteries on the "general interest" as the foundation of law. Submitting to government meant limiting individual freedoms and interests, for the sake of security and the common good. It added insult to injury to pretend that legislative debate could harmonize contrary interests, and that subjection to law required no compromise or sacrifice. Society was made up of men, driven by egoism and passions: government regulations established restrictions, proscriptions, tariffs, taxes, and sanctions. These, by definition, contradicted "the interests, inclination and desire of some." Inevitable confrontations over policy were aggravated by the multiple sovereignties that undergird federalism: activated by rival concerns, interests, or differences of opinion, political positions became more volatile because articulated by "clashing" sovereigns—"the people," the states, the nation—all asserting their supremacy.

Liberals scorned the Conservatives' dismal visions of representative government. They pointed to the alleged brilliant success of the United States in enacting legislation that benefited all, as was proved by the peaceful resolution of the 1830s nullification crisis. It is not clear if Mexican publicists were aware of what this resolution actually implied—a congressional compromise over tariffs, a force bill, and the president's threat to hang one of South Carolina's most prominent sons. Their adversaries argued, not without reason, that this was not an example of effective "transaction" but a vivid illustration of the vulnerability of a system based on sovereignty fragmented and delegated along indistinct lines, in which someone would eventually resort to the threat or the imposition of force.[65]

Public opinion or majority rule did not reconcile contending interests: it sacrificed those of the minority, regardless of their "import and legitimacy," to the "monstrous principle" of overwhelming influence. The "common good"—elusive, evolving, contentious—could not be the outcome of circumstantial arithmetic operations. Rather than taking up the impossible task of "combining" society's diverse impulses, governments needed to rely on "justice, reason and truth"—not numbers—as the guiding principles of their actions.[66]

Conservatives derided what they described as the Liberals' dogmatism, their blind faith in the abstract, radical, outdated "ideals of 1789," and pushed for a pragmatic, disenchanted view of politics. "Two levers," they argued, determined the development of societies: conservative and democratic impulses. In Europe, the clash between these equal and opposite forces had spawned revolution, with its "bloody battles and the screams of its victims." These conflicts, argued *El Universal*, did not set good against evil. They were engendered by political differences and ought to be settled through politics: if not through the give-and-take of judicious public debate, rooted in justice, then by alternating the values and visions held by those in power: "Would it not be Mexico's glory, if these two principles could battle each other, not with cannon fire, but with the arms of reason and intelligence? Wouldn't we give unquestionable proof that we understand civilization better than the peoples of old Europe?"[67] The Conservatives' proposed solution to the unsettled politics bred by people's ignorance, the tyranny of numbers, and the arrogance of demagogues was what we would describe as a stable, working two-party system.

Given these politicians' dismal vision of modern politics, it is surprising that they suggested a remedy of simple mechanics: improved party organization to allow two compact, disciplined, comprehensive "great parties" to alternate in office. It is not surprising, given the acerbic tone and insulting content of the critique they leveled against their opponents, that their one constructive proposal was rejected. Conservatives would not be recognized as legitimate adversaries on the political arena. The most radical of Mexico City's established newspapers, *El Monitor Constitutional*, changed its title to *Republicano* to emphasize the need to defend the republic from what was depicted as an insidious monarchist attack, despite the fact that *El Universal*, for all its defense of order and tradition and despite its censure of democracy's excesses, did not openly advocate for monarchy.[68]

The Liberal press accused its antagonist of writing with "political objectives," of pandering to a people it despised and whose sovereignty it denied, of setting up a "Jesuitical," monolithic, "frivolous and disorderly" political "gang," intent on monopolizing the spoils of government.[69] Tensions climbed when the Conservative Party won the elections to the Mexico City government in July 1849, which put them in charge of organizing elections in the nation's capital the following year. It was the municipal council's duty to oversee the election of two electoral colleges in which the final vote was taken, in a complex, lengthy—and therefore malleable—operation.

In September, after the popular election, the meeting of the city's electoral college was disturbed by cries of "Long live the Republic!" and "Death to the monarchists!" and had to be suspended. In December, Congress, with the support of the executive, reformed electoral law to exclude municipal authorities from the organization of elections. In response to a street riot in which the crowd, again calling, "Death to the monarchists!," broke the windows of a Conservative publicist's house and threatened to burn down *El Universal*'s press, the Conservative municipal council resigned.[70] The Conservative "party system" experiment was dead in the water . . . as was Conservative faith in the possibilities of modern electoral politics.

When *El Universal* bemoaned the events that had led to the aldermen's resignation, the moderate daily *El Siglo Diez y Nueve* scolded its colleague for making "too much noise" over some broken glass and the unsavory expressions of street urchins. Words were neither deadly nor physically harmful. They would soon be "blown away by the wind."[71] A few years later, this newspaper would, in turn, deplore the absence of modern party politics. In 1857, while most of the Mexico City press called for "a fusion between parties" or even the suspension of constitutional rule in order to prevent factional conflict descending into civil war, *El Siglo*'s editor-in-chief, Francisco Zarco, one of the most influential members of the constituent congress, defended the new order and called for two political innovations to bolster it: political parties and campaign platforms. Only then would suffrage—the "only act in which the people exercised sovereignty for themselves"—become an effective mechanism for the "legitimate expression of public opinion."[72]

Advocates of party politics saw the aversion they inspired as a cultural problem: a "false sense of modesty" prevented citizens from openly admitting they sought public office. This reduced campaigning to begging for votes in the dark, making inconsistent promises, and relying on dishonorable methods to manipulate elections. Candidates should be open about their "noble and patriotic aspirations"; they should publicize what they were running for: an electoral platform would stand as a solemn promise to voters and a guide for their actions in government if elected. Putting together a single, conciliatory "national party" meant surrendering "what men can never sacrifice: ideas and convictions." More important, "a transaction government, with no program, no vigor, no initiative . . . vacillating and uncertain," would satisfy no one. It would be unable "to do anything useful" and lock the nation into "a deplorable status quo."[73]

Distrustful of a government that was allegedly above and beyond partisanship, *El Siglo*'s editorials argued that, in other countries—and particularly in the United States, whose "continuous aggrandizement" Mexicans could painfully attest to—political parties did not seek to merge with each other. They fought for power, and, having conquered it, rightfully ousted those who did not belong to "their political communion" from positions of authority and influence, and surrounded themselves with "their own."[74] Political parties were not the enemies of public peace. Instead, they "battled openly, on the luminous field of argument." Those who lost one day could be victors the next, if they came up with a more solid, persuasive program. Political competition, disciplined by party organization and expectations, was always beneficial to the country.[75]

To *El Siglo*'s chagrin, open partisanship, blatant political ambition, and enthusiastic campaigning for oneself proved too exotic for Mexico's mid-century politicians. In 1857, Miguel Lerdo de Tejada, "a decided champion of social reform," former secretary of the treasury, and darling of the more radical Liberal press, abandoned the presidential race. He was impelled, he argued, by both principle and honor: he dreaded disunion and trusted Liberals would defend ideas, not fight over individuals or the spoils of government. He also refused to "expose his name to certain defeat," when he knew that it did not "derive from the free opinion of the people."[76]

Once the constitution was proclaimed on February 5, 1857, Liberal publicists—those calling for unity and compromise as much as those who encouraged vigorous partisan confrontation—disparaged "exclusivity" and claimed that public affairs were open to all men of good faith who sought the welfare of the republic.[77] Those who disagreed with Liberal law and policy were welcome to criticize and work for reform. But this celebration of "divergent opinions" had its limits: those who did not accept the new constitution had "declared themselves beyond the pale of the law."[78] The opponents—critics?—of fundamental law were not valid political players: so-called Conservatives lacked political vision and offered no viable alternatives, even as they "spoke without respite of religion, family, and property," defended "the principle of authority, without saying where it originated," and dreamed of "setting up a throne for a foreign prince."[79]

The Liberal press deemed its most radical political adversaries criminals and denied them even the label they had adopted, as members of a legitimate opposition. *El Siglo* claimed that "no political party in Mexico can be called Conservative. Those who claim that title are exclusively those who belong to the retrograde faction, whose banner is theft and debauchery, murder and treason."[80] A decade earlier, this newspaper had insisted that fighting words were not lethal. Those it published in 1857 meant to set up exclude Conservatives from the political arena. Mexico's contending parties would meet, weapons in hand, on another field.

Constitutional Tinkering

The Age of Revolution locked North American politics into the here and now by cutting them off from divine right and a transcendent order of things. They were validated by popular sovereignty, a formidable notion, as powerful as it was elusive. On a field made inherently unstable by revolutionary principles, constitutionalism figured prominently in the efforts of those who tried to build working governments. Older notions of the constitution as a frame of government resting on an intricate web of norms and precedents, customary rights and institutional equipoise, were replaced by its modern incarnation: a written document that set down the unvarying principles of government, proclaimed rights, and adjudicated power. Fundamental law was meant to give greater certainty to a political system in which the sovereign (the source of political authority, but also the last instance of public decision-making) was no longer a monarch or, as in the British case, the King-in-Parliament, but a protean abstraction: the people.[81]

Among those of the New World republics, the US constitution was practically alone in successfully weaving together theory and practice: it formed a union from sovereign states, defined the reach of different public authorities, and structured and delegated political powers.[82] Soon after it was ratified, it was recognized as the law of the land. Its stability spoke to its efficacy ... until it failed to prevent civil war. Conversely, on the other side of the border, recurrent efforts to reformulate the constitutional pact—1824, 1836, 1842, 1843, 1847, 1853—attest to Mexican statesmen's persistent faith in constitutionalism despite its consistent failures. In 1857, Mexicans were not able to test the constitution's efficacy; its subversive features set off a war that lasted almost ten years.

Despite widely different constitutional experiences, the outbreak of civil war in both North American republics was the outcome of a constitutional crisis, of fundamental law's incapacity, by the end of the 1850s, to channel political conflict toward peaceful resolution, grounding and containing divergence, providing the parameters that had made compromise possible and concessions acceptable.[83] Instead, the content and interpretation of constitutional precept became the object of heated disputes.

The Constitution as Obstacle or Instrument: Mexico

Unsurprisingly, it was in the southern republic, where no fundamental law had engendered enduring consensus, that struggles over the constitutional order proved most unsettling. In five years (1852–57), the Mexican government swung from that of an elected president under a reformed federal constitution to a centralizing, authoritarian Conservative dictatorship, followed by its revolutionary equivalent under Liberal leadership, and the proclamation of a constitutional, "democratic, representative, and popular republic," whose charter was abrogated after ten months by the president who had sworn to defend it.[84]

The 1850 election of Gen. Mariano Arista was the first since 1824 to allow for a peaceful transition in the executive office.[85] This regularization of republican government at mid-century could nevertheless not withstand the cycle of dissatisfaction, unrest, and contagious insurrection that had characterized Mexican politics since 1821.[86] In October 1852, the Plan del Hospicio, published in Guadalajara, deemed Arista's administration "unworthy of the public's confidence" and summoned a constitutional convention to refashion the national pact.[87] Liberals and Conservatives both called for radical political change and, as they jostled for power, sought out the same seasoned actor who, in Mexico's dramatic political theater, had alternately been hailed as the nation's savior and its most despicable villain.⁸⁸ Exiled military strongman Antonio López de Santa Anna was summoned to preside over the restoration of "order and justice" in the land.

The general took up the Conservatives' offer. Bitter, disenchanted, and radicalized, these politicians sought to reform Mexico's dislocated society without invoking its participation or even its consent. The nation would be modernized and transformed by the rigid execution of law conceived in reason and implemented with mathematical and uncompromising precision. Conservative luminary Lucas Alamán put forward a bleak, top-down, drastic program for government. Only by following its basic principles, he argued, could the nation elude the "dangers" stalking the "Spanish American race" in the guise of its voracious Anglo-Saxon neighbor. His first priority was to preserve and protect the Catholic religion, which had become the only thing "holding Mexicans together." The army needed to be strengthened, so that it could maintain order, ensure the safety and free movement of people and goods, and defend Mexicans against thieves, agitators, and "barbarous Indians."⁸⁹

Authority had to be reasserted: impulsive political experimentation had weakened the government and the nation, both morally and structurally, and endangered their very survival. Mexico's political geography needed to be redrawn, its sovereign states "confused and forgotten," representative government suspended, until "popular elections" could be organized differently. These radical measures could never be undertaken or enforced by a government of delegated, divided powers: the Santa Anna regime needed to be set up as a dictatorship.⁹⁰ Conservatives broke with precedent and, in the wake of the *pronunciamiento*'s triumph, did not call for an elected constituent congress, which had previously healed the nation's rifts by reconciling contending parties, realigning interregional relations, and articulating new visions of government.⁹¹

Instead, Conservatives published provisional "Bases for the Republic's Administration," which succinctly expounded the executive branch's ample powers, set up a twenty-one member Council of State, and shut down all representative bodies, with the exception of municipal councils in the larger cities.⁹² In their staunch rejection of politics and eagerness to consolidate authority, those who manned Santa Anna's government decided that the best constitution was—at least provisionally—to have no constitution at all. Mexican Conservatives had hoped to put together an efficient machine for government, one that would be above society and beyond politics. Their plans collided with widespread irritation, resistance to its arbitrary policies and the president's frivolity, and his flirtation with a monarchist conspiracy intent on provoking Spanish intervention.⁹³

In early March 1854, in a small town in the southern state of Guerrero—created only in 1849—the proclamation of the Plan de Ayutla ignited rebellion. Like most pronunciamientos, the movement sought to cast as wide a net as possible. Its long-term goals were vague and noncommittal: it called for the overthrow of the dictatorial government and the election of a new constituent congress.[94] Its adherents ranged from the radical federalists of Nuevo León to disappointed Santannistas. Once triumphant, insurrection was cast as revolution: its protagonists called for the deep transformation of the national polity.

The men surrounding Santa Anna had wanted to reform—redeem—a society they saw as distressed and unhinged. They saw constitutional law as an obstacle. Conversely, the Ayutla Liberals—many of them young, small-town politicians who had been harassed and displaced by Santannista despotism—called for founding nation anew.[95] They put forth a different understanding of what a constitution should do: fundamental law needed to go beyond brokering union between multiple sovereigns and ordering and systematizing what already existed. Adjustments to the structures of government were necessary but insufficient; an "absurd economic system" had to be destroyed. A poor and downtrodden people could never "be free, nor republican, nor remotely happy, even if a hundred constitutions and thousands of laws proclaimed abstract rights and beautiful but impracticable theories."[96]

These hopeful revolutionaries saw constitutions, not as legal frameworks, meant to stabilize politics, but as instruments for transformation. Because of the self-conscious radicalism of its designers, the 1857 constitution would be hard to sell as a consensus document. The Ayutla Liberals also broke with tradition by organizing, in the wake of military victory, elections that excluded the opposition.[97] Even in the absence of Conservatives, no common vision guided the assembly. The door almost closed on the possibility for momentous change when only one vote prevented the restoration of the 1824 confederal arrangement.[98] A radical minority had to work hard to convince their colleagues that simply restoring state autonomy was not sufficient to put the nation back on track. The more militant Liberals pushed for substantial reform through wily manipulation of parliamentary procedure, the strategic use of liberal and democratic tropes, compromise on both principle and practice, and the assertive actions of the Ayutla government on certain key issues: equality before the law and circumscribing the church's economic muscle.

The reformist impulse, however, was tempered by politicians' compulsion to temporize, evidence of deep-seated, popular attachment to Catholicism and older forms of property and social organization, which had been legitimate, if not efficacious, and the moderating influence of President Ignacio Comonfort's cabinet.[99] The farthest-reaching proposals—direct universal suffrage, trial by jury, religious tolerance—did not make it into fundamental law. But the 1857 constitution was, as we shall see in chapter 4, groundbreaking on issues of political representation, state religion, and the regulation of property. After almost a year (February 18, 1856–February 5, 1857) of heated discussions, the constitution disappointed almost everyone. Most *puros* felt it did not go far enough. Many who agreed with the fundamental law's modernizing spirit had practical concerns about its operation. The president would soon deem it an unworkable instrument of government.

Conservatives, discredited by their collaboration with the Santa Anna regime, did little but stand on the sidelines, criticize (often in hyperbolic, almost hysterical terms), complain, and conspire.[100] They found an ally among those adversely affected by constitutional dispositions—military officers and clerics who had lost their privileged legal status (*fueros*) and corporations threatened by the loss of property. In the midst of growing unrest, the disapproval of a crucial actor—the church—threatened the legitimacy of the new order. Most members of the clergy condemned what they perceived as the state's unacceptable intervention in ecclesiastical affairs. Some clerics were openly hostile to the reformers: during the Holy Week solemnities, the cathedral doors were shut on Mexico City's avant-garde governor, Juan José Baz.[101] Efforts to negotiate a mutually satisfactory arrangement, at least on the issue of selling off ecclesiastical property, foundered both on the church's defense of its autonomy and on what Treasury officials deemed was the bishops' lack of financial sophistication.[102]

Many Mexicans were concerned by the growing rift that separated temporal and spiritual authorities. For all its open condemnation of the constitution, church leadership did not confront the government directly, until a March decree ordered all political, civil, and military officers to swear to uphold the constitution. Conscientious objectors would lose their positions. The bishops cried foul: it was preposterous to appeal to God and conscience to bolster a law that was "impious, atheistic, and consequently unjust and immoral."[103] Those taking the oath were guilty of a "very enormous sin" and would be excommunicated.[104] The church decreed that the 1857 law violated that of God. Fulfilling one's civic duty meant doing evil. The bishops' condemnation and the government's clumsy attempts to warrant allegiance placed individual consciences in a moral quandary that crystallized the nation's schism: the good Catholic could not be a good citizen.

Compromises, Judicial Review, and Amendments: The United States

Unlike the constitutional discontent that had long pervaded in Mexican politics, the 1787 fundamental law was almost universally revered in the United States, rejected only by the more radical abolitionists—a minority within a minority. Their opposition was a symptom of their eccentricity and limited political relevance, not a symptom of the tensions that riddled constitutional consensus in the decade that followed the US-Mexico War. The US constitutional crisis that led to war was the result not of widespread rejection of fundamental law but of conflicting interpretations on a narrow practical question: that of congressional authority over slavery in the territories. The constitution's "ambiguities" and "gaps," Arthur

Bestor has written, "pricked out, as on a geological map, the fault line along which earthquakes were likely to occur."[105]

The 1850s witnessed a constitutionalization of politics, not unlike the one Jack Rakove has described for the 1790s: disagreements over matters of policy spawned corrosive debates over the reach and legitimacy of the powers of government.[106] In their eagerness to defuse the increasingly confrontational politics of the 1850s, lawmakers and statesmen, publicists and judges turned to the constitution. What began as a discussion of the powers of Congress to regulate slavery in the territories gave way to incompatible interpretations of the nature of the constitutional pact.

The US constitution offered no clear answer to the political predicaments of the 1850s. A particularly parsimonious document (when compared to other constitutions in the Americas), it set up a government of delegated powers, meant to check and balance each other. It was silent on the concept of sovereignty and on the issue of slavery. The constitution's advocates—Francis Lieber and Frederick Douglass then, Sean Wilentz today—argued that the founders were on the right side of history, that the constitution's silences embody a principled refusal to sanction either property-in-man or what Lieber called "State-egotism, envious localism" or "State-ishness."[107] But in practice these omissions—whether righteous reserve or clever ploy to enable compromise—allowed for flexibility, for the plausible constitutional defense of contradictory arguments on slavery and the Supreme Court's egregious verdict in the 1857 *Dred Scott* case.

In 1850, John C. Calhoun's remonstration against the legislative scramble to regulate the incorporation of conquered lands suggests that, for the glum veteran champion of Southern rights, what the constitution said was less important than what it was supposed to do. He commended its informal, operative underpinnings—parity in the state representation in the Senate—and the "fraternal feelings" that both cemented the Union and allowed for sectional peculiarities, such as the South's slave economy. What the advocates of the 1850 Compromise offered, he argued, put the Union on the path to ruin. California's entering the Union as a free state destroyed the Senate's "nearly perfect equilibrium," which had "afforded ample means to each [section] to protect itself against the aggression of the other." The South Carolinian foretold that an increasingly self-righteous, demographically more dynamic North would be free to leave its "constitutional duty" unfulfilled: a tyrannical majority would eventually assault the South, which would find no procedures or devices for its protection.[108]

In the midst of such tribulations, others looked not to the constitution's text but to the sources of its legitimacy: the states and the people. In defending opposite positions on slavery's expansion, each side vigorously waved the flag of state's rights.[109] Southerners insisted that they were entitled to the spoils of a war for which they had paid, bled, and died. The sanctity of property—in slaves as in any other form—imposed on both federal and state authorities the duty to protect it: the 1850 Fugitive Slave Law needed to be strictly enforced. Their opponents insisted on states' right to protect their free Black populations through personal liberty laws, and pushed back against a statute that had made the sin of slavery "national" and turned "hospitality into a crime."[110] The Fugitive Slave statute became a lightning rod for citizen anger. Southerners fumed against Yankee insubordination; indignation pushed the indifferent into antislavery politics in the North.[111] The solid constitutional ground that the law stood on did not quell the passions it unleashed or make its execution less problematic.[112] Its enactment revealed deep fractures in an irritated polity and the difficulties of upholding the constitutionally mandated protection of slaveholders' rights in federal court.[113]

In 1854, amid rising tensions, Congress debated the legal framework for the organization of the Kansas and Nebraska Territories. As a remedy for "existing evils," Illinois senator and leading Democrat Stephen A. Douglas marshaled one of the US political creed's key elements: popular sovereignty.[114] Pinning the determination of the slavery dispute to one of the most hallowed republican principles, to be resolved locally and on a case-by-case basis, would (hopefully) remove the contentious question from Congress, where it was wreaking havoc, and turn it over to those who were "immediately interested in it, and alone responsible for its consequences."[115] The epitome of the values of the United States, open-ended by nature, popular sovereignty theoretically enabled the much-coveted organization of the West, while delegating and postponing the unnerving decision on slavery's status in a given territory.

For all its conceptual punch, popular sovereignty proved slippery and volatile. Within the framework of federalism, its interpretation, and especially its implementation, was deeply problematic.[116] It had, as we already know, bolstered insurrection in Texas, Yucatán's drive for independence, and the Dorr rebellion in Rhode Island. Some despondent Southerners also argued that it had cloaked California's dubious bid for statehood with instant legitimacy, as if "every band of wandering men in any section of the country [who] choose to assemble together and adopt a so-called constitution" could bind the US Congress into recognizing "the validity of their sovereignty."[117]

This dangerous precedent had opened the doors of the Union to the fortune-hunting invaders of California, goaded by the officers of an occupying army, into establishing a state government to free themselves from being checked by the federal government. It could also eventually allow what many saw as an outlandish sect, settled on the shores of the Great Salt Lake, to set up a free and sovereign "state of Deseret." By bolstering the influence of numbers, popular sovereignty threatened the less populated South, as it inflamed the hopes and rhetoric of those who hoped to see the "slavocrats" mortally wounded by the votes of the numerous "unseduced, unpurchased, unawed" freemen of the North.[118]

In contrast, although all agreed that the people were sovereign, there was no consonance among US politicians as to who "the people" were, in this particular instance, and when they could exercise their sovereign prerogatives. Once again, the controversy hardened into a sectional divide. Northerners opposing the expansion of slavery argued that territorial legislatures could legally exclude the nefarious institution; Southerners derided this "squatter sovereignty" and insisted that only a constitutional convention could determine if a state was to be slave or free. When put into practice in Kansas, the principle of popular sovereignty had disastrous consequences. It did not take the corrosive issue of slavery out of politics: instead, the slavery dilemma infected the territory's colonization schemes, and pit, often violently, free-state against proslavery settlers.

Legislative and constitutional initiatives were warped by the competitive logic of electoral and representative politics.[119] The territorial census was packed and elections and constitutional referendums were manipulated and marred by extraordinary levels of violence and fraud. Artificial majorities were secured by unsightly means and legislatures pushed for extreme measures—an act of August 14, 1855, for instance, deemed it a felony to deny "the right to hold slaves."[120] Eventually, two constitutions were drafted and sent to Washington, where President James Buchanan endorsed the proslavery document, drafted in the town of Lecompton. The heated—and ultimately futile—controversy over Kansas's admission to the Union under a proslavery constitution—derided by its critics as the "Lecompton swindle"—split Congress along resolutely sectional lines, and pitted two influential Democrats, President Buchanan and Stephen A. Douglas, against each other.[121] Kansas's statehood had to be postponed until 1861. Rather than calming a storm-tossed sea, popular sovereignty, as both principle and process, hardened divisions and fueled the flames of conflict.

In the increasingly frenzied political climate of the late 1850s, one actor sought to shut down the slavery controversy by doing what its political colleagues had been unwilling or unable to do: ground its resolution in the constitution. In 1857, the Supreme Court took it upon itself to settle these thorny issues by ruling in the case of Dred Scott, a slave who sued for freedom on the grounds of his having been taken by his owner into places where slavery had been outlawed by the Northwest Ordinance: Illinois and the Wisconsin Territory. The decision, penned by Chief Justice Roger Taney, sought not only to determine the reach of federal authority over a peculiar form of property but also to permanently fix the place of African Americans—free and enslaved—within the republic.

Widely considered the worst in the Court's history, the *Scott v. Sanford* decision sanctioned the slaveholders' most extreme position and deemed all efforts to regulate slavery in the territories—including the 1820 and 1850 Compromises—unconstitutional: it affirmed that "the right of property in a slave" was "distinctly and expressly affirmed in the Constitution." Nothing in fundamental law gave

"Congress a greater power over slave property," or entitled "property of that kind to less protection than property of any other description. The only power conferred [was] the power coupled with the duty of guarding and protecting the owner in his rights."[122]

Taney's decision—with two justices concurring, four more writing separate opinions and another two dissenting—also denied Scott standing to sue a citizen in federal court, since he was not, and could never become, a citizen under the constitution. As "a negro, whose ancestors were imported into this country, and sold as slaves," he would have been regarded by the founders, whether enslaved, emancipated, or born free, as a being "of an inferior order, and altogether unfit to associate with the white race, either in social or political relations; and so far inferior, that they had no rights which the white man was bound to respect." Through a jaded reconstruction of the founders' worldview, Taney tried to put an end to the polemics about slavery's expansion. His opinion also took it upon itself to shut down the aspirations for inclusion and the sense of possibility and political agency that the rhetoric and experience of the United States had engendered, especially among marginalized populations. In ruling in the *Dred Scott* case, Taney sought to depoliticize what is perhaps the most political issue of all: the character of the republic, the shape—and color—of the body of the "sovereign people."

For all of Taney's ungenerous reading of the founding and the constitution, the justices' goal had been to quell a corrosive confrontation. Their hopes came to naught: the *Dred Scott* decision speaks to the still unsettled character of judicial review at mid-century. It did not settle the issue but became another source of division and indignation, another factor in political disintegration. The 1860 Republican Party platform vigorously condemned the "new dogma that the constitution, of its own force, carries slavery into any or all of the territories of the United States" as "dangerous political heresy."[123] Democrats split: Southerners embraced the Court's decision. Others clustered around Douglas, as he, somewhat inconsistently, clung to the principle of popular sovereignty, since, he argued, the people's right "to make a Slave Territory or a Free Territory" was "perfect and complete," regardless of the Supreme Court's position "on that abstract question."[124]

Taney's allegedly definitive interpretation proved counterproductive. The Court's guarantee to slaveholders notwithstanding, Republican success at the polls was perceived in the South as the "triumph of a sectional majority," spelling the "doom of our once happy and united confederacy."[125] Once again, those looking for a way out found it in the constitution, controversially interpreted. Unable to come together on fundamental law, they relied on it to come apart. Secessionists argued that the sovereign states that had come together to form the Union in the late 1780s had a constitutional right to leave it. Fundamental law no longer afforded them the security they craved, it had become "an engine of oppression" that sustained a "tyranny," all the more "galling" for its being "exercised through constitutional formulas."[126]

Most secessionists insisted that both the constitution and their nation's political principles—the people's rights to self-government and to alter the institutions "bequeathed to them by their fathers"—allowed them to leave, ideally in a dignified fashion.[127] It was wrong to construe federal authority as ruling "over all of the People." The government of the United States was a "Government of States." The latter had the power "inherently in them" to forsake what had become a less-than-perfect Union, through the same expedient as the one through which they had joined it: an elected convention. Since the North had broken "the bargain" on which "the compacts of the fathers" had been founded, the slave states could forsake them. The rights guaranteed to the states by the constitution were "political in their character, and not susceptible to judicial decision." It made no sense to speak of "rights and no remedies." Those affected by the North's transgression of the spirit of the constitution could "withdraw from the compact, by virtue of its own provisions."[128]

Their opponents argued that the United States was not "an aggregate of partners at pleasure."[129] They pointed out that establishing "a constitutional right to destroy the Union" in fundamental law would have made for "indeed a strange form of government."[130] The states were not parties to a contract but creatures of a covenant. "For the first time in history," the founders had endowed a "confederacy of states with the highest degree of self-government" by creating a "complete representative" central government, invested with all the "usual attributes of sovereignty." It was a "national law," grounded in "national necessity, national consciousness and national will, expressive of national destiny." The constitution had given birth to a national "organism," not to "a string of beads in mere juxtaposition on a slender thread that may snap at any minute."[131]

IN THE AMERICAS, theoretical and philosophical differences as to the nature of the political community engendered by constitutions had been a staple of political debate since independence. Different opinions became irreconcilable, and underpinned real—and incompatible—projects for the state and nation. In 1857, Chief Justice Roger Taney had argued that the "plain words" of the constitution supported the slaveholders' position. Three years later, Frederick Douglass, who had escaped from slavery, insisted that a "plain English" interpretation of the US constitution made it "bend for the cause of freedom and justice." The Black abolitionist and the Supreme Court justice both saw, in the law of the land, the bedrock and outline of the republic. Both insisted, passionately, that states and citizens, as members of the Union, were "responsible" for securing the version of the republic that was delineated in the constitution.[132]

A rarefied atmosphere engendered monsters. Tyranny, godless or theocratic, seemed to lurk over North America's republics. Mexican Liberals drafted a transformative constitution and believed it gave the nation new, more solid foundations. Their opponents were convinced that it destroyed them. Citizens of the republic to the north began thinking that the Union was not, perhaps, the exceptional political creation it was hailed to be. Fears of "Mexicanization," of passion overrunning Anglo-Saxon common sense, fed into growing anxieties.[133] In the end, the hallowed 1787 document proved as ineffective in preventing rebellion and war as the fleeting fundamental law of its weak, disorderly neighbor. There was no room, on either side of the Río Bravo, for the aspirations of the political other in the republican constitutional edifice.

The Politics of Emergency

In the decade that followed the peace of Guadalupe Hidalgo, political polarization eroded the unstable ground on which the North American republics had stood and once again put them on the brink of war, which this time would pitch compatriots against each other. Throughout the second half of 1857, popular discontent and bewilderment riddled the Mexican heartland.[134] Officers gave up their commissions and officeholders resigned rather than take a constitutional oath deemed sinful by the church. In the United States, by April 1861, secessionists had set up autonomous governments in seven states, established a confederation and organized—on paper—an army of over 60,000 men, "held in readiness" at home.[135] As confrontation loomed and arms were readied, politicians scrambled for a peaceful solution.

In December, President Comonfort, with the support of both Mexico City's radical governor, Juan José Baz, and the Conservative garrison, commanded by Félix Zuloaga, dissolved Congress and abrogated the contentious constitution. The *pronunciados* called for drafting a new fundamental law "according to the nation's will" that would protect the people's "real interests." In an unprecedented strategy in Mexico's tumultuous legal tradition, they promised this constitution would not be enacted until ratified by the votes of "the Republic's inhabitants."[136] But fundamental law would not be redrawn. The president's "system of vacillation"— his upholding reformist law—unsettled conscientious Catholics and irked military and ecclesiastical authorities. In January, Conservative officers struck against Comonfort, "to save the Fatherland" by preserving its religion, the army's well-being, and the rights of Mexican citizens.[137] Once in power, they sought to turn back the clock on political reform by abrogating the Ayutla government laws.

In the United States, fire-eaters in the South and radical abolitionists in the North hailed secession as deliverance, the former from the "Despotism" of a majority claiming to be "infallible and omnipotent," the latter from association with the "most lawless, desperate, barbarous, mobocratic, tyrannical, and profligate body of wrong-doers found in the world."[138] But most saw the destruction of the Union—the world's grandest democratic experiment—as a tragedy to be prevented at almost any cost. As Republican victory at the polls was confirmed, and the states of the Deep South began seceding—South Carolina led the way in December 1860, with Mississippi, Florida, Alabama, Georgia, and Louisiana seceding in January, and Texas on February 1—Southern unionists resisted and agitated, seeking to sway elections and manipulate conventions. They called for concerted action between all slaveholding states to delay, obstruct, or prevent secession.[139]

Politicians, including not only the consistently conciliatory senator John J. Crittenden from Kentucky but also Republican William H. Seward, who put his intransigence away when faced with the realization of the "irrepressible conflict" he had foretold, feverishly searched for the mutual concessions, symbolic and real, that would keep the "agitated and distracted" nation from falling apart. In Congress, some suggested that the constitution—preserved from intervention for fifty-five years by what Francis Lieber described as "extravagant and unhistorical exaltation"—be amended for the thirteenth time to "forever" safeguard states' "domestic institutions": Congress would be explicitly barred from legislating slavery in the territories, New Mexico could be admitted as a slave state, territorial expansion would require the concurrent vote of two-thirds of each house, the colonization of freedpeople abroad would be encouraged and financed, and African Americans would be constitutionally excluded from the franchise.[140]

In February, former president John Tyler convened a conference in the capital in which experienced statesmen from both free and slave states were charged with finding a solution to the crisis. In March, a joint resolution was passed to amend fundamental law so that that Congress would never have the power to abolish or interfere with slavery.[141] It was to no avail. Adversaries agreed on explicit constitutional protections for slavery where it existed, but the identity of the young Republican Party turned on its rejection of bondage's expansion.[142] In the midst of the secession crisis, even as he attempted to assuage Southern fears that the president-elect conspicuously described slavery as an "evil" to be "tolerated and protected" strictly out of necessity; it "could not be extended."[143] Southerners found that their exclusion from "equal enjoyment" of the conquered territories belied the indispensable equality between parties to the federal constitutional compact. These were not "the Union to which [they] were pledged," the constitution they had "sworn to maintain," nor the government they were "bound to support." There was "no agreement" on which all could stand.[144]

As he bid farewell to his colleagues in the Senate at the beginning of 1861, Jefferson Davis claimed the time for debate was past; the states had "gone out"; to discuss "their right" to do so was useless.[145] The only right that mattered now was the "last inherent right of man to preserve freedom, property and safety."[146] In Mexico, the overthrow of Comonfort in January 1858 also destroyed the possibility of a legislative, negotiated settlement. Although many state governors had adopted a wait-and-see attitude after the December coup, when the moderate president fell they rallied, weapons in hand, to the defense of the controversial 1857 constitution, which was preferable to the authoritarian, centralizing national government that Conservative officers were sure to establish. Politics collapsed on both sides of the border. Elections and representation no longer processed and defused political difference but became a stage for intransigent confrontation. Their outcomes were deemed illegitimate and unacceptable. In Mexico, the ritualized violence of pronunciamientos and recurrent rehashing of fundamental law gave way to all-out armed conflict. In the United States, the election of a Republican president provoked the disavowal of federal rule in seven states. Constitutions could no longer, as Oliver Wendell Holmes argued years later that they should, allow people "with fundamentally different views to live together." They became, instead, a cause of war.

PART TWO

IN THE LABORATORY OF POLITICS

CHAPTER THREE

REVOLUTIONARY REACTION

Confederate America and
Conservative Mexico

IN THE YEARS that followed the peace of Guadalupe Hidalgo, irreconcilable differences sundered the North American republics. Rebellion, first couched in terms meant to paper over an intractable breach—a *pronunciamiento* in Mexico; nonviolent, allegedly constitutional secession in the United States—split them in two. Southern secessionists claimed a new nation had been born; President Lincoln called for 75,000 militiamen to strangle it in the cradle. The Confederacy kept up the defense of its territory and institutions for four years. Union victory confirmed the emancipation of the South's 4 million enslaved and brought about a new constitutional order. In Mexico, President Comonfort was ousted by his more conservative associates, less than a month after they had brought the constitutional order down. For three years, the governments of Generals Félix Zuloaga (1858) and Miguel Miramón (1859–60) fought for "order" and "religion" against the defenders of the "godless," anarchic constitution.

In December 1857, Benito Juárez, chief justice of Mexico's Supreme Court, condemned the attack on Congress and the constitution; he was imprisoned by the rebels. A confounded Comonfort let him out a month later, before he fled into exile. In the absence of the president, the constitution vested executive power in the chief justice: the experienced politician from Oaxaca established his government in Veracruz, the country's main port. Over the next three years, he embodied the ideal of constitutional rule, rooted in the "democratic ideas" that "God had willed."[1] On the field, often improvised military commanders—at the head of what their foes derided as an "army of lawyers"—took to battle in their defense. The Reform War, violent and unforgiving, dragged on for three years. In December 1860, Liberal victory finally restored the constitution's rule. It brought neither order nor peace but a blood-spattered, uneven truce.

In 1861, a series of unexpected events—labeled providential and "admirable" by the Conservatives—remade the field.[2] As Mexico's Liberal government struggled with Conservative resistance, Liberal infighting, and bankruptcy, the United States collapsed into a protracted civil war. Across the Atlantic, the former starry-eyed *carbonario* who had become emperor of the French saw an opportunity to reestablish France's presence in North America. The handful of Mexican politicians who, since the 1840s, had unsuccessfully lobbied for European intervention against the "demagogues," suddenly had Napoléon III's attention. When, in July 1861, the careworn Mexican government declared a moratorium on the greater part of its foreign debt, the emperor used it as an excuse to mobilize other creditor nations. In October, France, Spain, and Great Britain agreed to send a military expedition to knock some sense of financial responsibility into the wayward republic.[3]

In early 1862, as foreign troops landed in Veracruz, the Juárez government quickly reached an agreement with the Spanish and British representatives on a new payment schedule.[4] But the French had bigger plans: Louis Napoléon's expeditionary forces, now posturing as an army of pacification and champions of the "Latin race" against Anglo-Saxon expansionism, marched toward the capital in order to establish a new government, indebted to the French Intervention. Their task took longer and was more difficult than expected, but in June 1863, after the Battle of Puebla that the Mexicans did not win, the French Army reached Mexico City. With the departure of the constitutional government, Conservative politicians set up a provisional administration, welcomed the invading forces, and convened an "Assembly of Dignitaries" charged with putting forth the form of government that the country needed.

In the face of the French Army's advance, President Juárez had, once again, packed up the constitution, the national archives, and most of his cabinet and gone north. After a hazardous journey, his government settled in Paso del Norte, on the US border, where it kept the republican flame alive. In Mexico City, under the auspices of the French expeditionary army, the Liberal constitution's enemies created a new order of things: they abandoned republican forms altogether and invited an Austrian archduke to cross the Atlantic and govern as Mexico's emperor. The nation once again split into enemy camps. Over the next three years, republic and empire fought, weapons in hand, over not only Mexico's political regime but also its character and destiny.

War—long, vicious and deadly—devastated the Disunited States for four years (April 1861–April 1865), and Mexico for almost a decade (1858–67). When it was over, these struggles were hailed as reiterations of the revolutions that had given birth to the North American nations: a "Second American Revolution"; Mexico's "Segunda Independencia." They confirmed the neighboring nations' republican vocation and consecrated democracy, equality, and freedom as their ideals. They also proved monumentally destructive of lives and property, political practices and institutions. But as they devoured resources and narrowed the grounds for political maneuvering, the stress and sacrifice spawned by armed conflict also radicalized political desire.

Embattled governments stood on fundamentally disputed grounds as they sought to persuade, mobilize, co-opt, and eventually coerce a divided people. High-stake struggles over territory, resources, and legitimacy made possible policies that had previously been, if not unthinkable, then politically unworkable. Crisis changed the ways key concepts—sovereignty, citizenship, property—were conceived and regulated. Rival governments put novel schemes into place: they were reconstructed or destroyed by war and often remade in its aftermath. Political experimentation, conflict, and trial recast North America. This chapter and the next will explore the visions and projects that unstrung nations tried to put together in the midst of violence.

Reactionary Revolutions

The Confederate States of America and Mexico's Conservative and Second Imperial governments failed spectacularly. In retrospect, it is easy to shelve them as the product of strange times and particularly asinine politics. Nevertheless, understanding these regimes, in line with those of their more successful opponents, clues us into the possibilities of politics at a time of profound crisis. Secessionists, Conservatives, and imperialists forcefully rejected the republic as it had become. Their breakaway projects meant to restore principles and ethical structures they believed were essential to the commonwealth. The Confederate States of America, in the words of their brand-new vice president, Alexander H. Stephens, were the first nation "in the history of the world" to be founded upon a "great physical, philosophical and moral truth": that of "negro" inferiority. In Mexico, Conservatives believed the true faith should be the foundation of the political edifice, and neither its principles nor its practices should be sacrificed to modernization.[5]

For all those conservatives' devotion to religion, tradition, unchanging "organic" law and "natural" social hierarchies, by the end of the 1850s they rejected what had become an unstable, even dangerous status quo. They engaged in a politics of sweeping transformation. In politics, asserted President General Miguel Miramón, staying put entailed only regression. "Great revolutions" were the expression of the nation's "great social needs": the Mexican republic's "beautiful call for reaction" demanded "radical change."[6] It was the duty of the upright to steer change in the right direction. Secession, reasoned its advocates, was "one of the greatest revolutions in the annals of the world," accomplished "without the loss of a single drop of blood." Confederate army chaplain William A. Hall waxed providential when he deemed the South's insurgency "the finest result of modern political philosophy": a revolution that was "eminently conservative."[7]

These reactionary revolutionaries took it upon themselves to recast North America's political landscape. Southern secessionists created a nation from scratch. In Mexico, the enemies of the 1857 constitution first tinkered with a military

Andrew B. Graham, lithographer, Seal of the Confederate States of America. Courtesy of the Library of Congress, Prints and Photographs Division.

dictatorship they hoped would be able to reorganize a society that was falling apart. Defeated in war by the end of 1860, "cast down but not destroyed," their fears of US intervention conveniently mitigated by the stranglehold that the Civil War had placed on US foreign policy, Conservatives swallowed their qualms about entangling foreign alliances and restored a monarchist regime, led by an Austrian archduke and sponsored by an invading foreign army.[8]

In their efforts to begin the nation anew, North America's conservative revolutionists knew they tread on dangerous ground. To conceal the untested nature of their political formulas, they stressed continuities with the past—real or idealized—and transcendent principle. The Confederacy presented itself as the true heir of the Spirit of 1776, which had been perverted by fanatical Northerners. Its seal was graced by George Washington riding horseback over the Latin inscription "Deo Vindice [God Our Defender]." Confederate claims to a glorious past were inevitably controversial. But even as Southerners rejected the "barefaced and transparent fallacies" of Declaration of Independence—the pretense that all men were created equal—they saw July 4 celebrations as an opportunity to "expose the North's failure to live up to the Revolution's ideals." Their own insurgency was construed as both an echo and an "improvement" on their ancestors'

Crest of the Mexican Second Empire, 1865. Archivo General de la Nación, Segundo Imperio, Gobernación y Relaciones Exteriores, Caja 2, Exp. 39.

feats.[9] Confederate nationalism, as Drew Gilpin Faust has written, meant to reconcile "revolution with tradition" and warrant "change without change."[10]

Maximilian's empire also tapped into Mexico's nationalist traditions and historical imagination. Unlike the divided, distracted Conservative governments that preceded it, the empire put forth an ambitious, comprehensive conception of the past, not as the object of angry disputes but as a source of unity. It put together a conciliatory version of *historia patria*, in which the recent troubles were but an accident in a long and venerable history, in which everyone was a hero: it glorified the extraordinary scientific and artistic achievements of precontact Indigenous civilizations and exalted both the popular revolt that set off the War for Independence in 1810 and the arbitrations of the former royalist officer—and merciless foe of the first insurgents—who had brought it to an end in 1821.[11]

In setting up the rituals of celebration, commemoration, and belonging that would weave the nation's past and future together and kindle people's affections, the popular feasts of Corpus Christi and of the Virgin of Guadalupe were marked out as civic celebrations, as was the emperor's birthday. Civic ceremonies would be solemnized by Catholic liturgy. The young emperor incorporated certain elements of Hapsburg heraldry into the imperial flag, but its colors and crest remained the same: the red, white, and green of Iturbide's army, symbolizing independence, religion, and union. At its center stood the "eagle of Anáhuac" standing on a cactus, tearing a serpent apart with its claws, the symbol of the founding of the great city of Tenochtitlán in the thirteenth century.[12] As they broke away from the young nation's republican traditions, imperialists sought to bestow on the new regime the prestige of an age-old imperial tradition that spanned two continents and many centuries.

Experimental Reaction

At mid-century, disunionists in the United States and opponents of Mexico's 1857 constitution drew from different philosophical, religious, and legal traditions to deal with particular challenges. Both faced the Conservatives' classic dilemma: a desire to appropriate modernity—"progress," "civilization"—and the need to purge it of its most unseemly, disquieting features, on both the practical and ideological levels.[13] These "retrogrades" feared the political principles and population dynamics that constituted them as minorities. They despaired at the arrogance of men intent on interfering with Providence and the "natural order of things." They bridled against an expansive, universalist language that jumbled the relationship between words and things and turned the heads of the poor, the ignorant, and the dependent. In rebuilding the political edifice, they hoped to separate the wheat from the chaff and discipline modernity through constitutional and legal engineering.

In their efforts to build a regime that was modern and stable, Confederates were also committed to upholding the legal and institutional precedents that their Mexican colleagues willingly threw overboard. Southerners equated their rebellion to that of the thirteen colonies against British tyranny and to the birth of the nation in 1787–89. To sever their relationship with the Union most seceding states relied on the same device they had used in the late 1780s to create a federal republic. Opting for flight rather than fighting over the character of state and nation with stubborn Northerners, secessionists upheld their legitimate claim to the founding—reloaded—and to the founders' constitution—perfected because rightly interpreted.

In Mexico, those who disapproved of the 1857 constitution drew from a more eclectic but shallower constitutional arsenal. While secessionists were leaving at least part of their troubles behind as they left the Union, Mexican Conservatives and imperialists were convinced that, in order to save the nation, they had to wrest it from the Liberals' hands. The Conservative military government (1858–60) pulled together a "provisional organic statute" to serve as fundamental law, but they dared not enact it. In 1863, a more ideologically diverse group of politicians aspired to a more profound transformation: it gave up on both constitutions and republican rule.

As they sorted out the characteristics of the new order, conservative advocates of revolution professed to be righting all sorts of wrongs, doing God's work and fulfilling His will. They argued that they were also heeding the people's mandate. Mexico's devout Catholics and the vigorous white citizenry of the South surely condemned the disturbing designs of fanatical demagogues. On these issues, radical conservatives were, nevertheless, more often than not as emphatic as they were unsure: on both sides of the border, "the people" had done things that belied their reasonable assumptions. In their enthusiasm for political meetings and electioneering that was far from sober, citizens had recently shown less than ideal judgment: in Mexico, many supported liberal radicalism with both votes and arms. In the United States, zealots had turned the heads of Northern voters and set the Union on the course of disaster, under the leadership of an untried, irresponsible political party. Even in the South, although voters had thoroughly rebuffed the Republican ticket, many had still backed moderate candidates who insisted on preserving the Union.[14]

Still, North America's reactionary revolutionaries insisted that they spoke for the people—or at least for their true interests and the common welfare. They feared that the people's voice would prove them wrong. Wary of popular intervention, the Confederacy's constitutional congress held its debates behind closed doors, as did the assembly that voted to restore a monarchical regime in Mexico City. Mexican authorities went further still: in order to prevent "bad passions" from "sowing seeds of discord among good Mexicans," they suspended newspaper publication in the capital during the "most solemn" days during which delegates discussed the fate of the nation.[15] Subsequently, the Confederate legislature frequently went into secret sessions; Mexico's military and imperial governments abolished almost all representative bodies and regulated the press. Legislation exalted the freedom of public writers but forcibly curtailed their "abuses" if they probed public figures' "private life" or endangered "morality" or the "public order."[16]

The architects of confederacy and empire wanted to ground the new order on both "truth"—eternal, immutable—and the people's will, inevitably volatile and unreliable, unless one assumed that the people could never be wrong. Conservative revolutionaries were under no such delusion. Their skepticism notwithstanding, they could not step away from the essential fiction of modern politics. The voice of the people seemed at once essential and detrimental to good government. These political innovators hoped that by purifying and restraining politics, they would be able to shape, channel, and induce the sovereign's voice and actions. It was an aspiration that generated tensions and contradictions, weakening the political structures they painstakingly set up.

The Confederate States of America: An Even More Perfect Union?

In the wake of Lincoln's election, secession became a hotly debated issue in all of the slave states. In South Carolina's stead, nine states called conventions to decide whether they should remain in the Union.[17] In the Deep South, they voted to leave, most by large margins; in South Carolina the vote was unanimous. Only in Texas, where disunion met with the staunch opposition of Governor Sam Houston, did the convention submit its ordinance to the "intelligence and patriotism" of the state's voters for ratification.[18] In Georgia and Alabama, where substantial minorities stood steadfastly for the Union, zealous—and not particularly scrupulous—secessionists organized strident campaigns out-of-doors and relied on "passion and extreme utterances" in convention debates, in order to pull, as politicians do, the mantle of a unified popular mandate over a fractured body politic.[19]

In the more socially and economically diverse Upper South, where disunion was less a long-caressed object of desire than a remedy of last resort, division and dissent had greater political traction. Lincoln's election was seen as an ominous sign, but neither the results of the 1860 election nor legislative debates that followed spelled out secession as a clear choice. Only the immediate threat of war, as the North mobilized after the attack on Fort Sumter, pushed the eight slave states along the Mason-Dixon line off the fence. As the "middle ground" between North and South buckled, Virginia, North Carolina, Arkansas, and Tennessee joined the Confederacy.[20] The outbreak of war wreaked havoc in the border states, where sympathies and loyalties were deeply divided, and whose strategic value forced the hand of military strategists. Slave states Delaware and Maryland remained in the Union. The latter became a testing ground for war legislation and the forceful imposition of loyalty.[21] Missouri and Kentucky were members of both the Union and the Confederate Congresses—as were Tennessee, Louisiana, and a split-up Virginia. For border state residents, however, civil war meant occupation by an enemy, regardless of whose troops held the ground.[22]

Even in the most desperate contexts, Southern disunionists stood on the US political tradition: they hailed its lofty ideals and relied on its more distasteful practices. The language of the rushed first secession—completed less than three months after Lincoln's election, a month before he took office—is redolent with the self-righteousness of a revolution that meant not only to transform but to redeem. It spoke of rules broken, of a covenant "violated and virtually abrogated," of fellowship betrayed. State declarations alluded to an impossible choice between "submission to the mandates of abolition or a dissolution from the Union," to the need to avert the destruction of "ourselves, our wives, our children, the desolation of our homes, our altars."[23] In drafting their statement, the South Carolina fire-eaters, who had been rehearsing disunion for years, were perhaps the most philosophically ambitious. As they invoked the principle of self-preservation, South Carolina's lawmakers deplored the stealth transformation of the Union from a "Government of Confederated Republics" into "a Consolidated Democracy, no longer a free Government, but a Despotism."[24]

For all their urgency, the artificers of secession and confederation were sticklers for procedural and constitutional soundness. To achieve the desired results, they resorted to maneuvers that were not unusual in US politics: electoral engineering and governors' activism, the intimidation of voters and representatives, fanning the deeply ingrained fears of slave insurrection and racial anarchy.[25] In the increasingly tension-fraught months that followed the election of 1860, they called for conventions, summoned them anew, or prolonged their sessions. In the face of dire circumstances in the border states, they called for new elections and referendums, as governors appointed new representatives and herded rump legislatures.

"Deratifying" the constitution theoretically entailed the same consideration and popular validation as those that had created the Union.[26] Like the men who met behind closed doors in Philadelphia in 1787, those who drafted the CSA's constitution in Montgomery felt authorized to wreck a Union meant to be "perpetual." They also submitted their creation for the people's sanction. It would, nonetheless, be difficult to argue that "one of the greatest and most probing public debates in American history" was replicated in the state conventions that ratified the Confederate fundamental law.[27] Disunionists sought not to discuss and compromise but to validate, to "impel and justify" the creation of a new government, committed to the defense of "the institution of slavery—the greatest material interest in the world."[28] On the road to secession and confederation, state conventions served as a means to reach a predetermined end: they stood as symbols of historical legitimacy and popular consent, not as arenas for discussion or devices for good governance.

An Old Constitution for a New Nation

In February 1861, "having dissolved their political connection" to the United States, seven newly independent republics sent some of their most proficient politicians—mostly large slaveholders—to Montgomery, Alabama, to give birth to a Confederate nation by endowing it with leadership and a fundamental law. The provisional Congress, stricken by what Emory M. Thomas described as a "mania for unanimity," elected two experienced statesmen from the booming cotton states to preside over the new government. Both the president, Mississippi's former senator Jefferson Davis, who had served the Union as secretary of war, and the vice president, Georgia congressman Alexander H. Stephens, had formerly steered a moderate course by Southern standards.[29] In November, in line with the Confederates' antiparty stance, Davis and Stephens ran for office unopposed.

At the ballot box, the people endorsed—having been presented with no other choice—the wisdom of their representatives at the constitutional convention.

Delegates to Montgomery hammered out, mostly behind closed doors, a provisional and then a permanent constitution. A radical minority considered fundamental law to be useless. Like some Mexican Conservatives, they found constitutions "not worth the paper they were written on." "God and nature" made states; the Confederacy needed little more than a simple, provisional treaty of alliance to bind them together. This small and cantankerous group, however, did most of its criticizing from the sidelines and to little effect.[30] Most Southern politicians considered a constitution essential. State representatives, then, faced a momentous, dangerous challenge.

In the words of Georgia's Benjamin Hill, the "formation of a new constitution" had to serve as "a very powerful agency for good," even as uncertainty and division proliferated. Some "anticipated a more radical democracy," "a fearful anarchy," "an aristocracy," "a slave-trade oligarchy," and "even a limited monarchy." Yet framing the new nation's constitution took less than a month: congressmen reviewed and selectively amended, line by line, the fundamental law whose rule the states had just thrown off, as they insisted on the defense of its spirit. They introduced only "necessary and proper" changes to the 1787 document.[31] The Confederacy's fundamental law was unanimously adopted on March 11 and then rapidly ratified. New York's *Harper's Weekly* hailed the reformed constitution, and asserted that its "principal alterations . . . would receive hearty support" from most people in the North.[32]

The Confederate fundamental law embodied the contradictory impulses of secession and confederation: the radical project of creating a new nation—jeopardized by the possibility of immediate war—and a conservative compulsion to avoid fixing what was not broken. It was drafted in an age of bold constitution-making: the short-lived constitutional iterations of the 1848 European revolutions, which had consecrated the nation as an organic political community, swept away the remnants of medieval serfdom to the borders of the Russian Empire, established parliamentary government or even republican rule, universal male suffrage, and "social" rights—such as the ephemeral French Republic's "right to work." Spanish America witnessed fundamental law restructure property rights, the relations between central and local governments, between church and state. Revolution flailed in Europe, while Spanish American constitutionalism struck out in new, eventually more stable, directions, often in the midst of war.[33]

In contrast, the secessionist experiment spoke of continuity and straitlaced constitutionalism. For all the admiration that the revolutionary generation inspired, no delegate suggested resurrecting North America's first experiment in bringing sovereign states together: the decentralized 1777 Confederation, in which the only politically relevant actors were the states. As befitted Southern statesmen's insistence that it was not they but the North that had betrayed the founders' vision, the seceded state constitutions remained unchanged, save some "unimportant" adjustments, like striking out all references to the "United States." David P. Currie has described the fundamental law that engendered the Confederacy as practically "a carbon copy of the constitution of the United States," meant to set up "a looking-glass variant" of the Union, "without the North and without Northern ideas."[34] The alterations made to the hallowed founders' constitution were, nonetheless, discreet but telling.

The Confederate statute established a "permanent federal government," not the evocative "more perfect" Union. But although it invoked "the favor and guidance of Almighty God," it drew its legitimacy, as did its predecessor, from "We the People," now of the confederated states. Constitutional design also suggests that the drafters wanted a—slightly—more flexible instrument: the amendment process was less convoluted, and the initiative for change was reserved to the states: conventions in "any three States" could call on Congress to open the amendment process, and changes could be approved in convention, with a vote by state. They would be ratified if approved by two-thirds of state assemblies or conventions.[35]

The states, placed at the center of the amendment process, nonetheless barely saw their powers enhanced. For all the Southerners' noisy devotion to "states' rights," state governments were only endowed with the—not particularly awesome—power of impeaching "a Federal officer, resident and acting solely within the limits of any State."[36] The CSA's constitution did not explicitly consecrate "states' rights" and pointedly did not sanction the right of secession. It has been argued, then and now, that this was unnecessary: the declaration that each state acted "in its sovereign and independent character" implied "right of secession at will."[37]

Some Confederate framers were not as confident: they tried—and failed—to introduce tighter safeguards for state autonomy. They endorsed striking out "We the People" and replacing it with an enumeration of the member states; they recommended that the right of secession be "expressly admitted" or "not denied." They wanted fundamental law to assert that upon a state convention's demand, Confederate forces would be removed and Confederate property restored to the state; that Congress be directed to "redress or accommodate" the grievances of the state that wished to leave. If conciliation failed to satisfy, an "equitable distribution of property" would be arranged and the state would leave peaceably.[38]

Other delegates construed the Supreme Court as an unreliable arbiter, acting invidiously in favor of the central government. This probably contributed to the government's never organizing a tribunal vested with the Confederacy's highest judicial power.[39] Nonetheless, in March 1862, a senator from Louisiana put forth a bill to repeal the appellate jurisdiction over the highest state courts of the—still nonexistent—high court. In the words of William L. Yancey of Alabama, assuming that state courts were of "inferior dignity" meant "[sapping] the main pillar of this Confederacy."[40] The provision was not rescinded, but the states' judiciary autonomy was inadvertently reinforced by the Confederate government's inaction. Yet in practice, in the cases that mattered most—conscription and impressment—state courts bolstered the authority of the Confederate government, given that it was fulfilling its constitutional mandate to defend the republic.[41]

Confederate delegates legislated to set up federal judicial review; statesmen's mistrust confined its agent—the highest court in the land—to remain lifeless, confined to a neglected constitutional provision. The men meeting in Montgomery also refrained from acting on a more abstract but pervasive constitutional conundrum. They did not put together a constitutional mechanism for the solution of a problem that had frequently disturbed—even jeopardized—Union politics: the adjudication, in a context of sundry possible constitutional interpretations, of the inevitable confrontations between the federal and state governments. Georgia's Benjamin Hill suggested a complex scheme for settling these disputes, which granted states, or "any citizen, body politic or corporate aggrieved," the right to try the constitutionality of offending laws in front of the Supreme Court, joined by the chief justice of the state that was the site of the conflict. His proposal also sanctioned the possibility of legitimate secession, were the plaintiff not persuaded by the decision of this ad hoc tribunal. This scheme was tabled and forgotten.[42]

Along the same lines, when meeting in Montgomery, John C. Calhoun's proud heirs forsook the opportunity to establish a constitutional vesting of states with "a veto or control on the actions of the general government, on contested points of authority," as the prominent South Carolinian had advocated in 1828.[43] Fellow Palmetto state native James Chesnut vainly put nullification of the table before the "Committee of Twelve," charged with drawing up the constitution's first draft.[44] For all the constitutional sophistication of Calhoun's schemes and the veneration he inspired, neither concurrent majorities nor nullification made it into fundamental law as a "rightful remedy" for federal overreach.

The most consequential changes to the 1787 document, then, did not entail renovating a constitutional tradition but dealing, concretely, with the issues that had driven polarization and secession. Ambivalent silences on slavery were swept away: the Confederate fundamental law asserted that "no slave" could be discharged from service or labor and that "the institution of negro slavery" was protected by Congress in all of the Confederacy, including the territories it might expand into.[45] As one of Alabama's representatives contended, "no euphony," dangerously open to interpretation, hid the real name of things: by calling "our negroes slaves," the constitution "recognized and protected them as persons and our rights to them as property."[46]

These essential innovations were, nonetheless, not pushed to their last consequences. The document did not normalize the presence of the enslaved in the republic, even in terms of how they should be counted for the purpose of apportionment. It preserved the three-fifths clause—a figure which outsiders found "most perplexing."[47] Politicians who had complained about it for years did not insist on counting the enslaved as inhabitants in order to bolster the political influence of large slaveholders or states with large enslaved populations. There was, perhaps, a powerful political reason for keeping things as they were. Confederates emphatically insisted on the political equality of white men: counting, for purposes of political representation, the "moral chattel" deemed radically unfit for citizenship proved too uncomfortable.

The framers, then, preserved the familiar fraction, agreed upon in Philadelphia, even if it defied conceptual soundness and belied the much-vaunted integrity and coherence of slave societies.[48] In another gesture of strategic comity, dressed up as paternalistic concern for the South's "four million improved, civilized, hardy and happy laborers," the Confederate constitution banned the Atlantic slave trade.[49] It forbid the importation of slaves "from any foreign country other than the slaveholding states or Territories of the United States" and gave Congress the power to ban their introduction from states that were not members of the CSA. This was meant, on the one hand, to reassure reluctant slave states of their place in the Confederacy, but it dangled over their heads the possibility of shutting down a profitable market if they refused to join the slaveholders' bold nation-building experiment.[50] On the other hand, as they prepared to launch the nation onto the world stage, the Confederacy's architects felt it was best not to provoke Great Britain and its abolitionists.

It is in some ways surprising that, having taken the solemn and dreadful step of secession, the builders of a republic premised on slavery and white supremacy enacted no constitutional provisions to shore up its most compelling elements. A majority of delegates either tabled or voted against proposals to explicitly exclude from the franchise those who had African blood in their veins; to forbid Congress from passing any law "denying the right of property in negro slaves"; and to keep free states out of the Confederacy, as long as they recognized the legitimacy of property in man.[51] The framers' restraint stemmed, in part, from their expectation that free border states would join the CSA; their more fanciful hope of luring some Midwestern states into the would-be powerful agricultural empire and a concern for the newborn nation's international reputation. They trusted, perhaps, that occasions for disagreement would diminish significantly, since Confederate legislative debates would be purged of the Union's most disturbing issues: protective tariffs and, intermittently but fatally (in 1820 and after 1846), the status of slavery in the territories.

Their discretion also spoke, perhaps, of peculiar conceptions of constitutionalism, federalism, and the right of property. According to their parameters, slavery was subject only to municipal regulation and property rights were something more than the product of convention upheld by law.⁵² Slavery, they contended, was a natural, "original institution": slaves were property and their title of ownership was not the creature "of human law," subject to debate, regulation, or restriction. Property—in man as in anything else—was beyond the purview of legislators, state or federal: it would never again become the "hobby of the political demagogue."⁵³

Experience, convictions, and an entrenched political culture, as well as particular understandings of key concepts and principles, kept Confederate constitutional innovation to a minimum. Moreover, fear of politics seemed to weigh heavier on the minds of members of the constitutional convention than their concerns for state sovereignty, the preservation of slavery or their exaltation of white citizenship. In their effort to restore the founders' vision of a republic idealized as virtuous, harmonious, and honest, the framers took steps to curb the factiousness and corruption which, in their opinion, had so marred Union politics. Their constitution sought to temper and elevate politics and limit their pollution by money and selfish interest.

The CSA's fundamental law therefore confirmed Congress's power to establish uniform legislation to deal with bankruptcies but barred it from discharging "any debt contracted" before its passage, thus bolstering creditor claims against potentially popular legislation mandating debt relief.⁵⁴ Of greater significance was the constitutional determination that only "the common defense" and the costs of government were worthy objects of public funding. The "general welfare" was eschewed as something worth spending the Confederacy's money on. With this, legislators meant to strike a blow against the spoils system and prevent Congress from unfairly boosting certain "class interests."⁵⁵ To further check politicking, lobbying, and pork-barrel legislation, Congress was designed to be smaller and less representative: each congressman would stand for 50,000 inhabitants, instead of the 30,000 established in the US constitution.⁵⁶

Consequently, the Confederate government would grant no bounties or impose protective tariffs to "foster any branch of industry." Despite Southerners' interest in free trade, the Confederacy would not fund infrastructure: any "internal improvement intended to facilitate commerce" would have to be paid for by the states, unless it was required for the river and coastal navigation vital to the cotton economy. The Post Office Department had to be "paid out of its own revenues." To prevent the "extravagance and corruption" of congressional logrolling, the constitution required a two-thirds majority in both houses to authorize appropriations not requested by department heads. It also granted the president a line-item veto on budget provisions.

In the face of the excitable, garrulous, perhaps corrupt people's representatives, the Confederate constitution set up the president as a stabilizing element. This more powerful chief executive saw his hand strengthened by a longer period in office: six years.⁵⁷ His informal influence was, nevertheless, abridged. The constitution curbed the president's—instrumental and much maligned—role as the great dispenser of political patronage. Although he could remove civil servants for bad behavior, unsatisfactory performance, redundancy, or obsolescence, he had to report and justify any dismissal to the Senate. Furthermore, amassing political capital would be useless, since the president could not be reelected.[58]

The Montgomery delegates voted unanimously for a constitution shaped by a distinctively Southern constitutional tradition, with its strong "contractual bend" and "persistent localism," its particular brand of republicanism and concern for the protection of slavery.[59] The architects of the new nation had "perfected their rebellion."[60] They rallied around fundamental law as they would around the flag, as patriots rather than constitutionalists. They hoped to show the world a nation born without fissures. Their aspirations were belied both by the contents of fundamental law and its application.

The South's conservative republican radicals sought to transform without undermining—at least not openly—the principles which, after independence, had become consubstantial with political legitimacy in the New World. They were intent on cleaning up public life, purging it of corruption and unseemly compromises, replacing self-seeking ambition with magnanimous virtue. They hoped to accomplish this by taking money out of politics and extinguishing factionalism, party machinations, and riotous electioneering. But they could only tweak rules and norms to limit what they saw as the undesirable consequences of a politics of consent and representation.

For all the Confederates' vehement condemnation of federal despotism, parties, job-seeking, and populist pandering, they too had to rely on a defense of federal supremacy, politicking, concessions, and compromise. As long as the sovereign people remained at the center of public discourse, elections proved contentious, even the absence of old party politics and the power of government was mobilized to protect "class interests." Even without the crushing pressures of war, then, Confederate design failed to do what it set out to do: secure states' rights by assertively reigning in federal authority, defuse majority rule if it threatened minority rights, and protect, in James L. Huston's words, a "legal definition that turned people into property."[61] Ironically, the Confederate constitution secured slavery by both naming it and setting it beyond the legislator's reach. The requirements of state-building and republican principles drew the limits of constitutional innovation.

Mexico: Desperately Seeking a "Wondrous Institution"

For all their inconsistencies, the architects of secession and confederation stood on firmer philosophical ground than did their Conservative and imperialist colleagues to the south. As Aaron Hall has written, would-be Confederates could credibly read "their present into the past" and weave "a cloak of historical legitimacy" to dress up their political project.[62] The Mexican politicians who rallied to arms—sword, pen, or law—against the 1857 constitution had no such luxury. The popular, federal constitution, they argued, was the "most imperfect copy of that of the United States," and was alien to Mexico's traditions and mores. It would lead to the disorganization and deterioration of an already weak state. It endangered the nation's most precious resource, the basis of national unity: the Catholic religion.[63]

Men who had served the republic their whole lives now found nothing in its painful legacy they could use: in three decades, five fundamental laws, over fifty administrations, and hundreds of increasingly violent pronunciamientos had only brought about frustration, economic stagnation, and territorial loss.[64] Nevertheless, when Conservatives glossed over the peace and prosperity of monarchical New Spain for contrast with the republican misadventure, they were uncomfortably aware of going against the grain of entrenched patriotic memory.[65] Unmoored from a usable past, bereft of an "ancient constitution," theirs was the unsteady, brittle politics of anxiety.

Paradoxically, then, those who had decided to call themselves Conservatives saw little in the past that they hoped, or were even able, to preserve. At the same time, they feared the change that the Liberals forcefully put forth. They had become suspicious of even the trappings of republican legitimacy. Having prided themselves in the past for their sophisticated, discerning, cosmopolitan constitutionalism, many Conservatives were ready, by mid-century, to sacrifice elections, political representation, and even fundamental law if this would allow them to set up an active and efficient public authority. They were nevertheless unsure of how much of the republican baggage they could throw overboard. After taking over the nation's capital by force of arms, both the military dictatorship (1858–60) and the imperial government (1863–67) forfeited constitutional rule and searched for alternative schemes for political representation and the expression of consent. When opportunity knocked, Conservatives leapt into political innovation, but they did so with very little faith.

Down with the Constitution

Rejection of an invigorated Liberal program coalesced around a document: the 1857 constitution, which Conservatives warned would bring about the nation's destruction. As former minions of a now much-maligned dictator, Conservative politicians were excluded from the 1856–57 congressional debates. Their newspapers voiced concerns over executive impotence, the suppression of the Senate—which would make for more passionate, less informed legislative debates—and the disorganizing effects of a radical conception of state sovereignty.[66] They despaired over the rift the constitution created between church and state. Militant

Catholics responded through an "exclusively religious" press, established *"ex profeso* to spread orthodox doctrines, and defend them from the dominant error."[67]

Conservative rejection of the 1857 law, for all the anguish it unleashed, was rooted in conceptual rather than practical issues: it did what constitutions should not do. Instead of putting a government together, establishing the reach and limits of its actions, and organizing territories and jurisdictions, it sought to transform society. In doing so, it contradicted basic principles and violated rights. It enacted revolution through law and would destroy society's foundations. Constitutions, argued an influential Conservative publicist, should be but "a declaration of what existed." They were not meant to set up an ideal for the people "to measure up to" but instead to organize the exercise of public authority along the lines of transcendent, unmovable natural law to ensure order and protect natural rights. A nation's fundamental law ought to be grounded in its history, which "could not be invented," on a people's habits, which "could not be improvised," and on their needs, "which would not be settled by abstract theory."[68] The Ayutla Liberals had not only legislated for a nonexistent Mexican nation, they had done worse: the 1857 constitution went beyond its appropriate object: it intruded upon civil society.

This charter delegitimized certain forms of property and interfered with the church's rights and prerogatives. It disturbed the natural, spontaneous, beneficial order of things. Instead of opening a field on which Mexicans could meet, debate, and legislate despite political differences, Liberals set up an overweening, unchecked, despotic state, militantly imposing its visions on the nation.[69] Their legal creature was categorically condemned by Mexico's bishops. The order it set up was unlivable. Conservative politicians and journalists who for a decade had derided popular sovereignty now insisted that "public outcry" and the people's "universal conscience" impelled to act against the Liberal constitution.[70] In December 1857, they supported the Mexico City garrison as it rebelled against Congress. The president dissolved the legislature and abrogated the fundamental law he had sworn to uphold in February. A month later, Conservative officers rose up again, this time against their former ally, and ousted Comonfort and the moderate Liberals from the government. They argued that since the factions that had riven the republic were "certainly not the organs of its will," the army had to embody the nation's "center for unity" until the "public conscience" was at peace.[71]

Once in power, President Zuloaga, professing his commitment to upholding "the true interests of the pueblos," took swift legislative action against Liberal policies.[72] Since 1855, reformist laws had ordered the dissolution of the Supreme Court, extinguished the pontifical university, provided for the privatization of civil and ecclesiastical corporate property, fixed parish dues, abolished special jurisdictions, created a civil registry—and demanded the clergy keep civil authorities informed of all sacramental activity—and dismissed government employees who refused to take the constitutional oath of office. The Conservative government declared all these regulations null and void.⁷³ In order to "systematize the order and regularity of political affairs," legislative assemblies were dissolved and states abolished and replaced with "departments," subject "in all matters and business" to the Supreme Government in Mexico City.⁷⁴

After demolishing federalism, eliminating political representation, and forcefully turning back the legislative clock on Reform, the Conservative government focused its attention on war.⁷⁵ It nevertheless legislated for the moral renewal of society by resurrecting statutes that had mandated resting on Sundays and going to Mass.⁷⁶ It tried to bolster the central government's control over particularly restless regions by carving out territories that it would administer directly: Iturbide, Tlaxcala, and Toluca in the central valleys; Tepic on the Pacific; in the Northeast, Nuevo León and Coahuila were split up on paper.⁷⁷ It publicly condemned the rival constitutionalist government's radicalized agenda.⁷⁸ It recurrently tried to shore up at least passive support from certain key constituencies by shielding them from the war's most dire consequences: forced conscription, especially of the Indigenous population, and the imposition of forced loans on foreign residents were forbidden by laws that would soon be ignored. The military dictatorship also promoted the creation of battalions of property owners, charged with protecting "their own interests" and exempt from being drafted into the regular army.⁷⁹

Even in the midst of a deadly armed struggle, some Conservatives fretted over the absence of a fundamental law to determine the government's attributes and warrant basic citizen rights. According to Gen. Miguel María Echeagaray, the government needed to write down and publish the ground rules for governance, to protect the nation from the dangers of "an absolutely discretionary government."⁸⁰ Zuloaga charged members of his Council of State—made up of a representative from each department, selected by the president—with framing a general statute that could serve, provisionally, as a constitution. The statute's authors included some of the most distinguished Conservative jurists: men like José Bernardo Couto, perhaps the most articulate lay defender of church prerogatives, and veteran statesman Luis Gonzaga Cuevas, who had written one of the most acerbic critiques of politics after independence. In the wake of the "ill-fated auspices" of 1848, he joined the growing chorus of voices decrying the ills wrought by modern politics and warned of the corrosive effects of the century's "monstrous contradictions": impressive material progress and the "government of all by all."

Unless adequately steadied and restrained, Cuevas argued, popular government engendered "authority without obedience and power with no means to hold its own." Forms of government—democratic, republican, or monarchical, either constitutional or absolute—were unimportant, as long as they were founded on the (Gospel) "truth." Only then could a "strong and energetic government" warrant the precious rights of the people, organized in distinct "classes."[81] With its vague references to God-given social structures and dismissal of constitutional formulas, Cuevas's political project was as forceful as it was nebulous and impractical. Still, it set out the theoretical groundwork for a "Provisional Organic Statute" meant to institutionalize and limit interim president Zuloaga's emergency powers. In the early summer of 1858, a draft of this bare-boned fundamental law was presented to the president's council and cabinet.

Conservative statesmen had little to fear from a document crafted by their own logicians, which they could discuss without entering into the unavoidable compromises of legislative negotiations. The statute hailed Mexican independence and resurrected its "Three Guarantees": religion, independence, and union. It upheld religious unanimity and an organic, centralist, and antiparty conception of the nation as a "single political family, with no distinctions of origin or locality." It declared the protection of individual rights and proclaimed the sovereignty "of the whole nation" and gave the president "absolute powers to pacify the country, promote its progress, and organize the different branches of the administration."

In a gesture to the tenets of separation of powers and political representation, the statute established elected councils to advise the president and department governors. These bodies were not to represent an abstract—faceless, voluble, irresponsible—people but would give a voice to concrete and legitimate social interests, local and national, economic or corporate. They would convene the most knowledgeable and virtuous: the owners of lands and mines, merchants, and industrialists would join military officers, lawyers, and men of letters to discuss laws and policies. "Provisionally," only municipal councils would be elected by the people at large.[82]

The statute relied on the structure and language of liberal constitutionalism but hollowed out representative bodies and decisively reinforced the powers of the president. Despite its stabilizing and authoritarian features, the Zuloaga government decided to neither publish nor enact it. Some of its members were discouraged by the fact that the people who were to live under the new frame of government had had no voice in setting it up.[83] They preferred that the military government remain a regime of exception, to be replaced by constitutional rule once the emergency was over. Others thought it futile to try to underpin community with fundamental law when the nation was so profoundly divided. The more radical elements considered that there should be no constitution of any kind. Political communities, these men argued—and the Southern author of *Cannibals All!* would have agreed—were endowed with inherent, historical constitutions painstakingly woven together, over centuries, from customs, beliefs, and societal and governmental norms. Written fundamental laws were artificial: useless at best, pernicious when they became an excuse for political confrontation or instruments for social engineering. Furthermore, according to Zuloaga's secretary of justice, intransigent priest Francisco Javier Miranda, a constitution would be seen by the enemy as a "concession." Revolution had to be crushed by force of arms, not met halfway.[84] The provisional statute went into the archives, to be discussed only by historians, over a century and a half later.[85]

In December 1858, Gen. Manuel Robles Pezuela joined Echeagaray in calling, once again, for an end to both dictatorial rule and civil war. Contending factions were drowning the nation in blood and tears; "equally exorbitant in their principles and pretentions," each lacked the strength to overcome the other. Violent confrontation would only end when the deadlock was broken. The nation hated both "licentiousness and tyranny": the two rivals needed to step back and stop "assassinating, banishing, or imprisoning half of those who called themselves Mexican." The army, whose duty it was to "sustain and assist" the nation's "sovereign will," had to put itself above this devastating dispute.

The insurgent generals proposed that a provisional government, headed by the army's commander, Miguel Miramón, call on "all citizens, with no exclusion of persons or classes," to elect a "national assembly," with three representatives from each department. This body would draft a new constitution, which would be submitted to the people six months after its completion.[86] The young general nonetheless violently rejected the idea of transaction: the great battle over the soul of the nation could not be resolved through elections, debate, and compromise. "The bandits who had torn the country apart" could not sit next to the honest men who had defended it, much less join them in charting the nation's future.[87] Miramón blocked the possibility of putting an end to the war through negotiations and a new constitutional beginning. In September 1860, President Juárez also rejected conciliation when Santos Degollado, commander of the Liberal forces, suggested foreign diplomats broker a truce between Liberals and Conservatives.

Echeagaray and Robles Pezuela's proposal failed; Zuloaga was ousted from office. Miramón assumed executive powers on top of his military command. The Conservatives' "Young Maccabee," who at twenty-six became the country's youngest president, would have no talk of constitutions: only a dictatorship was "fierce and active" enough to destroy the nation's enemy and set the republic on the right track, not by politics but through—he claimed somewhat anticlimactically—efficient on-the-ground governance. "The evils" that afflicted Mexico, he argued, were not in its form of government, its electoral practices, or its legislation, but in its bungling "administration." "Severe economies," a simpler tax system, well-organized departments, good police work, the swift administration of justice and a smaller, cheaper, and more disciplined army were the keys to "the reconstruction of the social edifice."[88]

Christian values, political reconciliation and compromise, administration, or brute force as antidotes to politics went untested, as Conservative designs were thwarted by internal division and, more bluntly, by military defeat. Miramón's army was crushed in December 1860. Its commander left the country, along with the country's bishops, who were ordered into exile. In January 1861, President Juárez returned to Mexico City in triumph and restored constitutional rule. Those who still rabidly opposed the 1857 fundamental law turned to conspiracies—local and transatlantic—against the Liberal government, while military strongmen sustained bloody, localized armed rebellions. Their political experiment had come to an end. Nonetheless, in the year that followed, a world turned upside down dealt the Liberals' disloyal opposition one last hand of cards to play.

Trying Monarchy on for Size

The arrival of Napoléon III's soldiers rekindled civil war: the nation was once again divided in two. As the republic "took refuge" in the northern desert, an "Assembly of Dignitaries" convened to decide the country's future in a city occupied by French troops. This convention was, paradoxically, perhaps more diverse, socially and ideologically, than the constituent body that preceded it.[89] The Conservative provisional government said it wanted to summon Mexican citizens endowed with common sense, with no distinction "of class or rank." Among the 215 delegates were numerous Conservatives with long careers in public service—most of them middle-class lawyers—but also two silversmiths, two painters, a shoemaker, a printer, and a weaver. Some experienced liberal politicians—former legislators, governors, civil servants—were also invited to join the deliberations; most of them declined. A few of the most distinguished would, nevertheless, later serve the regime whose founding they had refused to countenance.

The "dignitaries" also included at least four priests.[90] A regular feature in state and federal congresses during the first decades after independence, men of the cloth could not be voted into office after 1855, as part of the Liberals' legislative push to separate what was due to God from what ought to be given unto Caesar. Many Catholics saw the crisis that engulfed the nation in the late 1850s not as a struggle between different political principles but as a battle to the death between good and evil. In this uneasy atmosphere, some priests considered it their religious and patriotic duty to get deeply involved in the things of this world. They belied the bishops' wartime argument that the true faith was above and beyond earthly struggles for power, and they militantly entered politics.

Thus, Father Francisco Javier Miranda was an influential member of Zuloaga's cabinet. The nation's archbishop, Pelagio Antonio de Labastida y Dávalos, exiled in Rome since the summer of 1856, vigorously lobbied both the pope and reluctant Conservatives in favor of the French Intervention and the establishment of an empire in Mexico. He eventually returned from the Holy See to join the three-man regency that governed the country until Maximilian arrived. The church—or at least some of its clerics—actively sought, if for a short while, to restore the imbrication of the civil and the religious in the public sphere.[91]

The assembly—eclectic in its makeup, homogeneous in its ideological inclinations—came to a conclusion after a couple of days of half-hearted debate. It was as extraordinary as the circumstances that had brought it into being: the delegates asserted that the republican system had been nothing but a "fertile fountainhead" of evil. After forty years of mistakes, it was obvious that only the "monarchical institution" was "adaptable" to Mexico. Members of the assembly proclaimed, unanimously, that the nation should adopt a "hereditary moderate monarchy," ruled by a Catholic prince. The throne of the "Mexican Empire" would be offered, per Napoléon III's advice and in line with France's diplomatic strategies, to Ferdinand Maximilian von Hapsburg, the emperor of Austria's younger brother.[92]

During the very brief discussion that followed, two "dignitaries"—a general from Colima and a lawyer from Puebla—wondered why monarchy was qualified, vaguely, as "moderate" rather than "constitutional." Their timid call for grounding the new regime in fundamental law fell on deaf ears. The assembly's resolution praising the "astonishing system" of monarchical rule spoke of "statutes" and the action of councils and "different corporations" within the state as efficient—and sufficient—restraints on power. Councils would represent and defend "all the interests and rights" of the different "classes" that made up society, so that "the nobleman and the commoner, the opulent and the beggar," could all exert "direct influence on the politics of the country," according to their "real needs."[93]

Like the more radical Conservatives during the war, the imperial founders did not want to fetter the prince with the strictures of constitutional norms, or the interference of the people's representatives, who were so often pugnacious and arrogant. Constraints on the executive were often a "great hinderance to a sovereign who wanted to do good" but allowed him "to do evil."[94] Members of the assembly hoped Maximilian would rescue the nation from the abyss and offered him the freedom to do it as he saw fit. The archduke, however, apparently did not share his future subjects' fears and distrust: he committed to accepting the assembly's invitation to sit on "Charles V's throne," but only if its vote was ratified by "the whole nation." He also promised to "open up the wide road to progress, based on order and morality," through "a constitutional regime" and "wisely liberal institutions."[95] When he landed at Veracruz in May 1864, he carried under his arm both a meticulous and extensive rulebook "for the services of honor and Court ceremonial"—over 500 pages long in its printed version—and a constitution, made up of sixty-eight articles, handwritten by his wife.[96]

"Carlota's constitution" does little to shore up her husband's reputation as a Liberal. Under its precepts, the monarch remained an exceptionally strong executive, with little to check or balance his actions. Laws would be discussed by two deliberative bodies: a Council of State and a Senate. Members of the former would be selected by the "constitutional emperor," while the latter would be made up by the empire's luminaries—princes of the blood, bishops, university presidents, members of the Supreme Court—a hundred members chosen by the emperor, and another hundred elected by the people.[97] Given the "distracted state" of the nation, this fundamental law was neither publicized, discussed, nor implemented. In its place, another "Provisional Organic Statute" was proclaimed in April 1865 to put the relationship between "government and governed" on "reliable footing" and to ensure the uniformity of imperial rule.[98]

The Estatuto set down the empire's territorial and governmental structure. It established a Council of State, nine ministries, and an autonomous Court of Audits, charged with guaranteeing that public moneys were well spent. Municipal governments were elected by popular and—breaking with previous practices— direct suffrage. All Mexican citizens, twenty-one or older, had a right to vote, as long as they were literate, which left out most adult men.[99] Near the end of the document, the statute included "every Mexican's" right to an audience with the emperor or his ministers, as well as a list of "individual guarantees," which included—to many Conservatives' horror—freedom of worship. It also "provisionally" granted the emperor "the exercise of national sovereignty in all of its branches." This statute, like the French 1852 imperial constitution, meant to embrace modern, revolutionary principles—individual rights, popular sovereignty— while it shut down revolutionary politics. Maximilian's law went further than that of his French sponsor: it eliminated representative assemblies outright. As Georgina López has written, the Estatuto might have intended to legitimize a manufactured monarchy in the age of liberalism; instead, it effectively erected an administrative and paternalistic regime with a decisively authoritarian bent.[100]

THE IDEAL OF A STRONG GOVERNMENT appealed to those who, in an era of bewildering change, favored order over liberty. But it also proved seductive to those who were convinced that you could not have one without the other, and that only a government that was stable and powerful enough would be able to finally bring the two together. A monarchy would harmonize old and new and allow an agitated society to digest modernity. By putting politics on hold, it would cure progress of its ills. The monarch was a "sacred person": he was not the state but its "most august representation."[101] Consequently, the Crown would act as ballast on the tempest-tossed sea of politics. In the words of *La Razón*, a newspaper that described itself as both imperialist and Liberal, under the new regime Mexicans could be anything they wanted, "except ... emperor." The throne was placed above the machinations of the ambitious, the corrupt, and the unruly. It could not be the prize of armed rebellion or electoral fraud. Political parties—their men and ideals—would survive and continue to operate, but the empire would leave them "no field on which to fight, no arms to hurt each other, and no opportunity for revenge."[102]

These bloodless, passionless, uneventful politics required low-stake elections and entailed the abstention of a mettlesome, enormously influential actor: the armed forces. Many imperialists saw the military presence of the French as dreadful but necessary. They trusted that the presence of a foreign, professional, proudly apolitical army would stabilize politics. They assumed academy-trained French officers would be more trustworthy and less intrusive than the volatile, bellicose Mexican strongmen who had so often taken it upon themselves to monopolize the voice of the nation. Mexican advocates for the French Intervention were not wrong in conceiving the expeditionary army as the politically neutral arm of the state, but that state happened to be France. By 1866, when the cost-benefit analysis of Napoléon III's "Mexican adventure" yielded negative results, the French emperor withdrew his troops. The defense of Maximilian's regime was placed squarely in Mexican hands, deprived of the boots-on-the-ground that had made it possible.

The empire set itself up as a regime for national reconciliation. Putting the throne above partisan strife opened the door to broad collaboration and promised to insulate the state from the disruptive influence of politics. This prospect attracted both Liberal and Conservative statesmen who despaired at the republic's failure to put together an administrative apparatus that would—independently of who ran it—fulfill the basic tasks of government: guarantee order, protect rights, and command respect for the law. Some, often dismayed by foreign intervention and unenthused by the "sublime offspring of distinguished lineage" that sat on the throne, nevertheless saw the empire as an opportunity: a political truce that would provide the breathing space and stability needed for statesmen to devise and put together a machine able to act upon Mexico's intractable realities.

Some Liberals even thought that Mexico's momentous "social revolution," initiated by the men of 1857 but upended by administrative incapacity, Conservative resistance, and war, would finally be able to take root, given that opponents would be artificially restrained.[103] To the dismay of committed imperialists, these belated converts joined the ranks of Maximilian's government. With some of their Conservative colleagues, they resurrected long-standing administrative and legal projects that had broken down in the face of previous republican governments' inefficiency, instability, and lack of resources. Unlike the more romantic monarchists and staunch Catholics, they did not look back to a mythical golden age of good government. Instead, state-obsessed Mexican imperialists looked forward. They wasted no time on "the sterile noise of abstract questions"—such as the "so-called religious question." Government, they argued, was not an art or an exercise in righteousness; it was a science. It should be as objective, rule-bound, and eventually predictable as any other. It was not politics but administration that mattered, "instruments" with which to exercise authority, and not values, that were important.[104]

The empire's civil servants tried to be thorough and systematic where military dictatorship had been inchoate and haphazard. To direct government action and guarantee its regularity and energy, the empire's territory was divided into fifty departments, which would be governed by professional bureaucrats, organized in strict hierarchies and subject to the emperor's directives. "Scientific" criteria—"natural" borders, size, population, and ethnicity—were used to sweep away the irregular geography of power that had fractured the nation's territory, markets, and political loyalties.[105] They also perfected a previous law that created special courts, under the purview of the executive power, to review the actions of the "administrative authority," undertaken in fulfillment of its duties as society's "agent": infrastructure, taxes, concessions, patents, and privileges.[106]

The *imperialistas* believed in the vigorous promotion of economic development by the state. Some republican liberals had derided the need for a development (*fomento*) ministry—former Michoacán governor and celebrated anticlerical thinker Melchor Ocampo found it expensive and as ineffective as a "Ministry of Happiness." It was suppressed during the difficult war years. Imperial rule nevertheless revived this instance for state agency. The ministry multiplied the number of railway concessions, reviewed and authorized licenses for mining schemes and colonization projects, the exploitation of oil deposits, and the production and consumption of pulque, a popular fermented agave drink.[107] Even as members of the government debated inconclusively about what the empire's financial system should look like, Mexico's first commercial bank—the Banco de Londres y México—opened its doors in the capital in 1864.[108]

Maximilian's collaborators sought to set up a government of allegedly apolitical, professional bureaucrats, expertly handling a well-designed, well-oiled machine for government. Among the unfinished projects they picked up was the national civil code, drafted by a committee of jurists appointed by Juárez in 1861 and published in 1866. They took up an unenforced constitutional mandate and pushed for the rapid and uncompromising substitution of the country's diverse, customary systems of weights and measures with the "French" metric system. They set up a system of national public education that included elementary and secondary schools, explicitly secular higher education and programs for "special" graduate studies. Elementary education would be compulsory for children aged five to fifteen, and free for those who could not afford to pay a peso a year. The Ministry of Public Instruction would design school curricula, while local authorities would assess schoolchildren's "progress" and ensure they were treated with "gentleness." They hoped that, over time, the empire would rule over a modern, prosperous, well-ordered society, educated, organized, and disciplined from above.[109]

The advocates of monarchy—both true believers and recent converts—insisted that the system could fix a broken nation. They also argued that, as part of a three-century tradition, rooted in the nation's greatest treasures—religion and independence—it could only be what Mexicans wanted. But most did not trust elections. When Maximilian demanded "the whole nation" call him to the throne, the people's approval was not calibrated through suffrage or plebiscite. Instead, throughout 1863 and 1864, municipal authorities, leading citizens, and numerous "neighbors" drafted *actas de adhesión* (declarations of support) in villages, towns, and cities, usually—but not always—in the wake of the French Army's arrival in the region. These corporate bodies ("natural" communities, summoned by their civil and religious authorities) "freely and spontaneously," often "unanimously," recognized the new order of things, with everything from dispirited resignation to enthusiastic support. When the winds of war changed direction, many of these collective actors did the same for the republic.[110]

The empire claimed to be a government of and for the people, but the sovereign's voice—loud, confusing, unintelligible—would be carefully parsed out and curated. General voting was limited to municipal elections and, given the literacy requirements for suffrage in a country where so few could read and write, the electoral exercise would do little more than give a democratic veneer to firmly entrenched power of local elites. The issue of explicit, informed consent loomed larger when the imperial government tried to reform Mexico's disastrous public finances.[111] In each department, landowners, merchants, miners, and industrialists were summoned to vote for representatives who would join experienced civil servants in a Treasury Commission, charged with reorganizing imperial finances. As we shall see in chapter 6, its members served their constituents' interests well: they put forth no fiscal innovations that could affect them.

Public audiences meant to make Maximilian and his government available to the people.[112] The emperor was also perhaps the first of Mexico's rulers to travel the country and meet its inhabitants for politics' sake. He thought it especially important to reach out to the Indigenous population who, in his opinion, was, "and always would be, the best among Mexicans," but had been unjustly marginalized, exploited, and abused.[113] In April 1865, a five-member Junta Protectora de las Clases Menesterosas (Board for the Protection of the Needy Classes) was created, so that the empire's motto, "Equity in justice," could become a reality for its most unfortunate subjects. Presided by noted Nahuatl scholar and lawyer Faustino Galicia Chimalpopoca, the junta became a forum for the grievances of Indigenous communities, mostly from the central highlands. Indian pueblos sought its intervention to halt processes, often accelerated by Liberal legislation, that unsettled village life by privatizing communal lands and disrupting religious life.

The Junta Protectora was sympathetic but toothless: it advised and informed, tried to make sure that the prescriptions of law were respected, and instructed local archives to respond to villagers' queries and applications. It nevertheless had little interest in defending communal rights and practices or preserving Indigenous culture and traditions, for all the imperial couple's sympathies for their more exotic subjects. When communities asked that collective property and access to the commons be preserved, the junta reminded them that, as the rightful owners of these assets, they should proceed to "reducing" them to private property in order to properly exploit them.

When Indigenous parishioners complained about municipal governments' interfering with noisy, festive religious celebrations, such as the burial of "little angels"—babies who had died so young that they were thought to go straight to heaven—the members of the Junta Protectora sided with local government: these fiestas were uncivilized and irreverent; a waste of money, and an excuse for drunken, disorderly behavior. Like the Liberals who came before them, imperial advocates for the downtrodden were intent on securing for Indigenous people rights as citizens, individuals, and, ideally, property owners. They hoped to ease their cultural, social, economic transition to modernity, not preserve the identities, prerogatives, and customs that had characterized Indigenous populations "from time immemorial." Indians should disappear, "buried" in Mexican citizenship.[114]

Imperial policy and ritual sought to organize the people—unknowable, unreliable, and powerful—into discrete, dependable categories: municipalities, speaking clearly—and clearly in favor of empire—through their ayuntamientos; loyal subjects lining the streets to cheer imperial pageantry; the emperor's supplicant "children" looking to the Junta Protectora for guidance, protection, or relief; the agents of the nation's "material interests," advising and not approving the design and implementation of new fiscal policies. It is practically impossible to gauge the effectiveness of these initiatives. We don't know if the imperialistas' baroque engineering to both incorporate and control the people generated loyalty. We do know that the regime's collaborators pinned very different hopes on the imperial government. Some wanted it to set up an efficient machine for government, which would enact the law with mathematical precision, unencumbered by partisan passions or popular turbulence. Some hoped it would restore Catholicism as the basis of the political and social order. The empire could not fulfill these different aspirations; in trying to do so, it bungled them all.

It seems unlikely that the empire's commitment to the rule of law, its defense of its own version of liberty and rights and the contrived—but ineffectual—political truce that some found so attractive would have stabilized Mexico's erratic politics in less violent, contentious circumstances. Maximilian's loyal subjects, like the idealized citizen of the Confederacy—male, white, martial, and devoted—and both regimes' apolitical politics were unable to contain the dynamics that led to the wars that would destroy them.

Southern secessionists and critics of Mexico's 1857 constitution attempted to craft new states out of their fractured republics: a white slaveholding republic, on the one hand; a military dictatorship and a monarchical regime, on the other. These men, and their visions, were profoundly different. They were, nonetheless, connected. It was the slaveholders' rebellion that enabled their neighbors' radicalism. The different structures they put together were rooted in shared fears, stirred by similar aspirations. The new regimes' architects feared the republic's fragility: to avoid impending doom, they engaged in radical political experimentation but spoke of restoration. They hoped to stabilize, preserve, and protect society's core values, corroded by public debate and partisan manhandling. To do so, they refashioned state and nation. The politicians who hated politics realized that they were, in the words of the Mexican "dignitaries" who voted for monarchy, like doctors who could not attack "a patient's ailments, but only deal with his symptoms."[115] The "evils" of corruption, factionalism, and instability were perhaps, as one of the Montgomery framers pondered, inherent in institutions whose "cornerstone rests on the popular will."[116] To different degrees, these state-builders strove to integrate the aesthetics but not the substance of politics into systems of government. These contradictions probably contributed to the vulnerabilities they were hoping to alleviate.

CHAPTER FOUR

RADICAL CHEMISTRY
The US Union and Mexico's Constitutional Republic

I N APRIL 1865, the commander of the Confederate Army of Northern Virginia surrendered to Gen. Ulysses S. Grant in the Appomattox courthouse. In June 1867, on the outskirts of the city of Querétaro, Maximilian von Hapsburg and two of the most prominent Conservative generals, Miguel Miramón and Tomás Mejía, were executed, having been found guilty of plundering, usurpation, and treason. On both sides of the border, republican military victory was hailed as the decisive triumph of progress, civilization, and democracy over the dark forces of slavocracy, reaction, and imperialism. These ominous struggles bequeathed heroes and martyrs, hallowed "places of memory," some of the most evocative examples of republican rhetoric and perhaps the most emblematic and enduring symbols of civilian statesmanship in Presidents Lincoln and Juárez.

The outcome of this continental republican crisis has been scripted as the fulfillment of national destinies. This triumphalist narrative nonetheless waters down a capacious, profoundly transformative process and falsely stabilizes its contentious outcome. The cataclysm of the 1850s and 1860s restructured both national politics and continental geopolitics. The bloody civil wars of the mid-nineteenth century settled some of the issues that had shattered the republics: slavery in the "Land of the Free," a church that stifled the state in its neighbor to the south. Fratricidal violence destroyed a government "divided, half slave and half free" and the disruptive religious groundwork of the Mexican Republic. But it did more: before, during, and after the war, legislators assumed that they were not engaged in routine lawmaking. In the aftermath of such strenuous confrontations over the character of the commonwealth, the people's delegates were called to construe a "precise definition" of "the idea of a Republic" and act accordingly. Lawmakers in Mexico in 1856 and 1859 and their colleagues in the United States between 1865 and 1870 could not limit themselves to theorizing about its nature; they had to invigorate its "soul."[1]

Republican politicians on either side of the Rio Grande surveyed polities afflicted by different ailments but shared the common impulse to save them: they wanted to expand the body politic, institutionalize more potent notions of membership and rights, and set up efficient mechanisms for their protection. Their republican agenda, streamlined and radicalized by exceptional political circumstances, came to fruition through constitutional reforms that overhauled the federal pact and bolstered the central government, now charged with protecting citizens' rights. In Mexico a new federal charter, drafted in 1857, triggered an armed conflict that split the nation in two. The demands of war drove the republican government to radical intervention and aggressive secularization. When the guns fell silent, these retaliatory measures became legal—and eventually constitutional—precepts. In 1867, victorious liberalism proclaimed that the people's "love" and "blood" had consecrated contentious fundamental law into the embodiment of the nation.

Upon his return to Mexico City, Juárez nonetheless attempted to expedite constitutional reform by submitting constitutional amendments to the voters, in a move not unlike Napoléon III's recurrent "appeals to the People." He was met with fierce resistance from fellow Liberals.[2] The constitution's symbolic value made it difficult to conceive it pragmatically, as an instrument of government.[3] Still, for all its awkwardness, the 1857 charter became the stable framework that had eluded Mexican legislators since independence. Until the first decade of the twentieth century, it allowed for the operative, relatively stable national politics that ushered in the consolidation and imbrication of Mexican markets, within and without the nation's borders.[4] US Republicans also identified constitutional renewal as necessary to Union victory. The venerable 1787 document, untouched since 1804, was amended to abolish slavery, define US citizenship, and protect freedmen's right to vote. In the decades that followed, the reformed constitution undergirded the nation's westward expansion, its explosive economic growth, and its consolidation as a hemispheric power. North America's republican triumph had entailed profound transformations. As we shall see in this chapter, however, their artificers sought to codify revolutionary change into law. Innovation brokered into statute inevitably reflected conflicting priorities, partisan tensions, and the pressures of democratic politics.[5] Powerful visions undergird the North American republics' "new birth of freedom"; they inspired hopes and raised expectations, which the new order would often prove unable to meet.

Reluctant Revolutionaries, Crafty Constitutionalists

North American politicians in the 1850s and 1860s had ambivalent feelings about revolution. As discord grew, all claimed the mantle of the revolution that had engendered the nation, but revolutionary imperatives—the violence, illegality, and destructiveness of such movements—unsettled earnest republicans. As Lincoln wrote in the summer of 1861, revolution was never a "universal right": unless grounded in morality—which had grown increasingly difficult to pin down—it was "simply a wicked exercise of physical power."[6] On both sides of the ideological divide, North America's public men asserted their devotion to a government of laws: public opinion, deliberation, and legislation were the only legitimate catalysts for change.

In the northern republic, some states seceded and others went to war to preserve the constitution, jeopardized by what they condemned as their antagonists' unsound, revolutionary interpretations. On the other side of the border, Mexican Liberals made over their 1855 *pronunciamiento*—unexceptional in both its rhetoric and objectives—into a revolution, endowed with broad powers for reform.[7] Yet once the Juárez government committed to the defense of the 1857 constitution, it forcefully maintained that legitimate authority stemmed only from fundamental law. During ten years of armed confrontation, the vocal apologists of the Ayutla revolution, federalism, and democracy denied the legitimacy of power engendered by insurrection, military might, or territorial control. They also rejected political decisions validated by state sovereignty or even expressions of the popular will since, constitutionalists argued, war fractured and distracted the people and made suffrage unreliable.[8]

In both nations, the constitution was consecrated as the banner and object of a heroic struggle to save the republic.[9] Fundamental law—the bulwark of rights, custodian of essential continuities—would serve as the foundation of new political regimes, built on, as Bruce Ackerman has written, "higher lawmaking processes, and substantive solutions in the name of We the People."[10] These "solutions" often resulted from creative interpretations of the popular will: reformist republicans would, when circumstances required it, give the people what they needed rather than what they said they wanted. In Congress, the clash between reluctant revolution and insistent legalism warped the political arena, as men intent on transformation acted with what Greg Downs has aptly described as "a combination of punctiliousness and boldness."[11]

In both the United States and Mexico, those who imagined and then spearheaded the republics' transformation belonged to fledgling political organizations: the Republican Party was founded in 1854; Mexico's much less institutionalized Liberal Party was invigorated at mid-century by the leadership of younger politicians with no memories of the colonial regime, who had cut their teeth on local politics, opposition to Santa Anna, and exile. These party men were less committed to long-standing compromises and more willing to challenge the status quo.[12] To propel their visions forward, they engaged in grandstanding, electoral scheming, and parliamentary maneuvers. They also tried—not always successfully—to prolong their hold on power. In the heat of war, they wielded fundamental law to punish their enemies and discipline their allies, but they were also not above sacrificing some of its strictures to military or political necessity.

Thus, Mexico's elections to the 1856 constituent congress, organized by municipal authorities in the wake of the Liberals' triumphant "revolution," conspicuously returned no Conservative delegates. In a context of increasing political polarization, this set up the most ideologically monochromatic legislative assembly to date—and consequently perhaps the least representative.[13] The less numerous *puro* congressmen relied on their rhetorical skill, assertive sense of righteousness, and more effective organization to set up a reformist agenda and thwart more moderate proposals, such as a simple restoration of the 1824 constitution or the preservation of a senate. Radicals vigorously demanded greater democratic participation and control, but they endorsed legislation on issues—like religious tolerance—that were patently unpopular.[14] As members of a party that "legitimately aspired . . . to perpetuate itself in power," they tried, unsuccessfully, to enhance their future chances by eliminating birth and residence requirements for members of Congress.[15]

During the war, the constitution's champions hailed fundamental law as a source of legitimacy and practically unchecked authority. When, in 1859, the constitutional government decreed the nationalization of church property, it warned that those who opposed the law or in any way "enervated" its execution would be "expelled from the Republic" or tried for conspiracy.[16] In 1864, as the invading French Army moved North, Santiago Vidaurri, the fiercely independent governor of Nuevo León and Coahuila, summoned the state's citizens to vote and choose between fighting the French and negotiating a separate peace. An incensed Juárez government quoted extensively from fundamental law to accuse the ornery cacique of usurping national sovereignty and the war powers that belonged exclusively to the federal government. Vidaurri, and all who obeyed him, were outlaws, rebels, and traitors.[17]

In 1865, constitutional prescriptions for presidential succession were nevertheless ignored when President Juárez's term ran out, and the war against France and the empire made elections impossible. Jesús González Ortega, the dashing young general who had defeated the Conservatives in December 1860 and then been elected president of the Supreme Court, called on Juárez to hand over executive power. On Juárez's refusal, González Ortega left for the United States, where, like other Liberals, he tried to raise funds, buy arms, and recruit soldiers but also gain support for his presidential ambitions. The constitutional government charged him with abandoning his duties as an officer. Even after the empire collapsed, when González Ortega returned to Mexico, he was arrested and jailed until President Juárez had been reelected, just to be on the safe side.

Not unlike their neighbors to the south, US legislators resorted to parliamentary and legal maneuvers to run roughshod over their conservative critics, in Congress and in the public square. Even when the existential threat to the Union had passed, they continued to find opposition not only irksome but sinister.

Republican congressmen refused to seat former Confederate leaders whose voters sent them back to Washington; they passed legislation over the president's veto and, in early 1868, voted to impeach Andrew Johnson, who avoided removal by only one vote. They also tried to bolster their majority by authorizing western territories—Nebraska, Colorado, Nevada—to draft state constitutions and, in the South, a region in which their party had been practically nonexistent before the war, they stressed the "political necessity" of empowering "loyal blacks."[18]

In both North American republics, activists relied on exceptional circumstances, complex stratagems, and sometimes dodgy maneuvers to push their reformist, modernizing, democratizing agenda. They were conscious that, to materialize and endure, their visions needed to be placed, as a Kansas senator said, "beyond the reach of party legislation, removed from party politics," and enshrined in fundamental law.[19] This meant grafting significant change onto charters meant to ensure stability and continuity, and debating their amendment in legislative bodies. It is true that deological coincidence limited meaningful dissent in the 1856–57 Mexican constituent assembly and in the rump Congresses that sat in Washington during Reconstruction. Crusaders still had to steer parliamentary deliberations through a forest of principle, ambitions, and fears; electoral calculations and partisan chicanery; evolving strategies and shifting alliances. In the end, the principles they enshrined in the constitution were open to conflicting interpretations. Despite its advocates' efforts to preserve constitutional refounding from politics, it would bear the marks of the rivalries, compromises, and unintended consequences that marked a turbulent process.

A Fundamental Law That Is Not "Purely Political":
Mexico's 1857 Constitution

In mid-February 1856, the people's elected representatives met in Mexico City and were charged with "definitely"—and, hopefully, finally—"constituting the nation." For the fifth time since 1821, an elected assembly undertook the daunting task. Many of its members were now convinced that their mandate could not be limited to setting down "theory and ideals . . . dividing up powers, determining qualifications and attributions, and parsing out sovereignties."[20] In the shadow of an authoritarian, centralizing, and inefficient dictatorship, the reestablishment of federalism and representative government were essential but insufficient. Mexican society was weighed down by the "absurdities" of "gloomy centuries": it needed its constitution to not only address political organization but also trigger its transformation. Otherwise, fundamental law would remain "nothing but a piece of paper," bereft of "life, roots, or foundation."[21]

To rid the nation from the nefarious legacies of its past—the outrageous "advantages and benefits" enjoyed by certain classes—the structure and substance of governance both needed to change. All "power, direction, and authority" should be handed over to the people.²² Despite the Ayutla revolution's much-vaunted attachment to state sovereignty, a slim majority did away with the Senate. Critics of the Upper House selectively quoted Thomas Jefferson and argued that it was an "antidemocratic institution," embodying "aristocratic interests" rather than states' rights.²³ A single-chamber legislative, the true image of a horizontal, sovereign citizenry, was charged with the oversight of an inherently untrustworthy executive. The administration, reformers claimed, might have experience and "the science of the facts," but this did not make it "more enlightened or patriotic than the popular representatives." The constitution did not grant the president veto power. Unlike previous fundamental laws, the 1857 charter did vest emergency powers in the executive but only if they were authorized by a majority of the legislative body, even in the midst of rebellion or invasion.²⁴ Congress, as stand-in for the indivisible body of the people, stood as epicenter and engine of the political system.

The constitution's drafting committee included radicals such as Ponciano Arriaga, who had been a public defender (*procurador de pobres*) in San Luis Potosí, and José María Castillo Velasco, perhaps the most sophisticated advocate for municipal autonomy. Moderates like Pedro Escudero y Echánove and José María Cortés Esparza, who would later support Maximilian's empire, also underwrote the transformative text, with certain reservations. Committee members insisted that fundamental law needed to remind the nation's "poor, hardworking citizens" that they were not mere "sad machines" serving "big capitalists" but "free men, citizens of the Republic, members of the same family."²⁵ The constitution would protect freedom and equality, "consummated and perfected" by fraternity.²⁶ To prevent constitutional rights from remaining a "dead letter, scrawled on a piece of paper," they were entrusted to the federal Supreme Court for their protection.²⁷

Despite differences of opinion, the men who drafted, discussed, passed, and enacted the 1857 constitution all wanted to empower a national government that had remained poor, weak, unstable, and ineffective since independence.²⁸ To bolster the state's capabilities, Liberal politicians sought to circumscribe the influence of nonstate actors on public life—the church in first instance, eventually the army and regional strongmen—by reframing what was conceived as public and hence subject to governmental intervention. Dealing with the church was particularly difficult. Having rid itself of the Crown's officious patronage with independence, the Mexican ecclesiastical establishment had played an essential role in molding and transmitting modern political culture as it ministered to the faithful. From the pulpit and the printed press, clerics had both naturalized the languages of liberalism and defended ecclesiastical prerogatives.

The church also played an important, visible, and influential part in governance. Its actions as a public authority were both essential and contentious. It determined membership and status: the rituals of birth, marriage, and death were performed by its clerks and recorded in its registries. Only Catholic foreigners could become Mexican citizens. The church taught, censored, and administered justice. Diocesan and federal geographies shaped each other; the church's monumental buildings, its bells and processions drew the physical and sonorous landscapes of Mexican cities. Centuries of charitable donations had transformed convents into the largest landlords in central Mexico. In a country without banks, the church lent money and leased land and buildings.

Restructuring the relationship between church and state was a formidable challenge. Politicians of all stripes who were, for the most part, sincere, devout Catholics, saw the need for change. The more liberal members of the constituent congress believed that religious freedom was an unalienable, individual right that ought to be enshrined in the constitution. Others were more concerned with the future of the institution itself: if the church did not change, it would be unable to fulfill its evangelical mission. The constitution's first draft included religious toleration in the bill of rights warranted by fundamental law. It was nevertheless introduced rather timidly, in the negative, by establishing—like the US constitution—that no law could "forbid or prevent" any form of worship, as long as it was compatible with conventions and decency.[29] Because Catholicism had been the nation's religion, it would still be "protected" by "wise statutes."

This moderate position nevertheless unleashed noisy, widespread opposition. Numerous petitions reached Congress—many of them signed by women, whose intervention in the public sphere was described as shocking—decrying the "evils of tolerantism." A majority of the delegates voted against toleration, which they considered risky, ill-timed, or wicked. Although efforts to establish religious freedom foundered, the constitution did not mandate religious exclusivity. It curtailed the church's authority over education and publishing, and declared "inviolable" the freedom to teach, speak, write, and publish. Additionally, President Comonfort established a national civil registry to record births, adoptions, deaths, and individuals' civil status (single or married, in civil or religious ceremonies). It meant to include all the republic's inhabitants, and only those registered would be able to "exercise their civil rights."[30]

The men of Ayutla wanted to strengthen the national government so that it could act against the remnants of the colonial regime's hierarchical, corporate order. In their eyes, this was the only way to put an end to the nation's backwardness and poverty and bridge the abyss between the rich and poor. Endowed with extraordinary powers by revolution, the Liberal administration legislated to abolish exclusive jurisdictions—of special tribunals over mining or commercial interests, for instance—and deny ecclesiastical and military courts authority over civil matters: at least in courts of law, citizens were equal. Liberals also hoped to invigorate a stagnant economy: although they did not radically redefine property rights, as some had hoped, they did undertake significant reforms. To bring together a fractured, inefficient market, stimulate production and trade and increase taxable income, they ordered the disentailment of real estate owned by corporations: the church, municipal governments, and Indigenous communities. A strong, active state would jump-start the market, empower its citizens—as producers and consumers—and change the country for the better.

Transformative intervention required a healthy fiscal state where independent Mexico's had been profoundly deficient. A string of failed efforts to overhaul public finances embodied the brittleness of reformists' promises and their narrow possibilities for change. Like so many pronunciamientos, the Plan de Ayutla complained about "burdensome contributions" weighing down the pueblos. Atypically, the plan also called for "freedom of trade, both internal and external."[31] Nevertheless, the draft for a new fundamental law contained no proposals for tax reform. Personal contributions, such as the *capitación* (head tax) which so irritated poorer taxpayers, were the realm of state authority. The much-maligned *alcabalas* (duties paid on the movement of goods, levied by both the state and federal governments) had, for all their flaws, stood the test of time and survived revolution. Their sudden abolition would deplete state treasuries and further distress federal finances.[32]

Congressmen nonetheless insisted on a fiscal overhaul, with an enthusiasm usually reserved for loftier aspirations. They accused members of the drafting committee of breaking one of the "solemn promises" of Ayutla and of sacrificing the nation's future by taking the easy path.[33] The way forward was clear: the United States "owed half of its progress to religious freedom, the other to free trade." Mexican Liberals could no longer delay: *alcabalas* were "contemptible for a thousand reasons": they oppressed the poorest citizens, stole their sustenance, reduced them to "nakedness." Their collection was marred by procedures from the "semibarbarous ages," which were "an outrage to the dignity of men." They weakened the federal bond by encouraging "tax wars" between the states. Putting off their abolition because it was either untimely or unconstitutional was "unpatriotic." By a vote of 70 to 13, the constitution mandated *alcabalas* be abolished by June 1858. It established no new levies to replace them. War came in January and reform was postponed. *Alcabalas* were eliminated only in 1896.[34]

On February 5, 1857, Congress promulgated the long-awaited constitution. Some of its supporters thought it did not take reform far enough; others worried that it excessively weakened the executive and needlessly aggravated the religious and military establishments. Despite these concerns, Liberal politicians hoped fundamental law would underpin a new, peaceful, prosperous order, rooted in democracy, individual rights, capitalism, and secularism. Instead, civil war broke out and tore the republic apart. When Conservatives took power in Mexico City in January 1858, they moved to quash reform. From opposite trenches, Liberals sought instead to radicalize it.

In 1859, the Juárez government, bogged down in an inconclusive armed conflict, sought to punish the church for its role in inciting rebellion: free from the strictures of parliamentarian niceties and public opinion, the Veracruz administration consummated its separation from the state, nationalized its wealth, suppressed religious orders, and sought to secularize the public sphere by proscribing public religious displays. In December 1860, emboldened by the certainty of military triumph, Juárez decreed not toleration but religious liberty. Since it was "urgent" to put an end to the church's "compulsory and exclusive intervention" in the most important moments in people's lives, the state would be charged not only with recording and corroborating citizens' identities and status but also with their administration and validation. Sacraments—and notably marriage—would no longer be recognized as legal. Family relationships would henceforth be recognized by the state only if sanctioned by civil authority.[35]

The Liberals' attack on outdated corporations included the standing army. After defeating Miramón's troops on the fields of Calpulalpan, Jesús González Ortega decreed that the army be disbanded, for it had always been "a hinderance to all social advancement."[36] War and its hardships nevertheless thwarted the constitutionalists' intentions. Neither the young general's outrageous abolition of the nation's armed forces nor the privatization of ecclesiastical and Indigenous property became a reality in the immediate aftermath of their being decreed. Liberals thought the sale of corporate real estate—*bienes de manos muertas* (property placed in "dead hands")—would transform landless peasants into prosperous yeomen; instead, a protracted, uneven process fueled unrest in the countryside for decades and contributed to the concentration of land in the hands of the moneyed elite.[37] But despite its shortcomings and disappointments, the secular state was the Reforma's persistent achievement. Its independence from the church signaled a deep break with the nation's past. For all its importance, its reverberations throughout Mexican society were perhaps less expansive and transformative than what the architects of reform had hoped.

The Union as It Should Be? Amending the US Constitution

During the first half century of independence, Mexican politicians steadfastly but unsuccessfully sought a constitutional formula to warrant both "liberty and order," political stability and economic progress. The 1857 constitution was the most recent, and perhaps the most far-reaching, in a long line of unsatisfactory efforts. In contrast, their colleagues to the north hailed the eighteenth-century legal creation that had engendered the Union as a statute of "matchless perfection."[38] The rush to amend it, in the midst of the constitutional crisis sparked by the 1860 election, was a sign of desperation rather than the result of carefully considered aspirations for change. Nevertheless, five years later, in the aftermath of a war fought for the constitution, Republicans came together to call for its amendment.[39]

Some thought the nation's fundamental law needed a thorough overhaul. Columbia University's Francis Lieber put forth seven amendment proposals of "direct and urgent practical character." Had they passed, the federal government would have been declared the object of citizens' "plenary allegiance," and made responsible for the "full protection" of their rights. Secession, resistance to US authority, and any activity facilitating the "selling and buying" of human beings would be considered "high crimes." Abolition would have been enshrined in the constitution, along with the right of all free inhabitants to equal justice.[40] The professor's position was not particularly popular. Politicians in Congress, although intent on securing the freedom and rights of the formerly enslaved, were not eager to run roughshod over hallowed fundamental law. They nevertheless realized that if their vision—which their critics despised and their constituents did not always share—was to survive, it needed to be grafted onto the constitution and placed under the protection of an invigorated federal government.[41]

Constitutional debates surrounding abolition, citizenship, and suffrage stretched from late 1864—months before the war ended—to early 1870. Discussions were marked by the obduracy of Southern elites, the harrowing confrontation between Congress and President Johnson, and the grievous, pervasive conflicts that arose from military occupation, resistance to Reconstruction, and the violent intimidation of freedpeople in the South. Lincoln had pushed for gradual, compensated emancipation since the beginning of the war, then twice decreed that slaves held within the rebellious states were "henceforth and forever free."[42] In the end, slavery was destroyed by the war and by the actions of African Americans who took their freedom and left their enslavers or joined the Union army.[43] In 1865, an amendment inscribed abolition into fundamental law. It was made possible by the Republicans' artificial majority—a product of the secessionists' withdrawal in 1861—and President Johnson and other lawmakers' working for its ratification in Southern states, in a preemptive strategy to root the Union's reconstitution on a conservative version of Reconstruction, given that the Thirteenth Amendment constitutionalized a fait accompli without addressing the inevitable polemics of racial equality or political rights.[44]

Abolition meant to drive a constitutional nail into the coffin of slavery and put an end to the tensions and conflicts it had infused into the life of the republic. It aimed to wrap up the past. Further constitutional renewal intended to lay down conditions for the republic's future and steel the hand of its champions. Amendments were drafted, discussed, passed, and ratified amid growing strain. The Fourteenth is the longest amendment added to the constitution.[45] Tempered by concerns of constitutional overreach, its authors wove together hopeful visions of a more equal society with partisan ambition and a desire to punish the "recent rebels."[46]

The amendment established the principles of birthright citizenship—added at the last minute—and equal protection under law.[47] It also craftily conditioned the apportionment of a state's representatives in Congress to local respect for the political rights of formerly enslaved citizens. It excluded oath-breaking traitors from federal office and repudiated Confederate debt. The more circumspect Fifteenth Amendment banned states from restricting voting rights "on account of race, color, or previous condition of servitude." It explicitly protected African American male citizens' voting rights and implicitly reinforced the states' authority to regulate the privilege of suffrage. Furthermore, Republican majorities in Congress manufactured consent by requiring the unreconstructed states' legislatures to ratify the amendments before they could be readmitted into the Union, thus securing the three-fourths vote required.[48] All three amendments shifted the Union's center of gravity toward the federal government by conferring on Congress "the power to enforce" the amendments' prescriptions "by appropriate legislation."

As in Mexico, the new constitutional order in the Reunited States set up the federal government as the guardian of citizen rights. In both republics, the effects of this constitutionally mandated transformation were probably mitigated by the judicial process required for its enforcement, including the costs to plaintiffs and legal loopholes, the contentious nature and uncertain definition of states' rights, and, in the United States, the powerful backlash it provoked among those forcefully rejecting legal equality. Nonetheless, constitutional overhaul recalibrated the authority of nation and state: reformed fundamental law modified the structures of republican government as it reshaped its object and purpose. To restore and preserve the republic, its defenders thought it necessary to rethink its character and rebuild its moral and material foundations, which would lead to unconventional experimentation with key elements in republican political culture and institutions.

So That the Republic Can Stand: Citizenship and Property

To men like Ponciano Arriaga and Charles Sumner, a republic was more than a form of government. The dangers that threatened its survival at mid-century drove them to paint stirring visions of the commonwealth—as a nation, as a community of rights, as a family—and to endeavor to translate them into law. The republic's advocates needed to make membership more meaningful: they redefined citizenship and the rights associated with it. They laboriously wrestled to both demarcate and extend a right consecrated by revolutionary tradition as essential, "natural," and incommensurable: that of property. In economic contexts that were profoundly different—in terms of dynamism, markets, infrastructure, technology, and the availability of credit—reformists deemed certain forms of property sterile and illegitimate, even immoral: property-in-man in the United States; in Mexico property held in the "dead hands" of corporations, be they peasant communities, municipal councils, or ecclesiastical institutions. Reformist republicans also pursued policies that would endow a greater number of citizens with property. Ownership of land would, according to the Liberal creed, make citizens prosperous, independent, responsible, and committed to the republic . . . as well as to progressive parties.

New Meanings for Citizenship

Mexico's descent into civil war in January 1858 revealed a shattered nation. The new constitution had exacerbated political polarization and social confrontations to a breaking point. The men who drafted the 1857 constitution were, nevertheless, surprised. They had sought moderation and even-handedness, and, in redefining membership in the nation, had tried to cast as wide a net as possible. Eclipsed by the pyrotechnics of the "religious question," their secular, inclusive vision of the nation as a community of both origin and law, set out in a statute that meant to both discipline and protect, sparked little controversy, either within or without the walls of Congress.[49] The constitution recognized all those born to Mexican parents, within or without the republic's territory, as members of the nation. Foreigners became Mexican citizens if they chose to naturalize, bought land, or had children in Mexico, unless they explicitly stated they wanted to "keep their nationality"—and the right to request consular protection, which had proved so unsettling.[50] The most radical members of Congress had hoped to introduce religious tolerance into fundamental law. Although they had failed in the face of conspicuous popular repudiation, the constitution did not establish religious exclusivity. The bond between Catholicism and nationality, long thought essential, was quietly dissolved.

Paired with this open, secular view of political community was a more expansive vision of its members' rights. The honest, upstanding, hardworking *vecinos* of boroughs and villages were all citizens; they all had a right to vote: congressmen unanimously struck out the proposed literacy restriction to male suffrage, for "it ran against democratic principles." Not being able to read was not "the fault of the poor" but of the governments that had neglected public education.[51] As it established practically universal male suffrage, Congress also worked to streamline election procedures to both reduce the distance between legislators and their constituents and to make electoral colleges less vulnerable to manipulation by state governors.[52]

For all of Congress's democratic enthusiasm, those advocating for direct suffrage failed to convince a majority of their colleagues who feared that, if left to their own devices, citizens would follow the lead of "ignorant, superstitious priests" and elect "a child or an old bat" to speak for them in Congress.[53] Mexico's federal elections remained indirect until 1911. Paradoxically, despite their fear of popular political mobilization—especially for illiberal purposes, such as the defense of religion—the men who put the constitution together insisted that the people were not only the objects of government but its agents. If they were the "root" and "wellspring" of public authority, they also needed to be its executors.

Hence, membership in the nation's Supreme Court would also be determined by the vote of electors, who would choose its fifteen justices among men who, "in their judgement," were "knowledgeable in the science of Law." If the office of the president became vacant, the chief justice would take his place.[54] Congress's most radical members also tried to introduce trial by jury, which they considered "indispensable" to the administration of justice "in free countries." Juries would contribute to the painfully needed transformation of Mexico's dismal justice system, characterized by the "barbarous oriental despotism" of the colonial period. Jury duty would serve as a school for citizenship: the people would be charged with "protecting innocence and suppressing vice."[55]

Trial by jury proved too extreme an innovation for a majority in Congress. To counter this proposal, its critics relied on other tried-and-true tenets of postrevolutionary doctrine: they defended the right of sovereign states to organize their own judicial systems. They also praised the lawyer's specialized craft and insisted juries were foreign to Mexico's "habits and customs." But they mainly fell back on an ambivalent vision of the people. To great dramatic effect, they contrasted the reformists' unrealistic vision of the virtuous citizen who could act as governor, lawmaker, and judge with Mexican "reality": a motley "mass" of people who were poor, diverse, untrained, and ignorant.[56] Even as the unorthodox twostep election of Supreme Court members became a constitutional precept, the introduction of citizen juries in the administration of justice was removed from the constitution's draft before it could be voted on.[57]

Congress put the sovereign people at the heart of constitutional debate and at the center of fundamental law. It was understood in the most capacious sense, with its poorest members, the marginalized, the "proletarians," holding pride of place. Popular sanction was the source of legitimacy for all three branches of government, and the people were incarnate in the legislative power—a singlechamber assembly—conceived as superior to the other two. The constitution's electoral scheme nonetheless confirmed the role of popular elections in nineteenthcentury Mexico as visual and performative displays of community rather than effective exercises of choice.[58] Some puro congressmen, in their effort to liberate the republic's citizens from all forms of tutelage, tried to secure direct suffrage, trial by jury, and the noninterference of government in matters of religion. The majority rejected their unconventional proposals. War, when it broke out, radicalized the Liberals' project for secularization and invigorated the state's intervention in society, but did not bring about a reassessment of democracy. As José Antonio Aguilar has written, democracy as self-government "was devoured by civic and patriotic rhetoric." It became a powerful symbol rather than a formula for government or the basis of social organization.[59]

The constituents of Ayutla put forth a dramatically different vision of membership in the nation without causing any major upheavals. They claimed that the transformative potential of the new law lay in its promise to safeguard the rights of man rather than in greater inclusivity or democratic action. Mexican constitutions since 1836 had explicitly acknowledged the "rights and obligations" of the republic's inhabitants. The 1857 bill of rights was more extensive: it did away with ecclesiastical censure, safe-conducts, and the death penalty for political crimes; it recognized the right to bear arms and the freedom of fugitive slaves who crossed the border. It also established a mechanism that enabled the federal judiciary to grant relief to those whose "individual guarantees" had been infringed upon by the execution of law or the "actions" of "any civil servant, in local, state, or federal government." A federal judge could confer *amparo* (protection, shelter) and issue an injunction against legal or administrative actions that violated the plaintiff's constitutional rights.[60]

A few congressmen considered the bill of rights dangerous. Such exalted freedoms would shatter social hierarchies: men would feel entitled to miss work and breach their contracts. Espiridión Moreno apocalyptically predicted that "a true and most horrible communism"—another phantasm stirred by 1848—would sap society's foundations. Others were less alarmist but argued that federal protection of rights would both interfere with the local administration of justice and place a federal judge's opinion over the will of the sovereign people. Amparo suits, they warned, tarnished "the majesty of the law" and gave each citizen "the tools" to undermine and destroy it: norms were nothing, if not executed unyieldingly."[61] Their adversaries argued that this was not necessarily a bad thing: in a judge's hands, the bill of rights would become "a legal check" on ill-conceived law or unconstitutional government action.[62] Future chief justice Ignacio L. Vallarta hailed the *juicio de amparo* as rooted in the hallowed Anglo-Saxon institution of writs of habeas corpus, improved upon by Mexican liberalism. It kept the constitution's prescriptions from becoming "a lie." The enumeration of rights in fundamental law had previously been little more than a rhetorical exercise, especially when "the rights *of the poor*" were involved. The possibility of judicial relief made these rights real.[63]

By setting up the federal judiciary as the final arbiter in conflicts not only between individuals and public authorities but also between state and federal governments, the constituent congress sought to draw clear boundaries between spheres of sovereignty. It meant to institute a stable mechanism for the adjudication of the corrosive disputes that had marred Mexican federalism since independence. If the Supreme Court was recognized as the final interpreter of the constitution, "law would replace violence" and arbitration the use of "material force."[64] Advocates of the amparo mechanism, in the first throes of Mexican lawyers' long-lasting love affair with this judicial device, did not dispute their opponents' good faith and principles but censured their shortsightedness. They had not noticed the advantages of this judicial remedy, which was not only institutional, normative, and apolitical but also limited in its reach. A federal judge's verdict in an amparo suit suspended the execution of an unconstitutional statute only in the case of the particular plaintiff. It did not abrogate the law.

Suits, then, were legitimate, unobtrusive solutions to conflicts arising from the execution of laws. In the past, these conflicts had confronted different sovereign entities: they inevitably engendered "noisy initiatives . . . rash words and complaints" and often led to pronunciamientos and open rebellion. Disputes between those holding legitimate public authority needed to be "indirect, particular, negative." Amparo suits challenged the sovereign's law, but verdicts turned on legal technicalities, not principles: judges made no "general declarations" about the controverted statutes. They only protected the individual plaintiff from a statute's application. The lawmaker remained unscathed "in his high sphere as sovereign."[65] Even when granted, amparo suits would not upset the republic's unstable applecart, which needed to balance federalism, the separation of powers, and legislative supremacy.

In crafting this device, the 1856 Liberals invoked the US model of judicial review with quotes from "the gorgeous work" of Alexis de Tocqueville . . . and, with less flamboyance, that of French socialist Paul de Flotte.[66] They argued that the US constitution's "masterpiece" was the federal judiciary: while it acted in the name of the law, it dealt with individuals only. Admirers of the US system remarked that even when found unconstitutional, the law remained "intact"—they failed to mention that it was also abrogated. Just as they had when looking to Jefferson—the author of *A Manual of Parliamentary Practice for the Use of the Senate of the United States* (1801)—to legitimize the suppression of the upper house, Mexico's statesmen construed their own version of how the US constitutional order worked. The model republic, remarkable for its stability, energy, and mind-boggling prosperity, served less as a template than as a useful, flattering mirror in which Mexican constitutionalists saw themselves, and the future, at their best.

In February 1857, the Liberal Congress proclaimed a 128-article constitution—the first twenty-nine articles made up the bill of rights. It was conceived as a decisive—even revolutionary—break with the past. In the United States, legislators amended what many thought was a practically perfect constitution three times; the changes they wrought were equally dramatic. It is tempting to see the distinct legislative paths taken as the product of two profoundly different, self-contained, congruent political cultures and philosophies: one "Continental," Rousseauian, verbose, and idealistic; the other "Anglo-Saxon," Lockean, plain, and pragmatic. Congressional debates on both sides of the border point to a more complex reality, in which outcomes were shaped less by ideas and intellectual traditions than by context, institutional path-dependence, and the challenges confronting reformers.

In the wake of a movement they deemed revolutionary, Mexican Liberals crafted a groundbreaking constitution to found the republic anew. The ensuing ten years of intermittent war are proof of their exaggerated optimism. US Republicans also wagered on constitutional renewal as the country tried to come together, following what is still its deadliest armed conflict. They sought to remake federal authority over citizens whose primary allegiance was to their state. They needed to cobble together a new national community that would incorporate former slaves—previously thought of as unassimilable, even by many of slavery's critics, including Abraham Lincoln—and former slaveholders, who were doing their utmost to preserve the central hierarchies and tenets of the defeated order.

Even after the harrowing ordeal of the war, and the Union's decisive military victory, the need for drastic change was not obvious, beyond a circle of radical fellow travelers. Before the war, only five states had allowed African American men to vote; in late 1865 and early 1866, voters in four loyal states again rejected "impartial suffrage."[67] In March 1866, President Johnson vetoed the Civil Rights Act, which he described as "fraught with evil," for it would "sap and destroy our federative system of limited powers and break down the barriers which preserve the rights of the States."[68] As the rebel states were readmitted into the Union—Tennessee in July 1866, six more in the summer of 1868 and the last four in 1870—hostility to change grew in the capital. Republicans were well-aware of the electoral costs of pushing an excessively ambitious agenda.

In the face of resistance, Congress put boots on the ground: it ordered troops of the victorious army to occupy the former Confederacy. It created the Freedmen's Bureau for the protection—and tutelage—of the formerly enslaved. Conversely, in order to make Reconstruction legislation more acceptable, Radical Republicans—including John A. Bingham, Thaddeus Stevens, Jacob Howard, and Benjamin Wade—worked on separate, incremental changes: abolition, civil rights, and suffrage. Sweeping, far-reaching reform was mixed with circumstantial items that seemed particularly attractive in the aftermath of a costly, destructive Civil War, such as the disfranchisement of traitors and the repudiation of their debts. Against the background of violence and hostility in the South, African American activists insisted on the enfranchisement of Black citizens, not only as a matter of justice, but as a "question of life and death."[69]

The distressing testimony presented at the hearings called for by Congress's Joint Committee on Reconstruction proved them right, but would be unsympathetically described, even in the early twentieth century, as serving "a double purpose—first as an excuse for some proposed legislation, and second, as a kind of chamber of horrors ... an ominous warning to the northern voter."[70] Although less cynical, legislators in the 1860s proved ambivalent and sought to temper expectations of what constitutional innovation could do. They did so for different reasons: some believed the constitution was already an antislavery document; others upheld robust states' rights; and several rejected political equality on principle.

Lyman Trumbull, a former Democrat and sponsor of the Thirteenth Amendment, said of the Fourteenth that "the granting of civil rights does not, and never did, in this country, carry with it rights, or, more properly speaking, political privileges."[71] Even those calling for a more thorough constitutional overhaul insisted that theirs was a vision strongly rooted in continuity. Some of the most passionate legislators on the floor—Thaddeus Stevens, Samuel Pomeroy, and a self-righteous Charles Sumner—who called for "Equal Rights" for all, votes for women, and the right of all citizens to hold office, argued that the constitution would be amended only to better "embody the principles of its framers" and become the "transcript of their minds."[72] Reform would restore the founders' true meaning and "arm" Congress so that the constitution, "the whole of it, not part of it, *shall be the Supreme Law of the land.*"[73]

The foes of reform disparaged their adversaries' claims to continuity and respect for precedent. They decried the novelty and transgressive character of the proposed alterations, the dangers contained therein, and the speciousness of their sponsors' arguments. Underhanded activists, they admonished, hid behind devious "grammatical construction," "artistic" editing and "technicalities" in order to pass legislation that endowed the federal government with "monstrous" powers. Republicans had "mutilated" Congress and artificially created "a plurality" in order to pass measures that were "revolutionary" and should be "void." They promoted a forceful, ambitious central authority that sought to "convert" objectionable men into citizens and "annihilate" the right of sovereign states to regulate membership and suffrage. It would eventually be able to "abolish and modify all laws" and disproportionally "amplify and enlarge the jurisdiction" of federal courts.[74]

Critics of the amendments spoke, on the one hand, of the dangers threatening their nation's exceptional and uniquely well-balanced system of "divided sovereignties," checks and balances, and delegated powers. On the other, they warned of reform's dire reverberations, which would be felt far beyond the political realm. By outlawing discrimination, Republican legislation sought to "destroy" all the "regulations and customs" that conferred "privileged accommodations" on white people throughout the United States: on ships and railroads, in hotels, restaurants, and saloons. Assertions that Republicans sought "political equality alone" were false. The amendment's true objective was to "bring the two races upon the great plane of perfect equality."

African American activists fought for "public rights" as expressions of human dignity. Their detractors rejected "social equality" and invoked the ghost of sexual contact between Black and white. Opponents of the Fourteenth and Fifteenth Amendments described equality as a "detestable enterprise," repugnant to "the instincts and customs of the whole white race," incompatible, even, with "the unchangeable laws of nature." Their incendiary rhetoric meant to exploit racist fears prevalent both North and South: a law that granted civil and political rights to those who were obviously inferior would encourage "intermixture," "promiscuous marriages," and "miscegenation"—a term, they argued sardonically, made up by "amalgamationists" for a practice so appalling that there was no word for it in the English language.[75]

THE RECONSTRUCTED CONSTITUTION of the United States and Mexico's 1857 fundamental law have justifiably been described as expressions and platforms for the republics' second founding. At mid-century, crisis, disunion, and war required rethinking the nation. On both sides of the border, the architects of the new order trusted that a broader, more inclusive, more egalitarian political community would shore up a regime that was fragile by nature. An idyllic—and rather hazy—vision inspired Mexican Liberals: they wanted to implement "the social formula of Christianity" and confirm, in constitutional law, that members of the nation were all equal and free, because they were all "brothers."[76] The US lawmakers who stitched together the Reconstruction amendments and shepherded them through Congress also grounded citizenship in the nation. But as states remained the essential unit of belonging, they stressed the legal implications of membership by setting up the federal government as the protector of rights.

These new templates for community were not without their shortcomings. Mexican Liberals celebrated equality but balked at embracing its full consequences in the political realm: it was communion, not empowerment, that set the sovereign people at the heart of the new constitutional order. Citizens were conceived as voters, not electors or jurors. In the United States, the advocates of extending suffrage envisioned the ballot as a badge of manhood, as both a weapon and a shield, imperative for the defense of citizens' rights and interests, but also as a privilege, whose stewardship was entrusted to state authorities. Furthermore, constitutionalizing legal equality unleashed a fierce, pervasive resistance that animated a drawn-out, remarkably successful campaign to reinvent and separate the public from the private and deny the federal government any jurisdiction over the latter. In both North American republics, then, the protection of rights, warranted by the national government, gave new meaning to belonging, but the mechanics for safeguarding these prerogatives and securing the equal protection of the law were not self-executing: they had to be activated by judicial complaint. This limited the effect of constitutional innovation, even before legislation—such as the South's Jim Crow laws after 1877—and judicial interpretation watered down their meaning.

Conversely, those legislating for change realized that they needed not only to refashion the republic's "soul" but to provide it with a strong skeleton. Tangible, recognized, enforceable rights were needed to make citizenship meaningful, but it was access to property that would give it substance. Laws were drafted to recreate the republic as a compact, stable, prosperous community of small landowners. To multiply the number of independent citizens with a significant stake in the commonwealth, statesmen tried to eliminate forms of property they believed were injurious to the republic. On both sides of the border, lawmakers turned to the language of liberalism and political economy to redefine the nature and contours of property rights, hailed as the essential building block in the republican edifice.

Hitherto Shalt Thou Come, but No Further: The Complexities of Regulating Property

Throughout the Atlantic world during the Age of Revolution, the defense of the right of property had been a central tenet in the creation of new political regimes: rhetorically, it was hailed as an essential right, one with life and liberty. In practice, its protection, especially from arbitrary taxation, became a central tenet of the new order. Its importance, and the consensus that apparently undergirded it, belied its fractious nature. In the United States, discord over the morality and productivity of property in man, the contentious status of slavery within the framework of federalism, and the inordinate weight of slave property in national wealth made for an intractable combination that would lead to war.[77] In Mexico, the concentration of landed property in a few hands was seen as the determining factor that made the economy backward and sluggish and that was at the root of brutal social inequality. The young Liberals who came to power at mid-century were sure that these problems were aggravated by the vices inherent in corporate property: land held in the "dead" hands of the church or Indigenous peasant communities belonged "to all, and hence to no one": it would not become more productive through labor or investment and, since it was rarely bought or sold, it hobbled the market.[78]

For all the talk about its "sacrosanct" and "inviolable" character, politicians in both the United States and Mexico were aware that, as James L. Huston has written, it is the "unavoidable function" of governments to say what property is, and to legitimate and enforce possession.[79] After independence, both republican governments had regulated the sale of public lands, abolished rights of primogeniture, and tried to divide and allot the land of entailed and communal estates. After half a century of protracted, unsystematic efforts to privatize real estate, Liberals put together broad legislative schemes to rectify, extend, and protect property rights that would prove more far-reaching and significant.

Militant republicans sought to eradicate types of property they considered unproductive, inefficient, even wicked, and incompatible with a republican order:

property-in-man in the first model republic; Mexico's extensive, indifferently exploited landholdings, isolated from market forces because held by corporations. This land tenure system was all the more egregious because so many were landless. Mexican citizenship was made irrelevant by misery. In the United States, some saw the specter of just such a large, dispossessed, permanent underclass as a sinister possibility. In both cases, despite profound differences between the two republics' economies, calls for reform were met with similar cries decrying agrarianism and ungodly socialism. These attacks, as incendiary as they were unfounded, had limited impact: what really circumscribed reformist visions were constitutional and legal strictures, legislative practice, and crusaders' own conceptions of property.

In the United States, most antislavery politicians were convinced that the constitution gave Congress no authority over the peculiar institution where it existed; they would focus on limiting its expansion. On a different front, many in the country believed that the virile autonomy of citizens, essential to the health of their republic, had to be rooted in land ownership. During the 1850s, the call for granting homesteads to "actual settlers" in the West became more frequent and more popular. Between 1854 and 1860, a Homestead Bill passed the House five times, twice by a two-thirds majority, only to be brought down in the Senate, and, in June 1860, by President Buchanan's veto.[80] Legislative deadlock was common during the decade that led to war, but in the case of the Homestead Bill, it speaks to its supporters and detractors reading in circles around each other from the same script of republican virtue.

Arguments for and against granting land—misleadingly touted as "unoccupied"—to settlers mirrored and inverted each other. Some said Congress was the people's "trustee": it consequently lacked power to give away their patrimony. Others argued instead that it was the guardian's obligation to "place equity in the great mass of the people," by granting land to those moving west. All agreed that it was a "fixed principle" of the US republic to protect "the equal rights of all, rich or poor." A policy of "free farms," said the detractors of homestead legislation, would benefit only "one class": that of "cultivators of the soil." Their antagonists believed that only such a policy could break up the "land monopoly" and give all men access to "God's bounties," unjustly wrested from them by unfair laws and unresponsive governments.[81]

In 1860, Buchanan condemned the harsh blow that a policy of free land would deal to public revenue. But its most pernicious effect would be moral: such un-American profligacy would "go far to demoralize the people, repress [their] noble spirit of independence," and "introduce pernicious social theories that had proved so disastrous in other countries." The Homestead Bill's advocates argued that these policies would transform hardworking but propertyless men engaged in manual labor—the men that Senator James Henry Hammond had recently disparaged as "mudsills"—into ideal US citizens: "the middle class," "true friends of liberty," "reliable" at the ballot box, and "soldiers of peace" who would extend and sustain the nation by conquering "the elements, the wilderness and the savage."[82]

In Mexico in 1856, moderate and radical Liberals agreed—as would, a few years later, many of emperor Maximilian's collaborators—on the urgent need to rework a disastrous land tenure scheme. Property had to be made available to a landless majority: no republic could survive when most of its citizens could "neither produce nor consume."[83] The most radical politicians called on government to serve the Mexican peasants. In the small towns where most Mexican citizens lived, "indigence" blocked "the light of civilization." Members of the "wretched indigenous race" were "more miserable than slaves, more miserable than beasts even, because they [were] aware of their degradation and destitution." José María Castillo Velasco insisted on the need to guarantee the resources that would warrant the efficacy and autonomy of municipal governments, so that they could build basic infrastructure and provide enough land for the "common use" of its inhabitants. Unemployed citizens should have a "right to buy a piece of land that would secure their subsistence," for which they would pay 3 percent of its value until they were able to redeem the capital.[84]

Ponciano Arriaga, perhaps the most outspoken member of the constitution's drafting committee, wanted fundamental law to tackle Mexico's "monstrous division of landed wealth" by revising the legal definition of property and aligning it with "nature and God's will." Dispossessed individuals had a right to occupy empty land. Possession constituted property, but only "work and production . . . confirmed and developed" this essential right. As part of the poisonous colonial legacy, there were endless acres of "unoccupied land, deserted and entirely useless, barren." Since the origin of the titles to these landholdings was probably violent conquest, their deeds were "hollow, and perhaps illegal and depraved." Law could right these wrongs by recognizing that only "work, cultivation, or production" completed the right of property. If land lay fallow, property was "harmful to the common good and damaging . . . to a republican and democratic government." Arriaga suggested that those who owned estates larger than fifteen square leagues not be recognized as "perfect" landholders. Significantly higher taxes should be assessed on these large, often uncultivated, estates to encourage their sale at a lower price. If, after two years, these lands remained unsurveyed, untilled, and unenclosed, they should be considered vacant, and the state could sell them to the highest bidder.[85]

Congressional majorities rejected these proposals. Although intent on seeing the Indian—in their mind miserably poor, ignorant, backward, superstitious—disappear behind the citizen, the farmer, and the consumer, more timid delegates argued that the government lacked the information, instruments, and wherewithal to achieve Castillo Velasco's utopian municipalist vision. Arriaga's proposal was dismissed as an—inadmissible—attack on private property. But if congressmen were wary of disturbing individuals' property rights, they had few qualms about drastically curtailing those of corporations—parishes, convents, sodalities, and other religious associations; peasant communities—which they believed were anachronistic and detrimental to the republic. Financial experts like former treasury minister Manuel Payno argued that the disentailment of ecclesiastical property rightfully "gave back to the people what had come from the people," since it originated in the voluntary donations of generations of Mexicans.[86] Nevertheless, most members of Congress also believed that the rights of corporations had to be respected. Clergymen and Indian communities, seen as often inept economic actors, should give up their land and buildings, but they had to be compensated for their loss.

In June 1856, Comonfort's treasury minister, Miguel Lerdo de Tejada, scion of a wealthy merchant family from Veracruz and enthusiastic promoter of economic modernization, crafted a law meant to be both revolutionary and conciliatory. It ordered that all "rural and urban properties owned or managed by ecclesiastical and civil corporations" be allotted to those currently leasing or occupying them. Tenants would pay the former owners a yearly rate of 6 percent of the property's value. If tenants did not want to buy, lots would be auctioned off to the highest bidder.[87] The law meant to spur the redistribution of landed wealth, transform tenants into homeowners and poor Indians into independent landholders. As an added bonus, disentailment would bolster public finances by taxing sale transactions.

Lerdo's scheme laid out what was celebrated as a legitimate and fair procedure: it did not deprive corporations of their wealth but transformed it into a more convenient incarnation, one which allowed the church to focus on its evangelical mission and not on collecting rents. Its implementation would also root reform in "consummated facts" and enable social transformation to withstand its enemies' reaction. The more progressive members of Congress were less enthused by this conciliatory proposal. Some worried that the privatization of ecclesiastical and communal property—which a majority of Mexican statesmen considered to be a good thing—would deeply disturb the rural societies in which most Mexicans lived.

Critics of Lerdo's project were few but insightful. They believed that the June 1856 law was doomed to fail; it would accomplish the opposite of what it meant to: in a Catholic society that was profoundly unequal, in a market riddled by uncertainty, the forced sale of corporate land would concentrate real estate in the hands of the well-informed, the unscrupulous, and the cash-rich. It would fill the church's coffers with cash while the already miserable peasantry grew poorer and more dependent. According to Ignacio Ramírez, this "abstract" and "metaphysical" statute would replace the church's "dead hands" with those of "a thousand masters," whose very active hands would be set to exploiting "the life and labor of proletarians."[88]

Nevertheless, Lerdo's project for doing away with corporate property was met with enthusiasm by a majority of Congress and swiftly incorporated into fundamental law.[89] Liberal optimism for smooth reform soon proved unwarranted. Mexican bishops claimed they were unable to give up ecclesiastical property without the pope's explicit—and highly unlikely—authorization. To the Liberals' dismay, Pius IX was quick to condemn the Mexican constitution for its "numerous articles" that were in "open opposition to religion, to its healthy doctrine, its very holy precepts and its rights."[90] The head of the Church Universal condemned as decisively unacceptable the state's interference in the affairs of an institution founded by Jesus Christ.

Constitutional impediments, partisan rivalries, the moderates' ambivalence, and, in Mexico, the church's uncompromising condemnation, blocked a radical transformation of property rights. In the end, it would be brought about by war. In 1862, US lawmakers passed the Homestead, Morrill, and Pacific Railroad Acts, which provided land to settlers for free, established institutions of higher learning for their children, and sought to create a "truly national market" through the construction of government for their benefit.[91] Advocates insisted that these measures were "emphatically approved" of by the loyal citizens who had shouldered a musket to defend the Union and the constitution. Secession had extricated from Congress Southern opposition to what was touted as the universal aspiration of the "common man."[92] More radical endeavors—destroying immoral forms of property or endowing the nation's most vulnerable with land—did not follow immediately.[93] In both the United States and Mexico, military necessity pushed lawmakers into abrogating unseemly property rights. But responding to the urgencies of war also became an end in itself; more assertive social reform—such as more far-reaching, strategic land allocation—was sacrificed to national emergency; it would fall to the wayside once the crisis was over.

In Mexico, in July 1859, when the beleaguered Juárez government decreed the "perfect independence" of church and state and the confiscation of the former's wealth, it did so to punish a selfish, treasonous church. The language of capacious citizenship or expanding markets was gone. Unlike the much debated, carefully crafted, comprehensive, and conciliatory 1856 laws, the *Leyes de Reforma* of 1859–60, drafted by the president's cabinet, sought to chastise and cripple the enemy and marshal some badly needed funds. Nationalization of all ecclesiastic property, without compensation, entailed unprecedented governmental reach and a massive transfer of wealth into the hands of the state, destined to boost its fighting strength, not to transform society.

The magnitude and audacity of the 1859 decrees contrasted with their besieged authors' slim margin for action. Ecclesiastical property, expropriated on paper because most of it was in cities under Conservative control, had to be disposed of as quickly and for as much money as possible, under exceptionally strenuous circumstances. Properties were put up for auction; buyers had to pay for a third of their value in cash, another in government bonds. The law favored payments in coin, and tenants lost the preference they had enjoyed under the Lerdo Law.[94] Hurried sales benefited members of the moneyed elite who engaged in speculation: as moneylenders, they held most of the domestic public debt, had liquid assets, and could defer possession for an indeterminate amount of time.[95] Visions of a dynamic real estate market, energized by a growing number of industrious smallholders, were displaced by the exigencies of war. Once the nation's existential conflict was over and the disentailment of pueblo lands became a protracted, disparate process with uneven results, the ideal of a productive, equalizing, vernacular capitalism also faded into the background.

While Mexican Liberals, exasperated by war, had few reservations about turning bishops into criminals, Northerners in the Disunited States had a hard time drawing clear lines around their seceded former brethren. Were Confederates rebels, criminals, or enemies? If slavery was "the cause of the rebellion," shouldn't it be swiftly destroyed? Uncertainty about the semantics of war, often needled by Peace Democrats and Copperheads elected to Congress, revealed deep ambivalence about the conflict's nature, purpose, and protagonists. In Washington, those striving to fight the war by redefining the nature of property to destroy slavery followed a more convoluted path, thwarted by lawmakers' disagreements over the peculiar institution and the constitutional difficulties involved in prosecuting political crimes.[96]

Ambiguity also permeated discussions in Lincoln's cabinet, inside the War Department, and among officers and soldiers: Should fugitive slaves crossing army lines property to be returned to their owners, or were they "contraband" that should be put to use against the enemy?[97] "Gradualism and legalism" characterized the September 1862 Emancipation Proclamation, which limited the its territorial reach and deferred freedom by three months.[98] Equivocality also pervaded congressional debates. If, as James Oakes has argued, Republicans were enthusiastic emancipators, punctiliousness, quibbles about means and ends, reservations about what disloyalty entailed, and controversies over congressional, executive, or military overreach garbled the Confiscation Acts.[99] By setting the enslaved up as objects of confiscation, these laws implicitly recognized them as property. They also strove to assuage racist fears: the Second Confiscation Act promised provisions "for the transportation, colonization and settlement, in some tropical country... of such persons of the African race, made free by the provisions of this act, as may be willing to emigrate."[100] Intricate and unenthusiastically executed, these laws did, however, emancipate hundreds of slaves and legitimate the Union's actions against slave owners, without compensation, even if strictly as actions to prosecute the war. Because of both constitutional restrictions and lack of political traction, confiscated lands were not made available to freedmen, as either reparation or to ease the transition from slavery to freedom.[101]

On both sides of the border, these decrees meant to punish and weaken the republic's enemies. Their baroque language and dubious constitutionality speak to their visceral, exceptional quality. Anger and resentment, along with republican ideals, fueled these intimidating decrees, as did military necessity and the dire need of funds, rather than moral conviction or optimist visions of political economy. Their execution required territorial control, which neither government had when they were promulgated. But if their immediate impact was limited, they nevertheless became incarnations of the war's mission and harbingers of things to come. As such, they built a constituency for republican victory: the enslaved men and women who used their status as "enemy property" to seize their freedom in the United States; and investors who wagered on Liberal victory and bought church property in Mexico. Once the wars were over, however, these legal weapons became awkward and inappropriate instruments of government in peace.

THE STORM that engulfed the two North American republics at mid-century evidenced that, as Francis Lieber asserted, God admitted "no favorites in history."[102] The model republic's hallowed constitution, its vaunted stability, its enviable prosperity, did not prevent disaster: the United States was sundered by crisis and stumbled into war, just like its reprobate neighbor to the south. On both sides of the Río Bravo, war tested fundamental law and created a new constitutional order. It destroyed slavery in the United States and the *imperium in imperio* that was the Catholic Church within the Mexican Republic. Violence and confrontation refashioned a continent and reconstituted nations. It forged new, more generous polities on paper: citizenship became national in scope, more inclusive and more potent because of the rights inscribed in it. National governments were charged with protecting these rights, if as umpires rather than guardians.

In both republics, the defense of new constitutional rights turned on judicial decisions, which could entail expensive processes and be curtailed by judges' prejudices, their concerns for the delicate equilibriums required by federalism, or highly technical readings of the law and issues at stake. Rights were made fragile: too many of them, wrote Thaddeus B. Wakeman in 1890, were lost when they reached "that grave of liberty, the Supreme Court of the United States."[103] By the end of the nineteenth century, the promise of new, robust constitutional prerogatives had faded and frayed; economic freedom and untethered markets ended up being less advantageous and inclusive than what their advocates had imagined at mid-century.

On both sides of the border, republican efforts to bolster citizenship—to make it real—by grounding it in property followed choppy trajectories and had unexpected consequences. In Mexico, the hurried sale of ecclesiastical property benefited mainly those who were flush with cash, while in the United States the constitutionally dubious, politically fractious attempts at land expropriation to provide freedmen with "forty acres and a mule" came to naught.[104] Western expansion and the Republican principle of "free soil for free men" brought violence, dependency, and displacement to Indian nations on the Plains.[105] On the ground, homestead legislation in the US and policies for the privatization of communal land in Mexico were enacted in what Paul Gates has described as an "incongruous land system."

Consequently, previous sales patterns, market incentives, and, in the case of Mexico, interests within peasant communities, often fueled confrontation and benefited larger, better-endowed players.[106] If, during the last third of the nineteenth century, Mexican Liberals remained obsessed with "perfect property"—individually owned, registered, enclosed, its boundaries clearly demarcated—they no longer insisted on its redeeming virtues for citizen-landowners. The mobilization of landed property was a drawn-out, convoluted, highly heterogeneous process. It was shaped by local power imbalances and variegated economic impulses, by the social, legal, and political stratagems and concerns of actors within and without peasant communities and the weakness of state capacities. As Daniela Marino and Cecilia Zuleta have written, despite important transformations, the "modernization" of the Mexican countryside—home to three-quarters of the nation's inhabitants—did not engender a "capitalist agrarian revolution." Its promises remained an "optimist aspiration."[107] Hopes for a republican polity undergirded by solid citizen rights and prosperity, which had rallied legislators, publicists, and soldiers in times of crisis, were only partially and inequitably fulfilled.

PART THREE

TO WIN THE WAR

CHAPTER FIVE

THE RIGHTEOUSNESS OF OUR CAUSE

COURAGE. *Sacrificio.* Duty. *Honor.* Leadership. As violence tore through the two North American republics at mid-century, the ageless language of war was deployed to rally the people and turn fractious citizens into brave Hectors and virtuous Lucretias. North America's contending governments—the Conservative military dictatorship in Mexico City and the constitutionalist regime in Veracruz between 1858 and 1860; Unionists in Washington and Confederates in Richmond from 1861 to 1865; the imperialists and republicans who fought over Mexico in the 1860s—hailed the justice, even the sanctity, of their cause. All claimed patriotic virtue as their patrimony. But the stirring words, tropes, and images of martial heroism, anchored and perpetuated by ubiquitous memorialization, rang false, clashing with soldiers' on-the-ground experience, the painful effects of conflict on the home front, and the daunting challenges faced by political authority during these wars.

The scale of these conflicts was unprecedented: they spilled onto the sea and impacted practically the whole continent, unsettling even the staid Canadian provinces, who watched with horror as that "difficulty" called "states' rights" tore their neighbor apart.[1] They disquieted citizens' daily lives: split up families, confronted neighbors, divided nations. They mobilized, killed, and maimed a horrific number of men. Their drawn-out destructiveness, fueled by their scale and novel military technology, was unlike the ritualized violence of Mexico's pronunciamientos, the cruelties of "caste" or "Indian" wars, or the brutality with which the United States had fought in 1812, 1846, and 1847. The extraordinary devastation they wrought paradoxically contributed to the military deadlock that prolonged armed confrontation. Long, bloody, costly, and undecisive, these struggles placed tremendous stress on the people and institutions meant to steer them to victory.

War overwhelms, upends, feeds on itself. Its violence razes expectations, understandings, and norms. It devours men and wealth, transmogrifies landscapes and built environments, jostles social structures, hamstrings and often overwhelms institutions. Historically, we have been greatly invested—strategically, philosophically, institutionally—in trying to manage war: to endow it with meaning, limit its destructiveness, and direct the havoc it creates. To face the momentous challenges of civil war in the 1850s and 1860s, North America's governments had to muster men, money, and goods, in unprecedented quantities, with the capabilities at hand. So they legislated and prayed to God. Laws were drafted to draw resources both material and immaterial: to command allegiance, put boots on the ground, and raise public revenue. Statutes were deployed, manipulated, and sometimes ignored strategically, to fight and win the war.

These laws speak to legislators' intentions, to their perceptions of what was possible and permissible. Inquiring into their execution on the wildly uneven grounds of mid-century North America also allows us to throw light on government capabilities and popular sentiments. Marshaling men and money would, as we shall see in the next chapter, be the most imperative and influential task legislators faced. In the midst of the uneven advent of modern warfare, the outcome of these conflicts hung less on virtue, patriotism, strategy, and heroics than on numbers—of men, money, railways, munitions, supplies—and efficient logistics. As chaos engulfed the continent, however, statesmen turned to Providence and law to make sense of war's madness and to regulate citizens' actions and consciences. Their efforts to act upon the intangible, both human and divine, are the subject of this chapter.

It is impossible to gauge the effects of faith and prayer on armed conflict, but we can trace their effects on the war and its participants, as religion became another weapon in the antagonists' arsenals. We can also try to assess the effect of war, violence, and destruction on religious institutions, thought, and practice.[2] Legislators, civil servants, and officers in the field did not wait for Heavenly intervention, however, and acted forcefully to shape what happened on earth. On both sides of the Río Bravo, law was used to codify acceptable military behavior and endow it with meaning. It was also deployed to police the nation's citizens, as states tried to secure loyalty to fragile political projects born of circumstance and contention.

If God Is for Us, Who Can Be Against Us?

North America's armed conflicts were not wars of religion, but religion seemed to be everywhere. Faith steeped into war and raised its tone and stakes. North Americans facing each other on the battlefields prayed to the same God and, as Lincoln remarked, most read from the same Bible.[3] Catholics who celebrated the same liturgy in the same ancient language pledged allegiance to warring governments and fought in enemy trenches.[4] The issues dividing the children of the same nation were not theological or dogmatic.[5] They were nonetheless interpreted as clashing incarnations of God's will and mandates: on the frontline and on the home front, politicians and soldiers rallied to a cause they saw as sacred. Mexico's militant Catholics struck out against the enemies of the church, while Southerners called for the defeat of those who advocated for a law "higher" than Scripture and the constitution. Unionists condemned those who compounded the sin of slavery with that of treason. Mexican Liberals bemoaned their enemies' obstinate wickedness and refusal to recognize that "the will of God" was clearly in favor of "democratic ideas."[6]

Citizens of both republics had long considered theirs to be a special relationship with God. In the United States, in 1850, only one in seven denizens formally belonged to a church. But with its dynamic, democratic religious market and the effervescence of its churches, the United States was, nonetheless, held up as a "new Zion," a "shining city upon a hill" in which souls were "more awakened" and committed to "self-sacrifice for religious purposes than [in] any other country in the world."[7] In the constitutionally Catholic republic to the south, Mexicans thought of themselves as the Virgin Mary's favorite children. The 1531 apparitions of the Mother of God on the outskirts of Mexico City and the revered image she had left behind were proof of God's partiality.[8] It was, then, perhaps inevitable that religion would influence the ways the body politic, legitimacy, and the common good were conceived of and talked about in the North American republics.

In the 1850s, moral absolutes crept into politics and tainted religion. In the United States, slavery was fulminated by some as a national sin, defended by others as a divinely ordained blessing. In Mexico, men of faith antagonized over where the church would stand and what religion should do for the republic, while devoted women uncharacteristically entered the political fray to defend religious exclusivity: it was essential for the protection of the true faith and, consequently, to individual salvation and the preservation of the family and the republic. Religious strife strained the already fractious conversations about the nation's future; it was both cause and symptom of the erosion of the common ground that made politics possible.

Fifteen years before secession, disputes over slavery had already split two major US evangelical denominations, the Baptists and Methodists, while Mexican Conservatives warned that the political discussions of religious matters—which ought to be unavailable to lawmakers—frayed the only bonds holding the nation together.[9] When the war broke out, religion provided scripts, images, and rituals, as well as institutional and social networks, put to the service of fratricidal violence. Confederates and Unionists, Liberals and Conservatives, intent on seeing "the hand of Divine Providence" in the bewildering events that engulfed them, interpreted military victory as a sign of God's favor, defeat as a test meant to "purify their faith."[10] They were confident in the belief that, as Conservative general Miguel María Echeagaray contended, "God never protects the wicked." All claimed to have God on their side.[11] President Lincoln stressed the fallacious nature of this position: "In great contests, each party claims to act in accordance with the will of God. Both may be, and one must be wrong. God cannot be for and against the same thing at the same time."[12]

Logic notwithstanding, Mexican, US, and Confederate civil and military authorities called on ministers to bless regimental flags, organize processions, and hold religious services to thank God for His favor, atone for the nation's sins, or honor the "Christian heroes" who had fallen in battle.[13] In the Disunited States, presidents North and South dedicated days to national fasting, prayer, or thanksgiving. One of the changes introduced in the Confederate constitution's parsimonious revision of the 1787 text was its appeal to "the favor and guidance of Almighty God."[14] Union and Confederate churches mobilized to give Bibles to soldiers, provide chaplains to the army, and take the word of the Lord to camps, hospitals, and battlefields.[15]

Members of the Catholic hierarchy were distressed by the shadow that civil war cast on the unity of the Universal Church. Although leery of the nativist, anti-Catholic prejudices that often motivated abolitionists and Republicans, US bishops supported the war and hoped military service would prove Catholics worthy members of the nation, North or South. Pastors encouraged enlistment, even of those born on foreign soil, whose duty it was to serve the country "which has recognized them, as citizens." They called on the faithful to "weep over this calamity" and pray for it to end, but also to sacrifice "everything to sustain the power, authority and unity" of the government. Uncharacteristically, two Irish-born bishops, New York's John Hugues and Charleston's Patrick Lynch, served contending governments as emissaries to Europe.[16] In 1862, they probably coincided with some of their Mexican brethren in Rome at the particularly cosmopolitan canonization of the "martyrs of Japan," the twenty-six religious and laypersons—Spaniards, Portuguese, and Japanese and Mexico's first, much-longed-for saint, Felipe de Jesús—who died for their faith, nailed on crosses, in 1597 Nagasaki.[17] For many Catholics, the distressing politics of civil war were enmeshed in a broader, more transcendent and troubling process. As the New World republics were sundered by disagreement and confrontation, a beleaguered Church Universal insisted on unity, its global vocation, papal infallibility, and the "errors" of "modern Liberalism," as it sought to authoritatively lead its faithful down a narrower path.[18]

In the New World, men of the cloth of every denomination enthusiastically promoted conscription and support for the war effort, often contradicting the moderate, apolitical, and conciliatory positions many had held before the war: "patriotism," they now claimed, embodied the service owed by the citizen "to God, his Creator and Master."[19] Churches in the United States rallied to the Confederate or Union flags; Episcopalians and Evangelicals marched with the Catholics, Mormons, and Jews, whose faith they often considered suspect or distasteful. On the other side of the border, where Catholics fought Catholics, the tremors that led to the republic's collapse also shook the foundations of the One True Church.

After the triumph of the Ayutla movement in August 1855, Liberals discussed and enacted measures to curtail the church's wealth, influence, and administrative practices. Bishops and parish priests had cried foul, written incensed pastorals condemning the constitution, and denied the sacraments to those complying with its alleged anticlerical precepts. Prelates nonetheless called on priests to act with "the greatest prudence and circumspection" and "give Caesar his due," without surrendering their defense of church prerogatives. This proved an impossible balancing act. Instead, some parish priests fed the fire: from the pulpit, they described the constitution as "heretical and schismatic," threatened those observing its impious mandates with eternal damnation, preached civil resistance, and, in a few instances, hung up their vestments and took up arms against the constitutional government.[20] Others sought instead to keep the peace among their flock. A small minority saw an opportunity to reform Christ's church, whose mission had been betrayed by its hierarchy.

The war confronted those who defended a constitution under episcopal censure and those who refused to live under the new fundamental law. The latter did so for different reasons, but most agreed on its sacrilegious nature. The 1857 constitution frustrated a Catholic people's yearning for Catholic rule. Accordingly, Conservative general Tomás Mejía incited his troops—mostly Indigenous peasants from the Sierra Gorda—to fight against the "satellites of irreligion and despotism," under the banner of the Virgin of El Pueblito—a seventeenth-century representation of Mary, kept in a church on the outskirts of Querétaro—on whom he conferred a general's sash.[21] Other Conservative soldiers—in the valleys of Oaxaca and Puebla, in the mountains of Nayarit—were perhaps less concerned with constitutional violations than with the religious dimension of their struggles for greater autonomy and over the control of local resources. Fighting over the keys to local chapels, stealing saint effigies from Liberal towns and setting them up in their churches became acts of war.[22]

Constitutionalists did not counter their adversaries' religious visions with that of a secular society: they also aspired to upholding a Christian community, but one that was more equal, more democratic, and animated by "truly evangelical" spirituality, "rational, kind and full of gentleness," free from superstition and clerical abuse.[23] Santos Degollado, commander of the Liberal armies, called himself the "harbinger of Glad Tidings" and enjoined his soldiers to destroy the "diabolical alliance between scepter and cassock." He hailed his troops as bearers of "the laws that would save the republic," and restore the virtues of the primitive church when they secured the liberty—spiritual and political—that the Gospel had promised.[24]

Not all Liberals were as confident as this officer. Caught in the crossfire of a fratricidal war, many strove to separate religion from the church: they fought for change—the Reforma's semantic connection with the Protestant Reformation was unvoiced but not innocent—in terms that were both Christian and anticlerical. The severance of faith from structure was no easy task in a nation where sacraments had been conceived as citizen rights. The church excommunicated its sons and daughters for complying with constitutional precepts; the Liberal government reprehended an institution whose ministrations many believed were essential to the republic's health. There was, nevertheless, an essential contradiction, Col. Manuel Valdés argued, in expecting priests to tend to the spiritual needs of the same "heretics" who were committed to destroying their privileges.[25] Still, churchmen insisted on their opposition to reformist policies turning on principle and submission to authority only. They refused to budge without the Holy See's authorization. The conflict's religious dimension blocked the possibilities of reconciliation.

A few priests sought a different escape route. They embraced Liberal versions of nation and liberty, even at their most radical. Manuel Eleuterio Gómez, who served in a parish in the mining town of Taxco, collaborated with Liberal authorities to remove clerics who had been put in place by the intransigent bishop of Michoacán and had allegedly engaged in "seditious and antievangelical behavior." He also called for the "popular elections" of priests to parish positions, "in accordance with the practices of the primitive Church."[26] Along the same lines, in the fall of 1859, six priests in Mexico City undertook a more revolutionary— if inconspicuous and short-lived—experiment: in the face of the bishops' "abuses" and "sordid interests," they sought to establish a "Mexican Catholic Apostolic Church," to worship "Jesus Christ, who was poor, humble, indulgent, and kind," and not, as the Mexican prelates presented him, "cruel, tyrannical, rich, and rancorous." Released from the unreasonable dictates of Rome, the new church would teach its faithful obedience to civil authority and prove that there was no contradiction "between the new laws and the church's primitive doctrines."[27] The "constitutional priests" sparked the interest of President Juárez's cabinet but gained no momentum. Their project soon fell apart.

The constitutional government could not wait for the consolidation of a new church. Exhausted by a year and a half of fighting, it sought to break the political and military standoff by striking the old one. The Veracruz government claimed that the bishops' economic and moral support for the rebels, motivated by nothing but a selfish defense of wealth and privilege, had transformed a small mutiny of disgruntled, reactionary officers into a pervasive, nationwide rebellion.[28] To crush it they categorically separated church and state, expropriated ecclesiastical wealth, and suppressed the corporations and institutions that the church had relied on to structure and police society.[29]

In response to these punitive laws, Mexico's bishops vehemently denied having "conspired, armed, sustained, or authorized" a revolution. They deplored its painful consequences and accused Liberals of wanting the "complete destruction" of Catholicism.[30] These misguided politicians had introduced "the fabulous inventions of false history, false philosophy, false morality, and mendacious cults" into a "most Catholic and pious Republic." Reluctantly forced into the political arena by impending catastrophe, the bishops could only speak—sharply, authoritatively—"not as philosophers" but as teachers, whose authority came from Christ himself. They disparaged the possibilities of Liberal Catholicism and warned the faithful of those who "artfully" called themselves Christians instead of Catholics. Wily members of "Satan's synagogue, the Protestant Church, the band of Luther and Calvin's henchmen . . . thought as heretics, spoke as apostates, and acted as schismatics."[31] The Mexican people would not fall into their deceptive machinations.

The prelates reminded their flock that there was "only one God, one true religion, one set of morals." There was, consequently, only one "legitimate Church": neither salvation nor "lawful communication with God" were possible beyond its purview.[32] They accused Liberals of driving Mexicans to eternal damnation. Constitutionalists retorted that the clergy had betrayed the nation. The space—fractious but vital—in which civil and spiritual authorities had collaborated since independence lay in shambles. It would not be rebuilt. When the Juárez government returned to the capital in January 1861, it exiled Mexico's bishops, along with Luis Clementi, its first apostolic nuncio.

When the United States fell apart, secession and violence reverberated throughout the continent and beyond the Atlantic. On the international stage, the nation's collapse perhaps paradoxically broadened the spectrum of political possibility. In Mexico, Conservative despair, an exceptional sense of opportunity and Napoleonic ambitions fed into a stratagem to restore a monarchical regime, on the back of a foreign military intervention. Most of Mexico's banished bishops decided, once again, to play a political card. With varying degrees of enthusiasm, they threw their support behind the ascension of a young Austrian prince to Moctezuma's throne. The nation's prelates and the more militant members of their flock trusted that a Catholic monarch would restore harmony between church and state.

Their optimism was soon dashed. The imperial government pursued many of the Liberals' reformist project's objectives: modernization, property distribution, and market consolidation. It swiftly ratified the laws that the church had deemed intolerable, even as it sought to marshal the clergy into the service of state and nation. Maximilian wanted priests to be stationed throughout the Mexican territory, in small towns and villages, so that they would act as civilizers, educators, and celebrants of the regime's festive and solemn rituals. He also hoped to recover the patronage rights that the Spanish Crown had exercised over the Church of New Spain, which would allow him to select candidates to Mexico's episcopal sees and supervise the Roman pontiff's communications and instructions to the clergy and faithful.[33] Neither the papal envoy, Pedro Francisco Meglia, nor the Mexican bishops could accept his terms.

Efforts to iron out an agreement with Rome in 1865–66 foundered on the uncertainties surrounding the weakened imperial regime and the opposition of the two Mexican archbishops, who enjoyed exceptional access to the pope—an unexpected windfall of exile in Rome. Members of the Mexican hierarchy came to see the unfriendly independence set up by the secular republic as preferable to the interference of a meddling Catholic prince.[34] In supporting foreign intervention and monarchical restoration, they had paid a steep price. They nonetheless failed to heal the rift between religious and secular authorities. Their deep frustration would influence the Mexican church for decades.

IN 1850S AND 1860S, faith consecrated North America's antagonistic polities and transmuted their causes into moral absolutes. As the dramatic failure of Catholic support for monarchy's restoration makes clear, these massive, violent conflicts, conceived by some as holy wars, also transformed religion and its institutions, and the relationship between faith and politics. From the outset, some found the infusion of religion into war objectionable and ungodly. A priest in a small village in Mexico's central highlands pointed to the unbearable contradiction of praying for peace and "sacrificing to the God of Christians" only to urge your parishioners to march onto "always bloody" battlefields to slaughter their brethren.[35] Such "moral deconcoction" also provoked clashes between religious and political authorities, just as the passions of war made them more dangerous.[36] Military protagonists inevitably felt compelled to sacrifice religious principle to expediency: they occupied sacred spaces and chastised men of God for not fulfilling what those fighting in war conceived as a cleric's patriotic duties. On both sides of the border, armed conflict led to the anxious reimagining of God's place in the republic.

Like the faithful, most religious authorities responded enthusiastically to the drums of war. Many were soon discomfited by what they saw as politics polluting religion. In 1857, even before hostilities broke out, Guanajuato governor Manuel Doblado threatened to execute a priest for broadcasting the excommunication of prominent Liberals. In 1864, the bishop of Natchez, Mississippi, William Henry Elder, was removed to Louisiana for defying the Union officers who occupied the city and instructed him to introduce prayers for Lincoln's health and Union victory into the service. Elder argued that he would not allow his sacred ministry to become "an active instrument" in favor of "one side or the other" in a "deplorable" conflict. He "preferred banishment and insult to submission" and would not "preach politics or war."[37]

Catholics on both sides of the border appealed to Roman discipline to avoid deferring to local military or political demands. Priests—mostly in the occupied South—refused to fly the stars and stripes over their churches or pray for a cause that alienated their parishioners. They now contemptuously described these practices as "local"—when they were the imposition of an invading army—and insisted they wanted to conform "more closely" to the "approved usages" of the Universal Church: liturgy, church, and faith should be above political strife.[38] In Mexico, when Louis Testory, a chaplain in the French Army, suggested that, for the sake of peace and reconciliation, Mexican bishops abandon their "deplorable rigorism" and recognize the state's legitimate right to regulate property and citizenship rights, he was sharply chastised by one of his brothers in Christ. Father Basilio Arrillaga was emphatic: men of the cloth had nothing to say about the practical effects of laws but should speak only to their morality and legitimacy. "Catholic dogma, Christian morals, and evangelical precepts" could not get mixed up with "personal or local questions." Priests had to rise above worldly concerns: they did not belong "to the Nation or the State" but to God.[39]

Methodist minister William M. Leftwich would have agreed with the aged Mexican Jesuit. The "true Church of Jesus Christ," he insisted, was not of this world. It had existed "with slavery and without, in war and in peace"; it had "survived a thousand revolutions" and "would endure forever." "Religious questions *only*" were vital. Unfortunately, the polemics over slavery and then the war had blurred the lines between the essential and the accessory. This had engendered "too much control of citizenship in the interest of religion, too much religious proscription in the interest of loyalty to the state, too many partisan fanatics in the church, too many politico-fanatics in the country."[40] The dire consequences of this promiscuous mixture of religion and politics—or, rather, of the political use of religion—were nowhere as obvious as in the controversies surrounding oath-taking. In the North American republics, oaths had played an important part in patriotic ritual: civic obligations were entered into under the watchful eye of God. In the critical circumstances begotten by war, this familiar formality was construed as an instrument to correct wayward citizens and heal broken countries.

As such, these devices proved woefully deficient. In 1857 Mexico, it was disagreement over the constitutional oath that lit the flame of civil war. Against all evidence but with precedent on his side, Comonfort had hoped that requiring public officials to take the oath would warrant their abeyance to a controversial constitution. Instead, the president's prescription sparked open resistance and exhibited the chasm that the constitution had created: Mexican bishops decreed that invoking God in support of faithless law was not only ludicrous but a very grave sin. Resistance to the presidential mandate drew the geography of Conservative support: in the nation's central and western regions, officeholders, judges, and military officers refused to be sworn in. They resigned noisily, as villagers rioted rather than witness these ceremonies.⁴¹ In the occupied rebel territory, Union officers used loyalty oaths to signal and enforce the restoration of citizens' allegiance to the United States but also to punish and ostracize its enemies. In the subjugated South, "a solemn affirmation or declaration," made with an appeal to God, was required to avoid losing one's livelihood or political rights. It thus became an invitation to perjury, "the worst of crimes . . . the grossest insult, the most impious defense that could possibly be offered to Almighty God."⁴²

Just as the use of religion as a weapon moved pastors to call for the independence of church and state, civil servants conceded that religious belief and commitments should not be used as tools for government. According to a Union officer in Mississippi, appeals "to the Supreme Being," spurred by worldly interests, shrouded "dishonest hearts," and "unwilling minds." Such oaths were "necessarily offensive to Him and subversive to sound morality."⁴³ In 1860, Mexican law declared that "oaths and their retractions" were not the business of government.⁴⁴ In the United States, the Supreme Court came to the same conclusion, in the case of a Catholic priest who had been imprisoned and fined for fulfilling his pastoral duties without having taken the "iron-clad oath" mandated by the Missouri 1865 constitution. In 1867, the Court ruled that this constitutional requirement was unconstitutional: it inflicted a punishment "for a past act that was not punishable at the time it was committed." There was, furthermore, no connection between Rev. John A. Cummings's Confederate sympathies or his avoiding the draft and "his fitness to teach the doctrines or administer the sacraments of his church."⁴⁵

As the fires of war died down in both mangled nations, church and state relations settled into an unsteady equilibrium, which probably inspired as much skepticism as it did resignation. On both sides of the Río Bravo, citizens who had believed they were members of God's chosen people and had gone to war with the conviction that they were doing His work now found it best to keep God out of politics. Although He was present everywhere at the same time, many now assumed that God's place in the republic was not the public square but inside church buildings and the private consciences of men.

Republics at War

When the young New World nations built republican governments on imperial ruins, the world watched with fascination what they thought was a risky experiment. Republican mistrust of power drove constitutional efforts to disperse power, to check and balance it, to delegate authority differentially. Complex institutional machineries engendered weak federal governments that were often perceived as distant and purposeless. The execution of federal law was circumscribed by both constitutional mandate and circumstances on the ground, as states often assertively defended what they considered to be their concurrent or exclusive prerogatives.⁴⁶

Federal authorities had to follow convoluted roads to coerce, tax, and mobilize citizens. To architects and observers, this raised serious questions about how the modern republic would fare in war. The prospect of civil war—of some of the republic's own citizens taking up arms against it—seemed even more inauspicious.

The draftsmen of America's modern republics had a difficult time theorizing and legislating to either invigorate an untrustworthy central government or prevent aggression from within. Early North American federalism placed the political center of gravity in the states, whose powers were "numerous and indefinite," while those of federal authorities were "few and defined."[47] In Mexico, the federal government's proven incapacities pushed its politicians toward centralizing reforms: centralist constitutions were proclaimed in 1836, 1843, and 1853. For all their devotion to state autonomy, members of the 1856–57 constituent congress voted to endow the president with emergency powers to put down invasions and "serious" disturbances of the public peace, if conditional on congressional approval.[48] But innovative normative adjustments did not enable the national government to overcome resistance to the execution of its laws. Both the oppressive measures of Santa Anna's dictatorship (1853–55) and the radical laws of the Ayutla government sparked unmanageable defiance: in one case, it brought down the government; in the other, it unleashed a civil war.

The US experience—if not the nation's theoretical foundations—was different: stability and the early "constitutionalization of politics" established references, processes, and arbitration mechanisms that allowed for the resolution of contentious disputes and, often, for the effective execution of federal law, even when controversial.[49] But these devices were not fail-safe. In 1833, for instance, Congress responded to South Carolina's enactment of John C. Calhoun's clever but unacceptable nullification theory with a bill authorizing the president to use military force to collect the import duties invalidated by state law.[50] Negotiations and the lawful threat of force put an end to the tariff predicament. Nonetheless, two decades later, increasingly divisive statutes and judicial verdicts, such as the 1850 Fugitive Slave Law, the 1854 Kansas-Nebraska Act, and the *Dred Scott* Supreme Court decision in 1857, were met with more resolute—if perhaps less flashy—resistance. Legislation perceived as illegitimate could not be easily implemented.

If the architecture of federalism circumscribed the reach of the federal government, the principles of republicanism trammeled responses to political opposition when it crossed over the ambiguous line of lawfulness. Authority founded on popular sovereignty, volitional citizenship, and freedom of speech and association found it difficult to draw a line between the exciting and the dangerous, between critics of the government and enemies of the state. Under the logic of monarchical rule, modeled on that of the family, hurting or murdering the king, plotting against him, or conspiring to take his place were conceived as parricide, the "blackest" and "dirtiest" of felonies.[51] Construing the "sovereign" as an abstract entity, the monolithic embodiment of a diverse, far-flung citizenry made codifying "crimes against the state" more challenging. Republican law—and explicitly the US constitution—insisted on a strict construction of the crime of treason.[52] The prosecution of political opinion was condemned as a feature of the rotten politics of the past, just as attacks on the state appeared more dangerous, given its contingent foundations and ensuing vulnerability.

During the first decades after independence, North American republics found that criminalizing political dissidence in the halls of Congress or in court was at best an uncomfortable temptation. At worst, it discredited governments—which were limited by design—for going rogue and reaching for desperate, arbitrary devices. These illegitimate and often unconstitutional strategies generated contempt, unease, or resistance. The death threats often brandished in Mexican pronunciamientos were dismissed; in the United States charges of treason levied against rioters—angry at tax collectors in the late eighteenth century, outraged by the pretensions of the "slaveocracy" by the 1850s—were seen as misguided attempts to bully dissidents into submission.[53]

The dubious and devious character of these measures often deprived their victims of judicial protection: Mexicans legislated the expulsion of the Spanish population in the late 1820s and in 1833 decreed the exile of opponents of Valentín Gómez Farías's radical administration. In the 1790s, the extreme provisions enacted by the federalists in response to the US Quasi-War with France shut down Democratic Republican newspapers and landed editors and a lawmaker in jail.[54] Overblown threats and judicial overreach contributed to the opprobrium in which the state was held, not to any reputation for credibility and efficacy. Law proved a blunt instrument to deal with political dissidence in the republic. Nonetheless, as fratricidal conflict threatened the nation's survival, fear made such statutes seem unavoidable and necessary. It did not make them more effective.

Legislating Civil War

Between 1858 and 1867, North America's governments proved Cicero's dictum wrong: laws did not fall silent when swords were drawn. Instead, administrations-at-war sought to circumscribe, discipline, and channel mayhem through legislation. They did so in very different institutional contexts. In the shattered Union, Confederates deemed secession constitutional; the ensuing armed conflict was hailed as a war for independence. Unionists saw it as an insurrection to be crushed. Despite the cataclysmic nature of the conflict, the shaken structures of the divided republic remained operational. Constitutional rule, elections, political representation, the separation of powers, and a dynamic public sphere survived, even if anxious politics shored up one-party rule in the seceded states and led to undue process and the circumvention of rules and both North and South.[55]

In Mexico, by contrast, war overcame republican practice and unmoored legislation from precedent and constitutional constraints. In 1863, it justified the controversial restoration of monarchy. Benito Juárez, who successfully incarnated the defense of republican legality throughout a harrowing decade, presided over the Reform War as interim president. He led the fight against the empire and its French allies endowed with extraordinary powers, vested in him by Congress, right before it dissolved in San Luis Potosí in May 1863. When his constitutional term ran out, he did not call for an election.[56] Presidents Zuloaga and Miramón defended their use of dictatorial powers, while Maximilian, as the legal embodiment of "national sovereignty," justified his right to "exercise it in all its forms."[57]

Crises rocked and sometimes shattered assumptions, procedures, and instruments of governance. War divided the nation: it broke republican covenants, transforming citizens into foreigners, rebels, traitors, and enemies. Governments whose existence was the product of the dismantling of ordinary politics had to legislate the instruments of war that it would deploy against populations they claimed as their own. In the face of harrowing circumstances, contenders would, on the one hand, reach for the ready-made arsenal of the law of nations, which they adapted to meet their needs and aspirations. On the other, they engaged in vigorous, unconventional legislation to steel the nation for the tragedy of a conflict that set citizens, brothers, and compatriots against each other.

Nationalizing the Law of Nations

The venerable philosophy of natural rights had played a central if ambivalent role in the New World republics, both in shaping political culture and scripting the new nations' entrance onto the international stage. Once imperial bonds were broken, their rhetoric was used to push for a more equal society, made up of men who had been "endowed by their Creator" with the same "Unalienable rights." Natural law was also invoked to set clear limits on political transformation and protect the social hierarchies allegedly set up by the same Creator.[58] But the law of nations—and its corollary, the laws of war—were more conspicuous in the international realm, as the US-Mexico War made clear. Young nations valued the idea of systematizing principles and norms in order to make international relations less violent, arbitrary, and unpredictable. The first modern republic, wary of European interventionism and committed to the freedom of the seas, was its enthusiastic advocate from the get-go. Since the founding, US statesmen and diplomats ardently embraced the principle of neutrality, which shielded nonbelligerent shipping and commercial interests from other peoples' wars. As John Fabian Witt has shown, they went further still: by advocating for the "immunity of all economically productive private property on land as well as at sea," the United States cloaked property-in-man with the dignified mantle of iusnaturalism.[59]

The position of its unstable neighbor to the south was more conflicted: Mexicans had alternatively appealed to the law of nations as a shield from frequent foreign aggression and decried its pretentious, legalistic babble, that only justified the strong preying on the weak. The transnational character of North America's mid-century wars led to the law of nations' being reconceived and remade, by these two belligerents and throughout the continent. But before it was reconstructed as a means to balance, de-escalate, and "civilize" international relations, it was wielded as a strategic and symbolic resource. In Mexico in early 1862, the European powers' paradigmatic display of gunboat diplomacy and French aggression were proof that "the book of the law of nations," meant to apply to "the whole world," was closed to the republic.[60] Nevertheless, declared Manuel Payno, by repeatedly violating its principles and commitments, by infringing the principle of noninterference, explicitly ratified in the October 1861 London Convention and disregarding the settlement signed at La Soledad—and making war on a weak, disorganized, impecunious nation "with no truce, no rest, no quarter" and for "a miserable sum of money," France trampled both "reason and good law."[61]

Mexicans consistently argued that France's repeated infractions of the law of nations gave the invaded nation the moral upper hand. As they fought "the world's best soldiers," officers insisted on strict adherence to the laws of war, in both victory and defeat. It was, as Gen. Vicente Riva Palacio argued when negotiating a prisoner exchange in December 1865, the only way to abate the war's "vicious character" . . . and display the invaded nation's high degree of civilization.[62] Fuzzy—and fussy—distinctions between terms like *capitulation* and *rendition* mattered to generals like Jesús González Ortega—the hero of Calpulalpan who lost Puebla in May 1863—as much as to the Indigenous troops who captured and disarmed a Belgian company in Tacámbaro, Michoacán, in April 1865.[63] The republic's defenders were intent on preserving their honor and dignity: their legalism belied Europeans' arrogant disdain for the young American nation, confirmed its membership in a community of reason, honor, and law, and shattered the invaders' claims that theirs was a "civilizing mission."

On both sides of the Rio Grande, the vaunted commitment to universal, "Christian," humanitarian rules for warfare influenced relations between armed men and civilians, if only to censure enemy actions rather than shape how armies fought. Respect for the law of nations was seen as a badge of honor and civility: in New Mexico, Capt. Rafael Chacón, whose Hispano troops were disparaged by the officers and soldiers who came from the East, gave his "word as a gentleman" to women flying the Confederate flag over their house that they would not be disturbed: as "noncombatants," they could put their disloyalty on display "if it was their pleasure."[64] Conversely, those violating the "highest principles known to Christian civilization" were noisily reproached as barbarians.[65] In a conflict characterized by the general breakdown of conventions, Mexican Liberals were more effective in denouncing and publicizing Conservative and French atrocities. The cruelty with which Gen. Leonardo Márquez (the "Panther of Tacubaya") and the French antiguerrilla fighter Col. Charles-Louis Dupin acted, particularly against innocent civilians, was graphically and hair-raisingly described and publicized. "Enlightened" Liberals eventually won on both the battlefield and in the court of public opinion.[66]

International law also provided a way out of the complex quandaries involved in fighting enemies who were also fellow citizens. In the United States, as William Blair has argued, when confronted with alleged constitutional restrictions, Unionists who sought harsher sanctions against rebels reached for the laws of war tradition to distance themselves from the affected legalism of the war's detractors, who insisted that constitutional protections manacled the government and limited the reach of its war policies.[67] Conversely, in Mexico, when the empire fell in 1867, it was those who hoped to save the emperor's life who quoted de Vattel . . . and commended the triumphant Union's lenient treatment of the defeated Confederate leaders, and in particular of Jefferson Davis who, despite his responsibilities as leader of the rebellion, was not tried and punished.[68] Neither theory nor example prevented Maximilian's execution under Mexico's harsh January 1862 law "to punish crimes committed against the nation."[69]

Governments, in Mexico as in the Disunited States, also turned to law to discipline an actor who was a product of the war but escaped the logic of those trying to run it: the irregular forces who rallied to one of the contenders. They often fought fiercely but also engaged in larceny, kidnapping, and extortion. For the most part, these men took up arms voluntarily, if for purposes that were unclear and unstable. Sometimes nominally under the authority of the army, their lack of discipline and frequent escapades infuriated the officers they meant to "assist," while their violent attacks against both soldiers and civilians were decried as criminal. In Mexico, as the struggle against the French Intervention became a war of resistance and attrition, the republic's armies became, in their organization and conduct, armies of guerrillas.[70]

In the summer of 1862, Henry Halleck, general-in-chief of the Union army, was overwhelmed by the damage caused by irregular warfare and looking for a legal procedure to deal with it. He asked his friend Francis Lieber to elucidate how guerrillas fit into "the laws and usages of war." The Columbia professor distanced himself from the Mexican Republic's pragmatism amid the law of nations tradition to emphatically condemn guerrilla warfare. What distinguished the soldier from the criminal, he argued, was not his commission but the "working characteristics" of membership in the army: uniforms, provisions, salaries; belonging to a permanent body that answered to a centralized command structure. Consequently, irregular insurgents were not protected by the laws of war: they ought to be swiftly punished as dangerous felons.[71]

In Mexico, the feebler republican government was heavily dependent on irregular forces. It tried to discipline them by placing them under the command of republican officers and wishfully enacting regulations to guide their behavior. France's Expeditionary Army resorted to a strategy that was diametrically opposed: it armed and commissioned "contraguerrilla" forces who employed the same tactics of terror and violence they were charged with suppressing. The squadron led by Col. Charles Dupin, the "Red Butcher," famously dressed in the garb of the Mexican *charro*, provoked terror and indignation among the Mexican population and, eventually, French public opinion.[72] In the end, guerrilla forces made significant contributions to the Liberals' final victory, if only by making the French Army's stated objective of "pacification" impossible.[73]

"CIVILIZED WARFARE" proved an oxymoron. It also proved unequal to the task of putting down "rebellions" that had assumed "the character of war" in both North American republics.[74] John Fabian Witt's analysis of the Union's *Instructions for the Government of the Armies . . . in the Field* (1863) reveals how Francis Lieber, in his influential contribution to the literature on the laws of war tradition, was critical of its central premise of insulating everyday life and politics from the destructiveness of war. He deliberately rejected the law of nations as "sentimentalist" and flawed: by "separating the regulation of conduct in war from the justice of the war's aims," it created a "separate domain for war . . . with a moral and legal order of its own." Warfare's ethical dimension—the justice of its cause—required a proportional use of force and the sacrifice of romantic idealism.[75]

So while the author of the *Instructions* shared with iusnaturalists the urge to structure and regulate the means and strategies of war, he insisted that their nature and reach could only be determined by the conflict's purpose and ends. While he had forcefully denied the legitimacy of irregular forces, he defended the liberty of an army, as the military arm of the state, to do what it needed to in order to secure the objectives. All acts of violence and destruction were fair game in order "to save the country."[76] North America's governments-at-war apparently reached the same conclusions: for all the fanfare surrounding the law of nations, contenders relied on it as a convenient script: it rarely set limits on war policies that were molded by circumstance, perceived necessity, and the dynamics of politics.

Disciplining the Wayward: Caught between Independence, Rebellion, and Union. The Disunited States

To overcome a dangerous national crisis, North America's contending governments enacted unprecedented, contradictory, often redundant and constitutionally unsound legal statutes. They resorted to legislation to intimidate, cajole, or chastise a people whose will they were supposed to embody but whose allegiance they could not count on. Laws sought to protect civilians but also to constrain them, to police words and deeds, to compel loyalty. This legal munition reveals republican fragility and condenses the conundrums of civil war. In the sundered countries, formerly innocuous speech and action came to be seen as dangerous. Military necessity justified government overreach, the subversion of due process, and the abuses of armed men: newspapers were censored or shut down; passport systems put in place; property invaded, confiscated, or destroyed; civil liberties curtailed; justice expedited and militarized. The peculiar challenges faced by each government called for specific responses, often determined by state capacities.

In a severed United States, legislating war meant keeping disloyalty in check, or at least out of places where it could weaken or endanger the war effort. Union and Confederate authorities felt compelled to "identify loyalty and punish disloyalty on a huge scale."[77] In a Confederacy conscious of its recent, contentious birth, states enacted draconian treason laws: Georgia, for instance, mandated the execution of those who kept "enduring allegiance to the Union."[78] Both governments created a federal bureaucracy—the Union's provost marshals, the Confederacy's less well-known "habeas corpus commissioners"—charged with capturing deserters, weeding out traitors, stopping saboteurs, and silencing disloyal speech. In their crusade to save the republic, they often acted preemptively and disregarded revered legal recourses, even in the face of judicial disapproval. Presidents Davis and Lincoln both suspended the writ of habeas corpus, the former with the authorization of Congress—which voted three times to allow for suspension. The censure of Chief Justice Roger B. Taney in the North or that of North Carolina chief justice Richmond M. Pearson in the South did not lead to stricter observance.[79]

For all their similarities, Washington and Richmond were fighting different wars. Most battles took place in the South. For all the galvanizing effect of "Northern Aggression" after April 1861, the Confederacy, with its relatively smaller population and less developed infrastructure, bore the brunt of the conflict's destructiveness. An essential task for Jefferson Davis's government was keeping the Confederate states together and its citizens invested in a war effort that grew progressively more costly and less promising.[80] Rising prices, dramatic labor and food shortages, and a constant sense of fear and loss gnawed at Southern society. In this context, state and federal authorities legislated urgently to secure a home front subverted by two vital but uncomfortable actors whose previous relationship to the state had been mediated by father, husband, or master. Galvanized by war, white women and enslaved persons became more active and increasingly dangerous political subjects.[81]

Stephanie McCurry has meticulously documented how poor, rural Southern women, outraged by speculation, harassed by tax collectors, and unable to work their farms, acquire foodstuffs, or feed their families remade themselves into "soldiers' wives," entitled to protection and relief from the Confederate republic. By petitioning, organizing, and rioting, they became new, rights-bearing, "assertive constituencies." While elite women relied on the tropes of feminine weakness and vulnerability and used Confederate law—and particularly the Second Conscription Act's exemption of men in charge of plantations with twenty slaves or more—to safeguard their men and their interests, poor soldier's wives aggressive "politics of subsistence," and particularly the food riots in the spring of 1863, broke the mold of women's traditional political invisibility and forced a change of policy on local, state, and federal authorities.[82]

When relayed to the front, women's suffering demoralized fighting men and incited desertion, weakening the Confederate war effort.[83] Thus, despite an alarming scarcity of resources, the South's flimsy welfare systems were overhauled and expanded. The amount of money distributed to the poor by both public and private actors grew substantively. State governments took on the financial responsibility for social spending, provided tax exemptions, gave away basic foodstuffs like salt and corn and, in a move that speaks to their anguish, diverted supplies from the military to civilians. The Richmond administration forced planters to grow food instead of cash crops and eventually rewrote federal law to ease conscription's more onerous burden on the poor.[84]

If the pressures of recruitment and supply weighed so heavily on Confederate society—where military service claimed between 75 and 85 percent of able-bodied white men of military age, as opposed to 50 percent in the Union—it is in part because almost half of adult men in the CSA were enslaved and hence barred from becoming soldiers.[85] Because slaves were its leading citizens' most valuable property, the Confederacy also encountered significant resistance to their impressment. Enslavers feared losing their considerable investments and agonized over the dangers of slave rebellion encouraged by the disruptions of war. Commanders complained of the enslaveds' reluctance to dig trenches and build groundworks and their inclination to run away.[86] Crisis strained the painful ambiguities of property-in-man, as "moral chattel" consciously scuttled the institution: the enslaved slowed work down, spread rumors, accused their masters of Confederate sympathies, ran through Union lines, and took up arms against the enslavers' nation: of the 180,000 African American men who served in Union uniform, over half had been enslaved in the rebellious states.[87]

Legislating war in the Confederacy led to sweeping initiatives and ineluctable dead ends. Like the shocking action of poor women out-of-doors, the complex mobilization of enslaved persons and their dynamic information and resistance networks revealed the cracks in the foundations of a white republic that was materially and ideologically ill-equipped to meet the demands of war. Legislation to give soldier wives their due was groundbreaking but deficient. As the system of labor expropriation that the CSA had been established to protect gnawed at its entrails, its leaders debated laws to transform the "peculiar institution" so that it could both be preserved and serve the CSA's military needs. These discussions, unsurprisingly, came to naught.

In November 1864, Jefferson Davis called for the enrollment of 40,000 slaves for nonmilitary duties. He argued that they would enter the army not as property impressed but as "persons" who had a relationship to the state and could be rewarded for their "faithful service" with emancipation. These men would not serve as soldiers, much less be recognized as citizens, but since "local attachment" was "so marked a characteristic of the Negro," they would be entitled to request permission to reside in the state they had lived in once the war was over.[88] Despite the support of Confederate luminaries, such tortuous policies were rejected as "abhorrent to every southern sentiment and in conflict with all Southern opinion."[89] That the Confederate Congress and citizens debated the previously inconceivable possibility of legislating property into persons speaks to the depth of the crisis brought about by looming defeat. That these bills were dead on arrival confirms the structural limits of Confederate political imagination.

The Confederacy's invader was subject to similar, if less brutal, pressures. In Washington, when the war broke out, Congress endeavored to purge the disloyal from its midst. It deployed its power to expel, which it had previously used only once and would not be able to use successfully again until 2024.[90] Between 1861 and 1862, the Senate banished fourteen senators, while three representatives were dismissed from the House.[91] Some members condemned these extreme measures, which entailed the loss of states' representation. Critics argued that their embattled colleagues were being penalized for "honest" differences of "opinion" and "sentiment" over the nature of states' rights and the status of slavery under the constitution, the legality of secession, and the possibility of neutrality in the face of civil war.

Disagreements over these issues spoke to—or had reflected, until very recently—legitimate ways of conceiving a complex system of government. The besieged legislators had fulfilled their duty: at a time of uncertainty, excitement, and division; they had given voice to their constituents, as they stood on the sovereignty that "the constitution permitted . . . to remain to the states." Conversely, "tyrant" Republicans sought to "crush all opposition" by calling it treason. Committed Unionists rejected these accusations. "In reference to this rebellion . . . honest patriots" could not equivocate: it was illegitimate and needed to be crushed.[92] Thus, unwieldly, awkwardly written statutes resulted from republican quandaries—ingrained suspicion of politically motivated prosecutions and concerns with institutional impotence in dealing with crimes against the state—legislative debates trammeled by Republican radicalism and Copperhead obstruction and anxious soul-searching about the war's origin and nature. These laws aimed to strike against an enemy who, following the tortured logic of civil war, was also a citizen and compatriot.[93]

Things seemed less ambiguous to those fighting on the ground. As the seceded states became occupied territory, military impasse gave way to "hard war," intent on chastising the enemy and destroying his assets. As the Union became an army of occupation, it made "allegiance" a condition for "protection under the law," with the serious consequences in the moral and spiritual realms that the controversies surrounding loyalty test oaths attest to. Officers used these performances to discipline former rebels and ostracize traitors.[94] Formal, public declarations were required of federal officials and public servants, voters, and jurors, and, when military commanders or revanchist lawmakers thought it necessary, of witnesses; tavern keepers, merchants, and their customers; bank employees; attorneys; doctors; teachers; and men of the cloth.[95]

As Harold M. Hyman pointed out, public admission of the illegitimacy of secession meant access to "food, mail, and peace . . . liberty, and pardon."[96] Conspicuous Confederates who had sworn to "preserve, protect, and defend" the Constitution of the United States before 1861 were disenfranchised, but many former rebels took the new oath to avoid being ostracized. The conquering Union's imperious efforts to legislate consciences produced political theater rather than sincere conversion. "To swear, to lie," wrote a political prisoner, became a means to end "starvation, nakedness and all the ills / That Rebels [were] heirs to." "Love of ease"—he added—made "patriots of us all."[97] To no one's surprise, these oaths were not transformative. After the war, enactment of federal law required military occupation of the former Confederate states, redrafting state constitutions, and fighting protracted battles on the ground, in the legislatures, in court, at the ballot box, on the streets, and in public accommodations to block the reinstatement of the labor relations and racial hierarchies that had underpinned the peculiar institution that the war had destroyed.

The Union's most dramatic and momentous use of law as a weapon of war was emancipation. Its proclamation recognized the freedom of over 4 million enslaved persons, destroyed Southerners' most valuable asset and affirmed that the war's purpose was to annihilate its cause: slavery, the nation's original sin. By September 1862, military necessity trumped precedent, constitutional scruples, and electoral concerns, along with liberal convictions and the version of the law of nations proudly held in the United States. Lincoln's Preliminary Emancipation Proclamation was almost as convoluted as the previous congressional acts regulating confiscation. Freedom for the enslaved was brandished as a threat, not an aspiration; its materialization was contingent on the army's presence and muscle. The possibility of colonization and of gradual, compensated manumission were tendered to soften the blow in the loyal slave states. Nevertheless, on January 1, 1863, the "immediate and permanent" freedom of "all persons held as slaves" in the seceded states was proclaimed as "an act of justice, warranted by the Constitution, upon military necessity," as a consequence of rebellion.[98]

Disciplining the Wayward:
Fighting to Reconceptualize the Nation. Quarrelsome Mexicans

The breakdown of politics and polities in mid-nineteenth-century North America followed different paths. As the United States split up, rebellion called on principle and law as its watchwords: opinions were mobilized, votes marshaled, conventions strong-armed, and federal union re-created, allegedly stabilized and improved. In Mexico, crisis shattered the precepts and institutions that had—precariously—underpinned politics. In December 1857, a majority of state governments supported the Tacubaya pronunciamiento's call for a new constitution. They backtracked a few weeks later, in the face of the Conservatives' military takeover. As the wind changed in a war that raged in the country's center and west, state and local authorities alternatively abandoned their posts, summoned citizens to arms or sat still as they tried to weather the storm and protect their communities' lives and resources. Church and Army, accused of being symbiotically Conservative corporations, were torn apart by war; with members fighting in both trenches. For almost a decade—except for the months between January 1861 and May 1863, when the Liberals reinstated constitutional rule—rival governments functioned, intentionally, without legislative assemblies.

The Mexican laws of war bear the seal of greater urgency and intransigence.[99] Draconian decrees, designed to settle a struggle for the soul of the nation, sought to punish and browbeat the enemy and instill not only allegiance but patriotic fervor in untrustworthy citizens. Laws defined, classified, and severely sanctioned crimes against "the nation, order and public peace": perpetrators would be punished for aiding, abetting, or conspiring with the enemy; joining an invading army; organizing or participating in elections or otherwise endorsing "simulations of government"; engaging in piracy or slave trafficking; rebelling against "political institutions, calling for either their abolition of reform." These statutes also politicized and criminalized noncombatants' words and deeds: spreading rumors, meeting with more than one person after dark; engaging in business dealings with those now deemed to be enemies.

Lending credence to illegitimate political authority was also punished: performing bureaucratic acts of government—collecting taxes, adjudicating trials, tending to municipal services—in territories controlled by the enemy; negotiating the peaceful occupation of a city or town; participating in "commotions" that, intentionally or not, encouraged disrespect of public authorities. These laws demanded swift, exemplary execution and summary judicial proceedings, preferably in the hands of the military. The imperial government, in a cynical reach for expedited "justice," charged the Expeditionary Army's martial courts with prosecuting alleged crimes against order and safety, which included banditry, often described as the bane of Mexican society.[100]

Each government's laws often responded, mirrored, and escalated statutes enacted by its antagonist. Retaliatory, ever harsher punishments, engendered by increasing despair, were often in breach of the much-referenced laws of war. Their violation was justified by one side's greater legitimacy. Virtue could be defended by any means necessary. In October 1865, as skies darkened over the empire, Maximilian enacted a law that replicated the severity of the republic's January 1862 statute, aimed at deterring collaboration with the European invaders. The empire's "Black Decree" ordered the execution, after a swift court martial and within twenty-four hours, of anyone captured "with arms in their hands," whether or not they brandished a "political pretext." The imperial government argued—falsely—that President Juárez had crossed the border into the United States: the cause that he had sustained with "so much courage and constancy" had therefore perished, not only rejected by the nation—since Mexicans had called the young Hapsburg to the throne—but because the Juárez administration had disregarded the terms of the constitution it was allegedly fighting for. This decree invalidated the republican cause and sought to transform civil war into a struggle between "the Nation's honest men" and "criminal gangs and bandits."[101]

Conceived as weapons of war, these laws were as dreadful as they were unrealistic and overly ambitious. Jesús González Ortega's decisive triumph at Calpulalpan in December 1860 had brought about the fall of the Conservative dictatorship, the return of Juárez's government to Mexico City, and the restoration of constitutional rule. For all its bluster, his decree terminating the army was ineffectual.[102] The "enemy of the Nation" transmuted into elusive Conservative guerrillas whose violence was less visible, less conventional, and more vicious. In June 1861, as the constitutional government in the capital stood powerless, Conservative bands took the lives of three of the most prominent Liberals—influential ideologue and former minister Melchor Ocampo; Gen. Santos Degollado, who had led Liberal forces during most of the war, and brilliant young general Leandro Valle. These "heroes of the Reforma" were captured, summarily tried, and executed once the war was supposedly over and won.

The war's irregular prolongation marred the reinstatement of a progressive fundamental law, which explicitly forbid the death penalty for political crimes.[103] The Juárez administration took stringent, legally dubious steps against the enemies of the 1857 constitution who now "hypocritically" invoked its protections in order to plot its demise. It exiled the country's bishops and banished foreign diplomats whose "visible" sympathies for "reaction" had led them to interfere in Mexico's affairs.[104] It ordered that all "enemies, traitors, moderates" who had served "that farce which had been called the government" in Mexico City during the war be immediately fired.[105] Only those who could prove they had neither worked for the

Conservative government nor publicly objected to reformist legislation could be part of the federal bureaucracy. Lawyers accredited by courts under the purview of the Zuloaga and Miramón administrations had to seek recertification by state governors, after pledging obedience to the constitution and Reform laws.[106]

A flustered Congress, elected in February 1861, was torn between hopes of reconciliation and a desire to crush the enemy. Most of its members were indignant and deeply troubled by continuing Conservative depredations. Some congressmen deplored President Juárez's "characteristic leniency" and called for a "Committee of Public Safety" to prosecute the "enemies of public peace" emboldened by impunity.[107] Others repeatedly called for a general amnesty: those whom radicals branded "criminals" for having sided with the other camp during the war actually comprised a considerable portion of "the sovereign people." Were they to be tried and punished for their political opinions?[108] On the day after Ocampo's death, Congress declared seven Conservative commanders "beyond the pale of the law and its guarantees." Whoever rid the world of these "monsters" would benefit "all of humanity" and be rewarded with $10,000. On the eve of imminent foreign invasion, Congress amnestied those guilty of "political crimes" and called on them to take up arms against the French invader. It nevertheless excluded prominent Conservatives.[109]

Overwhelmed by Conservative resilience, lawmakers decided to prosecute the Liberals involved in the December 1857 Tacubaya pronunciamiento, which was now reprovingly labeled a coup d'état. Savvy former minister Manuel Payno defended the actions of the Comonfort administration: its suspension of constitutional rule was rooted in principle and had been accomplished "without firing one shot or spilling one drop of blood." The *pronunciados* had taken action against the "dead and inappropriate letter" of an impractical, ineffective, even dangerous, fundamental law. Their endeavor had, tragically, been highjacked by "reactionaries." But Comonfort and his associates had acted "under imperious necessity," as both Liberals and patriots. In hindsight, it was obvious that they had badly miscalculated, but they had done so without malice.[110]

An angry congressional majority had no patience for such explanations; delegates deemed pragmatism and the fog of dire circumstances worthless rationalizations. In politics, retorted fellow novelist Ignacio Manuel Altamirano, "mistakes were crimes," and the one that Payno and his accomplices had committed merited execution.[111] Looming political conflict, the intervention of the Supreme Court, and the threat of foreign war forestalled the process against Payno. Had Altamirano's verdict been carried out, Payno's *Los bandidos de Río Frío*, the most colorful, readable Mexican novel of manners, would not have been written.[112] Because of his skill and knowledge of public finances, this "traitor" would soon be called upon by the republican government. Harsh laws of war proved so ineffective that they had to be constantly reissued. In a divided nation, they engendered resentment, outrage, and sometimes fatal score-settling, but they brought about no change of heart or realignment of allegiances.

A good illustration of their intransigence and futility is the fate of Manuel Robles Pezuela, the Conservative general who had sought a conciliatory exit to the Reform War. In March 1862, having found about the unforgiving "new law" of January 1862, he did exactly what this edict hoped to prevent: he left Guanajuato, where he had been condemned to internal exile, and traveled toward Veracruz, where, like other Conservatives, he hoped to join forces with the foreign invaders. He was captured in Chalchicomula, Puebla.[113] The federal government ordered that he be tried for treason given his "suspicious and bad behavior." The general vehemently rejected the charge: he "yielded to no one when it came to patriotism and a desire for the people's well-being." He was convinced that only the "disinterested intervention" of the European powers could establish a "moral," orderly government in Mexico. His support for "the only political project" that could "save the nation from destruction" was proof of his patriotic devotion. His protestations were to no avail; he was swiftly executed, if for conspiracy rather than treason.[114]

The dramatic but generally spotty execution of dreadful laws did not weaken the enemy but transformed men-at-arms with dicey careers into tragic heroes and inspired calls for vengeance: Robles Pezuela's "distinguished services to the Nation" were applauded during the Second Empire.[115] In October 1865, the execution of republican generals José María Arteaga and Carlos Salazar, "the martyrs of Uruapan" who fell victims of the empire's Black Law, became a rallying cry for the growing, increasingly confident, more successful republican armies. Their gallant sacrifice, along with that of Ocampo, Degollado, and Valle, was consecrated in print and patriotic celebrations, as bloody civil war was transformed into an equally bloody but unequivocally virtuous struggle for liberty and nation.[116]

Once the empire was defeated, republicans acted with cooler heads. The dramatic but selective implementation of brutal patriotic law allowed the republic to eliminate its most threatening foes. The death by firing squad of Maximilian, Miramón, and Mejía became the awesome symbol of republican victory, propagated through striking images: photographs, photomontages, engravings, and, to great transatlantic effect, Édouard Manet's *The Execution of Emperor Maximilian*, completed in 1869.[117] The execution of the "stupid German" who had sat on a bogus throne meant to serve as a dire warning to other European expansionists. Domestically, draconian law, sparingly and strategically executed, rid the republic of some of the nation's most influential, exasperating, and possibly dangerous strongmen, while putting it aside dialed down the violence that had caused so much pain in the previous decade.

With the death of Generals Miguel Miramón and Tomás Mejía, the uneasy alliances between Conservatism, the army's officer corps, and Indigenous resistance came apart. Santiago Vidaurri was captured and executed in Mexico City in July

1867. His brand of extreme federalism, grounded in an armed citizenry, local control of resources, a brisk commercial economy, and access to the border, had no place in the triumphant Liberal republic. At the same time, the republic was magnanimous in victory. After eliminating the most threatening opposition figures and putting to death those who, in its eyes, had behaved most despicably when complying with the 1865 Black Decree—Generals Tomás O'Horan and Ramón Méndez—it extended broad amnesty to begin healing the nation's wounds. The strategic deployment of the laws of war once the war was over was perhaps their most effective use throughout ten years of bloody, continent-wide struggles.[118]

The Geopolitics of Loyalty

The efforts to govern loyalty made by North America's embattled governments revealed the brittleness and futility of their labor. They also exposed the delusive quality of the concepts we rely on to organize and interpret reality—ideology, nations—which we suppose are visible, bounded, and homogeneous. On the ground, clear ideological lines between contenders unraveled into irregular, unstable flashpoints. The disintegration of the common arena that had made national politics possible wrought anxiety and uncertainty as it paradoxically demanded absolute, unquestioning, and constant reactions from the nation's citizens. The tensions and urgencies of war dislocated and rearranged geographies of identity and allegiance. The shared visions, contentious aspirations, partisan rivalries, and disparate economic interests that crisscrossed the young nations shaped complex responses to division and violence.

Meandering Boundaries

After Lincoln's call for troops in the wake of the attack on Fort Sumter, Virginia joined the Confederacy. However, the Old Dominion's western counties rejected secession, even when the state convention's decision was confirmed by referendum less than a month later. Recalcitrant westerners convened at Wheeling in the early summer of 1861. A "Reorganized Assembly of the Restored Government of Virginia," elected in the loyal counties, was recognized by Washington. Despite an explicit constitutional proscription, this legislative body was granted permission to form a new state, within the jurisdiction of another, without the constitutionally mandated approval of its legislature. West Virginia was admitted into the Union in 1863.[119]

Other border states faltered. In May 1861, Tennessee governor Isham Harris called for the formation of a "military league" with other slaveholding states. On June 8, the state's citizens voted, in a highly contested referendum, to become a "free, sovereign and independent state," while waiving "any expression of opinion as to the abstract doctrine of secession."[120] After Sumter, the people of Kentucky and Missouri, distressed by fractious politics, still hoped they could preserve "the peace and amity between neighboring border states on both sides of the Ohio river." Impelled by the voices of "many good citizens," state governments attempted to maintain neutrality in the face of "deplorable war."[121] Unionists and Confederates alike condemned this desperate "fiction" as an immoral, theoretically unsound gamble. Neutrality nevertheless accurately reflected the perceptions and experiences of the inhabitants of the western Ohio Valley, who thought of their region as a land of moderation, physically and politically weaving North and South together.

Borderlander expectations were shattered in the fall of 1861, when these states were invaded by Union and Confederate troops. Political authority split, and rival governments contended for recognition and legitimacy. The latter was inevitably a fragile thing in the border states, and would be sacrificed repeatedly to the dictates of armed conflict. Missouri's loyal government, for instance, was eventually set up by a military coup d'état. It would twice postpone its gubernatorial elections during the war.[122] Secession upended social and political dynamics in all the border states, and the war displayed some of its most harrowing features in the region. When soldiers violently imposed hard categories of allegiance, they penalized citizens' flexible and complex political identities.[123] Confusion and confrontation inevitably arose in the states that upheld slavery but remained in the Union. As slaves acted to transform disruption into freedom, the—increasingly ambiguous—obligations of legal human bondage strained relations between officers and civilians and between local and federal authorities, even before the conflict explicitly became a war to destroy property-in-man.[124]

In Mexico's North and Southeast, war and regime change, wretched as they were, were also seen as opportunities to reset strained relations between periphery and center. Paradoxically, the propagation of violence, and the active and instrumental involvement of northern militias in national war, brought the disaffected North into Mexico, even as South Texas and northeastern Mexico became a single, integrated economic—even political—space. The experience of the states that came to border the United States in 1848 diverged from that of the rest of the country. Independence dismantled the Crown's military and diplomatic establishment, which resulted in greater isolation, instability, and exposure to Indigenous violence. Resentment toward a distant and incompetent national government was rife. Moreover, as the US border shifted south to the Río Bravo / Rio Grande, it spawned, as Miguel Ángel González Quiroga has shown, "myriad opportunities" for interactions with foreign neighbors, prompting increased trade and progress, conflict and cooperation, and both greater freedom and oppression.[125]

Fueled by cross-border incentives for commerce and stability, borderlanders (*fronterizos*) wrought a transnational space held together by the flow of Mexican silver and other goods, low tariffs, close-knit collaboration between political authority and moneyed interests on both sides of the border, along with the significant militarization of Norteño society, as it organized to contain Indian nations more aggressively.[126] This dynamic configuration sustained the rise to power of Santiago Vidaurri in Nuevo León and the formation of the state's effective national guard under his leadership. With their over 11,000 registered members, experience in the wars against the Indians, and arms imported from Texas, the Nuevo León *blusas* played a key role in the Reform and Intervention Wars.[127] The consolidation of political power in Mexico's Northeast—at least in Nuevo León and Coahuila—also set the stage for the reorientation of Southern commerce during the US Civil War and the momentous impact it had in the region.

When, as Luis Alberto García has explained, Vidaurri rebelled against the Santa Anna dictatorship in May 1855, he launched the Northeast onto the field of national politics. The key role played by Nuevo León's national guardsmen in the Liberal armies allowed Vidaurri to strengthen his position by alternatively supporting the Liberals in the national struggle and withdrawing his forces from the fray. Meanwhile, he buttressed his influence in the region and annexed the neighboring state of Coahuila—and its customshouse at Piedras Negras—with the blessing of the Liberal Congress that crafted the 1857 constitution and the assertion that the Coahuilenses wholeheartedly supported annexation.[128]

National crisis created occasions for settling regional problems and rivalries. Challenges to Vidaurri's authority at home and increasingly hostile relations with the federal government—primarily over tariffs, legally the federal government's purview but whose control was essential to the governor's power and the military and commercial arrangements that made the Rio Grande Valley work as an economic region—drove the northeastern cacique to join the ranks of the empire in 1864. Following a similar logic, when Coahuilenses mobilized to fight the French and Imperialists in the early 1860s, they did so to liberate their state from its neighbor's ascendancy. Locally, republican triumph meant the death of Vidaurri and the end of Nuevo León's experiment with radical government and subversive nationalism.[129]

At the country's other end, on the Yucatán Peninsula, the capital city's elite hailed the proclamation of empire. Like their call for secession in the early 1840s, the Emeritenses' conspicuous display of loyalty was part of a strategy to assert Mérida's autonomy from Mexico City and its pesky tariff policies. Their faith in imperial recognition of the Yucatecans' right to govern without outside interference would founder on imperial centralizing and rationalizing intentions, and on commissary José Salazar Ilarregui's energetic program and his plan to use the department's human and financial resources to fight Maya resistance.[130] Mérida's rival patricians, the merchants of Campeche, rallied instead to the republican cause. In April 1863, their loyalty was rewarded with the founding of a new republican state with the Gulf city as its capital.[131] To the north along the Gulf coast, in the lowlands of Tabasco, Liberal politicians swiftly defeated the French and *imperialistas* and turned their success in war over into enduring political power.[132]

In both republics, beyond persistent interelite rivalries and local aspirations of autonomy, exacerbated, enabled, or trammeled by violence and political experimentation, the topography of allegiance featured sites of particular fragility. In the Disunited States, federal governments had to contend with populations living in territories that had been torn away from another country less than two decades before: the Mexicans who had remained in the Faraway North as it became the US Southwest. Moreover, all North American nations had fraught relationships with the Indian nations that controlled extensive territories and maintained their independence despite state efforts to paper over—and sometimes physically crush—their autonomy. As citizens of Mexico, the United States, and the Confederacy fought over the fates of their nations, they unleashed a cycle of violence that impacted actors on its margins, altering the unstable ecosystem that sustained their relations with the center, at times opening new opportunities and more frequently shutting them down.

As violence reverberated across North America, it pulled frontier regions into the rhythms and interactions of overheated, spasmodic war capitalism. Money poured into California to finance the belligerent efforts and was reinvested in real estate and transportation, paving the way for more intense connections with the Eastern Seaboard and a heavier traffic of goods, people, and capital. As the Union army's men and provisions moved through the austere landscape of the poor, sparsely populated New Mexico Territory, they became an easy and profitable target for Indian raids. The demands of military mobilization accelerated, expanded, and then fractured what Lance R. Blythe has described as a fragile "borderland political economy" animated by "the reciprocal taking and exchanging of captives and livestock" between a variegated array of Anglo, Hispano, and Indigenous populations, sedentary and nomadic.[133]

To the south, the Río Bravo—which the Treaty of Guadalupe Hidalgo had designated as a neutral waterway—became the lifeline through which Southern cotton avoided the Union blockade and was reexported, mainly to Europe. Between 250,000 and 300,000 bales of cotton passed through the river's estuary, and the Confederacy's trans-Mississippi West was provided with everyday necessities and military supplies from the other side of the border. This economic boom remade—sweepingly if ephemerally—the eastern borderlands: the sleepy settlement of Matamoros (pop. 9,000), briefly became a bustling town of 40,000 and an important financial center; the makeshift port of Bagdad saw 450 ships loaded in twenty months, and thousands of Mexican muleteers, cart drivers, and freighters were recruited by this whirlwind of economic activity. Eight textile factories on the Mexican side, "capable of handling 1.5 million tons of cotton annually," provided uniforms to the CSA. Although the conspicuous effects of the cotton boom

Commercial activity exploded in towns along the Río Grande. "The War in Texas—Brownsville." From a sketch by L. Avery. Image taken from *Frank Leslie's Illustrated Newspaper*, December 5, 1863. Courtesy of the Texas State Library and Archives Commission.

would speedily disappear at the end of the Civil War, the capital left behind by its profitable trade was key to the industrialization of the Monterrey region from the 1880s onward.[134]

As armed conflicts grew more voracious, they raised the stakes of mobilization on the nation's margins and broadened the political stage for the individuals and communities who lived on the polity's edges. Thus, after being denied a commission in 1861—because the Civil War was, in the words of William Seward, "an affair between white men"—Towanda Seneca Ely S. Parker served in the Union army as Ulysses S. Grant's secretary and aide-de-camp.[135] In Mexico, Maximilian recognized sympathetic Indigenous military leaders and made them officers in the imperial army. Nayarit's Manuel Lozada, who had led the Cora and Huichol communities of the Sierra de Álica since the 1850s, successfully blocked Liberal consolidation and the control of Guadalajara over the region. At the head of an army of "good Christians . . . good Mexicans [and] good soldiers," Lozada was commissioned as a general, while Opata chief Refugio Tanori in Sonora became a colonel.[136] In the mountainous regions of Puebla and Oaxaca, Indigenous national guardsmen organized to support Liberal forces against the Conservatives and the French.[137]

When governments at war called their citizens to arms, they included men who had declared their intention to naturalize, and held out full membership in the political community to foreigners who were willing to fight for their future fatherland.[138] In the Disunited States, Union and Confederate authorities also drafted foreign residents. They argued that since they benefited from the protection of the state and its laws, they should contribute to their defense. As Paul Quigley has revealed, this claim to service was grounded in a performative, "reciprocal conception of citizenship that went beyond legal technicalities." Diplomats, however, were reluctant to abandon these normative minutiae. More often than not, a consul's intervention kept reticent foreigners from serving under someone else's flag, but this often engendered resentment, particularly in the increasingly desperate Confederacy, against men who shed "their nationality like a garment ... and [claimed] the protection of the very powers" they refused to defend.[139]

South of the Rio Grande, fear of foreign retaliation kept all governments from forcefully drafting resident foreigners. Still, the French Intervention put soldiers of a dizzying array of nationalities on Mexican battlefields, including the French members of the Expeditionary Army and the globetrotters who had joined its Foreign Legion; the Flemish, Walloons, Danes, Germans, and Central Europeans who voluntarily enrolled in the corps put together by Carlota's father and Maximilian's brother; and the Black, Muslim Sudanese members of the regiment recruited, at Napoléon III's behest, by the Egyptian khedive.[140] Men went to North America to fight, motivated by a thirst for adventure, financial need, or love for a cause. Felix de Salm-Salm, an indebted German prince, fought for the Union and then for Maximilian, whose life he earnestly tried to save. Styling himself a custodian of freedom and democracy, Argentine Edelmiro Mayer led African American troops for the Union army and, after Appomattox, joined Mexico's republicans, as did future African American historian, preacher, and activist George Washington Williams.[141] Polyglot, ethnically diverse, and ideologically heterogeneous, fighting forces in North America reflected the transnational nature of a struggle that its protagonists imagined as global.

Strangers on Their Own Land? Formerly Mexican Americans

Nowhere, perhaps, was the knot tying together citizenship and loyalty more tangled than in the territories of the Mexican Cession. After 1848, former Mexicans had become "foreigners in their native land," US citizens whose status was contested and whose political loyalties seemed suspect. As they entered the political arena, elite Californios, Tejanos, and Nuevomexicanos tried to navigate a challenging new environment. They strove to maintain power in a tense, convoluted political context. Slavery in the West was the bone of contention in the North-South antagonism. The new western possessions were, nonetheless and with the important exception of Texas, eccentric to the binary logic of a confrontation that eventually led to secession and war. The poignancy of Black bondage was blunted by peculiar configurations of race and regional investment in different incarnations of unfree labor, such as peonage and Indian slavery.

Nevertheless, new US politicians tried to manipulate these volatile issues to their advantage; they wagered on the Democratic Party and often collaborated with Southerners. Californio lawmakers supported both free-state status and discrimination against African Americans when California became a state in 1850, while the Nuevomexicano-dominated territorial legislature forbid the immigration of free Blacks in 1856 but passed a slave code three years later.[142] In contrast, in all the former Mexican territories, including Texas, the "conquered population"—and especially its poorer, more numerous members—suffered discrimination and dispossession. Consequently, former Mexicans' willingness to go to war for a nation in which their membership was called into question and they were often mistreated could not be taken for granted. When Col. J. R. West, commander of US forces in Arizona, called for the support of "the people" of the Mesilla Valley—which had been part of the United States for less than ten years— he spoke not of patriotism or the duties of citizenship, but of Texans' "perversity," the Union's commitment to the protection of life and property and the good price his outfit would pay for food.[143]

For all the ambivalence of their standing in the political communities that were reconstituted in 1848 and again in 1861, Californios, Tejanos, and Nuevomexicanos all served in the Civil War.[144] Like other men whose membership in the body politic nativists disparaged—immigrants, Catholics—citizens of Mexican origin proved as "American" as their less exotic countrymen. Although, in the words of patriotic Nuevomexicanos, they lived in "the least favored section of [their] country," Confederate or Union, they wanted to join the fight that would determine its future.[145] Like other US citizens of military age, former Mexicans enlisted for love of country and because they were compelled by law—to the indignation of Mexican diplomats, as Mexico's republican government, embroiled in a complicated relationship with the Lincoln administration, was not above using the travails of its former citizens to pressure the State Department.[146] These new US citizens also fought for inclusion, recognition, and social mobility. They were influenced by class and ethnic solidarities and antagonisms, by economic interests and family and social networks. Mobilization followed the push and pull of local playing fields on which they wanted to be acknowledged as players.

Consequently, Californios and Nuevomexicanos—with a few exceptions— followed their polity into the Union camp. The path to follow was less clear for Tejanos. As borderlanders, they belonged to complex transnational webs of family, economic, and political connections that tied them to networks in Nuevo León and Tamaulipas, and they could easily cross the border to avoid being drawn into the war.[147] Most fought for the Confederacy, which Texas had joined in March 1861 and whose men were drafted as soon as April 1862. As happened in the rest of the Mexican Cession, some members of the Tejano elite assumed leadership roles: Laredo's Santos Benavides, a brigadier general, was the highest-ranking Tejano in the Confederate army. Nevertheless, a substantial minority of his *compatriotas* joined the ranks of the Union, which meant, as Omar Valerio-Jiménez has written, "staking a claim for American citizenship" and defying the white-supremacist elites who treated them as second-class citizens even as they called them to arms. They also received a signing bonus of land and 100 pesos in gold.[148]

Former Mexicans fighting under Union and Confederate flags spoke of their "most sincere patriotism." A Texas state commissioner hailed Santos Benavides and his men for their "deeds of valor" and devotion to country, which refuted the racist "slander" against "citizens of Mexican origin." Former California state assemblyman Andrés Pico, who had actively lobbied for Democratic initiatives such as partitioning the state in 1858 and 1859, made his support for the Union public. He pledged "as a soldier my sword . . . as a citizen, my fortune." Nuevomexicanos vigorously condemned the people of Mesilla's support for "the South"—that "Eden of Liberty, equality and rights"—and the creation of a Confederate territory of Arizona. In San Miguel County, an orator anticipated Lincoln's sentiments by asserting that secession endangered the best of governments, "and with it the hope of the world, who are looking to our Union to solve the problems of man's capacity for self-government."[149]

Mexicanos in the Disunited States drew on the language and practices of republican politics old and new, from Mexico and the United States. As David Hayes-Bautista has shown, Californios deployed this hybrid, transnational, popular political culture most creatively and effectively. They conflated—as did Latin American diplomats in Washington—the war for the Union with Mexico's fight against European imperialism. Two convoluted, ensnared national tragedies were depicted as an epic continental struggle to save liberty and democracy from aristocracy, despotism and Old World intrusion. It was a momentous battle in which the Californios' former compatriotas and present countrymen were allies, bound together by "shared feelings about individual dignity and republican opinion."[150]

In 1862, as the Union's dismal military performance inspired frustration, Californios celebrated the news of the unexpected defeat of the French at Puebla and created what is today the quintessential Latino holiday, Cinco de Mayo. Transnational patriotism was sustained by conscious organization efforts: with the support of Mexican agents—Generals Plácido Vega and Gaspar Sánchez Ochoa—129 *juntas patrióticas* were established in California, Nevada, and Oregon. They met every month to mobilize patriotic feelings and Latin American solidarity, raise funds, and rhetorically tie together the destinies of the two nations wracked by war, just as US diplomacy wrestled to keep them apart. If, as the father of sons fighting in opposite trenches, Francis Lieber saw himself as the tragic "symbol of Civil War"; former Sonoma senator Mariano Guadalupe Vallejo, who had one son in the Union army and another fighting for the Mexican Republic, was the embodiment of enthusiastic New World republicanism.[151]

For all the resonance and sophistication of Mexicano patriotism, it often ran up against Anglo indifference or disdain: New Mexico's Spanish-speaking troops were blamed for the painful defeat at Valverde (February 1862) and their contributions to Union victory at Glorieta Pass (March 1862) were seldom acknowledged.[152] Capt. Rafael Chacón "raised and mounted," at his expense, a cavalry company in New Mexico's First Regiment. He was proud of his unit, made up mainly of family members and retainers, which had taken up arms so "that we may enjoy equal rights with others." The Union army acknowledged his "well-known energy," but his men received no pay and their horses no forage. To his disappointment, Chacón's sacrifice was "not well received or perhaps forgotten." In Texas, San Antonio native and Harvard graduate Capt. José Ángel Navarro crossed the border into Mexico in November 1863 because "those of Mexican extraction" did not "enjoy the same privileges as natives" in the Confederate army.[153]

Former Mexicans' involvement in the war was, like that of the rest of their countrymen, inspired and mediated by local feelings of attachment, solidarity, or hostility, and structured by family, patronage, and political networks. Deeply ingrained hatred of Texans stimulated both Californios and Nuevomexicanos to take up arms against the CSA. The latter's Union sympathies were reinforced by the *ricos* who, because of "flattery or vanity," supported the South.[154] The sacred cause of independence and the rejection of a despotic Union were not even mentioned in the letters that Confederate Tejanos Manuel Yturri y Castillo and Joseph Rafael de la Garza sent home. They were instead filled with homesickness, anecdotes from military life, an almost desperate longing for news from home, and affectionate but precise instructions: Yturri's wife was to kiss the children and teach them to read, count, and speak English, "a little every day." She should not spank them or let them spoil the dog.[155]

Most former Mexicans fought relatively close to home and, sometimes, as Phillip González has pointed out, to serve "local purposes." Members of the colorful California Lancers were sent to Arizona to support Union troops in pursuing Confederate bandits and Native Americans but most remained, doing "dull labor at Drum Barracks" in San Francisco.[156] In New Mexico, after defeat at Glorieta Pass effectively put an end to Confederate expansion in the Far West, Union policy and Nuevomexicano interests turned against the Indian Nations that their Hispano neighbors insisted—after over 200 years of tenuous collaboration, contentious exchanges, and intermittent conflict—had become an existential threat to their survival. Although the bulk of the Civil War's battles took place in the southeastern theater, the war materialized the nation in the faraway Western territories, hardened its policies toward defiant Native Americans, and backed them up with more men and greater firepower.[157] The tragedy of the Navajo's forced transfer to the Bosque Redondo reservation in 1864—which caused the death of almost 20 percent of this nation's population—was one of its consequences.[158]

Native Outlanders

"Wild," "*bárbaros*," "savage," "*indómitos*," "uncivilized": the brutal adjectives used to qualify the word *Indians* in nineteenth-century North America speak to the fears independent Indigenous nations inspired in settler communities on both sides of the border. As the nation crumbled into fratricidal conflict, the presence within its contested boundaries of entities at once familiar, foreign, and dangerous was perceived as increasingly threatening. In the Disunited States, those that law characterized, oxymoronically, as "domestic dependent nations" were seen as both potential allies in war and mortal enemies. In Mexico, where Indians—organized into corporate republics—had been part of the political community since the sixteenth century, they comprised an important if undetermined part of the population, since there were no fixed, objective criteria to distinguish the Indigenous from the rest of the peasant population.[159]

Indigeneity in nineteenth-century Mexico was, then, a slippery, subjective quality, ubiquitous but practically impossible to pin down or account for. Colonial administration had relied on the legal category of "Indian" for the collection of tribute, and its abolition at independence was a corollary of equality proclaimed. In a nation in which it could be surmised that most citizens had Amerindian origins, the Indian became was a key but ambiguous figure. Within the contentious work-in-progress that was Mexican nationalism, the precontact past was construed as glorious antiquity, but the Indian of the present—ubiquitous if elusive—became the nation's domestic Other, either poor and pitiful or barbarous and terrible.[160] By the 1850s, the Indian had become a problem to be solved: Norteños called for the death of Apaches and Comanches, while linguist Francisco Pimentel published a treatise on how to "remedy" the "situation" of Mexico's "indigenous race" through assimilation and miscegenation.[161]

The term *Indian* was inherently ambiguous, but its modifying adjectives—*indomitable, brave, peaceful, poor, helpless*—were relational and circumstantial. Thus the stigma of savagery was extended to those settled pueblos—in Yucatán, in Querétaro's Sierra Gorda, in Jalisco's Sierra del Nayar—who engaged in "caste war." The fearsome moniker was given to Indigenous insurrections, even when spawned by citizens' aspirations, fashioned by republican language and the defense of liberties and rights enjoyed "from time immemorial," and whose protagonists happened to be poor, rustic, and dark-skinned and spoke a language other than Spanish. Deployed by the ruling minority—perhaps, in some cases, more out of fear than as a purposeful tactic—the *caste war* label justified the appalling violence exercised against Indigenous insurgents.[162] Still, neither dread nor disdain permeated the century's legal categories: Mexican constitutions avoided ethnic classifications and recognized Indigenous people as citizens, endowed with the right of suffrage, including rebels and—nominally and implausibly—the members of the horse-riding nations who effectively dominated large swaths of the North.

In the New World, Indigenous communities that pushed back on the nation-state's pretense of assimilation and control presented a baffling challenge, which grew significantly in the midst of wars threatening the nation's survival. Indigenous communities traded, interacted with, and terrified settlers in the US West and Mexico's North and Southeast—where the rebel Cruzo'ob sustained their independence for over half a century—and simultaneously fueled and dislocated capitalist markets and networks. They upended notions of dominion as territorial and property as private, demarcated, and transferable. In the United States, relations between independent Indians and the federal government were built on contentious diplomatic negotiations, marred—in the opinion of republican officials—by archaic rituals and onerous mechanisms such as gifting and annuities that produced fragile agreements, often destroyed by betrayal, dispossession, and violence.[163]

Internecine war joggled and restructured the uncomfortable relationships of North America's nation-states with Indigenous peoples. Contending foes sought to entice those they considered untrustworthy, even dangerous actors. As the war overwhelmed them, they reached out to Native peoples in an effort to forge military alliances, or at least to ensure peaceful interaction. Among Mexico's northern warrior tribes, like the Opata and Mayo of Sonora, and peasant communities in the central highlands, interelite conflicts opened possibilities for alliances that could refashion power relationships. Some opted for the Conservatives, sometimes impelled by religious reasons; others followed the logic of an opponent's enemy being a friend.

Jean-François Lecaillon argues that many of Michoacán's Indigenous communities, often at odds with Liberal landowners who hoped to use disentailment legislation to acquire pueblo lands, supported the European armies by providing food, shelter, and information.[164] In Nayarit, Conservative and then imperial authorities recognized the power and influence of Manuel Lozada and formalized the autonomy of a region where his allies and associates clearly had the upper hand, in what Zachary Brittsan has aptly described as the "institutionalization of Lozadismo."[165] Tepic became a departmental capital, on par with Guadalajara, and Manuel Lozada bolstered his authority by distributing land among the Sierra's villages, because, he argued, it had been disentailed by Liberals, sold at an unfair price or to the wrong people.[166]

In the Yucatán Peninsula, however, imperial commissioner José Salazar Ilarregui called on the rebels of Chan Santa Cruz to stop making war on other "children of God and of this land" and submit to the imperial government. He promised that Maximilian, heir to the "great" Charles V, who had wisely ruled over their ancestors, was "as powerful as he was good." Flowery appeals to tradition notwithstanding, the imperial olive branch was rejected by the insurgents, who put the government's representative to death. The imperial government, like its predecessors, ended up supporting the Mérida elite and its Indigenous allies against the rebellious Maya.[167] In the mountains of Puebla and Oaxaca and the tropical lowlands of Michoacán, pueblos rallied to the Liberals. Many leveraged their contributions to republican victory into political autonomy throughout the century's final decades. Their heroic sacrifice in the fight against the foreign invader is an enduring source of local pride and proof of the pueblos' devotion to the nation.[168]

In the Disunited States, the Confederate government reached out to the nations that had settled in Indian Territory—present-day Oklahoma—during the summer of 1861 and negotiated and signed treaties of "Friendship and Alliance" to place them "under the protection" of the Confederate States of America.[169] Peter Pitchlynn, Choctaw chief and former delegate to Washington, argued that the Union's attack on the seceded states violated the republican principle of government by consent. War so absorbed Washington bureaucrats that they neglected the Union's commitments to Indian nations: the money due to them was not paid, forts were abandoned, and, in the Kansas-Nebraska territories, Indians were left "to the tender mercies of Kansas cutthroats and higher law leaders from all quarters of the North." Like the Confederate States, betrayed by the Union, the abandoned Indian nations were "contending for self-preservation" and "the right of self-government." Their "cause" and "interests" were "identical."[170]

In July, August, and October 1861, Confederate officer Albert Pike negotiated nine treaties with the Five Civilized Tribes and other groups: the Comanche, Osage, Seneca, Shawnee, and Quapaw. Perilous circumstances justified new arrangements, but these treaties also invoked the similarities and coincidences that bound together the "absolutely and unconditionally free and independent people" who were parties to new alliances: their commitment to self-rule and conviction that "the institution of slavery" was legitimate, that it had existed "from time immemorial" and should be "everywhere held valid and binding."[171] Other, less numerous, documents described how smoking the "pipe of peace" with Confederate agents and receiving from them "wampum of peace" had transformed the CSA into "friends and protectors."[172] These covenants speak to the diversity of the Indian universe and the perception that Native Americans could build different relations with federal authorities. The Confederate Congress shut them down by qualifying and circumscribing these agreements. As was the case with the recruitment of enslaved men as soldiers, the delegates' compunction illustrates the limits of political creativity, even when kindled by war.

Negotiations had followed a long and contentious tradition: treaties warranted protection, provisions (including rifles), and the payment of annuities. They were assumed to mediate in the Indian nation's trade and political relations. But Pike also offered potential Indian allies the right to send a delegate to the House of Representatives in Richmond and access the states' justice system on less unequal terms, by admitting Indian witnesses in court. Some nations would also have the privilege of enrolling their youths "to be educated at any military school" in the Confederacy. To fight against the Union, Indian "braves" could serve as scouts, runners, or soldiers, placed "under the orders of proper officers." The Confederacy would provide the money to arm, equip, and maintain these Indigenous troops.[173]

In the case of the Choctaw and Chickasaw, who had proved their "fitness and capacity" by establishing and preserving "a regularly organized republican government," the treaty set out the possibility of "the whole" of their country becoming a Confederate state, once their land was surveyed and a section of it devoted to "purposes of education."[174]

The amendments that Confederate legislators made to the treaties reveal the restrictions that prejudice—dressed up as political conviction—put on the transformation of the relationships between the nation-state and Native peoples. The role of Indian delegates in Congress would be circumscribed to those issues in which their nations were "particularly interested." Treaties could not "bind Congress absolutely to admit a state, or give people ... a positive and unqualified right to admission." Thus the incorporation of Choctaw and Chickasaw territory into a state was made contingent on circumstance and the lawmakers' will. Furthermore, the federal government lacked the power to make Indian citizens "competent witnesses in State courts." This, argued the treaties' negotiator, was a corollary of constitutional principle, and "in no matter prejudicial" to Indigenous people, as obstacles to political assimilation would disappear with time. Pike also argued, if not convincingly, that the states bordering on Indian territory would "cheerfully agree" to remove the disabilities that kept Indian witnesses out of court, for it was "equally unjust and ungenerous and quite as unwise and impolite."[175]

North America's civil wars might have—briefly, perhaps superficially—broadened perspectives for some Native American groups, but they tragically darkened the skies over others. In August 1862, the fatal attack of four young Dakotas on the town of Acton in Minnesota sparked a deadly war. The Dakota's desperate circumstances—displacement, a series of bad crops, overdue annuities—drove them to strike against white settlers in the hope of expelling them from what they still considered to be their land. The Indian uprising provoked hysterical reactions. When war ended with the surrender of 2,000 Dakotas, most of them noncombatants, the "united voice" of the people of Minnesota demanded Indians be removed from the state. Verdicts out of rushed, biased military trials—all of the commission's members had fought against the Dakota—condemned 303 men to death. Lincoln's intervention reduced the number to 38. They were hung in the largest public execution in US history.[176]

The Dakota War whipped up fears of attacks throughout white settlements in the West, where the war had disturbed an already violent region. In November 1864, in southeastern Colorado, in the midst of swirling rumors and bloody skirmishes between whites and Indians, John Chivington, a passionate abolitionist and devoted preacher who headed the volunteer Third Colorado Cavalry, rode into a camp of Arapahoes and Cheyennes, whose leaders had convened near Fort Lyons to try to broker new terms of peace. Instead, Chivington ordered the Union troops to attack the encampment, where they massacred, with conspicuous cruelty, callousness, and recklessness, over a hundred people, mostly women and children. The Sand Creek massacre, as Ari Kelman has skillfully shown, was profoundly contentious from the get-go. It prompted accusations from survivors, protestations from some of the soldiers involved, and a congressional investigation, which meted out no punishment. The incident is a deeply problematic memory site, which inevitably "unmakes"—the expression is Ned Blackhawk's—the history of the United States as that of different peoples' coming together to forge an exceptional nation.[177]

The Minnesota and Colorado disasters were products of the Civil War. The inefficiencies of an overwhelmed federal bureaucracy muddled Indian policy; the specious belief that Indian violence was part of a Confederate scheme heightened the panic it engendered and justified the violence deployed against "Indians," whose peculiar histories and circumstances were erased. In the words of John Pope, who led the fight against the Dakota Sioux, Native Americans were to be "treated as maniacs or wild beasts, by no means as people."[178] A bloody battle over the nation's soul erupted over slavery's place in the West, as the lands seized from Mexico were set up as an idealized—empty—stage, on which the promise of American freedom would come true. On the ground, men in blue, like John Chivington, surmised that this would not happen unless they got rid of the Indian Nations.[179]

White settlers argued that the South's "gigantic rebellion" exposed the dangers of the dysfunctional relationship between federal authority and Indian nations. As Jameson Sweet has shown, between 1820 and 1860, mixed-ancestry Indians in the Upper Midwest voted, held public office, and influenced territorial and Democratic Party politics. "Whiteness" was conflated with citizenship, not construed as its unequivocal condition.[180] By 1863, however, Minnesota's representative in Congress argued that the "experiment of maintaining one independent nation within the bounds of another" had failed: it could not be done "with safety to either." As Carol Chomsky has written, the military trials of the insurrectionaries were not just arbitrary and ruthless: charging the Dakota warriors with "civilian crimes" such as murder, rape, and robbery—which also spelled death for the perpetrators—denied their status as legitimate belligerents and citizens of independent sovereign nations. It negated their status as rebels and reduced them to felons.[181] It was the most negative interpretation possible of the Native nations' equivocal legal definition.

The dreadful violence of the Sioux War and the Sand Creek massacre throws light on the connection between the struggle for the Union and the battle over the West. As Kelman has aptly written, the former "midwifed 'a new birth of freedom'" as it "delivered the Indian Wars."[182] In Mexico, the relationship between the mid-century wars and the fate of Indigenous communities is less clear-cut. Still, the crushing defeat of Conservatism undermined communal autonomy by making the playing of dominant political actors against each other more difficult. Victorious Liberals acted swiftly to eliminate Indigenous actors they found partic-

The press distorted the actions of Native American troops, which were described as brutal, alien, and "barbaric." After the Battle of Pea Ridge in Arkansas (March 7–8, 1866), in which the Confederate army was reinforced by 800 members of the Cherokee, Choctaw and Chickasaw cavalry, the Northern newspapers' sensationalist descriptions of the scalping of eight Union soldiers scandalized public opinion in the North. Courtesy of the Shiloh Museum of Ozark History / Jim Miller Collection (S-96-2-665).

ularly unsettling: Tomás Mejía and Refugio Tanori died in front of firing squads; in 1873, a weakened Manuel Lozada was captured and executed by a hero of the fight against the French, the general and governor of Jalisco Ramón Corona. The war had a profound impact on North America's margins and borderlands and on their heterodox denizens. The arms, men, and animosities spawned by republican crisis and fratricidal confrontation jostled the nation at its edges; they expanded and circumscribed prospects. In some cases, they shattered them violently.

As it swept up a multifarious set of actors—individual and collective, near and far—the maelstrom of war's violence remade the character and geography of national politics. Contending governments used law as a weapon of war, to impose order on chaos, to mobilize their citizens, to identify and chasten the enemy, and to endow the war with sense. Liberal and Conservative, Confederate and Union, republican and imperialist authorities all tried to weed out and

"Zacapoaxtla" Indians on parade in Puebla, Mexico, May 5, 1962. The participation of the Sierra's Nahua Indigenous communities in the 1862 battle of Puebla was memorialized and applauded during the battle's centennial celebration. Reproduction courtesy of the Instituto Nacional de Antropología e Historia, Secretaría de Cultura.

disable internal enemies, refashion territorial hierarchies, and transform the national government's relationship with its citizens. In doing so, they reimagined, retooled, and sometimes betrayed their visions of polity and government. Laws aimed at policing conscience and enforcing allegiance were constitutionally dubious and, with the possible exception of their selective application in Mexico once the empire had fallen, consistently inefficient. Riding on war's violence, other laws transformed the nation: they refashioned the foundations of liberty and property, warped the nations' relationship to the Divine, and transformed the meaning of membership, if in uneven, contradictory ways. They also left behind the rough, jagged edges of communities divided.

CHAPTER SIX

MEN AND MONEY

NORTH AMERICA'S REPUBLICAN CRISES engendered powerful, contentious visions of political community rooted in principle, of the norms and policies needed to make it real. As debates grew increasingly intransigent, advocates construed their projects as the only way to redeem the nation and those of their adversaries as proof of their perversity. But when the war came, carefully drawn out, theoretically sophisticated plans were displaced by violence. Salvation would come by other means. For all the concern with loyalty and allegiance, it was not patriotism and heroism that saved the republic and the Union. On the battlefield and the home front, muscle and material resources mattered more than passion and imagination. These wars—so long, so sweeping, so lethal—were unlike any in which the North American republics had fought before.

Because of their mind-boggling scale, duration, and effects, these armed conflicts could not be won by spurts of patriotic enthusiasm, brilliant tactical displays, or gallant, reckless charges. They were won by numbers: of men mobilized, of money raised, of information, supplies, and reinforcements delivered on time, of weapons purchased, manufactured, or smuggled. Because rapidly evolving armament technology—minié balls and rifling, of breach-loading, repeating, and rapid-fire guns—and transportation infrastructure had such an important impact on how the war was fought, the Union, with its greater industrial capacities and over 20,000 miles of railroad track—to the Confederacy's 9,000—had a significant advantage. In Mexico, save for the eighty-mile track that the Expeditionary Corps hastily put together to get its troops out of the Gulf's disease-ridden lowlands, armies relied on human and animal locomotion and imported weapons.[1] In the end, capacities for the mobilization of human and material resources for war depended not only on economic potential but on politics: the structures of federalism, republican practices, assumptions, and innovation shaped enlistment and taxation policies and drove their execution, often determining the outcome of war.

Republican Predicaments: Recruitment and Taxing in America

North America's independent nations were born in war. Brutal, drawn-out conflicts—which lasted from 1775 to 1781 in the thirteen British colonies, 1810 to 1821 in New Spain—cast long shadows. Fueled by imperial rivalries, financial pressures, and revolutionary upheaval, they dislocated and sometimes shattered imperial circuits of trade and governance. Like the conflagrations that tore these nations apart at mid-century, those that gave them birth transformed compatriots into enemies, compelled the members of large, heterogeneous societies to take sides, and demanded the far-reaching mobilization of resources and manpower.

These wars were also revolutions: they disrupted social and racial hierarchies and refashioned the ways people thought and spoke about politics. The rhetoric of revolution wrought taxes—the "countless tributes, levies, and impositions" that so burdened North America's inhabitants—into tangible symbols of the arbitrary, tyrannical, extractive nature of the ancien régime.[2] Subjects became citizens, endowed with rights, duties, and a proportional share of the nation's sovereignty. Governance was challenged by a volatile combination of rights to equality and freedom and by sovereignty embodied by different entities—the nation, the people, the states—and exercised through the overlapping jurisdictions of federalism. Getting sovereign states, made up of sovereign citizens, to give up their money and the lives of their young men proved difficult for central governments endowed only with delegated powers.

The New World's republican founders were suspicious of standing armies, executive overreach, and the taxing power. They relied on constitutional engineering to keep dangerous actors in check, divide power up, and allocate authority selectively. The young nations' armed forces were organized on two levels: local militias, made up of citizen-soldiers who bolstered state sovereignty and provided a counterweight to the standing army and navy, led, for the most part, by professional officers, trained at the nation's war colleges. In both republics, the president was commander-in-chief of the armed forces, but only Congress could declare war. The legislature also had the power of the purse and that of mustering the armed forces.[3] Early constitutionalists put perhaps too much faith in their careful parsing out of power. Although they realized that swift, energetic military action would be required in cases of emergency—insurrection, invasion, or a threat to "public safety"—they did not provide clear constitutional guidelines for dealing with such situations.[4]

By mid-century, Mexico's federal government seemed better prepared to deal with these dangerous moments, if only on paper and for the wrong reasons. In the face of chronic instability, a treasury in shambles, and constant interference by a politicized officer corps, lawmakers tried to reign in the latter by endowing the executive with broader powers. They uneasily navigated aspirations to greater efficiency, affirmations of state sovereignty, and the Army's power and influence as they drafted constitutions that shifted from federalism to centralism and back. State militias were abolished and efforts made to create a smaller, more disciplined, more effective army. Reform floundered on the resistance of military strongmen, both in the professional corps and in the regions whose autonomy they jealously guarded. I contrast, the creation, during the US-Mexico War, of a national guard of citizen-soldiers, following the French model, reworked the relationship between civilian authority and the armed forces. For all their flaws—lack of discipline and preparedness, partisanship, clientelism—these local, semipermanent, and relatively democratic bodies could be mustered by the president and fight beyond their state borders. They effectively nationalized men-at-arms and offset the army's might.[5]

Constitutional schemes grounded in the coexistence and collaboration of different sovereign entities added a layer of complexity to mobilizing national resources. Different levels of government could legitimately lay claim to citizen contributions (in blood or money), which made determining and collecting what was due to the national government technically challenging and politically contentious. As enlightened, economics-inspired visions of flourishing national markets, dynamic transoceanic commerce, and a centralized fiscal state, the stipulations of republicanism and federalism narrowed policy choices for mandating and collecting public revenue. In Mexico and the United States, the people's representatives had to consent to taxes and public spending. The people's welfare was supposedly at the core of these laws, so that they would not stifle the creation and circulation of wealth. As free members of horizontal communities, republican citizens had to contribute to their upkeep and defense, but charges and duties had to be equal, uniform, and proportional to individuals' "ability to pay."[6]

In the wake of independence, both North American nations experimented with confederal fiscal regimes, which entrusted the states with collecting and forwarding the funds needed for the maintenance of the central government. The mechanisms laid out in the US Articles of Confederation—sent by Congress for ratification by the states in November 1777, enacted in March 1781, and superseded by the constitution in March 1789—and Mexico's 1824 federal constitution—enacted in January 1824 and superseded by the centralist Seven Laws in December 1836—recognized local authorities' more effective administrative capacities and granted them responsibility for assaying and collecting public money and sending the federal government its due.[7] This system did not work to the central government's advantage: its income depended on the goodwill of states it could not coerce.[8]

Both republics stepped away from these deconcentrated fiscal arrangements and established central governments that, at least on paper, could act—and levy and collect taxes—"directly on the people."[9] During the first fifty years after independence, however, neither national government relied on taxes paid directly by its citizens. Washington avoided direct taxation: on the one hand, constitutional precept denied Congress the power to lay a direct tax unless "in Proportion to the Census or Enumeration herein before directed to be taken." Direct taxes, like representatives in Congress, had to be "apportioned among the several states," which was inequitable and technically challenging.[10] On the other, when the federal government tried to collect direct taxes, it incensed citizens and sparked the Whiskey Rebellion (1791–94) and the revolt led by John Fries in 1799, both in Pennsylvania, which probably inspired circumspection. Authorities in Washington were also spared the need to call directly on the population for financial support: tariffs on imported goods and revenue from the sales of public lands furnished the federal government with enough to cover its expenses, pay its debts (including the consolidated financial obligations incurred by the states during the Revolution), bolster the nation's credit, and even fight and win wars.[11]

Conversely, the Mexican government would not get its financial bearings until the century's end.[12] In the words of Miguel Lerdo de Tejada, secretary of the treasury in 1856–58, his office was defined by "a lack of resources and excess of obligations." The Mexican government was born indebted when it assumed the viceregal government's financial liabilities at independence. In 1824 and 1827, it contracted two loans in London, whose payment schedule it was unable to meet by 1828.[13] Debt ballooned as the national state had to rely on credit extended on exorbitant terms. In a bankless, cash-poor economy, state creditors who enjoyed liquidity cornered an extremely tight financial market. They often played fast and loose with citizenship legislation and turned what was owed to them from personal to public obligations that were incorporated into Mexico's growing unpaid sovereign debt.[14]

Bound by diplomatic conventions, much of the federal government's income—that of tariffs on imported goods—went directly to paying interest on foreign debt and cover the standing army's expenses. Other federal contributions—leases of national mints, dues on mining and metallurgical assays and licensing—yielded, in Lerdo's words, an "absolutely nominal" amount. The one exception was the *alcabala* tax, which in Mexico City amounted to a few thousand pesos in cash a day and allowed federal authorities some immediate relief. With its panoply of checkpoints, inspectors, and fines, this excise was archaic, cumbersome, and antieconomic, but it was nonetheless a reliable source of income that state and federal governments were loath to give up.[15]

Throughout the first decades after independence, the strapped Mexican government repeatedly tried to come up with a less precarious system. It was unable or unwilling, however, to curb contraband or effectively collect property taxes on either urban or rural real estate. The *capitación*, a regressive and unequally levied state head tax, incited evasion, resistance, and sometimes rebellion. The general government lacked the information, administrative muscle, and legitimacy to tax its recalcitrant citizens.[16] Enthusiasm and conviction drove the 1856–57 Congress to abolish the alcabala, but politics, circumstances, and the opposition of state authorities made it impossible. The tax survived, despite its unconstitutionality, until 1896.

As was the case in all of the Americas, the fiscal mainstays of the two North American republics were tariffs on foreign trade, collected at a limited number of ports of entry by small, relatively inexpensive federal bureaucracies, while states remained the more assertive and efficient tax collectors. But if the systems' basic rationale and structures were similar, they played out quite differently on the ground. In Mexico, customshouses were the object of constant bickering among local, state, and national authorities. Their military occupation was an essential strategic objective in the country's frequent political disputes.[17] In the United States, the constitution's fiscal schemes were not particularly controversial, but legislating tariffs provoked significant, sometimes dangerous, sectional disagreements, of which the 1833 Nullification Crisis was the most consequential. At mid-century, both nations were debtor states devoid of a central bank. But while the United States had a vibrant, if unstable, banking system, Mexico had a restricted, rigid, and expensive credit market with no commercial banks at all. For all the institutional similarities, the US federal government could be described as the "model" of an understated central authority "that worked creatively, positively and effectively to unleash the nation's economic energies." Mexico's fiscal situation has aptly been labeled as one of "penury without end."[18]

In both North American republics, federalism engendered national governments that were meant to be small, invested with limited, delegated powers and charged with specific tasks. They were, nevertheless, animated by different logics. Throughout the fractious process of constitutional design in Philadelphia in 1787, the dangers of war from without weighed heavily on the minds of the founders. Forty years later, their Mexican colleagues seemed more concerned with securing regional autonomy against Mexico City's historical domineering tendencies. Consequently, as Conservative Lucas Alamán bitterly pointed out in his 1834 critique of Mexican federalism, the US constitution set up a strong central government and a powerful executive, elected by the people. Although charged with a small number of tasks, it enjoyed the powers to fund and execute them well. Across the border, he argued, the Mexican government remained hostage to the whims of the states: its fiscal and financial disabilities made it feeble, contested, and ineffectual.

Thus, while Washington ran surpluses between 1816 and 1836, which it used to pay down the national debt, Mexico's federal Congress was not presented with a budget until 1855 and would not vote on this financial instrument until 1869. Only in 1893 did Mexican lawmakers validate a surplus budget.[19] By enabling the federal government to contract loans and cover its financial obligations, the constitutional order of the United States transformed its public debt "from a liability to an asset." Interest and capital punctually paid became "an advertisement for America's creditworthiness." Loans and bond issues also proved an efficacious means for financing war without burdening taxpayers.[20] By 1850, the United States had successfully fought two major wars—that of 1812, against the former colonial power, and against Mexico in the 1840s—without increasing taxes.[21] Conversely, Mexico's public debt remained very much a liability: along with military spending, trying—and mostly failing—to keep up with interest payments on loans old and new swallowed up much of the federal government's scant resources. In 1861, the republic's financial incompetence served as a pretext for armed invasion.

Every Citizen a Soldier?
Putting Armies Together for Civil War

Legislating Recruitment

The experience, in war and peace, of the two North American republics had been dramatically different. Their paths crossed, nevertheless, in the violent clash of 1846–48. They converged for at least the next two decades: both nations fell apart, were devastated by war, and had to be put back together again. No one was ready for the wars that came: these conflicts lasted for years—four in the United States; almost ten, intermittently, in its southern neighbor. Hundreds, sometimes thousands of men faced each other in pitched battles. On both sides of the border, trained officers followed the same tactical prescriptions, drawn up by Antoine-Henri de Jomini, a veteran of the Napoleonic wars, while battles proved as deadly as they were undecisive. In the end, the war was not won by "Strategy, Great Tactics and Military Politics," but by the state's capability to put soldiers in the field.

Potent nationalist discourses—often expressed in enduring marble and bronze—and conventional histories of war identify the bravery and persistence of citizen-soldiers, "motivated not by fear of their officers but by passionate love for their cause," as essential to putting armies together, maintaining their discipline, and keeping their fighting spirit alive.[22] Heaven, Mexico's national anthem asserted forcefully, had given the "beloved *patria* ... a soldier in every one of its sons": their boundless patriotism would win the war. At the root of successful mobilization lay citizen enthusiasm, commitment, and resilience: Confederate nationalism and Conservative allegiances had clearly not been up to the task. It was never that simple.

As Mexican society fractured, men took up arms to defend God or the people's constitution. After the firing on Fort Sumter, young volunteers North and South eagerly rushed to arms, the former to save the Union, the latter to defend home, hearth, and family.[23] Love of country is a powerful but unstable, intangible, and immeasurable element. No party had a monopoly on it, and it is probably a mistake to identify emotional intensity with efficacy. Once early excitement faded as the possibility of swift victory vanished and the frightful number of dead and wounded climbed, neither the small US standing army nor Mexico's top-heavy, inconsistent military establishment had the mechanisms to reliably put boots on the ground, for all the courage and patriotism displayed by its members. Military outfits had a hard time keeping men from abandoning the ranks when grain needed to be sowed or harvested, families pleaded for their return, or they could not be paid. All the combat forces involved needed replacements who had to be enrolled, trained, equipped, and transported. Patriotism would not be enough.

In his magisterial social history of the armies that fought in the US-Mexico War, Peter Guardino notes that the advent of "modern war"—propelled by nationalism, its means of destruction maximized by the Industrial Revolution—was more drawn-out than prevailing wisdom suggests. Prior to the overwhelming turmoil at mid-century, the regular army in both North American republics had been manned by society's poorest, most marginalized men, often rootless individuals who joined the ranks out of desperation or, in Mexico, because they were forcibly taken from streets, taverns, and homes by the dreaded *leva* (press gang). In both republics, officers subjected soldiers to despotic treatment and degrading corporal punishment.[24] State militias (in Mexico, after 1846, the National Guard), with their elected officers, colorful flags, and uniforms, their masculine, horizontal, festive conviviality, were closer to the mobilized citizen-soldier ideal. But with some exceptions (Mexico's fierce, well-paid, and well-equipped Norteño guards, created to defend populations against Indian raids), they were also inconsistent and unreliable, because of their lack of discipline and training, and their disdain for the grunt work involved in making war.[25]

North America's mid-century wars mustered an unprecedented—and, in the case of the Disunited States, astounding—number of men, but maintained the two-track (federal/state) system of recruitment. In both republics, war rent the armies' leadership: one-third of US Army officers resigned to join the Confederacy, along with all but one of the heads of the army's eight bureaus, four previous secretaries of war, and most of the War Department's clerks.[26] This rift in leadership notwithstanding, military establishments grew exponentially: in 1860, there were 16,000 men in the US Army, most of them disseminated in western outposts. Over the next four years, almost 600,000 served in the Confederate armies and over 1.5 million in the Union's.[27] By the end of the war, the standing army had increased its numbers to 41,819.[28]

Domestic conflict strengthened the regular army in the United States; it wrought havoc on its counterpart on the other side of the border. Many Mexican officers, aggrieved by the Liberals' equalizing reforms, rebelled to protect religion and the hierarchies and privileges of the ecclesiastical and military corps. Still, a significant number chose to fight for the new, more democratic order promised by the 1857 constitution.²⁹ As hostilities broke out, a new generation of intransigent generals, dubbed the "Young Maccabees," led by Luis G. Osollo and Miguel Miramón, many of whom had cut their teeth fighting against the US invader, displaced the army's older, more ingratiating, more experienced leadership.³⁰

European intervention reshuffled military allegiances: some Conservative generals (Manuel González, Miguel Negrete) put ideology aside and joined their former foes to defend their beleaguered nation. A number of Liberals joined the monarchical project, in an effort to preserve regional autonomy (Santiago Vidaurri) or when faced with the "absolute futility," given French military superiority, of their troops' "sacrifice." Gen. José López Uraga, for instance, joined the ranks of empire, trusting Maximilian to keep his promise and preserve the nation's most "precious assets": independence and reform. These officers were, to their discomfort and sometimes disgust, placed under the authority of the French commander.³¹

The breakout of hostilities in Mexico coincided with the disarray of its already dysfunctional military establishment. The national government had repeatedly and unsuccessfully tried to discipline and downsize an army led by too many officers, most of whom had risen through the ranks through political meddling rather than battlefield exertions. Its troops were poorly and infrequently paid, often mistreated, and constantly depleted by desertion. In the unnerving atmosphere of 1857, the search for a solution revealed insurmountable differences. The contentious negotiations between the Liberal government—headed by Gen. Ignacio Comonfort—and the recalcitrant military establishment that had supported the Santa Anna dictatorship ended with the understanding that the Mexican Army would be comprised of 30,841 men, commanded by 1,833 officers. Seven hundred of these military leaders would be discharged for rebellion against the constitution. The settlement was difficult to reach and impossible to enforce. The Ministry of War apparently operated on a different plane altogether: in 1857, it optimistically reported—and budgeted for—a standing army of 10,000 soldiers and 12,000 National Guardsmen.³²

It was probably naive to think armed forces could be brought to heel in the midst of a crisis that would soon descend into war. Despite the conflict between civilian and military authorities and the disarray that riddled the armed forces, Liberal and Conservative commanders managed to cobble together armies for battle. Mobilized through violence and concessions, these battalions were recruited, undone, and remade to the rhythm of available resources and military fortunes. Although far from the numbers of Antietam (132,000 men on the ground) or Gettysburg (158,300), Mexican officers repeatedly accomplished impressive feats in marching troops onto the field.

Thirteen thousand men fought at Salamanca in March 1858, where the Conservatives' smaller contingent—5,000 troops—routed its less experienced rivals. Led by Liberal Santos Degollado, derisively called "the hero of defeats" by his foes, 7,000 men could not hold Guadalajara in November 1858; while President Miramón's armies, 5,000 and 7,000 strong, failed to take Veracruz in 1859 and again in 1860.[33] But since no one was able to maintain large bodies of fighting men for extended periods, much of the military action during both the Reforma and Intervention Wars was performed by smaller, more mobile, often irregular forces, who struck at the enemy and ran.[34]

Recruitment in war-torn Mexico was, more often than not, the result of forceful negotiations, in which recent military success, as a harbinger of more to come, was a determining factor. As war wound down, during both 1860 and 1867, Conservative and Imperial commands were unable to bring enough men into the ranks, while the accretion of Liberal victories sealed their triumph and the nation's political fate.[35] In December 1860, Jesús González Ortega's 20,000 men obliterated Miramón's 8,000 soldiers in two hours.[36] Seven years later, once the French Army had been repatriated, the empire's supporters managed to gather 9,500 troops to defend what was left of the empire at Querétaro. The city, besieged by Mariano Escobedo's Army of the North, fell in May, after a two month-long siege, during which republican troops grew from 25,000 to 35,000 men. The emperor and his generals were captured: the war was over; it had killed Mexico's monarchical experiment.[37]

On both sides of the border, recruitment on such a gigantic scale required bracketing republican assumptions, abandoning practices of old, and changing the army's relationships with society. Citizens needed to be turned into soldiers at great speed. In the Disunited States, relying on volunteers soon proved insufficient. In May 1861, as confidence in a quick victory evaporated, the Confederacy, which in the early days of the war had to turn back enthusiastic men keen to fight, called for 400,000 to enroll for three years, in addition to the 100,000 who had enlisted for a year in February. To the 75,000 men Lincoln had summoned after the firing on Fort Sumter, he called for 300,000 in October 1863, and for half a million in July 1864.[38] Both governments offered bounties to men who signed up.

As the costs of war climbed, enthusiasm faded and resistance festered. More drastic measures became necessary. Massive mobilization required the general government to compel, rather than call upon, men to fight. In federal republics that prized state sovereignty and distrusted standing armies and conscription laws, redolent of European tyranny, this was not an easy feat. In both Richmond and Washington, the implementation of mandatory military service was deferred and whitewashed, and finally enforced with difficulty.

On March 28, 1862, Jefferson Davis spoke to the Confederate Congress of a "resistance so general, so resolute and so self-sacrificing" among the South's population that it needed to be "regulated" rather than "stimulated." He charged Confederate lawmakers with coming up with a "simple and general system for exercising the power of raising armies," to ensure that the "burthens" of service not fall "exclusively on the most ardent" and warrant efficiency on both the battlefield and the home front.[39] The CSA enacted the first draft law in US history in April 1862, which "placed in the military service of the Confederate States" all white men aged eighteen to thirty-five for three years. It passed three more conscription statutes: each expanded the pool of those liable to serve and the duration of their terms. In September 1862, the law included thirty-five-to-forty-year-olds and, in February 1864, those aged seventeen to fifty, who were to fight for the duration of the war.[40]

The Union had a much larger pool of men of military age to draw from: over 3.5 as many white men, and it would also call on African Americans to volunteer after January 1863.[41] It nevertheless also, if more gradually, moved toward compulsion. As the president renewed his call to patriotic men to join the ranks on their own initiative, laws were drafted to pressure the eligible into service: the July 1862 Militia Act put all able-bodied men at the disposal of the president for a nine-month stint of service, while the March 1863 Enrollment Act called for the registration, by the federal Provost Marshal's Bureau, of "all able-bodied male citizens" between the ages of twenty and forty-five, and foreigners of military age who had registered their intention to naturalize. The enrolled would constitute the "national forces," subject to being called for service for two years, if rebellion persisted. Lincoln also issued a call for new troops in July 1863 and three times again in 1864.[42]

Crafting conscription legislation North and South required navigating ideological quandaries, vested interests, and the susceptibilities of sovereign states—including those of governors who had been, according to one Confederate senator, "exceedingly partial" in the organization of regiments.[43] That the draft was a military necessity was obvious to most lawmakers.[44] Still, some found compulsory federal enlistment repugnant to republican sensibilities: it violated state sovereignty and forced soldering on free citizens. In the words of an alarmed Virginia lawyer, conscription would "oppress the people, destroy the individuality of the states, crush individual rights under the iron heal of military despotism," and bring about "the extinction of all true manhood."[45] Breaking with republican principles and traditions also exposed national governments to the sharp barbs of the opposition. The "new-fangled *war power*," contended a Democratic congressman, mangled the constitution and turned the Union into something "fit only to be sneered at."[46] Notorious Copperhead Clement C. L. Vallandigham pointed to conscription as proof of a failed war, fought for the wrong reasons: the bill "virtually [admitted]" that the war was not "one to which the people give, freely, themselves and their sustenance" but one in which the sacrifices of war had to be "enforced by arbitrary power."[47]

The laws' authors put philosophical scruples and partisan bellyaching aside. They had no choice but to send soldiers to the front and try to keep the economy going and the home front from falling apart. This tenuous balancing act made for baroque, cumbersome laws that tried to do many things at once. Their centralizing traits were condemned as "subversive" of the sovereignty of the states, while national governments had to rely on state and local authorities for enlistment, given that they were more competent at identifying, gathering, and enlisting men to fight.[48] As Rachel Shelden has shown for the case of the Union, the federal government depended, for the execution of its policies, on the advice, support, networks, and tried-and-true methods of public officials who were "closer to the ground." Local authorities similarly looked to the federal government to enact measures that were both unpopular and indispensable to win the war, such as the draft.[49]

These statutes intended, on the one hand, to preserve some features of local, grassroots, voluntary organizations, like the election of officers.[50] On the other, the federal government threatened coercion to both pressure and incentivize local authorities to muster as many men as possible. The 1863 Enrollment Act, for instance, established that the draft would be necessary only if district quotas were not met. As James McPherson noted, this law, for all its "dubious legality" and "confusing arithmetic," established a working "carrot and stick" mechanism. When combined with the 1862 Militia Law and Lincoln's calls for volunteers, the threat of being drafted increased the number of troops who enlisted on their own accord, at least in July 1863 and March 1864.[51]

This legislation called on all "able-bodied" (and "white" in the Confederacy) men of military age to enlist. It also established exemptions for humane and strategic reasons. The Union's more vigorous demography allowed it to release men who were their family's sole breadwinner—the "only son" of "a widow" or "aged or infirm parents," the "only brother of children not twelve years old," "the father of motherless children under twelve years of age dependent upon his labor," and men whose families had already sent more than two of their members to the front.[52] Conscription statutes North and South also exempted high-level civil servants—the president and vice president, cabinet members, governors, and judges—and allowed drafted men to provide a substitute. The Union also sanctioned commutation of service for $300. Confederate law shielded men thought necessary to secure "order and good government at home."[53]

Modern war demanded a modern economy. For the South, this meant industrializing against the clock: the Confederate economy desperately needed "operatives" to make munitions and arms, to work the foundries, mines, tanneries, and paper and textile factories. The seceded states also needed mail carriers, telegraph operators, railroad, and river workers: these essential workers were exempt by law. Political scheming, grandstanding, and ingrained fears also lengthened the list of the privileged: all sorts of public employees did not have to serve in the military; physicians, ministers, and teachers were also excepted. Law infamously shielded men who, on plantations, were responsible for "twenty negroes" or more. Governors who were critical of conscription—Georgia's Joseph Brown, North Carolina's Zebulon Vance—appointed more civil servants to shield them from the draft.[54] The laws' contradictions and perceived injustices turned their execution into, in George Rable's words, "a legal and political nightmare."[55]

For all the cries decrying a "Rich Man's War," Civil War recruitment was not particularly skewed against the "poor man." As Tyler Abinder has shown, some of society's most downtrodden, such as the poor immigrant men who lived in cities, had a better chance of evading the draft—by failing to report, claiming an exemption, or failing to show up for duty—than did native urban skilled workers, farmers, or agricultural laborers.[56] But conscription laws, which meant to compel military service as they balanced out its burdens, wove together partisan strategies and cronyism along with good intentions. They explicitly provided an exit ramp for the rich and, in the South, the slaveholder; they were widely perceived as unfair.

A sense of injustice, controversies over slavery, and the weight and consequences of federal intrusion in citizens' lives inspired significant evasion. Desertion was common in both camps. In the North, over 20 percent of men called to serve did not report for duty. Draft avoidance grew as the war unfolded, even as the Union's military prospects brightened.[57] The numbers generated by the actual operation of the draft suggest that it was particularly ineffective: of the 776,829 men summoned, only 46,347 served.[58] In the Confederacy, by March 1864, Vice President Alexander Stevens stated that conscription was "useless . . . dangerous . . . unnecessary and unconstitutional." As the Yankee advance sowed terror throughout the South, state governments gave up on federal conscription and concentrated on their own defense.[59] In hindsight, volunteer enlistments and local organization proved significantly more successful . . . as long as the prospect of victory was believable.

THE GOVERNMENTS that fought over Mexico between 1858 and 1867 had fewer resources to draw upon and moved on a narrower stage than their northern neighbors. To mobilize men and increase government revenue, they turned to old methods that often contradicted vaunted republican principles and had, as a general rule, not served them well in the past. There was, nevertheless, a significant exception. The defeated Conservatives opted for a policy as radical as its outcome was catastrophic: they brought in someone else's army. With the continent's hegemonic power incapacitated by its own internal struggle, Mexican Conservatives wagered on foreign invasion and monarchy to defeat their enemy, forcibly make peace, and put the beleaguered nation on the path to progress and prosperity.

Although the few who had been committed monarchists before the 1860s were convinced that the country needed permanent, conspicuous European support, the presence and sway of foreign troops were deeply discomfiting. Nevertheless, for all its high costs, in terms of optics, reputation, and money—since the Mexican Empire pledged to cover the French Army's expenditures in the Treaty of Miramar (April 1864)—the idea of relying on a modern, well-equipped, professional army, free of the weaknesses and vices that plagued Mexican forces, proved overwhelmingly attractive. Theoretically, the presence of the French Army disentangled the Mexican state from constant, expensive, debilitating negotiations with military strongmen. It was a risky, brazen move; Conservatives hoped it would yield proportionate results. The invasion of "the world's best soldiers," undefeated since Waterloo, would—paradoxically—finally "pacify" the nation.

The French disembarked in Veracruz in January 1862. After the 6,000 soldiers commanded by Charles de Lorencez failed to take Puebla in the famous battle of May 5, Louis Napoléon's government sent over 30,000 reinforcements, drawn from experienced colonial regiments, headed first by Élie Forey, then by Achille Bazaine. The volunteer Austrian and Belgian Legions were also placed, nominally, under Bazaine's command, as were the Conservative officers and troops who joined the Intervention, about 7,000 men led by die-hard enemies of the Liberals and their constitution: Leonardo Márquez, Tomás Mejía, Juan Vicario, and eventually Miguel Miramón. These troops were supposed to be the seed of a Mexican imperial army that would grow to be as disciplined, well-trained, and proficient as that of its European "ally."[60]

The French treated Mexican officers not as partners but as subordinates, and untrustworthy ones at that.[61] To prevent insurrection in the Mexican ranks, Bazaine continuously changed the leadership of Mexican divisions so that troops would not be "more loyal to one general than to another," enabling the former to "undertake a *pronunciamiento* every time it got into his head."[62] The emperor himself was always suspicious of the more successful Conservative commanders, leaders who could stand on their own prestige and the loyalty of their men. He sent two of the most prominent, Miguel Miramón and Leonardo Márquez, into exile dressed up as diplomatic missions. The former president was tasked with learning about military tactics and new armament in Prussia; the "Panther of Tacubaya" became Maximilian's representative to Istanbul and the Holy Land.[63]

While it hampered the organization of its armed forces on the ground, the empire legislated meticulously: an "organic" law put all armies under the authority of the emperor. The land army would be 23,538 strong in times of peace and increase to 31,208 if there was a war. It would be furnished with 7,607 horses and mules. To prevent the politization and careerism that characterized the Mexican officer corps, the emperor "alone" would grant commissions; there would be no more than six major-generals and fourteen brigadier generals. In a context in which concerns about violence and insecurity overwhelmed public opinion, the army would also serve as a platform for the creation of a constabulary—almost 2,000 strong—and a rural guard tasked with securing law and order. The former would be deputized to cities, while the latter, paid for in part by local landowners, would subdue the much-disordered countryside.[64]

Imperial law also divided the nation's territory—organized into fifty administrative departments—into eight military districts. Each of its commanders was ordered to "assist" civil authorities whenever they asked for help. Another law described and regulated the army's uniforms in 271 articles.[65] Exacting rules and regulations contributed little to building the effective fighting force they laid out on paper. In the end, when Napoléon III ordered the withdrawal of the Expeditionary Army in early 1866, the empire's military strategy imploded. Maximilian was left with fewer than 10,000 men, entrusted with doing what 30,000 hardened French soldiers had been unable to accomplish.[66]

Mexico's governments-at-war—including the one that outsourced the conscription of soldiers—repeatedly condemned forced impressment. In January 1861, the triumphant Liberal commander publicly announced the end of the "hateful system of the leva," which had been "tolerable" when the people suffered under the reaction's onslaught. The time had come to turn constitutional guarantees into reality: men and their dignity could not be "diminished and discounted" by forcing them to serve against their will.[67] Two years later, the imperial regency government strictly forbid forced impressment. The new regime recognized that one of society's "most precious guarantees" was "individual security." No one who "obeyed the law and made a living by honorable means" should be "torn away from his work" and forced to take up arms.[68]

Even in the midst of war, public authorities tried to legislate conscription based on principle and equity. In May 1862, as French troops advanced toward the central highlands, the government of the state of Puebla ordered "all" citizens, aged sixteen to sixty, to enlist in the National Guard and defend "independence, territorial integrity, freedom, the democratic republican system, and local peace and quiet." Only those "who had certified physical impediments" would be exempt, and hiring substitutes was not allowed.[69] In November 1865, the imperial government established a draft mechanism to cover the army's quotas, so that citizens served the fatherland "under the unchanging laws of equality and justice."[70] The men who drafted these laws probably knew they were unrealistic; they would be quietly sacrificed to military necessity.

During the summer of 1861, as the government that reinstated constitutional rule braced for further Conservative aggression, Congress decreed that "all individuals could be compelled to furnish personal services" when the "national public interest" demanded it, despite a constitutional ban on forced, unremunerated labor.[71] Some legislators condemned this underhanded effort to legitimize forced impressment and elevate "abuse to the rank of law." The majority voted for the unconstitutional edicts.[72] For all the statesmen's qualms, Mexican armies had been and would be, for the most part, put together through forced impressment. This explains their precarity and the way they grew and shrank, as men were forcefully marched onto the battlefield but left to scatter after the fight. It also sheds light on why irregular warfare played such an important role during this violent decade.

After the Cinco de Mayo victory and until late 1866, the Mexican armies' successes in formal battle were few and far between. Nonetheless, the resilient bands of armed men who hassled interventionist forces, local authorities, and regular citizens made pacification and the regular operation of the imperial government impossible, outside of the central highlands and the road from Veracruz to Mexico City, which, despite being heavily guarded, was sometimes disturbed by murderous assaults on stagecoaches.[73] Many military commanders complained about the ignorance and lack of discipline of irregular forces, and condemned their unruly—and sometimes criminal—behavior. Other republicans saw in "the guerrilla system" the promise of final—if far-off—victory. Far removed from the battlefields, diplomat Jesús Terán insisted that guerrillas inevitably spelled defeat for would-be conquerors. Irregular forces were all the more "frightening" in that their power was "never revealed": they won "by virtue of losing." The enemy trusted triumph was around the corner until "slow exhaustion and annihilation" revealed his impotence.[74] If the striking, fearsome, and celebrated *chinacos* did not crush the enemy or tear the empire down, they did cripple its foundations and make its predominance impossible.

Soldiers into Citizens

In November 1866, after winning the battles of La Carbonera and Miahuatlán, general and future president Porfirio Díaz, commander of the Army of the East, hailed the "sons of the pueblo," who had taken up arms by "their own will" and "turned themselves into soldiers." They had resoundingly beat "the French, the Austrians, the Hungarians, and the Mexicans."[75] Díaz's a posteriori celebration of enthusiastic popular participation in battle—which, at the time, he had disparaged in his reports—runs through the patriotic narrative spun by the triumphant Liberals. On the ground, things were, as they always are, more complex. In Mexico and the United States, men fought for a myriad of reasons, and governments-at-war could not rely on patriotism alone. As Héctor Strobel has written, civilians did not "turn themselves into soldiers": they were aggressively driven to fight by recruiters, commanders, the heat of battle, and—not particularly successfully—the law.

Conscription laws were the product of urgent military necessity. They also speak to lawmakers' potent, often contradictory visions of the national polity, and to equal citizenship conceived as a source of rights and duties. These notions were severely strained by war. Even if they were unevenly executed on the ground, baroque statutes meant to create armies signaled an important transformation of political imagination and of the relationship between the national state and its citizens. Civic virtue played a smaller part than expected in building the awesome war machines of what have been described as "modern wars." Local dynamics remained decisive on both sides of the Río Bravo. In the divided northern republic, the draft provoked resistance and anger rather than orderly recruitment. In Mexico, it was the much-maligned leva that got most men to the front. This, according to a French observer who was shocked that there was no operative conscription law in Mexico, led to desertion "at the first opportunity": forced recruits lacked "enthusiasm, military spirit, and any hope of seeing their miserable condition change."[76]

This onlooker was only half right. Men, even when forcefully sent to the front, could still fight bravely, for honor and love of country, for God and political ideals. They were sometimes motivated by passions less lofty, but perhaps more pressing: in the town of Mascota, perched in the western mountains over the Pacific, for example, young women "promised their hand in marriage as a prize to those who took up arms to defend religion." In contrast, those who shirked their duties as Catholics would feel "their everlasting disdain."[77] Soldiers spoke of solidarity and of defense of community. They also took up arms in pursuit of self-interest, driven by a thirst for adventure, a surfeit of necessities, or a dearth of options. Disparate and evolving feelings and incentives moved men to march off to the long, unpredictable wars of the 1850s and 1860s. James McPherson recorded how the sentiments among Union soldiers often changed, sometimes following intricate patterns that mirrored the war's developments.[78] The same can be said for the Mexican experience. When Puebla fell in May 1863, almost exactly a year after its brilliant defense, not one of the 1,400 Mexican officers accepted the amnesty extended by Forey to those who would lay down their arms. To do so would "diminish the dignity of military honor" and contradict "their convictions and personal opinions."[79] Over 500 were taken to France as prisoners of war. As they marched to Veracruz, they sang "La Marseillaise," the French revolutionary anthem that had been banned by Napoléon III.[80]

Enthusiastic displays of martial honor were not reserved to the officer corps. In recent decades, historians have revealed the valor and steadfastness of the members of the National Guard contingents organized in the small, rural, mostly Indigenous communities of the mountainous regions of Puebla, Oaxaca, and Guerrero, who flew to the Liberals' side.[81] Intense convictions and similar emotions moved the men who fought as Conservatives in Nayarit, Querétaro's Sierra Gorda, and Oaxaca's Mixteca Baja.[82] There was more to these mobilizations than patriotism, or devotion to vernacular versions of national ideologies. The intransigent violence of wars with uncertain outcomes drove men and women on the ground to collaborate with, as Stathis Kalyvas has written, "the political actor that best [guaranteed] their survival."[83] Hostile relations with surrounding haciendas or intervillage rivalries could push a community into one camp and not the other. In the aftermath of war, military support could be leveraged into respect for the pueblo's autonomy and protection of its political, material, and spiritual resources.

Local tensions and hierarchies, economic inequality, group rivalries, and social pressures, along with political convictions, shaped, and sometimes determined, responses to war.[84] They probably explain why approximately 100,000 natives of Confederate states served in the Union army.[85] Sometimes, circumstances and not structural dynamics were at play: an individual could be in the wrong place at the wrong time; the insult, mistreatment, or death of a loved one could turn a perpetrator into an enemy; an accusation of cowardice could push the indifferent into taking sides.[86] In turbulent times, support for a cause would hardly be set in stone: Héctor Strobel has meticulously documented how peasant communities in Guerrero, Michoacán, Puebla, the State of Mexico, Jalisco, and Querétaro who took up arms in 1854 and 1855 against the Santa Anna government to secure their access to land and water and lower taxes and religious tithes rallied to the defense of religion in 1858, in part out of frustration.[87] Reversals of position, individual and collective, were a common feature throughout the war.

Motives for taking up arms—or trying to stay home, deserting, or switching sides—were, then, extremely diverse. Nonetheless, debates, laws, and patriotic discourse to promote and secure mobilization recast society's imagination. Wars that asked so much of so many inevitably molded the way people thought of soldiers and of their place in society. They also challenged the roles women played, as wives, mothers, and sisters of soldiers, and also, if controversially, as patriots in their own right. At mid-century, servicemen—often poor, rootless men—were, in both republics, objects of derision, contempt, and fear. In the United States, in the early days of the war, swaggering militiamen from the South scoffed at the North's "hirelings" and foreign "mercenaries" who "enlisted for the pay."[88] The undercurrent of hostility against men-at-arms was perhaps stronger in Mexico, where the armed forces were visible, disruptive, and costly. The Mexican Army had proved undisciplined and inefficient in its defense of the nation—it was thought to be responsible, in great part, for the loss of half of the nation's territory—but proficient when stoking division among countrymen.

Sentiment and perceptions changed as war swept up sons, husbands, and brothers. In the United States, recruiting posters called on "good men and true." "Mechanics and working men" who were "patriotic," "sober, reliable and able bodied," should "rally" to serve their country, to fight for Liberty and the Union, to "avoid the draft."[89] Soldiers were flatteringly portrayed in illustrated magazines, their dignified martial air and valiant deaths immortalized in prose, verse, and image. Julia Howe's "Battle Hymn of the Republic" exalted the heroes who would "die to make men free." In Union and Confederate states, people suspended their mistrust of standing armies, which had led most state constitutions to ban all "soldier[s], seam[e]n, marine[s]" from the ballot box. Most Civil War legislatures not only recognized recruits' right to vote but allowed them to cast their ballots from the field. Southern lawmakers did so almost immediately, as they drafted their "new" constitutions after secession in seven states. Northern state congresses followed suit, if more haphazardly, as some Peace Democrats resisted this "revolutionary" innovation.[90]

In the Union states, the soldiers' vote—and its "controlling influence upon the home vote"—was seen, "like the bullet or the bayonet," as another instrument to "destroy the Southern rebellion."[91] Once the Emancipation Proclamation transformed the Union's fight into a war against slavery, it put an end to many soldiers' ambivalence about what their mission was: to break, in the eloquent words of a sergeant in the 107th US Colored Infantry, "the chain and exclaim 'Freedom for all!'"[92] As members of massive armies, both fighting for "Liberty" dissimilarly interpreted, Confederate and Union soldiers had become the republic's ideal citizens, construed as such not only by their rights but by the sacred duties they fulfilled.[93] The nation was in their debt.

Mexico's institutional weaknesses and the turmoil brought on by war makes it more difficult to trace a shift in conceptions of citizenship and military service in law. But literature and art speak to the efforts of the Liberal intelligentsia to redeem the common soldier. In the popular novels of Ignacio Manuel Altamirano and Juan A. Mateos, young men of humble origins, moved by patriotism to join the fight against the Conservatives and the French invaders, become gallant soldiers, pillars of a nation delivered from darkness by its heroes . . . even when betrayed by women's faithlessness.[94] The dignified, disciplined, and stoic soldiers of painter Primitivo Miranda or engraver Casimiro Castro stand in sharp contrast to the vulgar, slovenly, drunk, and abusive soldiers that Agustín Arrieta painted in the 1850s. The image of valiant chinacos countered the ubiquitous disdain for *el vulgo* (the populace) displayed by members of the elite, even those claiming to defend "the people."[95] During the French Intervention, satirical newspapers gleefully contrasted the foppish, effeminate, Frenchified traitors who swooned over Maximilian with the manly, plain-speaking, leather-clad men of humble origins who had taken up arms to fight against the Austrian's ridiculous regime.[96]

War was a man's business, but it discomfited the lives of women. In both divided republics, family units were also, in most cases, units of production: if torn apart by conscription, a family's well-being, sometimes even its survival, was imperiled. Women were pushed to assume the roles and responsibilities of those who had left. Some were forced come up with different strategies to get by, which included recasting their relationship to the governments that had taken the men away, as did the South's "soldiers' wives" and, less dramatically, the women who, on both sides of the border, claimed a pension for the sacrifice of their loved ones.[97] Women also followed men into the field.

José Agustín Arrieta, *El requiebro* (Flirtation), c. 1850. The painter captures a soldier's clearly unwelcome amorous advance. Courtesy of Wikimedia Commons.

For the duration of the war, and sometimes beyond it, women managed farms and plantations, worked the land, took care of the account books, drove goods to market, supplied contending armies, went to work in factories—for wages consistently lower than men's—and made arms, uniforms, and other war provisions.[98] In Mexico City, Empress Carlota also took her husband's place when he left, not for the front but to take the empire to its subjects in the countryside.[99] By most accounts, she ruled competently as regent, the first woman to do so in Mexican history.[100] Gender plotted the ways women stepped up to serve in the nation's momentous ordeal, even as emergency loosened some of these boundaries.[101]

Casmiro Castro, *Chinacos during the Reform War*, 1855. Castro paints a flattering picture of the Pintos, the feared militia men of southern Mexico. C. Castro, G. Rodríguez, and J. Campillo, "Trajes mexicanos, soldados del Sur," 1855, in *México y sus alrededores:* Colección de vistas monumentales, paisajes y trajes del país; Dibujados al natural y litografiados por los artistas mexicanos. Mexico City: V. Debray, 1869. Courtesy of New York Public Library.

Like all nineteenth-century military outfits, North America's civil war armies included women camp followers, who were often related to soldiers and performed various tasks, as nurses, sutlers, laundresses and seamstresses, wives, partners, and prostitutes. In the Disunited States, the shocking human costs of the war led to the increase and formalization of women's presence close to the battlefield. Several thousand joined the war effort to tend to the sick and wounded. Female nurses, in the words of Victoria L. Holder, went from doctors' "hand maiden to right hand," and women like Dorotea Dix, Clara Barton, Mary Livermore, and members of religious orders such as the Sisters of Mercy displayed remarkable administrative and leadership skills in running hospitals and relief agencies.[102]

Observers were often shocked at the number of women—of "whole families"— who followed Mexican armies, mounted or on foot, "with a child in front / . . . a parrot on her shoulder / and a squirrel hanging at her side."[103] These "armies of women" speak to both the poverty of the households that soldiers came from and the precariousness of Mexican military institutions: armies were unable to provide basic services such as the provision and preparation of food, cleaning and repairing clothing, and caring for the sick and wounded. It was the *soldaderas* who took up the slack.[104] Tortillas also made women's presence indispensable. As the Mexicans' staple food, their plate and spoon, tortillas had to be made daily, and this labor-intensive and time-consuming task could only be performed by women.[105] Mexican women's labor among men-at-arms, then, was a mark of continuity rather than the product of exceptional times.

North America's mid-century wars mobilized whole societies. Most women contributed to the war effort by supporting fighting men—most often those to which they were attached by the bonds of family. But the language of civil war, the glorification of a higher cause, and the reinvention of the nation pulled them into the public realm. In both republics, before hostilities broke out, predicaments had already led some women to trespass into the realm of men and engage with politics. Feminine support for certain causes (Indian removal, abolition, and women's suffrage in the United States; the defense of Catholicism in Mexico) was brandished, on both sides of the border, as a reason to ignore, condemn, or dismiss them.[106] When the war came, women were expected to support the most public of causes, but their patriotism had to follow the script of womanly virtue. In Mexico, the wives of prominent politicians—Liberal and Conservative—raised funds for "Blood hospitals," rolled bandages, sent provisions to the front, and visited wounded soldiers. In the United States young women's wearing mourning—or not—became a way to express devotion to the cause, while in Mexico they put red or green bows in their hair to signal their political position. Others capitalized instead on their allegedly apolitical nature to move between adversaries and to trade with armed men of all affiliations, as many served as spies and informants.[107]

A small number of women bucked the limitations of gender by posing as men and joining the army: over 400 women fought as soldiers in the US Civil War.[108] Like the men in their families, they joined for a variety of reasons: so as not to stay behind, to earn more money, and for love of family, comrades, country, and cause.[109] In Mexico, a few women, derisively called *barraganas* (concubines) fought against the European invaders, usually at the side of their life partners. One of the war's heroines was aristocratic Ignacia Reichy, a Guadalajara native who served in the Western Army and displayed remarkable skills in combat and command.[110] According to Liberal lore, this "romantic" and "nervous" heroine, who had stared down "the world's best soldiers," shot herself through the heart in 1866 after hearing a fellow officer's joke about her making yarn and keeping house.[111]

In 1890, radical Mexico City journalist Daniel Cabrera published a handsome illustrated volume that told the life histories of those who had contributed to "the triumph of democratic institutions" during the nation's mid-century trials. These literary "crowns of laurel," meant to honor the "champions of liberty," referred to over sixty men and four women: the wives of two Liberal luminaries, Margarita

Maza de Juárez and the wife of Gen. Nicolás Régules, who had "suffered their in no ways small part of calvary" with a smile; Agustina Ramírez, a poor woman from Sinaloa who had lost her husband and twelve of her thirteen sons to the defense of the republic, which they had taken up at her behest; and Ignacia Reichy, the heroic, ruthless, but suicidal female soldier.[112] Expressions of women's patriotism and sacrifice—like those of transvestite "distaff soldiers" north of the border—that came unmoored from expectations of domesticity, complementarity, and feminine virtue kindled unease. At the heart of this apprehension lay not only disapproval of their unseemly behavior but also concern that it might forge a relationship between women, politics, and the state unmediated by men. In the midst of a war that changed so many things, martial masculinity and the idealization of ancillary feminine sacrifice show how these conflagrations shifted, but did not break, the ways gender was construed.

WORDS AND PICTURES painted heroic peoples fighting in the most momentous of national conflicts and dying for the most sacred of causes. These powerful images papered over the complexities, tensions, failures, and contradictions that characterized these massive mobilizations. The wars' numbers were appalling: there were an estimated 1.5 million casualties of the US Civil War—620,000 dead, 476,000 wounded, and 400,000 captured or missing. Of the men who left to fight the war, approximately one in four did not come home.[113] There are no reliable statistics for the Mexican conflicts: Will Fowler surmises there were between 100 and 200 dead at each of the seventy-one formal battles of the Reform War, which yields between 7,100 and 14,200 combatant casualties, without taking into account civilians, in a war during which large cities like Puebla, Guadalajara, and Veracruz were repeatedly besieged. In 1867, former Liberal congressman Basilio Pérez Gallardo painstakingly reconstructed the number of dead, wounded, and captured republican soldiers from officer reports of 1,020 actions of war. His *Martyrology* concluded that 31,962 "defenders of Independence" had died and 8,304 had been wounded. The number of fatalities, which is surely underestimated, is almost equivalent to that of the troops who came with the French Expeditionary Army.[114]

These basic statistics, their lacunae and errors, speak to the transformation of the relationship between the state and society and to the different capacities of those involved in these cruel trials by combat. Casualty lists, seventy-three national cemeteries, and the publication and subsequent revision of documents like the *Final Report of the Provost Marshal General to the Secretary of War* (1866) and the 128 volumes of the *Official Records of the War of the Rebellion* (1880–1901) tell of Union authorities' assuming the responsibility of informing soldiers' families, recording the fate of fighting men, and honoring the fallen. They are also proof of the state's bureaucratic competence to fulfill these novel duties.[115] The creation of Southern memorial associations, Confederate graveyards, and the Southern Historical Association's efforts to account for Confederate losses stand as evidence of the same sense of obligation to those who sacrificed for the cause, but, like Basilio Pérez Gallardo's book of martyrs, whose data were compiled not in military archives but from the enemy's official publication, *El Diario del Imperio*, they speak not only to their patriotic commitment but also to the dearth of administrative capabilities to back it up.[116]

Money Is Always the Issue: Taxing for War

In the treatise that is most often cited to associate Machiavelli with unscrupulous politics, the Florentine famously quipped that men would "sooner forget the death of their father than the loss of their patrimony."[117] In North America at mid-century, those charged with managing the war effort were put in an untenable position: national calamity required the sacrifice of both life and purse. Mustering material resources for such long, unforgiving armed conflicts proved a daunting task, whose complexities were also compounded by republican strictures and the practices for determining and collecting public revenue that had developed in the New World. In both Mexico and the United States, embattled governments-at-war had to navigate the premises, expectations, and mechanisms of peculiar fiscal systems.

The Sinews of the State: Paying to Keep Up the Fight

When the nation splintered and war came—to Mexico in January 1858, to the United States in April 1861—contending governments anticipated a short conflict and saw no reason to abandon their familiar fiscal scripts. They planned to rely on tariffs, debt, and, only if need be, taxes. In the case of Mexican governments, the term *plan* is a euphemism: past experience did not bode well for their possibilities of obtaining either credit or additional levies. When Conservative general Félix Zuloaga toppled President Comonfort in January 1858, Mexico's constitutionalist administration fled Mexico City and gave up its de facto government status. This weakened its legitimacy on the international stage and downgraded its already flimsy creditworthiness. But by establishing its base in the Liberal port city of Veracruz, the nation's point of entry for the bulk of the Atlantic trade, the Juárez government secured access to the tariffs paid by the ports' traders, the most productive and reliable source of federal income throughout the nineteenth century. What was seen as a sign of weakness throughout the war surely contributed to the Liberals' victory in 1860.

In the Disunited States, both the Union and Confederate Congresses broke with precedent—and, in the case of Southerners, with entrenched convictions—

to raise tariffs on foreign trade. In 1860, even before hostilities broke out, the Republican majority in Congress voted for a moderate increase in duties on imported goods, which had been steadily declining since the protectionist schedules of the late 1820s incensed Southerners. Lawmakers tried to compensate for their regressive nature by establishing a low rate—10 percent—on goods deemed "necessary to most consumers."[118] After the shocking Union defeat at Bull Run, only thirty miles from Washington (July 1861), Congress raised tariffs on these products—sugar, tea, and coffee—despite the unpopularity of the measure.[119]

In Montgomery, and then in Richmond, Confederate lawmakers overcame their distaste for tariffs. In March 1861, they voted a 15 percent levy on various imported goods. In May, Congress expanded the list of taxable items and established differential rates of between 5 percent—on articles for dyeing and tanning, including indigo, unmanufactured metals (brass, copper, tin ore, zinc, spelter), unset gems, gums, and rubber—and 25 percent—on, among others, alabaster, fish preserved in oil, confectionary, precious woods, wines, cigars, and snuff. Other products could enter the Confederacy duty free: books, scientific apparatuses and specimens, works of art, coin and bullion, garden seeds, meats and grains, gunpowder, lead, arms, and ships paid no duty.[120]

The tariff schedule's gradations and exemptions reflected congressmen's concerns about their overwhelmingly agricultural economy's war capabilities, but also their aspirations—modeled on previous state policies—to promote education and discourage bad habits among the citizens of a virtuous new nation. Southern aversion to taxing imported goods relaxed, but Confederates doubled down on their belief that cotton's importance to the global economy strengthened their hand on the international stage. They believed withholding cotton from the European market would force the Old World powers to recognize their new nation. Consequently, in February 1861, Congress imposed an export duty on raw cotton, despite this type of excise being anathema to states growing agricultural commodities for sale abroad.[121] Two years later, a similar toll was levied on cotton and tobacco, if it was exported to countries that had not acknowledged the Confederacy as a sovereign state.

The Confederacy's diplomatic and economic strategies had no success. British and French industry had stockpiled cotton, lessening the impact of the collapse of Southern exports in 1862. Furthermore, the Union blockade of Southern ports, ordered by Lincoln in April 1861, and the fall of New Orleans in May 1862 made these fiscal innovations practically irrelevant, except for the cotton exported from the Mexican bank of the Río Bravo.[122] Mexican governments operated under even more harrowing circumstances. They dared not tinker with tariff schedules but lowered excises on the internal circulation of goods in order to mitigate the "heavy burden" of war on "the needy classes." "Essential" goods—rice, chiles, beans, flour, salt, lard, pigs, cows and calves, wood and coal—paid no taxes and could be introduced into cities even if they were under siege.[123]

THE YEAR BEFORE THE WAR, the relatively small, inconspicuous US government had spent $63 million. By 1865, the Union-at-war was spending as much every twenty days.[124] In response to the unprecedented and persistent spike in government spending, Washington and Richmond contracted loans, in the hope of avoiding the irritating effect of taxation. For all North American contenders, borrowing money to fight proved a vital—if not equally productive—instrument to finance the war. In the Mexican case, government frailty and precarity, coupled with the urgencies of war, distorted credit markets and even the meaning of words. "Loan," usually qualified with the adjective "forced," became a stand-in for confiscation. With public debt bonds priced at between 2 and 3 percent of their value on the open market, authorities—Conservative and constitutionalist, imperial and republican—repeatedly threatened those unwilling to lend them money with prison, impoundment, or confiscation.[125]

In May 1858, the Zuloaga government attempted to extract money from Mexico City's foreign residents, in violation of the law of nations and despite serious diplomatic repercussions.[126] The church, because of its wealth and territorial presence, was preyed upon by both its enemies and defenders. Until the nationalization law of June 1859, it probably suffered more in the hands of the latter: Conservatives siphoned off its cash in the form of loans that would never be repaid and used ecclesiastical property as collateral for credit. Troops, regardless of their political affiliation, set up barracks in church buildings and stole, melted down, or sold church bells and liturgical "sacred vessels." The church, argues Jan Bazant, land-rich but cash-poor, having for centuries played an important, often stabilizing role in the viceroyalty's and then Mexican credit market, became an insolvent institution.[127]

Possibilities for credit became increasingly scarce and demanding. Urgency justified intemperate practices on the field; force proved less futile than legislation. Mexican officers impressed goods, demanded money, and occupied buildings. They had little choice but to allow their dismally equipped, irregularly paid, and insufficiently fed troops to plunder occupied territory.[128] Beleaguered political and military authorities engaged in increasingly desperate measures. Under growing pressure, Zuloaga's government delivered bonds worth 15 million pesos to Juan Bautista Jecker between October 1859 and March 1860. In exchange, it received not quite 620,000 pesos in cash, 368,000 pesos in clothing, and almost 790,000 in older public debt bonds.[129] After the Conservatives' defeat, the Swiss-born Jecker, a longtime Mexico City resident, relied on his friendship with Napoléon III's illegitimate half-brother, the influential duc de Morny, to become a French citizen and include what the Liberal government deemed an "absolutely illegal transaction" in the long list of French claims against the Mexican state.

As the third year of the war dragged on, Liberals and Conservatives frantically and ineffectually sought fresh funds. In September, "political considerations" overwhelmed the "delicacy and moral duties" of constitutionalist commander Santos Degollado. Because Liberal forces needed "strictly to survive," he ordered the "occupation" of over a million pesos, belonging to foreign and Mexican merchants, deposited in the hacienda of Laguna Seca in San Luis Potosí, while it waited for safe transport to Veracruz.[130] In November, Conservative general Leonardo Márquez, allegedly acting under direct orders from "General-in-Chief"—and then-president—Miramón, "subtracted" the "Mexican funds"—660,000 pesos—deposited in the British Legation in Mexico City.[131]

In 1861, because of his financial acumen and despite his recent indictment for crimes against the nation, Manuel Payno was charged with tracing, registering, and crunching the numbers on the "damages caused by revolution" that had prompted diplomatic complaints. The war and its imperatives, argued a despondent Payno, had forced Mexican authorities to violate their most sacred duty: the protection of property. The administration had to compensate those whose rights had been violated. It recognized 493 claims, with indemnities that amounted to over 1.2 million pesos.[132] The armed struggle over the 1857 constitution left behind death, destruction, financial mayhem, and a bewildering trail of receipts, recycled government bonds, promissory notes, and IOUs.

ON THE OTHER SIDE of the Río Bravo, governments steeled themselves for violent confrontation by borrowing money. Unlike their neighbors to the south, they enjoyed the luxury of not factoring inevitable catastrophe into their calculus. They believed there would be plenty of people willing to lend them money. Even before the war started, the Confederate Congress voted to place a $15 million loan, in February 1861, guaranteed by the—soon to become inoperative—export duty on raw cotton.[133] In the summer of 1861, the Union's secretary of the treasury, Salmon P. Chase, asked Congress to authorize three separate loans, for a total of $240 million, to be offered to domestic and foreign investors.[134] Between the spring of 1863 and that of 1865, the sale of interest-bearing bonds financed the brunt of the war, covering between 65 and 75 percent of the Union's federal expenses.[135] Conversely, the Confederacy obtained 54 percent of its revenue from non-interest-bearing bonds and approximately 36 percent from other forms of debt.[136] By 1865, the US national debt had increased from $90 million in 1861 to $2.7 billion: from 2 percent of gross national product to 15 percent, a proportion it would not reach again until the last decades of the twentieth century.[137] The duration and outrageous costs of North America's civil wars and the difficulties faced by contending governments forced them to explore some untried, even objectionable, alternatives for payment.

Uncharted Waters

Foreign credit played an important part in the economic life of the United States: between 1852 and 1869, nearly half of its public debt was held overseas, principally in Great Britain. It made sense for the embattled Union and Confederate administrations to look abroad for financial relief. Nonetheless, during the better part of the 1850s, the sectional dispute cooled the market for US bonds, and 1860 unleashed a panic in the stock exchange whose origins were, according to *The Economist*, "wholly political."[138] Given the cautious withdrawal of British investors, the Union's projected 1861 European loan did not materialize. At the same time, secession and the French sponsorship of Mexico's monarchical experiment distorted the transatlantic market for North American debt. While uncertainty and violent upheaval increased investors' risks, the remarkable geopolitical shift appeared to open new opportunities. The two governments that lacked a credit record—the Confederacy and Mexico's Second Empire—attracted the interest of some European investors, prompted, perhaps, by political incentives rather than market signals.

Most Confederate bonds were bought by foreign investors, and Confederate agents successfully floated a loan in Europe in 1863, through the firm of Émile d'Erlanger, with £5,000,000 in bonds redeemable in cotton. It was oversubscribed five times, and produced £1,759,894 for the CSA to spend on desperately needed war matériel. John Slidell even dubbed its success the "financial recognition of our independence." Nonetheless, the enthusiasm inspired by this operation was short-lived, as the near-impossibility of exchanging these bonds for cotton became evident—it required twice running the Union blockade to retrieve and transport cotton across the Atlantic. The bonds' price plunged.[139]

The Mexican government had been unable to obtain fresh European capital since it defaulted on its 1820s London loans. Republican efforts to drum up resources or buy arms and equipment in the United States on credit largely failed, with the exception of the two shipments negotiated in 1866 and 1865 by José María Carvajal and Matías Romero, respectively, for 2 million pesos in all. Dire market conditions forced other Mexican agents into deals that were so "abusive and disastrous" that the republic's minister in Washington had to intervene to stop and repudiate them.[140] Conversely, during the first year of Maximilian's reign, French and British bankers—who hoped to leverage their management of the loan into a concession for establishing Mexico's first commercial bank—vied with each other to place Mexican bonds in European markets.

Buyers—almost 70,000—in London and Brussels, but mostly in Paris, paid over 100 million pesos for Mexican Empire bonds. Most of this capital went to cover the costs of the French Expeditionary Army; Mexico's imperial government received less than 6.5 million pesos. Maximilian's *petits bleus* ("little blue" bonds) turned out to be a very unsound investment: their holders were not able to cash in on this venture until the 1900s, after arduous negotiations.[141] Perhaps popular but deluded visions of "white gold" and other fabulous New World riches, coupled with a misplaced faith in France's civilizational and modernizing influence, drove small investors to bet on the Confederacy and Maximilian's regime, to their later chagrin.[142]

In contrast, the Union raised almost $2 billion. Its war debt was remarkable, not only for its size but because it was sold, almost exclusively, on the domestic market. In late 1862, Chase insisted that the product of the first loans be deposited in specie in federal subtreasuries, which depleted bank reserves as the deficit ballooned and financial crisis loomed. In response to bankers' outcry, the federal government distanced itself from traditional creditors, established a national banking scheme (February 1863), and issued a large number of bonds that were aggressively marketed—with a diligent, persuasive Jay Cooke leading the charge—directly to regular people in Union states. Buying government bonds became part of the war effort. Treasury bills were sold as badges of patriotism. Significantly, these financial operations transformed the Union's citizens into its stakeholders.[143]

The monetary toll of war was massive: the classic account of the cost of the US Civil War puts government expenditures and the value of destroyed human and physical capital in the Union and the Confederacy at almost $6.7 billion.[144] When in 1868 Manuel Payno had to assess the financial "damages" caused by foreign war, he estimated that the military costs of the imperial adventure amounted to almost 65 million pesos, even without taking into account the death, suffering, and destruction that befell the nation between 1862 and 1867 or the imperial couple's frivolous expenses. The national debt, which in 1861, after forty years of stormy independence, came to 184 million pesos, had reached 350 million by 1865.[145]

For all the governments involved, adjusting tariff schedules and increasing public debt—even in the case of the Union's pathbreaking success—proved woefully inadequate to cover the massive demands of war. Contending governments reached for mechanisms that had previously not been part of North America's fiscal toolbox, either because of the political risks they implied, the material obstacles to their implementation, or their questionable legality: taxes, paper money, and expropriation without appropriate compensation. We know that Lincoln and Juárez, who would lead the republic to victory, engaged in radical intervention in the economy: the former abolished slavery; the latter nationalized church wealth. However, for all their "great political results," these momentous, revolutionary strokes did not bolster the capacities of the fiscal state.[146]

Confiscation by presidential decree was a repudiation of the liberal principles that allegedly stood at the center of modern taxation. Direct taxes, in contrast, were its true embodiment, in particular when levied on property, which grounded extraction in "equality, uniformity and proportionality" and the consent of the people's representatives. Moreover, in the words of republican secretary of the treasury José María Mata, "when citizens can feel how much the government costs them, they become interested in knowing what it spends their money on, and why."[147] Nevertheless, North America's federal governments had stayed away from direct taxation for almost half a century. In the face of war, beleaguered treasuries tried to implement direct contributions, if with little cause for optimism.

In 1861, and despite their discouraging past experience, Mexico's triumphant Liberals sought "a complete divorce with the past" in matters fiscal and financial.[148] As soon as the Juárez government returned to Mexico City, it legislated ambivalently to both palliate the ills of a troubled present and secure a brighter future. In February, it decreed all alcabalas would be abolished on January 1, 1862. It passed a law that established wide-ranging federal levies on varied incarnations of property: it taxed urban and rural real estate, mortgages, patents on commercial and industrial establishments, and licenses for tradesmen and professionals. In April, the cumbersome, regressive tolls paid on roadways were replaced with increased property taxes on rural properties, since it was their owners who would most benefit from safe and efficient ground transportation.[149]

Although the situation of the nation's coffers was desperate, Juárez's young, radical secretary argued that the solution was actually simple: law needed to replace "chaos." Then "order would follow confusion, economy would replace extravagance, and morality would displace waste." Order, virtue, and morality would heal the nation's financial woes. Liberal hopes in metaphysical virtue would soon be dashed. The tangled state of public finances resisted all systematization, and new levies, despite being in "harmony with universally recognized economic principles," produced no revenue.[150] The Juárez government, furnished with the most meager of resources, had to deal with Conservative violence, growing pressures from creditors, and the threat of foreign war. To face this crisis, the president was invested with the "broadest powers." Once again, the Mexican federal government would try to rely on extraordinary, illiberal, and arbitrary excises.

The Juárez administration decreed a tax on capital, four times; it ordered the collection of a general contribution meant to involve, "more or less directly," all the republic's inhabitants. It also mandated a one-time, "personal contribution" of 100 pesos, to be collected by state governors, who were free to determine who had to pay this substantial amount, foreigners excepted. When the foreign occupation of Veracruz blocked its access to the product of tariffs on imported goods, the government doubled the capital's alcabala fees and all direct contributions; it resurrected the colonial duty on stamped paper and imposed a federal tax on the local consumption of cotton.[151] None of these aggressive, controversial measures prevented "bankruptcy." In July 1861, with the republic's survival at stake, Congress voted to interrupt payments to foreign debtors. This law, which meant to allow the beleaguered republic to take a breath, set off a chain reaction in Europe, engineered by the ambitious emperor of the French, that resulted in armed intervention and the blockade of Mexican ports, aggravating the financial crisis.[152]

Three years later, in the midst of violence and upheaval, some perceived the French-sponsored ascension of a Hapsburg prince to a newfangled Mexican throne as an opportunity to put the fiscal house in order. The state of public finances screamed for intervention, but experience—as was proved by the Liberals' most recent efforts—suggested not much could be done. Moreover, even before Maximilian sat on the throne, the empire's financial situation was objectively more compromised than the republic's. At its inception, Maximilian's government assumed responsibility not only for the debt that the republic had struggled to pay but also for the costs of intervention. In the treaty the empire signed on April 1, 1864, the Hapsburg pledged to cover the French Army's expenses up to July of that year—54 million pesos at an interest rate of 3 percent a year—and, after that, 200 pesos a year for every soldier, plus 8,000 per ship, for the transatlantic transport of troops. The Mexican Empire had to turn over 13 million pesos immediately, from the loan floated on European markets, and then send 5 million a year in cash to cover these payments and "war expenditures in excess."[153]

Even with these obligations weighing down the newborn regime, imperialists thought they could place public finances on more solid ground. As Carlos Becerril Hernández has astutely observed, these statesmen juggled three different options: in matters of public revenue, its legislation, collection, administration, and disbursement, they could "repeal, reform, or innovate."[154] In July 1864, to set things off on the right note, the imperial government called on members of the "productive classes"—merchants, miners, planters, and industrialists—to elect representatives to the Treasury Commission, charged with overhauling Mexico's hobbled public finances.[155] The empire's initiative was predicated on the understanding that the new regime was strong, modern, reasonable, and impartial. Harsh reality would drastically circumscribe the reach of its proposals, in both their conception and execution.

While commissioners debated, the government introduced new tax laws. As others had, briefly, half-heartedly, and unsuccessfully before him, Maximilian turned to property: his administration attempted to improve the assessment of real estate values by creating local committees, made up of landowners and public servants. The imperial government also tried to make property taxes more progressive by levying dues on plots of land that it considered oversized, so as to encourage the sale of uncultivated land and the partition of large estates.[156] Landowners objected vehemently: the law was "ruinous" and "degrading." It was antieconomic: duties fell on capital, not its returns. It was inequitable: it intentionally harmed "a determinate class"—the one they belonged to.[157] In the face of their publicized indignant protest, these laws were immediately abrogated.

It soon became apparent that neither the government nor the Treasury Commission was willing to engage in thorough, necessarily contentious fiscal reform: given the state's precarious economic situation, innovations were "extremely dangerous." Best not disturb an old, complicated, rickety machine—even if it was obviously broken. Members of the commission argued candidly that customary taxes on the movement of goods had their advantages, since consumers protected both producers and the government. They paid the alcabala fee only when they had money to spend; if it upset them, they cursed at the hustling trader, not fiscal authorities.[158] Like the Liberal revolutionaries before them, imperialists appealed, just as unproductively, to "order" and "morality." They "legislated to organize" and tried to spend carefully, but did little else. Imperial tax policy turned into another ill-fated effort to improve the management of Mexico's disastrous public finances.[159]

NORTH OF THE BORDER, federal authorities in both the Confederacy and the Union were also wary of exasperating recalcitrant taxpayers. The Union government nevertheless broke out of its complacency as early as August 1861, driven, perhaps, by the jolt of defeat at Bull Run. In a special session, Congress approved a direct tax apportioned—as was mandated by the constitution—among the members of the Union. State war expenses could be offset against these payments to the federal treasury, with states contributing to federal expenses with no more than $5 million a year.[160] The Lincoln administration had to come up with new sources of income.

In 1862, Congress passed currency and tax laws that transformed the relationship between the previously distant and practically invisible federal government and its people. The Legal Tender Act (February 25, 1862) authorized the issue of $150 million in non-interest-bearing notes—the enduring greenbacks—receivable as "lawful money . . . in payment of all debts, public and private." As Max Edling has noted, what was revolutionary—and what many, Republicans included, found deeply disturbing—was not the emission of notes but the fact that public and private creditors were forced to accept them.[161] By war's end, the government had printed $250 million worth of greenbacks, which accounted for 18 percent of government revenue between 1861 and 1865.[162]

During the spring of 1862, Congress legislated the creation of a new federal tax system. In the words of Senator Justin Morrill, the exigencies of war drove his fellow citizens—temporarily—from their idyllic "untaxed garden" into a vigorously taxed reality, similar to that of other modern nation-states. Lawmakers skirted the constitutional restriction on federal direct taxation by conceiving levies on income as an indirect tax. They imposed a duty of 3 percent on revenue above $600, and a 5 percent levy on a second bracket whose income surpassed $10,000. This doubled the amount of taxes paid by the wealthiest residents of Union states. The law also created a 3 percent sales tax on manufacturers and the receipts of some corporations—including railroads—and levied excises on professional licenses and a broad variety of goods and services.

Until the end of the war, the Union Congress raised taxes every year: tariffs reached 47 percent, the sales tax rose to 6 percent and, by 1865, taxes on liquor had reached ten times the cost of production. Taxes on income grew from 3 to 5 percent, imposed on revenues between $600 and $5,000, 7.5 percent on the next bracket—up to $10,000—and 10 percent on incomes that exceeded that sum. Given the manpower required to assess and collect these moneys, the federal bureaucracy—which before the war had consisted basically of military and postal personnel—grew to unprecedented size. In the end, revenue from taxes covered 25 percent of the Union's costs of war.[163] The Union government had proved remarkably effective at financing the war. By making money that kept its value and by remaking its citizens into the nation's creditors and taxpayers, it mobilized and channeled the North's financial resources toward the war.

The same cannot be said for the Confederacy, whose empty coffers were, by the end of the war, both cause and effect of its looming defeat. In marshalling resources, the Confederate government, which had precociously instituted general conscription in February 1862, dragged its feet on raising revenue through taxes. Although in the summer of 1861 Congress voted a onetime half-a-percentage-point tax on property—broadly conceived to include not only real estate but securities, cattle, carriages, and even, for all its controversial nature, slaves—its collection was postponed for a year, and its product—$17 million—was woefully inadequate.[164] In July 1863, the CSA Congress voted a "tax in kind" provision law, which covered increasingly aggressive impressment and confiscations on the ground with the cloak of legality.[165]

During the first years of the war, then, income from taxes remained low. The Confederate Treasury relied instead on the emission of notes. One million dollars was issued in March 1861, $2 million in August. Congress then voted to authorize the emission of as many notes as were needed, up to $100 million. This cap was raised three times, to $218 million in October 1862. In March 1863, Congress authorized the emission of $50 million worth of notes per month, contributing to runaway inflation: by the mid-1863, prices had multiplied by thirteen. Monetary woes were compounded by military catastrophe, as prices rose sharply after defeat at Gettysburg and with the fall of Vicksburg and Atlanta. By the end of the war, the value of the Confederacy's currency was close to zero. These notes represented a third of the South's revenue.[166]

Despair drove the Confederate government to tax. Congress passed three increasingly aggressive laws in February and June 1864. They lay progressive rates on different types of capital: 5 percent on all property, including slaves, stocks, and monies; 10 percent on gold, silver, and jewels; and between 10 and 25 percent on profits. Despite a shrinking tax base, given the advance of the Union armies, Confederate authorities—unlike their Mexican counterparts—were surprisingly effective at collecting these monies, bringing in $118 million. But it was too little, too late: taxes paid only for 11 percent of the war's costs, and their increase in 1864 could not prop up the flailing CSA.[167]

THE NINETEENTH CENTURY has been consecrated as the century of nations and nationalism, of revolution, of devoted citizen-soldiers, of enthusiastic *levées-en-masse*. North America's civil wars reveal the fragility of these vivid images, their artificial nature: nations shattered, a republic became an empire, patriotism faltered, citizens dodged taxes, and soldiers deserted. Conflicts so long, so bloody, and so costly created similar challenges for the beleaguered governments fighting over the United States and Mexico. Despite different contexts, experiences, and access to resources, similar devices were deployed to respond to the challenges of crisis and war: laws were proclaimed to police loyalty, bid people to fast and pray, and compel them to fight and pay taxes. Public authorities demanded oaths be taken, shirked due process, forcefully drafted men into the army, and engaged in punitive dispossession.

Laws were wielded as weapons in these momentous contests, but it was their implementation and results, not their content and tone, that were significant. Many of the laws of war were not useful, some were counterproductive, and their effectiveness owed less to their nature and legitimacy than to the government's capacity to sustain and execute them over a significant length of time. It is in this arena, that of state power deployed, not conceived, that the North American civil war experiences diverge the most. It is also perhaps these differences that hold the key to deciphering the logic of victory and defeat. The Union government in Washington was able to build a war machine that outlasted that of the Confederacy.

At Appomattox, Grant provided three days' worth of rations to Lee's wretched and hungry soldiers.[168] During the next couple of years, the Union army circuitously furnished the bedraggled but hopeful Mexican republicans with arms and equipment. It effectively ended the war that had threatened the survival of the Union and contributed to shutting down the cycle of violence and foreign intervention that had plagued its southern neighbor for a decade. The capacity to extract, galvanize, and influence historical processes, even beyond its borders, revealed that the Union government had acquired the structure and muscle of the modern nation-state and the potential for regional predominance in North America. It would not irreversibly or automatically put them to use.

PART FOUR

PUTTING THE REPUBLIC BACK TOGETHER AGAIN

CHAPTER SEVEN

FROM WAR TO NORMALIZATION
North America Reconfigured

WHEN RICHMOND FELL to the Union army in early April 1865, Matías Romero, Mexico's extremely competent minister in Washington, was quick to inform his government. No other country, he declared, "would draw more advantages" from the end of the US Civil War than Mexico.[1] With the resounding defeat of disunion, Washington would abandon its cautious foreign policy, openly condemn European encroachment in the New World, and pressure Napoléon III into abandoning his nonsensical Mexican adventure. Romero's optimism was not entirely justified: diplomatic reflexes proved less swift and forceful than he expected. Relief did not come to the Mexican Republic until two years later. Nevertheless, the young envoy was right to sense that, through the ordeal of war—and in part due to his assertive diplomacy—Mexico's relations with its northern neighbor had grown closer, more complex, and more relevant.

The two North American republics emerged from crisis transformed. So did the ties that bound them. The bilateral relationship, shattered by war in 1846, had been rebuilt on the shallow foundations of Mexican vulnerability and US appetite for territorial expansion. Only five years after signing the Treaty of Guadalupe Hidalgo, mutual dissatisfaction drove the two countries to reassess the obligations and territorial limits it had set. Growing sectional tensions in the United States and civil war in Mexico (1858–60) strained relations and led to a diplomatic impasse, riddled by interventionism, the severance of relations, and negotiations marked by old grievances, innovative proposals, and threats of invasion. The massive, entangled conflagrations that broke out in the 1860s spurred both desperate initiatives and cautious strategies that eventually led to reimagining Mexico-US relations.

Other People's Troubles:
The Diplomacy of Leverage and Desperation

In 1847, as they embarked onto difficult negotiations with an enemy invader poised to take the nation's capital, Mexico's commissioners unrealistically demanded that the peace treaty stipulate the US motives for attacking another republic and then claiming a large part of its territory.² They did not get what they wanted. The northern colossus's war of conquest shattered many Mexican statesmen's faith in a republican New World order, structured by right and reason, not unthinking force.³ War represented a dramatic milestone in the history of US-Mexico relations, but it did not alter its basic grammar, which turned on asymmetry and US hunger for land, even as legislative support for expansion weakened in the midst of sectional disputes. The Treaty of Guadalupe Hidalgo brought about the end of war, but it proved an unwieldly instrument for dealing with the many problems that arose from vicinity and conflicting aspirations.

In the United States, some found the war's territorial gains inadequate, especially along the Sonora–New Mexico border, where the new boundary line interfered with a projected southern transcontinental railway line. With the excitement of California's gold rush and the United States now stretching from one ocean to another, establishing efficient and reliable communications between East and West became more important, heightening the intensity and political traction of investors' quarrels over intercontinental communications, particularly in Mexico's Isthmus of Tehuantepec. Moreover, the United States had proved incapable—or unwilling—of fulfilling its treaty obligations: it had not suppressed Indian raids in the borderlands, and neither federal nor state authorities seemed keen on stopping filibustering expeditions. In the fall of 1853, in the middle of renewed diplomatic negotiations, William Walker invaded first Sonora, then Baja California.⁴

James Gadsden's mission as minister to Mexico between 1853 and 1856 was to resolve these issues to the advantage of the United States. The Charleston native was quick to detect and exploit the Mexican government's weakness and financial distress. To pressure and intimidate, he called for the mobilization of US troops on the border and insisted on the immediate satisfaction of US citizens' claims. At the same time, he offered large indemnities and flexible schemes for payment as incentives for the sale of land. He negotiated a treaty that established a new territorial settlement and transferred over 88,000 square miles to the United States. The pilfering of Mexico's assets outraged the nation's public opinion and stumbled in the US Senate. In the midst of heated disagreements over the Kansas-Nebraska Act, a good number of senators reacted negatively to a treaty furthering Southerners' irresponsible and unchecked appetite for expansion. In the end, the agreement was ratified on June 29, 1854, but, for the only time in its history, the Senate reduced territorial gain to a third of what had been originally agreed upon the treaty's negotiators.⁵

For all the turbulence that attended his diplomatic endeavors, James Gadsden secured the Mesilla region (29,640 square miles) for the United States for $10,000. When the Ayutla rebellion broke out in April 1854, he undertook a further-reaching, more cunning strategy to bolster US ascendancy in the affairs of its next-door neighbor: he supported the insurrection against the government with whom he had successfully negotiated. He shared Mexican Liberals' enthusiasm for free trade, immigration, infrastructure, and the possibilities of establishing a US protectorate. Leaning into his brash, antagonistic style, the US minister disputed the government's blockade of Pacific ports and threatened military intervention. He delayed the Mesilla payments, sought his government's support for the insurgents, and, it was rumored, used legation funds to finance the rebellion.[6] But victory transformed rebels into government men, and Gadsden's involvement into unacceptable meddling. President Comonfort asked for his removal, given that his interference was "hampering" harmonious relations between the two countries. The pugnacious minister left Mexico City in the fall of 1856.[7]

As confrontation and factionalism grew on both sides of the border, politics increasingly plagued the republics' foreign policies and ensnared their diplomats' designs. From 1858 to 1861, with civil war and the menace of foreign invasion threatening Mexico's survival, the United States and its enterprising ministers saw in their neighbor's failed state an opportunity to further an agenda in which the "fixation" with acquiring more territory still held pride of place.[8] President Buchanan called for military intervention to prevent Mexico's further descent into "hopeless anarchy and imbecility," while Washington's ministers—John Forsyth Jr. (1856–58) and Robert M. McLane (1859–60)—tried but failed to lever the desperate need for funds by the Mexican governments-at-war into diplomatic and territorial gains for the United States.[9]

In January 1858, when the constitutional government fled the capital, John Forsyth followed convention and, like the rest of the diplomatic corps, stayed put and recognized Zuloaga's military dictatorship as Mexico's de facto government. He then set out to exploit its financial woes and contested legitimacy. Given the violence and disorder on the border—whose "unhappy state" justified, in Buchanan's opinion, the establishment of a "temporary" US protectorate—and the utter helplessness of Mexican authorities, Forsyth suggested the Mexico City government give up its abstract dominion over Baja California and parts of Sonora in exchange for a concrete, substantial influx of funds. The Zuloaga administration was emphatic in its refusal, which it made public through the Mexico City press: it could not redraw the nation's boundary lines when there was no representative assembly to validate such a momentous decision. Furthermore, for all its "advantages," the arrangement proposed by the US minister was detrimental to both the republic's "true interests" and its "good name."[10]

A disappointed Forsyth did not conceal his frustration and protested vigorously against the government's war policies. In May 1858, he decried the imposition of an emergency tax on all capital—including foreigners' property—and broke off diplomatic relations a month later. In December, in his message to Congress, President Buchanan recommended that the United States "employ military force in Mexico" to "redress the wrongs and protect the rights" of its citizens, "restore peace and order," and prevent European intrusion.[11] On the other side of the border, Mexico's Liberals and Conservatives sought to break the military quagmire by scoring points in the diplomatic arena.

Rival governments vied for international recognition to shore up their frail legitimacy. Both undertook risky negotiations and signed unfair treaties. Washington—like Madrid—sought to profit from diplomatic initiatives grounded in despair. The Buchanan administration broke with diplomatic tradition and practice: in 1859 it held out diplomatic recognition to the beleaguered rivals so as to bolster its negotiating leverage. Encouraged by the enthusiastic report sent by the special agent who had sounded out the constitutional government in Veracruz, Buchanan appointed free-trade champion Robert M. McLane to hammer out a new treaty with the southern neighbor. In early April 1959, the US envoy sat down with committed reformist Melchor Ocampo, Juárez's minister of foreign relations.

As they entered negotiations, the two parties had clear but flexible priorities. The United States hoped to buy Baja California; the Juárez administration wanted to establish a formal military alliance that would bind the signatories to intervene next door if "order" was disturbed or if the "legitimate government" asked its neighbor for support. According to McLane, it also refused "to cede a foot of territory, whatever might be the consequences."[12] Neither party got what it most wanted, but both secured part of their objectives. On December 14, the US diplomat and the Mexican minister signed the transit and commerce treaty that bears their names. It granted free passage through the Isthmus of Tehuantepec, "in perpetuity," to people and goods coming from the United States and authorized Washington to use force, if necessary, to protect the trans-isthmian route. To compensate Mexico for the loss of revenue from customs duties, the US government would pay its counterpart $4 million, of which half would be used to cover the claims of US citizens against the Mexican government. The treaty also gave US troops transit rights between Nogales—about sixty miles due south of Tucson—and the port of Guaymas on the Gulf of California, and from any point along the Río Bravo to the Pacific port of Mazatlán.

The treaty's commercial clauses meant to bring the two neighbors closer by exempting certain goods from the payment of duties. The impact of this innovation was to be rather modest, since it applied only to exchanges across the border—when the bulk of Mexican foreign trade went through its ports, and, overwhelmingly, through Veracruz—but the principles of reciprocity and free trade were set down as the foundations for a new relationship. The spirit of partnership was, however, blatantly contradicted by the authority granted to the US Congress, which could unilaterally set, review, and exempt the tariffs to be paid by goods entering Mexico and their exemptions.[13] McLane, who had not achieved his mission's central objective, nevertheless felt a sense of accomplishment: by sowing the seeds of "commercial intimacy between the two Republics," the agreement prepared "the way for admission of all Mexican States into our Union."[14]

The McLane–Ocampo Treaty was not a dramatic departure from previous arrangements; the transit rights conferred on the United States developed and diversified the Gadsden Purchase's concessions. The negotiators did, nevertheless, attach a convention to the treaty—an off-kilter version of the Mexican Liberals' vision of a republican defensive alliance—in which the parties agreed that the United States could intervene to fulfill the treaty's stipulations or to protect US citizens in war-torn Mexico. In the midst of a bloody, undecisive domestic conflict, this clause anticipated and justified Washington's armed intervention.[15] When, in the overheated atmosphere of war, the treaty was made public, it provoked a scandal that the Conservative government eagerly exploited. The agreement was denounced as illegal, because—paradoxically—that "farce called the constitutional government" lacked the authority to conduct foreign policy and had not followed constitutional precepts and submitted the treaty to Congress for ratification.

More important, argued the treaty's censors, the agreement mutilated Mexico's sovereignty and left it at the mercy of the Protestant, racist, slaveholding nation that had already swallowed up half its territory. The Mexico City government protested against a dangerous arrangement, "extracted from a defeated party." In an address to the nation, President Miramón condemned the faction that was willing to "sell the *Patria*'s integrity, honor, and security, in exchange for a despicable treaty that marks the forehead of those who signed it with the indelible seal of treason."[16] The document also sparked an incensed popular reaction: in towns large and small, *vecinos* and municipal authorities railed against the "demagogues" who meant to sell Mexicans off "as if they were humble and defenseless lambs" and destroy "our forefathers' beloved religion" for "a handful of coin."[17]

The treaty caused a commotion in Mexico because it allegedly gave outrageous advantages to an unfriendly power. When it was submitted to the Senate in January 1860, it was rejected. Its failure is often attributed to sectional confrontation; yet the debates surrounding ratification contradict simple dichotomous dynamics and instead display the complexities of the anxious politics that, in the fraught run-up to the 1860 election, engendered uncertainty, decomposition, and dispersion rather than clear-cut division. As Pearl T. Ponce has noted, ratification was not forthcoming—despite the best efforts of the Mexican minister in Washington—for a variety of reasons unrelated to opposition to Southern expansion: the off-putting hostility between two of the democracy's most conspicuous leaders, President Buchanan and Illinois's Stephen Douglas; concerns about the "erosion" of congressional authority in foreign policy and for the impact of this modest free trade agreement on more muscular commercial partners, who would demand most-favored-nation treatment; fears of getting sucked into the Mexican quagmire; and wariness in the face of the heated dispute among US companies over the Tehuantepec concession.[18]

In the end, all Republican senators voted against the treaty, but it was Democratic dissent—with five Democrats joining the opposition and thirteen, mostly from the South, not voting—that sealed its fate.[19] The treaty's advocates in the United States were defeated, and it seemed that the Veracruz government had made a risky gamble for naught. But the Juárez administration's aggressive US diplomacy had already delivered, although perhaps by no merit of its own. In March 1860, as two armed steamers purchased in Cuba by the Conservative government advanced toward the port, the constitutional government warned that "pirates" were approaching Veracruz. After a brief scuffle, two US ships captured the vessels and took them to New Orleans, where their crew was charged with piracy.

A few months later, the boats' officers and crew were found not guilty. The district court sentenced that, for all the "strong sympathies" that US ship commanders naturally felt for the Mexican government that was acknowledged by Washington, these did not justify their seizing vessels that were clearly not pirates but belonged to a "hostile faction" in a civil war. Maritime nations were required to observe the strictest neutrality in the face of such domestic disputes.[20] The Conservatives' vindication in a US court was useless: by then, the deed was done. The siege of Veracruz had failed. It is unclear if two hastily armed warships—one of which, until very recently, had been a mail packet—could have made much difference in a difficult military operation. But tangible military gains for the Liberals offset the smear of pandering to US interests. And in the end, for all the indignation that it triggered, the McLane–Ocampo Treaty never went into effect.[21]

North America Aflame: There Be Dragons

Relations between the Juárez and Buchanan administrations were fraught with tensions and danger, but this served the constitutionalists well. Thus, the election, in November 1860, of a Republican who had been a critic of the Mexican American War was greeted with optimism by Mexican Liberals. According to Matías Romero, who arrived in Washington in December 1859, Lincoln's presidency signaled that "new ideas" and "different politics" would replace the old: US relations with Mexico were about to undergo "radical change." Seward spoke to the young diplomat of the new "disinterested spirit," stripped of all ambition, that was to shape relations between their two countries.[22] The appointment of another outspoken opponent of the Mexican War, Thomas Corwin, as minister to the constitutional government recently reinstated in Mexico City was seen as another reason for optimism: the Ohioan was a welcome change from the Southern slaveholders who had historically held sway over the US legation in Mexico City.[23]

As Corwin made his way south in April 1861, however, dark skies hung over both North American republics. By this time, secession and war had broken up the United States, while the restoration of constitutional rule in Mexico faltered in the face of Conservative resistance, Liberal infighting, and the perennial lack of public funds. In the US minister's opinion, it was a moment of extraordinary danger: the US tribulations' overlapping of the crisis in Mexico made European intervention not only possible but likely, since creditor nations grumbled on the other side of the Atlantic and Conservative exiles plotted regime change in Mexico. Like his Mexican counterparts, Corwin saw US intercession—or at least US money—as the only possible way to save the beleaguered republic. He also believed that this critical situation made the acquisition of more Mexican territory possible. To obtain the funds it so sorely needed, the Juárez administration should sell Baja California to its northern neighbor, especially since, he insisted, repeating his predecessors' arguments, the peninsula held no value for Mexico.[24]

Thomas Corwin displayed great energy and inventiveness to achieve his policy goals, for all their contradictory character and despite his government's monumental crisis.[25] He worked hard to present himself as a friend of Mexico: he showed little patience for his compatriots' supercilious belief that foreigners should not pay property taxes and allowed his opinion to be published in the press by the Mexican government.[26] He negotiated four agreements with its beleaguered authorities: two standard documents, one regulating postal services, the other, extradition. The latter had, ironically, been made possible by secession, which had taken Southern interests out of the equation and enabled negotiators to leave out an issue that had repeatedly been a deal-breaker in US-Mexico dialogue: the request, consistently rejected by Mexican diplomats, that treaties include the obligation to capture and return fugitive slaves crossing the border.[27]

Additionally, two treaties were signed by Corwin and different ministers of foreign affairs: the Corwin–Zamacona treaty, in November 1861, and the convention between Corwin and Doblado, endorsed in April, when French troops were already marching toward the central highlands. Both documents meant to secure the money needed to cover Mexico's debt obligations—to destroy the European powers' specious excuse for military intervention—and effectively fight the invaders. These instruments also sought—if in drawn-out fashion—to transfer Mexican territory to the United States. The two documents promised Mexico a loan, the first for 9 million pesos, the second for 11 million. Payments were underwritten by levies on economic assets that potentially interested US investors: mining rights and the public lands that had been owned by the church which, it could confidently be predicted, would fall into US hands once Mexico defaulted on its loan.[28]

As had happened before, these prejudicial treaties had no impact because they did not go into effect. Corwin was working in an increasingly tense and demanding context: the possibility of recasting US-Mexico relations—if in their method rather than their content—would soon be shut down. The "new and important complication of affairs in Mexico," wrote William Seward, and the attention and resources demanded by Confederate insurrection, made consideration of Corwin's treaties "inexpedient."[29] The Juárez government was left to scramble alone, and try to reach an inevitably unbalanced settlement with the invading creditor nations.[30] In Corwin's opinion, there was a real danger that this would transform Mexico into a "colony in fact."[31]

The minister had hoped to put together an alliance to fend off Europe's intrusion in the New World, with a nation whose territory the US government meant, yet again, to dismember. His efforts faltered, however, not for their inconsistency but because of the circumspection of the Lincoln administration, incapacitated by the overwhelming predicament of civil war. Whatever momentum there might have been for a republican reset for US-Mexico relations was lost. The prostrated Mexican government lost faith: it had given up much in exacting negotiations; it had received nothing in return. When, in May 1862, Corwin tried to promote a scheme for the colonization of emancipated slaves on land in the Tehuantepec isthmus, the Mexican government would not yield. Manuel Doblado, minister of foreign relations, replied that no new international commitments could be taken up until a treaty with the United States was ratified.[32]

CIVIL WAR IN THE UNITED STATES and French Intervention in Mexico transformed North America's international relations into an uneven, dangerous battlefield. In quick succession, terrible events reshuffled priorities, restricted resources, and narrowed possibilities.[33] Trade (in cotton, grain, and silver), debt, imperial ambitions, and an unsettled balance of power pulled foreign actors into the North American morass.[34] As players in a complicated, multidimensional, transatlantic game of chess, Unionists and Confederates, republicans and imperialists angled and maneuvered to avoid the pitfalls of a treacherous global stage. For all the bluster displayed by some of the actors involved (Seward's call for wrapping "the world in fire"), caution stayed foreign policy initiatives: its goals became increasingly modest, intent on avoiding disaster rather than securing diplomatic triumph.[35] Once chaos subsided, it became apparent that impassioned rhetoric, convoluted diplomacy, and confounded actions on the ground had produced what Matías Romero described as a "revolution in the world's international relations": Mexico-US relations had changed, this time in both tone and substance; continental geopolitics were transformed and the Americas stepped onto a different place on the world stage.[36]

Fighting by the Book

The US collapse into a devastating, protracted civil war garbled international interactions in the Atlantic world: it revitalized the Old World's colonial ambitions by making them seem viable once again. Spain and France attempted to regain a foothold in continental America. The former occupied the Chincha Islands off the Peruvian coast, made war on Perú and Chile (1864–66) and reestablished its rule over the Dominican Republic (1861–65). The latter invaded Mexico. The warring Union and Confederate governments engaged in sparring policies on the international stage. Led by the pugnacious antislavery former governor of New York, William H. Seward, the Union's foreign policy concentrated on "counteracting and preventing," with "the greatest possible diligence and fidelity . . . the designs of those who would invoke foreign intervention to embarrass and overthrow the republic."[37] Confederates, confident in the righteousness of their struggle for national independence and in the leverage provided by the global hunger for Southern cotton, expected to be "acknowledged . . . at once in the family of nations." They would be sorely disappointed.[38]

The Mexican Republic, overwhelmed by civil dissention and foreign invasion, looked to the North for relief, just as its relationship with Washington tumbled down the scale of Union foreign policy priorities. The French-sponsored imperial government established diplomatic relations with the European powers and monarchical Brazil, endorsed colonization schemes involving European migrants, defeated Confederates, and enslaved workers. It also consistently sought Washington's recognition, to no avail.[39] Bewildered and hampered by circumstance, Union and Confederate statesmen, like Mexican republicans and imperialists, reached for international law to navigate these stormy seas. As a "system of right and justice," the "law of nations" (*el derecho de gentes*) had striven, since the eighteenth century, to govern what, by definition, was ungovernable: the relations between "sovereigns" recognizing no superior and sharing no common body of rules. In the words of Emer de Vattel, who by the nineteenth century had become the school's most prominent author, international law, grounded in men's nature and "the views of their common creator," could preserve civilians' "safety . . . happiness [and] dearest interests," even in the midst of war.[40]

In a postrevolutionary context in which "state" and "nation" were welded together and a sharp distinction was drawn between a monarch's "private" negotiations and the "public" diplomacy of nations, the advocates of international law argued that this body of principles and norms provided a script for international relations that anchored and shielded diplomacy from being distorted by patriotic passion.[41] Despite divergent precedents, in both North America's republics, in times of extraordinary emergency, civil and military authorities appealed to the law of nations, refashioned to serve their struggle over nation and dominion.[42] Men-at-war did not envision its principles as "natural and divine, universal and unchanging, previous and superior to any human convention" but rather as a set of respectable, practical, malleable ideas and policy options.[43] One of its virtues was its legibility on both sides of the Atlantic: the law of nations provided the language and devices that allowed contenders to organize protean conflicts into categories that foreign actors could understand.

Thus, Lincoln's decision to blockade Southern ports, although controversial, was, in the words of the British minister in Washington, "less objectionable," since the "rules of a blockade" were "determined and known."[44] As Howard Jones has written, the British and French declarations of neutrality "placed the American struggle within the dictates of international law." To Washington's distress, this automatically elevated the status of both contenders into that of belligerents, endowed with rights to trade, incur in debt, fly their own flag, blockade ports, and board and search ships for contraband. But if this temporarily strengthened the Confederacy's hand, it favored the Union in the long run. Universal rules lent respectability and intelligibility to its blockade and contraband policies.[45] At the same time, violation of the precepts of international law could escalate conflict. When the Union Navy forcefully boarded the British mail packet *Trent* in November 1861 and arrested the Confederacy's envoys to Europe, Washington was accused not only of violating Britain's neutrality but also of insulting its honor, which strained its relations with London to the brink of estrangement.[46]

Those fighting North America's civil wars construed law as a weapon to be wielded against the enemy, but they also turned to international law to stay their arms and prevent the contagion of war. Opting for neutrality put foreign policy in the hands of unexciting, lawyerly diplomats—or mollified formerly fiery politicians. For all the French Empire's authoritarian bent and Napoléon III's thirst for prominence, it was his staid ministers of foreign affairs, Édouard Thouvenel and Édouard Drouyn de Lhuys, who steered French policy in the face of the US Civil War. If by late 1862 the emperor's circle called for recognizing the Confederacy, because it considered that the success of secession would be "particularly favorable" to France and its Mexican adventure, members of his cabinet shut the initiative down, as they stolidly pursued France's national interests, realistically construed, and the dictates of a tradition that valued stability and the balance of power on both sides of the Atlantic.[47]

In Washington, William Seward had vehemently warned of "irrepressible conflict" and cultivated an image of recklessness during the early days of the war, when he floated the possibility of confrontation with Europe as a "remedy" for national conflict. As secretary of state, he strove, above all, to avoid misunderstandings and provocations when dealing with the European powers.[48] He used his copious and vigorous correspondence to restrain the Union diplomatic corps.

In the face of Mexico's troubles, even with Congress and the press forcefully condemning France's intervention in Mexico as antirepublican and inimical to US interests and principles, he insisted on maintaining "a strict line of forbearance and neutrality." The Lincoln administration adhered to the "practical and purely executive decision" it was constitutionally entitled to make, despite the people's "unanimous sentiment" against Louis Napoléon's attack on the neighboring republic.[49]

The Union, Seward insisted, was "engaged in suppressing a dangerous rebellion" and would not be "unnecessarily diverted" by "foreign wars or foreign politics." Its government conducted itself in the same hands-off manner it believed other powers should cultivate in relation to the purely domestic troubles of the United States. Only in late 1865 did Seward move to pressure Paris into abandoning its "Mexican folly." In a winding, drawn-out manner, the secretary of state asked his minister, John Bigelow, to signal to the imperial government that the "earnest [US] desire to continue and cultivate sincere friendship with France" would be jeopardized unless Louis Napoléon's government "could deem it consistent with her interest and honor to desist prosecution of armed intervention in Mexico."[50]

In continental geopolitics, the Union's State Department policy of strict neutrality toward the French intervention in Mexico mirrored that of its neighbor in the face of secession and civil war breaking out in the United States. Neither government swayed from its initial decision: both consistently rejected appeals for recognition from insurgent regimes, kept each other informed, warned of potential disturbances, and acted to contain unrest at the border, where the economic bonanza brought about by the reexportation of Confederate cotton greatly contributed to the borderlands' "disturbed condition."[51] But if neutrality served to stabilize and defuse conflict, it could not fulfill its promise of evenhandedness.[52] While the French Army was able to purchase food, horses, mules, and carts in Union ports, Mexican republicans could not ship the arms they desperately needed. Gruesome domestic conflict had driven the Treasury Department to prohibit their exportation. Seward's legalism, the long-standing US commitment to commerce remaining "free and independent," isolated from "the whims of war," and the State Department's determination to avoid any confrontation with the French hampered war efforts in the assailed republic. The Union's policies, confirmed its secretary of state, could not be determined by the needs of other belligerents but only by the US "military situation." [53]

Even after Appomattox, Seward persisted in restraint. He insisted to Matías Romero, the republic's young minister in Washington, that Mexico's republicans needed to save themselves through "their own efforts": "foreign intervention" would weaken the integrity of their cause and put them "in the hands of friends who could inflict greater harm upon them" than the enemy.[54] Romero bristled at Seward's "most extraordinary" doctrines, and what he described as the US "hypocrisy" and "selfishness." Seward's argument against foreign intervention made sense only as an "abstract question," which the presence of French troops in Mexico was definitely not.

Furthermore, Romero deplored the State Department's willingness to engage in "the greatest degradations, the most improper condescension" to avoid irritating Napoléon III. The Mexican minister believed the Union government was ready to "sacrifice not only Mexico but the whole continent" if it would help them keep the French at bay. He was especially frustrated by the State Department's obliviousness to the intimate connection between the Union cause and Mexico's plight, to the "excellent parallel between Mexico's reactionary party and that of slavery in the United States": republicans on both sides of the border defended "the interests of the masses" and sought to rid their commonwealths of "privileged classes."[55] Not only was Mexico's cause that of the Union but each nation also depended on the other for salvation. In the summer of 1866, while reporting on the "sad outcome" of the Fenian "conspirators" who had invaded Canada and New Brunswick in the hope of weakening Great Britain's hold on Ireland, Romero retrospectively mused about the effect of Mexican republicans' organizing a similar expedition to aid the Union as it fought the slave power's rebellion. Little could be expected from exclusively rhetorical republican solidarity.[56]

For all of Romero's frustration, the diplomacy of neutrality—cautious, pragmatic, subdued, structured by the law of nations—in which North American republican administrations engaged—Juárez's as much as Lincoln's—proved to be a sound strategy. Although imposed on the Union by the policy decisions of the European players, neutrality circumscribed their interference in the Civil War and defused a volatile situation in the North Atlantic that could have descended into confrontation. In North America, where the politics and violence that shattered the two republics were densely connected, neutrality built a conceptual wall between the two conflicts that perhaps contained the war's reach, if not its horrors. Nonetheless, Matías Romero and his fellow travelers tried to circumvent the inertia engendered by the precepts of neutrality. They drew from a tradition invented in the New World to forge a transnational republican alliance that recast US relations with Mexico, and the rest of the continent, in unexpected ways.

Reinventing Monroe

Washington's neutrality trammeled the Mexican Republic's efforts to defeat France and Maximilian's empire. In the words of Jesús Terán, Juárez's envoy to Europe, Mexico needed "arms, and arms exclusively."[57] To secure the "elements of war" that the republican armies sorely needed, Mexico's resourceful minister in Washington launched a sweeping, sophisticated information and networking campaign that broke diplomatic conventions and intervened in Union politics and public debate. To get around the Seward's legalistic obduracy and self-righteousness, Romero considered it "his duty to exploit the people's sympathies" without implicating the government.[58]

It is difficult to overstate the caliber and influence of Romero's unorthodox activities. Tireless, sociable, creative, and bold, the young diplomat—he was twenty-four when the US Civil War started—wrote "nonstop" to provide friends of the Mexican cause with strategic information and solid evidence, so that they could speak to the neighboring nation's predicament in Congress or the press; he lobbied key actors around restaurant tables or at rallies at the Cooper Union. He put together a potent, ideologically diverse network that included former—and soon-to-be-again—Democrat Montgomery Blair, postmaster general until September 1864; commander of Union forces Ulysses S. Grant; radical Republican senator Benjamin Wade; and his rogue Democrat colleague James McDougall. He kept the Juárez government abreast of all news and changing circumstances, and sounded out and reworked his—sometimes excessively—daring stratagems in dialogue with the president and his minister of foreign relations.[59] He intrigued during the 1864 US presidential election: given that Lincoln's Mexico policy "would not change one iota," he "wanted . . . any other candidate" to win. He floated the possibility of sending Union soldiers to Mexico—euphemistically described as "an armed emigration of citizens"—to form the "nucleus for our armies" and make US sympathies for the Mexican cause "more fruitful."[60]

But perhaps the most significant achievement of Romero's intense activism was his allies' success in resurrecting James Monroe's 1823 declaration and its consecration as doctrine.[61] As Jay Sexton has shown, the Virginian's 1823 blustering but toothless foreign policy statement, tucked into a "routine presidential message," was seen, by the late 1840s and throughout the next decade, as a "contested and partisan symbol." During the windup of the Civil War, it became "national dogma." Paradoxically, the forceful validation of "America for the Americans" principles—that Latin American anti-imperialists would clamorously decry half a century later—resulted from the initiative of the "other" Americans in Washington—with Matías Romero foremost among them—as much as from opposition politics in the United States at the end of the Civil War.[62]

During the densely connected crises of the 1860s, the resurgence of European expansionism in the Americas pushed beleaguered Spanish American statesmen to call on an embattled Union for support. They pressed for the enforcement of, in the words of Chilean Benjamín Vicuña Mackenna, a Monroe Doctrine "of our own": anticolonial, republican, and Pan-American.[63] As we might surmise, such an ambitious strategy had no place in the careful, noncommittal, risk-averse diplomacy of the Lincoln administration, for all of Seward's explicit hope that "Liberty and republican institutions" would be preserved "in all the other countries in the hemisphere."[64]

The United States, it seemed, was no longer "a revolutionary nation" and would do little for the rest of the world's revolutionaries.⁶⁵ Still, memories of its early enthusiasm for the New World's becoming a continent of republics proved uncomfortable. The convoluted declarations of Union diplomats committed to neutrality were maliciously interpreted as sympathy for Europe's incursions in America. In Paris, John Bigelow was cornered into saying that "Americans wished to see Mexico's monarchical 'experiment . . . to be fully tried,'" so as to determine "finally and forever whether European systems of government suited Mexican people best."⁶⁶ A pamphlet calling for Washington's timely recognition of Maximilian's empire described the 1823 declaration as "speculative doctrine, utterly without immediate of practical application," mistakenly interpreted as a "great principle in our national life," when it was but a "pouting policy," alien to the sound judgement and material interests of the United States.⁶⁷ Critics condemned it as the work of the State and War Departments' "well-fed favorites . . . employed in arguing away" the Monroe Doctrine.

With the rise of the Union's military star in 1865, it became politically productive to decry Lincoln's cautious, pragmatic diplomacy of neutrality as foolhardy, dishonorable, cowardly, and unpatriotic. It was not only a question of principle: if, in accordance with Napoléon III's wishes, the "Latin race" gained "ascendancy," it would "absorb Central America, hold the isthmus, separate [the United States] from the Pacific States by ocean route . . . [and] rob us of our Sister Republics of the Far West." The "long-settled, well-approved policy" of the country, laid out by President Monroe, ought not be abandoned for "fear of France, nor corruption of stockholders or jobbers, nor blandishments from political aspirants, nor their political machinery."⁶⁸ Frustrated by the administration's "sterile sympathies," which, "even if genuine, were of no use," Romero eagerly supported these campaigns to sacralize US interference in the New World.⁶⁹

In Richmond, Congressman Daniel C. De Jarnette called for an alliance between Union and Confederacy, grounded in Southern independence and the vindication of the Monroe Doctrine, "for the expulsion of England and France from the continent of North America."⁷⁰ While the Virginian dreamed of reconciliation grafted onto shared conquest, radical Republicans in opposite trenches wove the Monroe Doctrine and the Emancipation Proclamation together, as "olden principles" whose implementation would fulfill the true destiny of the United States.⁷¹ In a meeting at the Cooper Union, Rev. Joshua Leavitt, committed advocate of many of the nineteenth century's moral causes, recast the fearsome developments of the 1860s in the Americas in terms of political philosophy: Southern rebellion and European intervention were spawned by the "antagonism" in ideas "concerning the origin of valid governments."

The great powers across the Atlantic "utterly rejected" the American tenet of popular sovereignty as the only foundation for legitimate government. They considered republican regimes "a mere aggregation of individuals, from which men may come and go at pleasure." This disdain justified France's attack on the Juárez government and European equanimity in the face of Southern secession. It was manifestly dangerous to New World nations. In such a context, Monroe's statement was not the product of particular circumstances, or designed to pursue a single policy goal. It was an "axiomatic truth in political science," proclaimed for all times, a principle upon which there could be no compromise. It was a flag for all real patriots to rally around, in the United States and other American republics.[72]

Monroe Qualified: "Beautiful" Confusion at the Border

For all the risk involved, the fields of diplomacy and politics lent themselves to functional fictions, premised on the conviction that law and doctrine would govern international relations and foreign policy. These were grounded in the belief that an international border is an "easily discernable line" that separates "two distinct actors, with clearly defined personalities: two countries, two cultures, two economies, and historical developments that are full of contrasts."[73] This is probably only exceptionally true and, as we already know, it was and is untenable along the river with two names that runs between Mexico and the United States. It was glaringly false during North America's mid-century crisis.

The economic, social, and political ties woven between Mexico's Northeast and South Texas after 1848 grew exponentially in the early 1860s, stimulated by war, and by the impact that this complex relationship had on the fate of the two nations. But the sunbaked US-Mexico borderlands, distant from centers of power and decision, held a multitude of shifting sites in which political, ideological, and military alliances were made and unmade. The reverberations of what took place in the borderlands turned center-periphery relations on their head. They speak to the fragility, on the nation's margins, of even the most coherent national policy. They also suggest that, when studying the entangled histories on the ground on which transnational actors, interests, and dynamics do much of the intertwining, the shape and strength of the knot is sometimes more important than the threads it ties together.[74]

The creation of a unified economic space along the Mexico-Texas border was vital to the Confederacy's survival and to the conduct of war on both sides. It was engendered by economic opportunity but also influenced by political factors: the long-term cooperation between members of the Tejano elite who had become part of the ruling establishment in Texas and Norteño politicians on the other side of the river, of which the potent alliance between Laredo's Santos Benavides and Nuevo León's Santiago Vidaurri is the best example. These men used their formal and informal influence and their military capacities to facilitate the transit of goods, defuse incidents involving border authorities (without the interference of the federal government), punish cattle rustlers (with particular cruelty in the case of the Lipan Apache), and return stolen property across the border. The inner workings of this partnership, Luis Alberto García tells us, set up the region as an "undivided, quasi-independent state in all but name."[75]

War acted as an accelerator: on economic bustle, on struggles for power in a region of growing significance, and on frenzied diplomatic activity. In the context of a relentless movement of people, goods, and soldiers, scuffles and provocations could have easily blown up, as five different armies moved across a relatively compact space: local Confederate battalions and the Union troops that landed at Port Isabel, Texas, in November 1863; Mexico's imperialists under Tomás Mejía; their French allies; the myriad of republican guerrillas led by local caudillos like Servando Canales, Francisco de León, José María Carvajal, and Juan N. Cortina, who refused to cooperate with each other. But neither the French soldiers' "saucy and insulting" shenanigans from across the river, nor the bloody ambushes, raids, and seizure of supply trains and steamers, nor even the destructive January 1866 binational republican raid and plunder of the port of Bagdad, changed the course of war in the Rio Grande Valley.[76]

The attack on Bagdad, which involved almost 200 US soldiers, recruited by a former Union officer on the streets of Brownsville, produced scandal in Washington and Mexico City. The Johnson administration, which had little control over what happened on the nation's margins, had to deal with an irate French minister and over a hundred merchants from Matamoros decrying a flagrant violation of neutrality. Matías Romero unsympathetically side-stepped the raid issue and smugly observed that, in returning sequestered arms and artillery to General Mejía, "chief of the traitors in Matamoros," US officers had entered into unseemly negotiations with a government whose flag the Union allegedly did not recognize.[77] In the imperial capital, the Conservative press was horrified: anarchy and plunder, it contended, were one of the dreadful results of US democracy and of its emancipation. "Subalterns," who agitated to obtain "the support of the masses," and "thousands" of "freed blacks" who had "acquired a taste for theft and the rape of girls and white women" rampaged the small Mexican port.[78] For all the shock it generated, the incident had little effect on the commercial movements and resilient trade circuits that animated the river frontier.

The coexistence of bloody violence and economic bonanza was due, as Miguel Ángel González Quiroga has noted, to everyone's "focus being on commerce."[79] Military commanders, local strongmen, and well-connected merchants sought each other out across the river, regardless of nationality or ideological affiliation, which, moreover, proved surprisingly malleable.[80] When the Union blockade affected the South's economic and fiscal health, it forced the Confederate government to look for a viable alternative. President Davis sent a capable agent to Vidaurri in Monterrey, and José Agustín Quintero, a Havana-born Texas patriot, successfully negotiated lower tariffs with Nuevo León's governor, in the midst of rumors of his state's joining the Confederacy. In early 1864, when the controversial radical federalist cacique abandoned his post to join the ranks of empire, Quintero managed to secure the protection "of our interests" by the Juárez administration, which, during the brief period that the republicans controlled the northeastern border, was also intent on preserving a booming business that generated over $40,000 a month at the Piedras Negras customshouse alone.[81]

East of Vidaurri's territories, the Tamaulipeco republican leaders who, to the despair of the republican leadership, had such a hard time fighting together, proved nonetheless effective in negotiating with the diverse cast of characters who inhabited the borderlands. Juan Cortina, champion of the Mexicans in Texas and short-lived *imperialista*, corresponded with John S. Ford, Confederate officer and former commander of the despised Texas Rangers, to suppress hostilities, exchange prisoners, and preserve free passage on the river.[82] In June 1866, José María Carvajal, poised to take Matamoros by force, hammered out the surrender of the imperial forces led by Mejía with the support of the city's US merchants. The fact that this cost him his commission and political future in the eventually triumphant republic was a sign that, imperceptibly for some, the borderlands' zeitgeist had changed.[83]

Carvajal, whose career as a *fronterizo* Liberal had relied on a network of "friends and family" living on both sides of the river, should be excused for not recognizing that the borderlands' logic had shifted.[84] Confederate defeat and the abrupt end of the cotton-fueled boom did not subdue the borderlands, or break up the apparently unnatural alliances it had engendered. Some Confederate soldiers refused to recognize even Edmund Kirby Smith's belated surrender at Galveston in June 1865 and set out to cross into Mexico and keep up the fight . . . although it was not particularly clear against whom. So that "the unsheathed sword . . . remain unsullied and victorious," Gen. Joseph O. Shelby invited loyal Confederates to "march into Mexico and reinstate Juárez or espouse Maximilian."[85] During the last days of the war, Union officers and their Confederate foes—including John S. Ford—enthusiastically discussed a plan to drive the French out of Mexico together, once the trans-Mississippi region had been pacified.[86] In the words of Philip H. Sheridan, who in May 1865 was sent south to "restore" Texas and Louisiana to the Union, things "on the Rio Grande frontier" had a tendency to get "beautifully mixed up."[87]

National policy, like so many other things, twisted and splintered on the border. The French Intervention in Mexico had cornered the Lincoln administration into a guarded and uncomfortable foreign policy, but Grant and those who thought like him were convinced that intervention and empire were "part of the rebellion itself" and that triumph over the Confederacy would "never be complete" until the European "invaders" were "compelled to quit" Mexican territory. Military necessity, then, called for circumventing the "slow and pokey methods" of Seward's

State Department.[88] Teresa Van Hoy has described the efforts made by radical US Republicans and Latin American liberals in Washington to recast Monroe's message into honorable doctrine, "disinterested and principled," a "call-to-conscience" rather than "a call-to-arms." Actors on the ground—Mexican agents in the United States; friends of the beleaguered neighbor, such as Col. George M. Green, Gen. Lew Wallace, and arms manufacturer Herman Sturm—insistently called for soldiers, weapons, and munitions and lobbied, negotiated, organized, and eluded domestic and international law to get them over the border.[89]

Robert R. Miller's thorough study of US aid to the Mexican Republic follows the diverse, geographically scattered, and sometimes misguided endeavors of its agents to draft men and secure and dispatch equipment and resources for its war against the French without flagrantly flaunting the US neutrality policy, which persisted for months after the end of the war. Brigades of recently demobilized volunteers were put together and disguised as emigrant societies. Herman Sturm managed to purchase and send a considerable volume of military supplies to Mexican republicans: more than 20,000 rifles, over a million cartridges, and almost 3 million percussion caps.[90] In the Rio Grande Valley, Philip Sheridan hassled the French for the return of captured Confederate munitions and Union property, conspicuously prepared for a military campaign, and made "a formidable show of force" by parading troops along the river and meeting with Juaristas "with some ostentation." He also supplied arms to Mexican republicans by leaving them "at convenient places on our side of the river to fall into their hands."[91]

In Washington, Grant, Romero, and future secretary of war John Schofield, who had led the Union's Army of the Frontier, conspired: the general would go to Texas and cross over the border at the head of an "auxiliary army"—four well-armed divisions, three infantry, one cavalry—made up of "emigrant soldiers."[92] These stratagems yielded mixed results. The state-of-the-art weapons and munitions supplied to armies that sorely needed them certainly bolstered Mexican republicans. It is even more remarkable that some were purchased on the "paper-thin credit" of the Juárez administration, as Sturm juggled discounted Mexican government bonds, the possibility of acquiring land and mining concessions in Mexico, and his own funds and influence to buy and ship this matériel.[93]

But no auxiliary army came to the Mexican Republic's rescue; hundreds, not thousands of US troops fought alongside their Mexican neighbors. Significant military involvement, behind the State Department's back, was unrealistic, and floundered when Seward commissioned Schofield to Paris. Furthermore, US soldiers, for all their transnational republican enthusiasm, expected their salary be paid in full and on time, which the Juárez government was in no position to do.[94] Even a self-satisfied Sheridan suggested that the impact of US support was, above all, psychological: when the Mexican Liberals "saw their cause [. . .] under the

A cartoon in the Catholic newspaper *Doña Clara* depicts Gen. Philip Sheridan guided across the Río Grande by a dog that looks like President Juárez. He exclaims, "With this guide-dog, I will bring down the Mexican Empire very soon." Biblioteca Nacional de Antropología e Historia. Reproduction courtesy of the Instituto Nacional de Antropología e Historia, Secretaría de Cultura.

influence of such significant and powerful backing," they grew "so strong" that they delivered a "deathblow" to "Imperialism" . . . effective two years later.[95]

Diplomatic pressure, military displays of force along the border, and the state-of-the-art armaments that came across it contributed to France's retreat and republican victory against intervention and empire. Wrought by radical republicans on both sides of the border who conceived and publicized the North American wars as a common struggle for freedom, democracy, and progress, these policies and resources also came late, stingily, and after much unconventional pulling and prodding. While US mythography adopted the seamless tale that "Americans had saved republicanism in Mexico and . . . forced a great European power to bow before the Monroe Doctrine," Mexican politicians—and their colleagues further south—remained skeptical, and even resentful.[96]

As Paolo Riguzzi has shown, the appropriation of the Monroe Doctrine by Mexican statesmen was part of a "survival strategy."[97] Desperation called for the flamboyant consecration of an 1820s tagline in a presidential address as American Scripture. Concerns for the character of US-Mexico relations in the long run, however, drove a more careful diplomacy, wary of construing strategic responses to specific events as dogmatic principle: in his instructions to Romero in late

1864, Minister of Foreign Relations Sebastián Lerdo de Tejada authorized an alliance treaty with the Union "to repel the present invasion," an accord that could enshrine "Monroe's doctrine" as a "permanent principle in exclusively American matters." He nevertheless argued that it would be preferable if "effective assistance in the present struggle" could be obtained, without entering into "commitments for the future."[98] Chile's envoy to the United States, Benjamín Vicuña Mackenna, echoed Lerdo de Tejada's sentiments but was harsher in his assessment: a year after hailing the Monroe Doctrine and calling for its implementation, he derided this formula as "a humbug . . . a farce and an iniquity."[99]

A New Order?

By the end of 1867, at least on paper, Canada, the United States, and Mexico had stabilized the borders they shared and adopted the basic structures of the modern nation-state, with its centralized state, bounded territory, and market economy.[100] The violence and political experimentation, on the grand and radical scale that had characterized the previous decade, were over. A period cartoon shows a muscular Uncle Sam, flanked by Union generals, scarred and disheveled by war, surrounded by a motley crowd which hailed the American as the "champion of the world." The image speaks to Northerners' pride in a Union destined to do great things, but it also suggests that the unilateral initiatives of the United States reshaped the continent's—and the world's—political structures and reset the coordinates of its diplomacy. Instead, dramatic transformation was the product of the diverse aspirations and complex interactions of a multitude of actors, trying to deal with the maelstrom of crisis.

In trying to avoid disaster, Unionists and Confederates, Liberals and Conservatives, republicans and imperialists tried to forge risky international alliances and invoked and reinterpreted rules they knew were unenforceable. In doing so, they transformed the script of Mexico-US relations and the ways the Americas' character and their place in the world were imagined. Although both were enthused by republican triumph, Mexico and the United States did not become the "Sister Republics" hailed by optimistic propaganda.[101] But bilateral relations were stabilized and standardized, even if they remained—and remain—lopsided and often fraught with tension. At the same time, other Americans began speaking, with a distinctive voice, about the nature of the international realm.

As US ministers to Mexico McLane and Corwin devised mechanisms to acquire more land—by, for instance, using church lands to underwrite US loans on which Mexico was sure to default—they paradoxically sketched out a different binational relationship, grounded in the potential of trade, continental solidarity, ideological partnership, and even the fiction of sovereign equality. On becoming secretary of state, William Seward spoke of the "Spanish American Republics"

Once the Civil War was over, public opinion in the North called for action against European intervention in the New World. In this cartoon, which appeared in a New York newspaper circa 1865, a tall and rough-looking Uncle Sam, flanked by Ulysses S. Grant and cheered on by the crowd as the "champion of the world," intimidates Napoléon III and Maximilian, who looks like a sulky child. At the bottom of the cartoon is this line: "Louis Nap (to Little Max): 'You must not say nothing to 'im; zat is the man vot von ze fight.'" Courtesy of Barry Lawrence Ruderman Antique Maps Inc.

being "entitled to greater forbearance and more generous sympathies from the government and people of the United States." Diplomatic envoys to the continent's other nations should assume "a spirit more elevated than one of merely commerce and conventional amity, a spirit disinterested and unambitious, earnestly American in the continental sense of the word, and fraternal in no affected or mere diplomatic meaning of the term."[102]

These generous visions crashed into the upheaval and destruction of civil war. As US-Mexico relations was reconstructed after 1867, they did not speak to a "special" relationship, beyond what vicinity and a porous, convoluted, refractory borderland required, nor did they foster greater economic interaction, as trade and US investment increased only in the 1880s, a product of market integration, not republican affinity. But with the abolition of slavery, the eclipse of Southern diplomats and a focus on Reconstruction, economic growth, and the West, territorial expansion faded from the Mexican agenda of the United States. Washington abandoned its strategy of exploiting weakness, instability, and citizen claims to satisfy its hunger for land: its relationship to its southern neighbor became like the ones it pursued with other friendly countries. Thus, for example, to resolve the numerous disputes that emerged during the war years on both sides of the border, Mexico and the United States relied on the same mechanism the United States set up to process the frictions that the war had also engendered with Great Britain and France. A binational claims commission was established in 1868, chaired first by Francis Lieber, then by the British minister in Washington. It met over eight years and resolved, to the satisfaction of both parties, over 2,000 complaints by Mexican and US citizens.[103]

As violence and fear reverberated throughout the Americas in the 1860s, they unsettled the ideas and diplomatic routines, predicated on asymmetry, that had coalesced after independence. Crisis would lead to reformulation and adjustment. Ironically, the US fall from exceptionalism and into constitutional crisis and civil war, and the unorthodox instruments Unionists and Confederates relied on to defend their positions on the transoceanic stage, built up the diplomatic arsenal of New World nations. In his defense of the Monroe Doctrine, Joshua Leavitt excoriated inhabitants of the United States for abiding by rules established by "the crowned heads of Europe," intent on destroying "republican liberties." He particularly reviled the tradition of recognizing "any faction in possession of the capital," as the de facto government, instead of supporting legitimate authority, "originated solely in the voice of the people." De facto recognition could bind the nation to the acts of "transient usurpers" like Jefferson Davis.[104] The Juárez government had spent almost a decade making the same argument: in 1864, Jesús Terán, the republican government's representative in Europe, censored European powers for recognizing Maximilian's as a de facto government, given that the constitutional administration had not "ceased to exist" but only "changed its residence."[105]

American nations could argue they were only following the northern colossus's financial lead. As Matías Romero noted, the US government refusal to "consider itself obliged to pay a single cent of the Confederate cotton loan," regardless of British demands, constituted "a precedent we ought not to lose sight of when expected to recognize Maximilian's loans."[106] Actions taken in the aftermath of war were justified by referencing the US experience. Even in the face of sharp criticism from foreign opinion, North America's triumphant republics rejected the commitments and laws of rival governments—whose illegitimacy had been confirmed by defeat—and (selectively) chastised rebels as criminals. Mexico ostentatiously tried and executed a Hapsburg prince for filibustering, usurpation, and the murder of republican prisoners-of-war.[107]

In contrast, the cautious (some would say cowering) war diplomacy of the United States, followed by its politically driven, low-cost, and low-risk enthusiastic embrace of Pan-Americanism, inspired little confidence in the Spanish American republics that had suffered renewed European aggression. The statesmen who had invoked Monroe's spirit with rather poor results called for making over an international system in which weak, unstable, often insolvent states were particularly vulnerable. Even as war raged in Mexico, the republic's envoy to Europe, trusting the nation's arms would eventually triumph over the French, foresaw in that moment "perhaps the only opportunity . . . to modify the treaties with the European governments that have been so detrimental to the nation."[108]

With the North American crisis looming large in their minds, conscious of how an uneven, densely connected sphere of international relations had shaped both its origins and consequences, publicists and diplomats from the other America called for the world to be organized differently. In the words of Colombian José María Torres Caicedo, "The weak and ransacked, or those who are in danger of being plundered," should join forces against "the strong and predatory."[109] Latin American unity, then, was not only needed to collectively build strength: it was a moral necessity. The other America was called to

> Defend genuine liberty,
> The new idea, divine morality,
> The holy law of love and charity.
> The world lay in deep darkness:
> In Europe despotism dominated,
> From North America, egoism,
> Thirst for gold, and insincere piety.[110]

WHILE THE COLOMBIAN JOURNALIST AND DIPLOMAT waxed poetic from Paris, his Argentine colleague, Carlos Calvo, pursued two interrelated goals in his extensive publications: on the one hand, to condemn the "absolute lack of international law principles and the most complete arbitrariness" that had characterized European interventions in the affairs of the American states. On the other, the noted jurist wanted to establish "well-defined and constant" principles to deal with "very serious conflicts between states," so that justice and law, not caprice and might, would prevail.[111] He hoped to "correct" the work of his predecessors and peers by including the theoretical reflections and experiences of "the vast American continent, whose influence and power" was increasingly important.[112]

Calvo's 1868 systematic compilation of theory and fact about international relations scrutinized the positions of the most prestigious law of nations scholars from a New World perspective. In 1863 Manuel Payno had lamented that the "book" of international law was shut for countries like Mexico. By the end of the decade, his Argentine partner had published one that was Latin American in its content and purpose.[113] As various scholars have suggested, the resurgence of European expansionism in the New World in the 1860s inspired statesmen and publicists to reconceive continental identities, call for American solidarity, and promote, as Tom Long and Carsten-Andreas Schulz have argued, a republican internationalism grounded in association, separation of powers, and the rule of law.[114] The nationalist focus on patriotic saga has missed the significance of the inclusion of a new, potent, New World–flavored republican version of the law of nations into the Mexican state's diplomatic and political arsenal.

Latin American authors celebrated the continent's republican solidarity and called for a stable, righteous code to govern the relations between sovereign—if in some cases weak and unstable—states. Nevertheless, like Mexico's diplomats and statesmen, they were wary of the Anglo-Saxon republic. Even as they contributed to the Monroe Doctrine's consecration as dogma in the United States, diplomats from the other America sought to distance themselves from a policy whose original intention and meaning, they argued, had been perverted and transmuted into the belief that "only the United States had the right to conquer the territories in Latin America that they find convenient."[115] Nations who only recently had "categorically . . . invoked Monroe's Doctrine" as "a shield, a weapon for combat and even a principle of government," as well as an essential element in the definition of the relations between Europe and the New World, now sought to step away from it.[116]

EPILOGUE

THE REPUBLIC, RESTORED AND RECONSTRUCTED

APRIL 9, 1865. June 19, 1867. On these days, the wars that remade the continent came to an end. In the Disunited States, military commanders met in a courthouse in Virginia; in Mexico, the emperor and two of his generals were executed at dawn, on the outskirts of Querétaro. These symbolic moments did not, however, put an end to the fighting: Lincoln was assassinated six days after Lee surrendered to Grant, and it was months before Confederate troops lay down their arms in the trans-Mississippi west; Porfirio Díaz lay siege to Mexico City even as the firing squad's shots rang out. In the Reunited States, Reconstruction entailed the military occupation of former rebel states in what Greg Downs has described as "post-surrender wartime."[1]

Appomattox and the Cerro de las Campanas are convenient but artificial markers. They allow us to wrap up our story nicely: the war was over. But when peace came, it did not tie up loose ends or smooth down the jagged edges left behind by destructive violence. Still, the ways the transition from devastating war to precarious peace was construed in each of the two republics set the framework and basic terms for reconstruction and restoration: for dealing with the war's unresolved issues and confrontations, for how nations broken and put back together again would metabolize the legacies of a calamitous, decade-long storm.

The North American wars ended with no formal surrender documents, no peace treaties. The defeated were no longer able to make war; they were deemed incompetent to conclude peace. The Confederacy and the Mexican Empire became nonentities. If, however, nations shattered by war were to heal once arms were laid down and soldiers sent home, they had to, on the one hand, process what had happened and, on the other, decide how former rebels would be brought back into the fold. Conflicts so violent, deadly, and ruinous had to be countenanced and endowed with meaning. In the wake of national tragedy, who would be held responsible? Would the guilty be identified, their crimes prosecuted, and perpetrators indicted and sanctioned? In both the United States and Mexico, the verdict of the battlefield was compelling. But, as Cynthia Nicoletti has argued, for all its forcefulness, the wars' outcome did not automatically and transparently seem compatible with the rule of law, whose restoration so mattered to the triumphant republicans.[2] Defeat had incapacitated the enemy and destroyed, at least on paper, the contentious issues—slavery, the religious foundation of politics—that had driven crisis and sparked war. Silence on the battlefields did not destroy the animus that had sustained war. On both sides of the border, victors moved to ascertain the legitimacy of their success by proving, in a court of law, the iniquity and illegality of their rivals' cause.

In Mexico, the Juárez administration, bolstered by emergency powers and unfettered by legislative injunctions, marshaled the severe January 1862 law to "Punish the Crimes against the Nation, order, public peace and individual guarantees" to prosecute the insurrectionary leaders captured at the fall of Querétaro.[3] In what was conceived and presented as a sober, dispassionate exercise of republican justice, the Hapsburg prince and Conservative generals were brought before a military tribunal, as mandated by statute. Despite the same law's calling for a summary trial, the defendants were provided with competent counsel and given time to prepare their pleas. Although Maximilian refused to appear before the military tribunal, Miramón and Mejía put up a vigorous defense. The lawyers for the generals who in 1858 had gone to war to preserve the exclusive jurisdiction of military tribunals now underscored their rights as citizens rather than their prerogatives as officers. They argued that, as stalwart opponents of the 1857 constitution, they had never recognized the government it created. They had fought against it, arms in hand, for ten years. As contenders in a civil war, they could not be prosecuted for what the enemy alleged was a crime. The law of nations was clear: when a state split in two, each of its parts "recognized no superior on earth" that could "judge or decide" where "grievance or justice" lay. The prominent Liberal jurists who had been engaged to represent the "traitors" also called on the court to follow the example the much-admired "great people" to the north, who had refused to submit Jefferson Davis, the patently guilty president of the extinct Confederacy, to an unconstitutional process by taking him before a "court of exception."[4]

For all of these lawyers' talent and creativity, the war council's verdict was swift: it was preposterous for the "so-called generals" to assert that their refusal to recognize the constitutional government excused them for serving the nation's enemy. Their argument was "but a confession of their having rebelled against the republic's institutions, which was, precisely, a crime."[5] With a handful of unscrupulous agitators, Mejía and Miramón incited a rebellion, which had persisted only because of ill-gotten support, first from the church, then from French imperialism. The army's "Young Maccabee" and the Otomí strongman were found guilty of treason and condemned to death, along with the filibustering, murderous "usurper" who sat on the "so-called empire's" ridiculous throne. Republican justice—if substantiated by laws of war, desperately written up—had determined execution "right, necessary, urgent, and inevitable."[6]

The Americas' public conscience "imperiously demanded putting to death a would-be colonizer," even if he happened to be a European prince.[7] Maximilian's execution meant to serve as a warning; it provoked an international scandal. Among the numerous pleas for mercy was that of Lewis Campbell, Seward's envoy to the Mexican Republic. He called on the republic for the "humane treatment" of prisoners of war, as befitted "civilized nations."[8] The US government's message was resented and ignored. The republic's "terrible" actions were grounded in "reason, prudence, and the required tranquility" as well as the defense of "the world of Washington, Hidalgo, Arteaga, Bolívar, San Martín, and the thousands of other heroes who gave Americans a homeland and independence."[9]

The spectacular application of justice at Querétaro was part of the Liberals' dual strategy of severity and magnanimity. The "expiatory sacrifice" of the guiltiest allowed for the reconciliation of the rest. Between July 1867 and October 1870, the Juárez administration enacted progressively broader amnesty laws to restore the empire's former collaborators to their citizen rights.[10] Eventually, even former conspirator and short-lived imperial regent Archbishop Pelagio Antonio Labastida y Dávalos and infamous general Leonardo Márquez returned from exile, the former in 1871, the latter in 1895. In the wake of the 1867 verdict, national memory recast civil war as a struggle for national dignity and sovereignty, a "Second Independence." Conservativism could only play the part of the irrational political option of a misguided, criminal few, who now—fortunately—lay dead.

In Mexico, constitutional crisis had not engendered a new nation that claimed to be sovereign within the Union's territory, asserting that secession was warranted by fundamental law. Antagonists had not fought over two versions of the same constitution. Foreign intervention, brazen and cruel, made fratricidal war easier to sanitize, if not to fight. It was thus simpler for Mexican republicans to take their case to court. Their radical counterparts in the United States faced a more difficult challenge not only in bringing judicial closure to the national trauma inflicted by civil war but also in resolving broader constitutional issues. Fundamental law had not checked a crisis from spiraling into war; Southerners had plausibly argued the constitutionality of secession, and, while Radical Reconstruction was deemed necessary and legitimate, its constitutional soundness was dubious. If the fall of the empire had brought about the political death of Mexican Conservatives, in the Reunited States the men committed to a revolutionary second founding faced the resistance of entrenched Southern elites and their less staunch colleagues—Democrat and moderate Republican—and the opposition of states' rights and white supremacy enthusiast President Andrew Johnson.

Jefferson Davis's trial for treason had larger implications: it would settle the issue of secession's constitutionality. Cynthia Nicoletti's brilliant analysis shows how, as the Davis affair dragged on for four years, riddled by the tensions of Reconstruction politics, trammeled by contradictory visions, and warped by the ambition of the lawyers, prosecutors, and judges involved. It risked several dangers: the looming possibility that its outcome would undercut "the moral weight of Union victory" by disturbing the "verdict of war"; uncertainty over the outcome of the trial-by-jury of the president of the extinct Confederacy, held in its former capital; and concerns about due process touching on the proper venue for treason trials, the inclusion of African Americans on the jury, and the possibility that the Fourteenth Amendment precluded prosecution for treason, since it already disenfranchised oath-breaking rebels. Discrepancies and doubts led to recurrent deferments.[11]

Moreover, some of Davis's most fervent foes did not want him tried. Military Reconstruction was grounded in the "doctrine of conquest": the premise that Southern states had left the Union and become foreign enemies. If secession was deemed unconstitutional, rebels had remained under the constitution's purview and the justification for Reconstruction's vigorous policies fell apart.[12] In a series of colorless cases involving blocked ports during the war and public debt bonds once it was over, secession was discretely, gradually, and somehow inconsistently reckoned unconstitutional. In 1863, courts concluded that the federal government could impose a blockade—an act of war—on ports it claimed as its own, for it sustained "the double character of a belligerent and a sovereign." In 1869, the Supreme Court "reconciled the irreconcilable" by "declaring secession unconstitutional": it recognized that rebel entities had remained federal entities—sovereign states—but affirmed that they were, nevertheless, subject to federal "supervision" under military Reconstruction.[13] Jefferson Davis was released from prison; neither he nor any other prominent Confederate were judged in a court of law—and much less punished—for breaking up a country and setting up a new one.

In both Mexico and the United States, judicial decisions in the wake of war—including, in the case of culpable Confederates, the ones not taken—lay down a basic script for interpreting the nations' ordeals. Mexican Conservatives and monarchists were to blame for the war. Their defeat, chastisement, and banishment were merited: this would safeguard the republic's future. In the United States, it was determined that secession had been wrong but no one would be held liable for it. During the last third of the nineteenth century, victors and vanquished set out to embroider on these elemental narratives, to mark the days, publish the books, and erect the statues that would shape the memories and interpretations of these national ordeals and how these reconstructed pasts would undergird the North American republics' idea of themselves and their future.[14]

Jefferson Davis, released from prison in 1869, wears the clothes he was captured in to refute the rumors, broadcast and caricaturized by the press, that he had been dressed as a woman when arrested by Union troops in May 1865. American Civil War Museum, under the management of Virginia Museum of History and Culture (FIC2009.03220).

Maximilian's corpse after being embalmed for the first time. Photograph by François Aubert, 1867. Courtesy of the Metropolitan Museum of Art.

IN THE AMERICAS, the nineteenth century's central decades—the revolutionary fifties and sixties—activated crises and political experimentation. The continent's boisterous, popular, territorially scattered postrevolutionary politics gave way to constitutional innovations and different territorial arrangements, propped up by the carefully curated rhetoric, rituals, and fundamentals of the republic.[15] After the violence and vibrancy of the 1860s, politicians and citizens settled into a republicanism of the possible, grounded in more sober and stable politics—less pugnacious, less festive and popular, in some cases authoritarian—often paired, by the final decades of the nineteenth century, with more dynamic economies, more firmly bound to the rest of the world.[16]

By 1867, as the flames of war died down, North America had become a continent of federal nation-states. The destabilizing tensions and conflicts that had riddled their politics for decades seemed settled. In this new configuration, the central government held sway. National boundaries were set, even if borderlines ran across porous, disorderly, and sometimes violent borderlands. Canada, the United States, and Mexico set up comparable, fairly sound institutions, at least on paper. Purified through trials by fire, the region confirmed its liberal, reasonably democratic, capitalist vocation. Things, apparently, turned out the way they ought. Some could argue that this story's ostensibly happy ending is not unlike that of the better-known patriotic tales of destiny fulfilled. Does this book only paint a bigger, busier, more intricate version of the same picture? As such, will it be able, like Rivera's colorful, now lost *Portrait of America*, to unsettle its readers, encourage them to rethink geography, and reimagine the past? Will it replace certainties with curiosity?

The North American story of republican crisis and resilience is, perhaps in the first instance, that of entangled experience: of how a war between neighbors set both on the road to division and internecine conflict; of how domestic strife consumed the United States and opened the door to European aggression in the New World; of efforts to recast the meaning of citizenship, the nature of property, and God's place in the republic; of war policies remaking far-flung territories and markets. This dynamic confluence was obvious to contemporary actors: to Ralph Waldo Emerson when he warned that Mexico would "poison" its aggressor and to Matías Romero when he applauded the Monroe Doctrine. It is tangible in the fear of "Mexicanization" in the United States and in Mexican politicians' strategic, discerning references to their neighbor's institutions. These parallel experiences, mutual influences, and connections and the appropriation and reinterpretation of the other's experiences have been obscured by patriotic navel-gazing and ignored in the national histories we have written, obsessed with our own exceptionalism, often with our backs to each other. It is probably time to turn around.

Does broadening our scope and shifting perspectives contribute to a better understanding of convoluted processes? It sets up a more expansive stage; displays a larger, more eclectic, perhaps more balanced cast of characters; accounts for the perplexing twists and turns generated by two governments becoming four, by war turning territories near and far into battlegrounds and nationalizing violence even as the nation fell apart. This book's most banal contribution is that it throws light on the almost overwhelming complexity of relatively well-known historical processes by highlighting how they unfolded across a continent and were punctuated by uncommon levels of violence.

It sometimes seems that the historian's mission has become that of smugly reminding the uninitiated that things are much more complicated than they seem. There is, nonetheless, more to this than a wonk's delight in ruining a good story.

Insistence on intricacy and interconnectedness is rooted in and reflects the consciousness that human action is never seamless, self-contained, or scripted. It calls for skepticism in the face of soaring tales of right vanquishing wrong, of consequences intended and endings expected. Heavy-footed, cautious belief is perhaps especially useful when delving into the history of the republic, a protean, potent political community that both constitutes and governs itself and that is vitally relevant today to those who live in both sides of the Rio Grande / Río Bravo.

This is a study of civil war in nineteenth-century North America: what it entailed for political community, what it said about state capacities, and what it did to them. It is also a book about republican crisis, shared by two nations that we insist have little in common, save the border that divides them. But contingency and circumstance wrecked the unsteady, impecunious, incompetent republic to the south with the same effectiveness with which they brought down its stable, prosperous, successful northern neighbor. If, as James Kloppenberg has lucidly written about the history of democracy, "different preexisting cultural and institutional topographies . . . helped determine the forms of popular governments," North America's simultaneous, contiguous crises remind us that it is sometimes not landscapes but the fault lines and erosion in the ground that sustains them, oblivious to national borders and different cultural makeups, that decisively shape republican polities.[17]

This is also a story of republican resilience. For all the audacity of their political imagination, the North American politicians who sought to shore up the crumbling edifice of the republic or tried to lay down new groundworks for the nation had to stand on the "foundational fiction" of popular sovereignty, even when, in Mexico, some gave up on the republic altogether. This book explores the contradictory schemes they hastily put together, and the nuts and bolts they desperately replaced and readjusted to face the formidable challenges of war. In an attempt to heal the rifts and avoid the pitfalls that had torn the republic apart, governments were restructured, the meaning of membership recast, and political community recreated.

US Unionists and Mexico's *republicanos* beat, respectively, a regime committed to slavery and a government of undivided powers, sponsored by an invading foreign power, both engineered to discipline and contain democracy and secularization. Their triumph has been naturalized by national memory. The righteousness of these outcomes did not, however, make them inevitable. I hope that pulling apart the different political experiments that crisis wrought in the past will help us think about republican fragility, the allure of its alternatives, the costs of compromise, and the reach and boundaries of collective action. This is an invitation to reflect on the limits of politics but also on its possibilities, to loosen the hold of the present and push us to imagine different futures.

NOTES

Introduction

1. Rivera, *Portrait of America*, 31–32, 126. See also Lear, "Diego Rivera"; Ugalde, *"Maintenant"*; Azuela, *Diego Rivera*. Most of these panels, which were purchased by the International Ladies Garment Workers Union and displayed at its Unity House resort in the Poconos, were destroyed by a fire in 1969. I am grateful to Bertha Cea for introducing me to this fascinating work of art, and to Daphne Cruz for sharing her knowledge and insights on the work of the Mexican muralists in the United States.

2. Rivera, *Portrait of America*, 113, 123–33.

3. See, for instance, Rivera's murals depicting the *Epic of the Mexican People*, painted between 1929 and 1951 in Mexico City's National Palace; www.gob.mx/cms/uploads/attachment/file/796710/1_Palacio_Nacional_QR.pdf, 15–23.

4. Rivera, *Portrait of America*, 32, 13.

5. García Martínez, "El espacio," 49; García Martínez, "En busca." See also Werner and Zimmermann, "Penser l'histoire croisée."

6. On the transnational reverberations of the 1848 revolutions and the US Civil War, see Thomson, *European Revolutions*; Bender, *Nation Among Nations*, 116–81; Fleche, *Revolution of 1861*; Doyle, *Cause of All Nations*; Doyle, *Age of Reconstruction*; Kelly, "Lost Continent"; Downs, *Second American Revolution*; Rothera, *Civil Wars*; and Izecksohn, *Dos guerras*. On the polyvalent nature of civil war, see Canal, "Guerras civiles," 36.

7. Honeck, *We Are the Revolutionists*. Spanish Carlistas had been politically active in Mexico at least since the War against the United States, when priest-turned-guerrilla-leader Celedonio Domeco Jarauta rebelled against the Treaty of Guadalupe Hidalgo; for their involvement in the US Civil War, see Cancio, *España y la Guerra Civil*. On Marx and the US Civil War, see Nimtz, "Marx and Engels on the US Civil War." Hugo's messages to the Mexican republicans can be found in Hugo, *Actes et paroles*, 2: chap. 57, www.atramenta.net/lire/oeuvre5658-chapitre-57.html, and *Lettre de Victor Hugo à Juárez*.

8. For the impact of foreign participation in Mexico's war against the French, see Miller, "Arms Across the Border"; Taylor Hansen, "Voluntarios extranjeros"; For the convoluted effect of the continental crisis on US foreign policy, see Terrazas y Basante, "¿Dónde quedó la doctrina Monroe?"; Sexton, *Monroe Doctrine*, chap. 4; and Sweeney, "Sobre su cadáver."

9. For the construction of "Latin America," see Quijada, "Sobre el origen"; Gobat, "Invention of Latin America"; and Tenorio, *Latin America*. For three paradigmatic examples of Latin America construed as really existing and morally superior to the northern continental hegemon, written throughout the twentieth century, see Rodó, *Ariel*; Morse, *Prospero's Mirror*; and Veliz, *New World*. On the Rio Grande / Río Bravo, see Aguilar Rivera, *El sonido y la furia*, 292.

10. Cosío Villegas, "México y Estados Unidos"; O'Gorman, "Do the Americas Have a Common History?" In his invitation to write the shared history of Mexico and the United States, Mauricio Tenorio calls for avoiding the reification of national differences. Tenorio, "On the Limits," 568. For the possibilities of North American history, see the dossier "Débats: Transnationalizing North American History"; and Demers and Vézina, *Historias conectadas de América*.

11. Maier, "Consigning the Twentieth Century," 814, 816. On the continental scale of this transformation, see Spangler and Towers, *Remaking North American Sovereignty*; Schoen, Spangler, and Towers, *Continent in Crisis*.

12. Abraham Lincoln, "The Gettysburg Address," November 19, 1863, www.abrahamlincoln online.org/lincoln/speeches/gettysburg.htm.

13. The phrase is from David Ramsay, South Carolina delegate to the Constitutional Convention and historian of the American Revolution; Ramsay, *Dissertation*, 3. For the politics of independent Spanish America as radically innovative, see Sanders, *Vanguard*.

14. For recent work that analyzes the republic as a historical problem, see Entin, "Catholic Republicanism," 106, 109–10, 117–21; Thibaud, "Para una historia," 153–55; Ávila, *Para la libertad*; Lempérière, *Entre Dios y el rey*; Rojas, *Las repúblicas de aire*; and Hilda Sabato's exceptional *Las repúblicas del Nuevo Mundo*.

15. In his authoritative *Imagined Communities* (49–68), Benedict Anderson pointed out the precocity of a nationalist imagination in Spanish America. Studies of nationalism abound in Mexican historiography. See, among others, Vázquez, *Nacionalismo y educación*; Brading, *Los orígenes*; Sommer, *Foundational Fictions*; and Tenorio, *Artilugio de la nación*. Studies of nationalism are perhaps less prevalent in the United States. See Waldstreicher, *In the Midst*. For liberalism, see the paradigmatic Reyes Heroles, *El liberalismo mexicano*; and Charles A. Hale's critique in "Los mitos políticos." The liberalism paradigm has been less pervasive in the United States, but it is the central thesis in Harz, *Liberal Tradition*.

The republic's inherent contingency—its subjection to fortune and secular time, its awareness of its own "temporal finitude"—is productively examined by Pocock, *Machiavellian Moment*, vii. It also underpins François Furet's insistence on the primacy of politics during the French Revolution (Furet, *Penser la Révolution*), Elías Palti's reading of the nineteenth century as an age of "politics" (Palti, *El tiempo de la política*, 11–18), and Rafael Rojas's vision of intangible republics (Rojas, *Las repúblicas de aire*). See also Kloppenberg, "From Harz to Tocqueville."

16. The formulation is Daniel Rodgers's in *Contested Truths*.

17. For the peculiarities of the US model of church-state relations, see Onuf, "Thomas Jefferson's Christian Nation"; and Madeley, "America's Secular State." For the Chilean case, see Serrano, *¿Qué hacer con Dios?*; on Mexico, see Connaughton, *La mancuerna discordante*; and Mijangos, *Entre Dios y la República*.

18. Sabato, *Las repúblicas*.

19. Schlereth, "Privileges of Locomotion"; Schlereth, "Voluntary Mexicans"; Sabato and Lettieri, *La vida política*.

20. James Madison, *Federalist Papers*, no. 10 (1787), https://avalon.law.yale.edu/18th_century /fed10.asp.

21. Mauricio Tenorio has pointed this out in "Riddle of a Common History," 95. For a particularly intelligent and polished analysis of irreconcilable difference, see Riding, *Distant Neighbors*. There is now a very solid, provocative historiography of shared experiences on the US-Mexico borderlands. See Ceballos, *Encuentro en la frontera*; Tinker Salas, *In the Shadow*; Truett, *Fugitive Landscapes*; Truett and Young, *Continental Crossroads*; St. John, *Line in the Sand*; González Quiroga, *War and Peace*; and Gurza and Torget, *These Ragged Edges*.

22. Valéry, *Les fruits amers*, 16 . All translations are mine unless otherwise indicated.

23. Rosanvallon, "Para una historia conceptual," 126, 129.

24. Thompson, *Whigs*, 267, 259, 265.

25. Thompson, *Whigs*, 263–64.

26. Fowler, *La Guerra*, 21. Two excellent road maps to the copious historiography of Civil

War are Towers, "Partisans, New History"; and, more recently, Woods, "What Twenty-First-Century Historians."

27. Pani, *El Segundo Imperio*.

28. Ceja, *La fragilidad*; Becerril Hernández, *Hacienda pública*; León Garduño, *Entre tradición y modernidad*; Arroyo, *La arquitectura*; Luna Argudín, *El Congreso*; and the essays in Pani, *Estado, nación y constitución*. In contrast, Paco Ignacio Taibo II's nationalistic and melodramatic *Patria* was a bestseller and is now a docudrama streaming on Netflix.

29. This historiography follows in the footsteps of W. E. B. Du Bois's bold, groundbreaking *Black Reconstruction*. See, among others, Litwack, *Been in the Storm*; Hahn, *Nation Under Our Feet*; Hahn, *Political Worlds of Slavery*; Glymph, *Out of the House*; Oakes, *Freedom National*; and Pinheiro, *Families' Civil War*. See two useful reviews in Mathisen, "The Second Slavery"; and, for Marxist interpretations, Kelly, "Slave Self-Activity." Because grassroots politics is beyond its scope, this book will not engage with this fertile literature.

30. Charles and Mary Beard described the Civil War as the "Second American Revolution" in the late 1920s; Beard and Beard, *Rise of American Civilization*, 2:52–121. See also McPherson, *Abraham Lincoln*; Downs, *Second American Revolution*; and Foner, *Second Founding*.

31. New histories have sought to account for the impact of the war beyod the eastern theater: Arenson and Graybill, *Civil War Wests*; Nelson, *Three-Cornered War*. Steven Hahn and Alan Taylor have published beautifully written histories of the United States within a continental framework in Hahn, *Nation Without Borders*, and Taylor, *American Civil Wars*. Raymond Jonas has written a global history of Mexico's Second Empire, *Hapsburgs on the Rio Grande*. Others have probed the transnational impact—often interpreted through an optimist interpretative framework of liberal, democratic progress—of the US Civil War: Doyle, *Cause of All Nations*; Doyle, *Age of Reconstruction*; Kelly, "Lost Continent"; Downs, *Second American Revolution*; Rothera, *Civil Wars*. This book engages with this turbulent period as a moment of radical political experiments in nation-building, as do Mijangos, "Guerra civil"; Spangler and Towers, *Remaking North American Sovereignty*; Schoen, Spangler, and Towers, *Continent in Crisis*; and Izecksohn, *Dos guerras*.

32. Peter Guardino forcefully and effectively argues against this in *The Dead March*.

33. Torget, *Seeds of Empire*, 57–96.

34. Guardino, *Dead March*, 90, 91–101, 151–68.

35. González Navarro, *Anatomía del poder*; Vázquez Mantecón, *Santa Anna*; Sinkin, *Mexican Reform*.

36. Potter and Fehrenbacher, *Impending Crisis*; Holt, *Political Crisis*.

37. Faust, *This Republic of Suffering*, 9; Bensel, *Yankee Leviathan*.

38. Pani, "La innombrable."

Chapter One

1. For the 1848 revolutions, see Aghulon, *La République*; Sperber, *European Revolutions*; and Karl Marx and Friedrich Engels, "Manifesto of the Communist Party," February 1848, 14, 34, 67, n5, www.marxists.org/archive/marx/works/download/pdf/Manifesto.pdf.

2. Osterhammel, *Transformation of the World*, 543–57. Osterhammel does not mention Mexico's Reform and Intervention Wars as part of this "great disturbance."

3. Hahn, *Nation Without Borders*, 121.

4. Winders, *Mr. Polk's Army*, 87; Guardino, *Dead March*, 91.

5. As Conrado Hernández López's research shows, it is difficult to determine the size of the Mexican standing army during the first half of the nineteenth century, especially since its numbers on paper often diverged significantly from reality. He surmises the army was

20,000 strong throughout the 1820s and 1830s. In 1841 and then in 1845, the Ministry of War registered 32,000 and 75,492 men, respectively, but a more realistic estimate is Manuel Balbotín's 12,000. Hernández López, "Militares conservadores," 34, 44, 33. See also Archer, "Militarization." On the National Guard, see Santoni, *Mexicans at Arms*; Guardino, *Dead March*, 159–68; Ortiz Escamilla, "La nacionalización"; and Héctor Strobel's important *El ejército liberal*.

6. Peter Guardino has masterfully shown this to be a rather flat rendition of a complex continent-wide process in which nationalism did not overrun other loyalties but was powerfully and intimately imbricated with individual and local conceptions of membership, status, and self-interest. As would happen again later in the century, patriotic fervor—present on both sides—did not necessarily entail efficiency in war. Guardino, *Dead March*, 352–64.

7. Guardino, *Dead March*, 141–47, 192–202.

8. Nevertheless, the US-Mexico War has the highest rate of desertion (over 8 percent) and casualties (over 10 percent) in US military history. Greenberg, *Wicked War*, 15.

9. I follow Edling, *Hercules in the Cradle*, 145–76. On the "Polko" rebellion, see Santoni, "Where Did the Other Heroes Go?" On the war indemnity practically "vanishing" because of the postwar governments' efforts to pay off Mexico's astronomical debt, see Fowler and Santoni, "Setting the Scene," 13–14.

10. Thomas Jefferson, First Inaugural Address, March 4, 1801, https://avalon.law.yale.edu/19th_century/jefinau1.asp.

11. James K. Polk to the Congress, May 11, 1848, *Congressional Globe*, 29th Cong., 1st sess., 782–83.

12. On reform initiatives, see Andrews, "Discusiones"; on the popularity of the antifederalist Plan de Cuernavaca (May 24, 1838), see Fowler, *Independent Mexico*, 181–87. On the Seven Constitutional Laws, proclaimed in December 1836, see Sordo Cedeño, *El Congreso*.

13. For the regime of exceptions carved out by Anglo settlers in Texas, see Torget, *Seeds of Empire*, 97–178. The Texan pronunciamientos of June 22 and November 7, 1835, can be found at https://arts.st-andrews.ac.uk/pronunciamientos/regions.php?r=28&pid=57 and https://arts.st-andrews.ac.uk/pronunciamientos/regions.php?r=28&pid=87 and the Texas Declaration of Independence (March 2, 1836) at www.tsl.texas.gov/exhibits/texas175/declaration.

14. For the convictions and motivation of Anglo immigrants, see Schlereth, "Privileges of Locomotion"; and Rodriguez, "Greatest Nation." For the influence of Indigenous nations, see DeLay, *War of a Thousand Deserts*, esp. chaps. 3 and 7; and Hämäläinen, *Comanche Empire*, 141–238. For national disputes over annexation, see Hietala, *Manifest Design*.

15. Hietala, *Manifest Design*, xvii, 2, 10–131.

16. Guardino, *Dead March*, 186–87; Greenberg, *Wicked War*, 121.

17. Senator Calhoun, January 4, 1848, *Congressional Globe*, 29th Cong., 1st sess., 49–53.

18. "Puntos que deberán tratarse en las conferencias con el Comisionado de los Estados Unidos y que deberán servir de bases a los de México, propuestos al Excmo. Sr. Presidente por el Ministro de Relaciones y aprobados por S.E. en Junta de Ministros," August 24, 1847, "Instrucciones para los comisionados mexicanos, acordadas en Juntas de Ministros de 25 de agosto de 1847, en vista de las propuestas hechas por el comisionado de Estados Unidos," August 30, 1847, in Castillo Nájera, *El tratado de Guadalupe*, "Apéndice," 53–55, 63–65.

19. "Exposición dirigida por varios señores diputados a la Corte Suprema de Justicia, intentando el recurso establecido por el artículo 23 del Acta de Reformas, para que se someta el Tratado de paz al examen de las legislaturas de los estados," Querétaro, May 19, 1848, *Algunos documentos*, 248–61, 248.

20. Circular del Sr. Lafragua, November 27, 1846, *Algunos documentos*, 40–44, 44.

21. "Comunicación," *Algunos documentos*, 97. In fact, art. 50, secs. 4–7, of the 1824 constitution gave Congress the power to admit new states, establish state boundaries, turn territories into states, join two or more states, or establish a new state within the border of another, with the approval of three-quarters of Congress and ratification by three-quarters of the state legislatures.

22. "Observaciones del diputado saliente Manuel Cresencio Rejón, contra los tratados de paz, firmados en la ciudad de Guadalupe el 2 de próximo pasado Febrero, precedidas de la parte histórica relativa a la cuestión originaria," *Algunos documentos*, 300–347, 339.

23. "Observaciones," *Algunos documentos*, 328–29.

24. "Comunicación," *Algunos documentos*, 97–98.

25. "Exposición," *Algunos documentos*, 97–98.

26. Treaty of Peace, Friendship, Limits and Settlement, Art. 9, ex. doc. no. 50, 30th Cong., 2nd sess., 1849, 32, 16.

27. See DeLay, *War of a Thousand Deserts*.

28. Treaty of Peace, Friendship, Limits and Settlement, Art. 11.

29. Treaty of Peace, Friendship, Limits and Settlement, Art. 11, ex. doc. no. 50, 30th Cong., 2nd sess., 1849, 17, 33, 45.

30. James Buchanan to Luis de la Rosa, Washington, March 18, 1849, ex. doc. no. 50, 30th Cong., 2nd sess., 1849, 45.

31. "Exposición," *Algunos documentos*, 256.

32. "Expediente: Resolución Suprema Corte de Justicia sobre el pedido de once diputados sobre la validez o nulidad del tratado de paz entre México y Estados Unidos," México, June 27, 1848, July 10, 1848, *Algunos documentos*, 263–68, 268–72.

33. "Exposición con que el Ministro de Relaciones presenta al Congreso Nacional el Tratado de Paz," Querétaro, May 9, 1848, *Algunos documentos*, 168–92, 179.

34. "Comunicación," "Exposición," *Algunos documentos*, 68, 85, 101.

35. "Comunicación," *Algunos documentos*, 79–80.

36. "Circular de la Secretaría de Relaciones Exteriores, Gobernación y Policía a los Gobernadores y Asambleas Departamentales," December 11, 1845, *Algunos documentos*, 248–61, 248.

37. "Exposición de motivos presentada por los comisionados de México," March 1, 1848, *Algunos documentos*, 139–68, 161, 142–43.

38. "Exposición con que el Ministro de Relaciones presenta al Congreso Nacional el Tratado de Paz," Querétaro, May 9, 1848, *Algunos documentos*, 168–92, 184, 186.

39. "Exposición con que el Ministro de Relaciones presenta al Congreso Nacional el Tratado de Paz," *Algunos documentos*, 167–68.

40. "Comisión de Relaciones, Cámara de diputados," Querétaro, May 13, 1848, *Algunos documentos*, 192–204, 199, 201.

41. "Dictamen: Comisión Cámara de Senadores," Querétaro, May 21, 1848, *Algunos documentos*, 205–26, 221.

42. Sordo Cedeño, "El Congreso y la guerra," 102.

43. Mexico, *puro* legislators had argued, deserved the tragedy that befell it. Its citizens had been unable to defeat 10,000 soldiers from "the world's least renowned" military power. "Comunicación," "Exposición," *Algunos documentos*, 68, 85, 101.

44. Senator Cass, January 3, 1848, *Congressional Globe*, 30th Cong., 1st sess., 17:86–88.

45. Senator Hale, January 6, 1848, *Congressional Globe*, 30th Cong., 1st sess., 17:122–26.

46. Senator Foote, January 20, 1848, *Congressional Globe*, 30th Cong., 1st sess., 17:217–21.

47. Senator Foote, January 20, 1848, *Congressional Globe*, 30th Cong., 1st sess., 17:217–21.

48. Senator Calhoun, January 4, 1848, *Congressional Globe*, 30th Cong., 1st sess., appendix, 17:49–53.

49. Senators Allen and Rusk, February 24, 1848, *Congressional Globe*, 17:387–88. For the gag rules put in place by Congress, see Miller, *Arguing About Slavery*.

50. Senator Hale, December 21, 1847, *Congressional Globe*, 30th Cong., 1st sess., 17:63.

51. Congressman Hilliard, July 24, 1848, *Congressional Globe*, 30th Cong., 1st sess., appendix, 17:938–43.

52. Congressman Hilliard, July 24, 1848, *Congressional Globe*, 30th Cong., 1st sess., appendix, 17:938–43.

53. Senator Morse, February 1, 1848, *Congressional Globe*, 30th Cong., 1st sess., appendix, 17:152–53. The senator quotes a letter to the editor published in the *New York Herald* in October 1846.

54. Varon, *Disunion!*, 1–2, 13–14.

55. Schlereth, "Privileges of Locomotion"; Schlereth, "Voluntary Mexicans"; Reséndez, *Texas Patriot*; Bowman, *Mormon People*, chap. 4.

56. Despite the intervention of prominent citizens—including army officers and the archbishop—the San Patricios were flogged and branded, and over fifty were publicly hanged. Hogan, *Irish Soldiers*, 92–101, 159–96; Miller, *Shamrock and Sword*, 32–34; Sanders, *Vanguard*, 64–68.

57. Such was the case of Chihuahua's José Francisco Chávez, scion to one of the state's most distinguished families. Gonzales, *Política: Nuevomexicanos*, chap. 2; Smith, "El contrabando."

58. Santoni, "Where Did the Other Heroes Go?"

59. A wonderful study of the city during the war is Granados, *Sueñan las piedras*. For a fascinating eyewitness account by an erudite historian and moderate politician, see Ramírez, *México durante su guerra*. See also Berge, "Mexican Dilemma"; and Sánchez de Tagle, "Un protectorado americano."

60. Suárez Iriarte, *Defensa pronunciada*, 17–19, 7, 120.

61. Suárez Iriarte, *Defensa pronunciada*, 40–43.

62. Treaty of Guadalupe Hidalgo, Art. 8, February 2, 1848, www.docsteach.org/documents/document/treaty-guadalupe-hidalgo/5274/1.

63. Reséndez, *Changing National Identities*; Pérez Tisserant, *Nuestra California*.

64. Gen. Stephen W. Kearny, "Proclamation to the People of Santa Fe," August 22, 1846, in Crutchfield, *Revolt at Taos*, 169–70.

65. Governor Juan Bautista Vigil's Response to Kearny's address, August 19, 1846, in Crutchfield, *Revolt at Taos*, 167.

66. Lewis Garrad's account, in McNierney, *Taos in 1847*, 65–66.

67. Treaty of Campo Cahuenga, January 12, 1847, at www.militarymuseum.org/Cahuenga.html.

68. The *Saint Louis Republican* saw "the Mexicans'" insurrection as futile but destructive of life and property, especially because of their alliance with Pueblo Indians. *Niles National Register*, April 3, 1847, 72–73.

69. Proclamation, Santa Fe, January 25, 1847, in McNierney, *Taos in 1847*, 42–43.

70. Lewis Garrard, who wrote *Wah-to-yah and the Taos Trail* (1850) about his experiences on the Santa Fe Trail, exclaimed, "Treason indeed! What did the poor devil know about his new allegiance?" McNierney, *Taos in 1847*, 75–76; Crutchfield, *Revolt at Taos*, 102, 103–4, 106–7.

71. Governor Donaciano Vigil to James Polk, Santa Fe, March 1847, in McNierney, *Taos in 1847*, 78–79.

72. Griswold del Castillo, *The Treaty of Guadalupe Hidalgo*; de León, *They Called Them Greasers*; Montejano, *Anglos and Mexicans*.

73. Martínez, "El Paso y Ciudad Juárez"; Ceballos, "Los dos Laredos"; Tinker Salas, "Los dos Nogales." For the case of La Ascención, Chihuahua, see Hernández, *Mexican American Colonization*, 163–223; for the lower Rio Grande Valley, see Valerio Jiménez, *River of Hope*. On New Mexico's repatriation commission, and the leadership of Fr. Ramón Ortiz, see González de la Vara, "El traslado de familias"; and Sisneros, "Los Emigrantes Nuevomexicanos."

74. I have delved into these issues with greater detail in Pani, "Aquellos hermanos nuestros."

75. *New Mexico: Convention of Delegates*, 1–2. In February 1850, thirteen of the nineteen delegates meeting in the New Mexican territorial convention had Spanish surnames The prevalence of certain last names (Armijo, Baca, Vigil, Otero) speaks to a small, tight-knit elite. Conversely, of the forty-eight members of the California constitutional convention, which met in September and October 1849, only seven were Californios, six of them native-born. *Report of the Debates . . . California*, 517–18.

76. *New Mexico: Convention of Delegates*, 10–13. See also Gonzales, "Mexican Party, American Party."

77. Between 1889 and 1895, New Mexican politicians introduced four statehood bills in Washington, which Congress voted down because they believed the majority of the state population "was not prepared for self-government." Valerio Jiménez, *Remembering Conquest*, 95–101, 96.

78. Gwin, in *Report of the Debates . . . California*, 16.

79. Carrillo, in *Report of the Debates . . . California*, 22–23. The delegate from Los Angeles advised that, given the enthusiasm for establishing a state government in the north of the state, California be divided by running a line west from San Luis Obispo, and establishing a territorial government in the south. His position, he argued, did not contradict the fact that he considered himself "as much an American citizen" as Gwin.

80. Notably through the "foreign miner tax." See Pitt, *Decline of the Californios*, 48–68.

81. *New Mexico: Convention of Delegates*, 4.

82. Some of these men were experienced politicians. See, for instance, on William Gwin, St. John, "Unpredictable America."

83. Botts, in *Report of the Debates . . . California*, 66.

84. See Pérez Tisserand, *Nuestra California*, 251–56.

85. De la Guerra (who is mistakenly identified by his father's maternal surname, Noriega—misspelled as Noriego), in *Report of the Debates . . . California*, 63, 70.

86. De la Guerra, in *Report of the Debates . . . California*, 63. Some Californios did protest the discrimination against African Americans and Chinese. See Benavides, "Californios! Whom Do You Support?"

87. People ex. rel. Kimberly v. De la Guerra, 40 Cal 311 (1870).

88. Carter v. Territory; Quintana v. Tomkins, 1, 1853 NMSC 2.

89. People ex. rel. Kimberly v. De la Guerra.

90. United States v. Ritchie 58 U.S. 525 (1854).

91. Roberts, "United States," 77.

92. Thomson, introduction to *European Revolutions*, 1–18.

93. Roberts, "United States," 99.

94. Roberts, "United States," 78, 99.

95. "Exposición con que el ministro de Relaciones [Luis de la Rosa] presenta a Congreso Nacional el Tratado de Paz," Querétaro, May 9, 1848, *Algunos documentos*, 168–92, 190–91.

96. Careaga, *De llaves y cerrojos*. Between 1840 and 1843, the Yucatecan government sought the support of the Lone Star Republic.

97. Justo Miguel Flores Escalante argues convincingly that historians have exaggerated Yucatecan separatism, and that the peninsula's elites never sought "absolute independence" but used it as a bargaining chip in order to defend the state's "exceptionalism" and sovereignty within a federalist framework. Flores Escalante, *Soberanía y excepcionalidad*, 143–62.

98. Acta de independencia de la península de Yucatán, October 1, 1841, www.biblioteca.tv /artman2/publish/1841_144/Acta_de_Independencia_de_la_pen_nsula_de_Yucat_n_1390.shtml.

99. This was the mission of politician and prominent man of letters Justo Sierra O'Reilly, which he described in his *Diario de nuestro viaje*.

100. Rugeley, *Rebellion Now*, 59–68; Campos García, "La invención," 159–63.

101. Notable exceptions are Rugeley, *Rebellion Now*; Taracena, *De héroes olvidados*; and Campos García, "La invención." For the agrarian roots of the rebellion, see, among others, González Navarro, *Raza y tierra*; and Güemez Pineda, *Mayas, gobierno y tierras*. For classic accounts of the war as a defense of Mayan identity, see Reed, *Caste War*; Dumond, *Machete and the Cross*; and Careaga, *Hierofanía combatiente*.

102. Campos García, "La invención," 169–70; Sierra O'Reilly, *Diario de nuestro viaje*, 116–18.

103. I closely follow Terry Rugeley's argument in *Rebellion Now*.

104. See Jacinto Pat to John Kingdom and Edward Rhys, February 10, 1848; Cecilio Chi to John Farcourt, April 23, 1849; Jacinto Pat to Modesto Méndez, July 11, 1848, in Rugeley, *Maya Wars*, 52–56.

105. "Message from the President," April 21, 1848, *Congressional Globe*, 30th Cong., 1st sess., 709.

106. Senator Calhoun, April 29, 1848, *Congressional Globe*, 30th Cong., 1st sess., 712–13; Sexton, *Monroe Doctrine*, 94–97.

107. Congressman Root, April 29, 1848, *Congressional Globe*, 30th Cong., 1st sess., 711–12.

108. Senator Houston, May 8, 1848, *Congressional Globe*, 30th Cong., 1st sess., 603–6.

109. Falcón, "En medio del asedio"; Fowler and Santoni, "Setting the Scene," 19–20; Fowler, "Sierra Gorda Pronunciamientos"; Meyer, *Esperando a Lozada*; Van Osterhout, "Popular Conservatism in Mexico."

110. Jan Rus has suggestively argued the for another caste war: the violence against the Tzotzil-speaking communities of the Chiapas highlands in 1869; Rus, "Whose Caste War?" For a careful reconstruction of this "invention" for the Yucatán rebellion, see García Campos, "La invención."

111. Gettleman, *Dorr Rebellion*.

112. *Report on the Trial of Thomas Wilson Dorr*.

113. *Rhode Island Question*, 4; *Rights of the People*, 7.

114. *Rights of the People*, 28, 54.

115. *Rhode Island Question*, 8–9; *Opening Argument*, 10.

116. *Rhode Island Question*, 6–8.

117. *Opening Argument*, 22–23.

118. Luther v. Borden, 48 U.S. 1 (1849), https://supreme.justia.com/cases/federal/us/48/1 /case.html.

119. As Gettleman notes, this optimism was surprising in the face of such "unmistakable expressions of judicial hostility"; Gettleman, *Dorr Rebellion*, 175–76, 186–89.

Chapter Two

1. As the senator from Mississippi put it, in *Speech of the Honorable Jefferson Davis* (1850), 15.

2. See Michael F. Holt's careful, detailed description of the political crisis of the 1850s; Holt, *Political Crisis*.

3. For the contentious nature of federalism during what she calls the "Interbellum period" (1815–61), see Alison LaCroix's *The Interbellum Constitution*, chap. 1. For the tensions riddling federalism as both "ideology" and "historical experience," see Piqueras, *El federalismo*. For political violence, see Joanne Freeman's masterful *The Field of Blood* and Salvador Rueda's fascinating *El diablo de Semana Santa*. In his dystopic novel, Conservative man of letters José María Roa Bárcena mocked Mexican radicals who, to imitate their idealized American neighbors, tried to start fistfights in Congress. Roa Bárcena, *La quinta modelo*, chap. 1.

4. Beckert, *Empire of Cotton*; Huston, *Calculating the Value*; Finkelman, *Slavery and the Founders*; Fehrenbacher, *Dred Scott Case*.

5. Connaughton, *Entre la voz de Dios*; Lira, "Patrimonios hereditarios"; Mijangos, *Entre Dios y la República*.

6. Political representation allowed for the voice of the sovereign to be heard while "refining" and "enlarging the public views." James Madison, *Federalist Papers*, no. 10 (1787), https://avalon.law.yale.edu/18th_century/fed10.asp.

7. In the words of Carlos Garriga, modern constitutionalism undergirds a "political culture of rights and the institutional devices that warrant them." Garriga, *Historia y constitución*, 11–23, 14.

8. In contrast, seventeen projects for constitutional laws were drafted in the United Provinces of La Plata / Argentina between 1811 and 1853; twenty-three in Colombia between 1811 and 1886; and eleven in Chile between 1811 and 1833. Perú and Uruguay were more stable, with four constitutions each during the nineteenth century. See Biblioteca Virtual Miguel de Cervantes, *Constituciones hispanoamericanas: Catálogo de constituciones y otros textos jurídicos*, www.cervantesvirtual.com/portales/constituciones_hispanoamericanas/catalogo_paises/.

9. LaCroix, *Interbellum Constitution*, introduction. I am very grateful to Pablo Mijangos for his comments on the issue of constitutionality.

10. LaCroix, *Interbellum Constitution*, introduction.

11. Altschuler and Blumin, *Rude Republic*, 47–86, 82.

12. Carmagnani and Hernández Chávez, "La ciudadanía orgánica mexicana"; Aguilar Rivera, *Elecciones y gobierno*. For the most thorough, systematic analyses of Mexican elections in the nineteenth century, see Gantús, *Elecciones . . . Las fuentes* and *Elecciones . . . Las prácticas*; and Gantús and Salmerón, *Cuando las armas, Contribución a un diálogo*, and *Prensa y elecciones*.

13. Illustrative examples of this have been recorded by Noriega, "Elecciones y notables"; and Hernández Jaimes, "La estrategia de los caciques."

14. Noriega, "Los grupos parlamentarios."

15. Crespo, *Del rey al presidente*.

16. Costeloe, "Mariano Arista."

17. Vázquez, "Los primeros tropiezos."

18. Andrews, "Discusiones."

19. Fowler, *Independent Mexico*, 29.

20. Fowler, *Independent Mexico*; Guerra, "El pronunciamiento en México."

21. Pocock, *Machiavellian Moment*, vii; Rakove, "Thinking Like a Constitution."

22. Eissa-Barroso, "Mirando hacia Filadelfia." The favorable critique by future Conservative luminary Lucas Alamán is especially interesting. Alamán, *Examen imparcial*, 195–99.

23. Shelden and Alexander, "Dismantling the Party System." I am very grateful to Greg Downs for his comments on the issue of political parties.

24. Shelden and Alexander, "Dismantling the Party System," 447–48.

25. Shelden and Alexander, "Dismantling the Party System," 421. For the crucial role

played by the press and by editors who acted as businessmen, citizens and partisans in Mexico City, see Suárez de la Torre and Castro, *Empresa y cultura*; and the wonderful Zeltsman, *Ink Under the Fingernails*.

26. Guardino, *Time of Liberty*, 156–222; Trejo, *Redes*, 48–78, 136–206.

27. Ávila and Salmerón, *Partidos, facciones y otras calamidades*.

28. Quoted in Hofstadter, *Idea*, 247. As Jabez Hammond, chronicler of New York's political parties, explained, these institutions clarified public issues, underwrote liberty by giving latitude to the opposition, checked corruption, and provided institutional, nonviolent means for channeling conflict and changing administrations. Hofstadter, *Idea*, 262. For the persistence of antipartyism, see Shelden and Alexander, "Dismantling the Party System," 432–33.

29. Quoted in Shelden and Alexander, "Dismantling the Party System," 431.

30. McCormick, *Second American Party System*; Holt, *Rise and Fall*.

31. Douglas, "First Joint Debate," 123.

32. Fehrenbacher, *Dred Scott Case*, 28–47, 74–208.

33. As described by one of the Compromise's harshest critics, John C. Calhoun of South Carolina. Since Calhoun was too ill to deliver his speech, it was read by Virginia senator James Mason, March 4, 1850; see also Henry S. Foote, January 16, 1850, *Congressional Globe*, Senate, 31st Cong., 1st sess., 451–55; 166.

34. Fehrenbacher, *Dred Scott Case*, 43.

35. John Crittenden, December 18, 1860, *Congressional Globe*, Senate, 36th Cong., 2nd sess., 113.

36. These "doughfaces"—as they were derisively called—were defined by Bartlett's *Dictionary of Americanisms* (1848) as "the northern favorers and abettors of negro slavery." Freeman, *Field of Blood*, 63.

37. Benjamin Wade, February 6, 1854, in *Nebraska Question*, 66–67.

38. John P. Hale, December 18, 1860, *Congressional Globe*, Senate, 36th Cong., 2nd sess., 116.

39. Salmon P. Chase, February 3, 1854, in *Nebraska Question*, 61.

40. Seward, in *Nebraska Question*, 22.

41. Wade, February 6, 1854, in *Nebraska Question*, 66–67, 61.

42. *Speech of Mr. Thaddeus Stevens*, 2.

43. Guy M. Bryan (Texas), April 28, 1860, in *Official Proceedings*, 62.

44. Davis, *Speech of the Honorable Jefferson Davis* (1850), 3, 16.

45. Davis, *Speech of the Honorable Jefferson Davis* (1850), 10–11. For the "doctrine of noninterference" as a free-standing principle that could preclude Congress from legislating on the matter and keep slavery out of the Mexican Cession, see Baumgartner, *South to Freedom*, 138, 143–45, 171–72. Mexico followed a convoluted road to abolition, proclaimed in 1829. See Olveda, "La abolición de la esclavitud."

46. Henry Clay, January 29, 1850, *Congressional Globe*, Senate, 31st Cong., 1st sess., 246.

47. George Badger, February 16, 1854, Stephen A. Douglas, January 30, 1854, in *Nebraska Question*, 92–93, 45–46.

48. Henry Clay, January 29, 1850, *Congressional Globe*, Senate, 31st Cong., 1st sess., 244–46.

49. Holt, *Fate of Their Country*, 83, 92; Maizlish, *Strife of Tongues*.

50. Letter from a Democratic congressman to Speaker Nathaniel Banks. The writer shows how the arrival of an "explicitly Northern opposition had an enormous impact on Congress": the number of fights grew and their dynamics changed, as Republicans proved willing to fight back against Southern bullying. Quoted in Freeman, *Field of Blood*, 225, 209.

51. Stephen A. Douglas, January 30, 1854, in *Nebraska Question*, 46; *Speech of John J.*

Crittenden. In David Goldfield's opinion, "The political system could not contain the passions stoked by the infusion of evangelical Christianity into the political process. Westward expansion, sectarian conflict and above all slavery assumed moral dimensions that confounded political solutions." His argument speaks to the growing tensions and sense of moral urgency of post-1848 politics but takes the "compromisers'" censure of their more radical colleagues as an objective diagnosis rather than partisan rhetoric. Goldfield, *America Aflame*, 1–103, 1.

52. John Crittenden, December 18, 1860, *Congressional Globe*, Senate, 36th Cong., 2nd sess., 112.

53. Smith, *Stormy Present*, 68–88.

54. Foner, "Wilmot Proviso," 278; 276; Holt, *Fate of Their Country*, 19–49. The proviso was part of the Northern Democrats' defensive strategy in the face of their constituencies' growing antislavery sentiment, resentment of Texas's annexation as a slave state, and feeling of betrayal by the Polk administration for its concession in the Oregon negotiations with Great Britain.

55. Guelzo, "Houses Divided," 401; *Kansas: The Lecompton Constitution*, 12.

56. Alfred P. Nicholson, December 24, 1860, *Congressional Globe*, Senate, 36th Cong., 2nd sess., 186; Cox Richardson, *To Make Men Free*, 7.

57. The expression is James Buchanan's. President's message to Congress, December 3, 1860, *Congressional Globe*, Senate, 36th Cong., 2nd sess., appendix, 1.

58. Truman Smith, February 9, 1854, in *Nebraska Question*, 84; Seward, in *Nebraska Question*, 29.

59. "Situación," *El Universal*, June 27, 1849.

60. "Aniversario del grito de Dolores," *El Universal*, September 16, 1849.

61. "Rerógrados: Liberales," "Los conservadores y la nación," *El Universal*, January 3, 1849; January 9, 1850.

62. For the most groundbreaking reading of mid-century Mexican conservative thought, see Palti, *La política del disenso*, 7–58.

63. "Chispa," "Soberanía popular," *El Universal*, November 18 and December 17, 1848.

64. "Soberanía popular (Cuarto artículo)," "Soberanía popular (Tercer artículo)," "Soberanía popular (Segundo artículo)," *El Universal*, December 17, 13, 10, 1848.

65. "La cuestión de prohibiciones," *El Monitor Republicano*, March 7, 1849; "La Federación defendida por *El Monitor*," *El Universal*, April 24, 1849.

66. "Más contradicciones (Segundo artículo)," "Más contradicciones (Segundo artículo. Concluye)," *El Universal*, March 11, 12, 1849.

67. "Partidos. Liberalismo. Servilismo. (Concluye)," *El Universal*, September 8, 1849.

68. "Popularidad: Opinión General. Preocupaciones," *El Universal*, April 29, 1849. On monarchy as an almost embarrassing political option, which was only defended under exceptional circumstances after the fall of Agustín de Iturbide's empire in 1823, see Pani, "La innombrable."

69. "Más contradicciones (Segundo artículo. Concluye)," *El Universal*, March 12, 1849; "Más sobre gobiernos," *El Monitor Republicano*, August 31, 1849; "Las constituciones y los gobiernos [tercer artículo]," *El Siglo Diez y Nueve*, April 8, 1849.

70. A mob attacked the house of the minister of foreign relations, Manuel Díaz de Bonilla, future negotiator of the Gadsden Purchase. Alcántara Machuca, "La elección de Lucas Alamán"; "Crónica interior: Reflexiones sobre las últimas ocurrencias en la capital," *El Universal*, December 6, 1849.

71. "Variedades," *El Siglo Diez y Nueve*, December 9, 1849.

72. "Elecciones," *El Siglo Diez y Nueve*, February 15, 1857.
73. "Elecciones," "La fusión de los partidos," *El Siglo Diez y Nueve*, February 15, 25, 1857.
74. "La fusión de los partidos: El *Heraldo*," *El Siglo Diez y Nueve*, March 4, 1857.
75. "La fusión de los partidos: La *Nación*," "Orden Constitucional," *El Siglo Diez y Nueve*, March 5 and February 14, 1857.
76. "Crónica electoral: Manifestación al público," *El Siglo Diez y Nueve*, June 17, 1857; Tapia, "Competencia electoral."
77. Johansson, "El imposible pluralismo político."
78. "La fusión de los partidos: La *Nación*," "Orden Constitucional," *El Siglo Diez y Nueve*, March 5 and February 14, 1857.
79. "Orden constitucional," *El Siglo Diez y Nueve*, February 14, 1857.
80. "La facción demagógica," *El Siglo Diez y Nueve*, March 25, 1857.
81. Fioravanti, *Constitución*; Bailyn, *Ideological Origins*, 198–229; Rojas, "Constitución histórica."
82. During the first half of the nineteenth century, the other relatively stable constitution is that of Chile, proclaimed in 1833, preceded by four more ephemeral fundamental laws (1818, 1822, 1823, 1828). As Alison LaCroix has written, the constitution's "subject-matter vision of sovereignty," designed to "de-pathologize" a system with multiple sovereigns, was "the paramount innovation of the American federal republic." LaCroix, *Interbellum Constitution*, introduction.
83. Bestor, "American Civil War."
84. "Constitución federal de los Estados Unidos Mexicanos," February 5, 1857, www.orden juridico.gob.mx/Constitucion/1857.pdf.
85. Costeloe, "Mariano Arista."
86. Fowler, "El pronunciamiento mexicano."
87. "Plan del Hospicio," Guadalajara, October 20, 1852, in *The Pronunciamiento in Independent Mexico, 1821–1876*, https://arts.st-andrews.ac.uk/pronunciamientos/getpdf.php?id=656.
88. Fowler, *Santa Anna*.
89. Lucas Alamán to Antonio López de Santa Anna, Mexico City, March 23, 1853, in García Cantú, *El pensamiento*, 341–45.
90. Alamán to Santa Anna, Mexico City, March 23, 1853, in García Cantú, *El pensamiento*, 342.
91. For the Mexican and Iberoamerican constitutional tradition, see Garriga, *Historia y constitución*; Luna, Mijangos, and Rojas, *De Cádiz al siglo XXI*; and Andrews, *De Cádiz a Querétaro*.
92. "Bases para la administración de la República hasta la promulgación de la Constitución," April 22, 1853, www.ordenjuridico.gob.mx/Constitucion/1853.pdf.
93. Fowler, *Santa Anna*, 289–316; Vázquez Mantecón, *Santa Anna*. Right before the Mexican American War, some Conservative and military leaders, with Salvador Bermúdez de Castro, Spain's minister to Mexico, were involved in a surreptitious monarchist movement. See Soto, *La conspiración monárquica*.
94. O'Gorman, "Precedentes y sentido."
95. Prieto, *Viajes de orden suprema*.
96. Ponciano Arriaga, June 23, 1856, in Zarco, *Historia del Congreso*, 387–404.
97. For the election results, see Zarco, *Historia del Congreso*, 21–25. Noriega, "Los grupos parlamentarios," shows how the experienced legislators who had been a regular feature of previous assemblies were left out of the 1856–57 Congress.
98. 39 votes against 40. *Actas oficiales*, 19.

99. For the *moderados*, see Villegas Revueltas, *El liberalismo moderado*.
100. See Pani, "Cuando la ley fundamental desbarata."
101. Aguilar y Marocho, *La Batalla de Jueves Santo*.
102. Payno, "Memoria sobre la revolución," 49–50.
103. Labastida y Dávalos, *Carta pastoral*, 26.
104. Munguía, *Opúsculo*, 18.
105. Bestor, "American Civil War," 343.
106. Rakove, "Thinking Like a Constitution," 22–24.
107. This is the central argument of Wilentz's important book, *No Property in Man*. See also Lieber, *What Is Our Constitution?*, 33, 35.
108. Calhoun was too ill to deliver this speech, which was read by Virginia senator James Mason, March 4, 1850, *Congressional Globe*, Senate, 31st Cong., 1st sess., 451–55.
109. LaCroix, *Interbellum Constitution*, chap. 9; Suárez Argüello, "De los esclavos fugitivos."
110. Seward, in *Crittenden Compromise*, 7–8.
111. Smith, *Stormy Present*, 43–67.
112. Only 150 cases were prosecuted in 1850 and 1851, while thousands of slaves made their way to Canada. Downs, *Second American Revolution*, 69.
113. In the case of the Christiana Riot in 1851—during which a Maryland slaveholder died while trying to capture some fugitive slaves—one of the ringleaders was charged with treason. The judge instructed the jury that the prisoner's "transaction" did not rise "to the dignity of treason or levying war." He found it "dangerous . . . to extend the crime of treason by construction to doubtful cases." Robbins, *Report of the Trial*. For the controversial nature of interstate noncooperation, denial of interstate comity and state opposition to federal law (often related to slavery), see Finkelman, "States Rights."
114. Stephen A. Douglas, January 4, 1854, in *Nebraska Question*, 35–36.
115. Stephen A. Douglas, January 4, 1854, in *Nebraska Question*, 36.
116. Childers, "Interpreting Popular Sovereignty," 61–65.
117. Davis, *Speech of the Honorable Jefferson Davis* (1850), 15, 13.
118. *Crittenden Compromise*, 2, 12.
119. Etcheson, *Bleeding Kansas*; Sutton, *Stark Mad Abolitionists*.
120. *Act to punish offences*, August 14, 1855.
121. Fehrenbacher, *Dred Scott Case*, 449–84.
122. Dred Scott v. Sanford (1857), 19 Howard 393, 15 L.Ed. 691.
123. Republican Party Platform of 1860, May 17, 1860, www.presidency.ucsb.edu/documents/republican-party-platform-1860.
124. As Don Fehrenbacher argues, *Dred Scott*, the first decision to invalidate a major federal law, forced the United States, for the first time, "to consider the operational scope and meaning of judicial review in national politics." Fehrenbacher, *Dred Scott Case*, 4.
125. Palmer, *South*, 4–5.
126. Palmer, *South*, 12.
127. Benjamin, *Speech*, 2.
128. Benjamin, *Speech*, 7–8, 10.
129. Lieber, *What Is Our Constitution?*, 5–6.
130. *Kansas: The Lecompton Constitution*, 8.
131. Lieber, *What Is Our Constitution?*, 29–30, 32–33.
132. Douglass, *Constitution*, 2–4.
133. Smith, *Stormy Present*, 168, 172. For the use of this term, see Greg P. Downs's suggestive

"The Mexicanization of American Politics" and Joshua T. Tracy's chronologically and thematically broader analysis, "The 'Mexicanization' of the United States."

134. For the geography of political dissent, see Mijangos, *Entre Dios y la República*, 237–75; and Strobel, *El ejército liberal*, 76–155.

135. Thomas, *Confederate Nation*, 74–75.

136. Plan de Tacubaya, December 17, 1857, in *The Pronunciamiento in Independent Mexico, 1821–1876*, https://arts.st-andrews.ac.uk/pronunciamientos/dates.php?f=y&pid=1006&m=12&y=1857.

137. Modificaciones al Plan de Tacubaya, January 11, 1858, in *The Pronunciamiento in Independent Mexico, 1821–1876*, https://arts.st-andrews.ac.uk/pronunciamientos/dates.php?f=y&pid=1269&m=1&y=1858.

138. *Address of the People of South Carolina*, December 25, 1860, 4, 13; "Southern Secessionists and Northern Disunionists," *The Liberator*, April 19, 1861.

139. Thomas, *Confederate Nation*, 41–43.

140. [Lieber], *Amendments of the Constitution*, 5; Vorenberg, *Final Freedom*, 11–13; Foner, *Fiery Trial*, 147–49, 156.

141. "H.J. Res. 80, proposing to amend the Constitution of the United States (Corwin Amendment)," February 28, 1861, www.visitthecapitol.gov/artifact/hj-res-80-proposing-amend-constitution-united-states-corwin-amendment-february-28-1861.

142. Holt, *Fate of Their Country*, 3.

143. Abraham Lincoln, "Cooper Union Address," February 27, 1860, www.abrahamlincolnonline.org/lincoln/speeches/cooper.htm.

144. [Davis], *Speech of the Hon. Jefferson Davis* (1861), 15, 12.

145. [Davis], *Speech of the Hon. Jefferson Davis* (1861), 2, 11.

146. Benjamin, *Speech of Hon. J. P. Benjamin*, 11.

Chapter Three

1. "Manifiesto del presidente constitucional interino," Guadalajara, March 16, 1858, in *The Pronunciamiento in Independent Mexico, 1821–1876*, https://arts.st-andrews.ac.uk/pronunciamientos/regions.php?r=13&pid=1550.

2. "Dictamen acerca de la forma de gobierno que, para constituirse definitivamente conviene adoptar en México; presentado por la Comisión especial en la sesión del 8 de julio de 1863, fue nombrara por la Asamblea de Notables reunida en cumplimiento del decreto del 16 de junio último" in "Documentos relativos," 1144.

3. On the French Intervention, see Hanna and Hanna, *Napoleon III*; Black, *Napoleon III*; Lecaillon, *Napoléon III*; Cunningham, *Mexico and the Foreign Policy*; and Shawcross, *France, Mexico*. On the Spanish expedition, see Pi Suñer, *El general Prim*.

4. An agreement that Mexico would resume debt payments and foreign intervention come to an end was signed in the highlands above the unhealthy coast in La Soledad, Veracruz, in February 1862.

5. Alexander H. Stephens, "Cornerstone Speech," Savannah, March 21, 1861, www.battlefields.org/learn/primary-sources/cornerstone-speech; see, for Mexican Conservatives, "Moralidad pública," *La Sociedad*, October 1, 1864; *Manifestación que hacen al venerable clero*, August 30, 1859, 1–2.

6. "La hermosa reacción," Chapultepec, July 12, 1859, in García Cantú, *El pensamiento*, 1:502–12, 502, 505.

7. Hall, *Historic Significance*, 37–38. In one of the most suggestive analyses of Confederate politics, George C. Rable has described a "conservative revolution" as an "oxymoron"; Rable, *Confederate Republic*, 44–63.

8. The reference to 2 Corinthians, 4:8–9, was common to Conservative language. See García González, "Vencidos pero no convencidos."

9. Quigley, "Independence Day Dilemmas"; the quote from Charleston's *Daily Courier* is at 257; 245–46. Quote of George Fitzhugh on the "Confederate Revolution" improving on the American Revolution from Rubin, *Shattered Nation*, 18.

10. Faust, *Creation of Confederate Nationalism*, 21.

11. "Discurso inaugural del Emperador ante la Academia imperial de ciencias y artes," *El Diario del Imperio*, July 7, 1865. To the Conservatives' dismay, Maximilian derided the period of Spanish domination as a "three hundred year-long artificial night." The fateful events that contributed to independence and the nation's rival founding fathers—Miguel Hidalgo and Agustín de Iturbide—were to be memorialized on the same day, since the new government considered that Mexicans took too many days off work. To the dismay of many Conservatives, the emperor—in a decision that settled the date of the national holiday for the future— picked September 16, the anniversary of the insurgent rebellion, as Independence Day. Duncan, "Political Legitimation"; Duncan, "Embracing a Suitable Past"; Pani, "El proyecto de Estado." For a brilliant analysis of the construction of a visual repertoire for this patriotic history by Mexican artists under imperial patronage, see Acevedo, *Testimonios artísiticos*.

12. "Parte oficial," *El Diario del Imperio*, November 13, 1865. The crest was surrounded by a ribbon inscribed with the imperial motto: "Equity in Justice."

13. This is Edmundo O'Gorman's central argument in *México, el trauma*. He depicts the US model, embraced by Mexican Liberals, as the seamless epitome of modernity.

14. Egnal, "Rethinking Secession."

15. "Suspensión de periódicos," "Cesa suspensión de la prensa," June 11 and 15, 1863, in *Boletín de las leyes del Imperio* (1863), 1:36, 40–42.

16. Practically all republican administrations had regulated freedom of the press. Coudart, "La regulación," 680, 635, 630. In the United States, the Lincoln administration also restricted freedom of the press, by suppressing newspapers it considered to be "organs of treason," as part of its efforts to win the war. Holzer, *Lincoln*.

17. Alabama, Mississippi, Georgia, Florida, Louisiana, Texas, Arkansas, North Carolina, and Virginia. Dew, *Apostles*, 22.

18. Conventions in Mississippi, Florida, and Louisiana voted to leave the Union with majorities of almost 80 percent. McCurry, *Confederate Reckoning*, chap. 2; Joe T. Timmons's analysis of the Texas popular vote—with an overwhelming majority ratifying secession— casts doubt on the referendum having been "properly held" and its results "correctly recorded"; Timmons, "Referendum in Texas," 20.

19. Hill, "Speech Delivered at Milledgeville, Ga.," in *Senator Benjamin H. Hill*, 237–50, 237; McCurry, *Confederate Reckoning*, chap. 2.

20. Thomas, *Confederate Nation*, 93–95; McCurry, *Confederate Reckoning*, chap. 2.

21. Rehnquist, *All the Laws but One*; Farber, *Lincoln's Constitution*, 157–63, 188–92; Neff, *Justice in Blue and Gray*, 34–44, 52–55.

22. Phillips, *Rivers Ran Backward*, 83–168, 125, 139–14.

23. "A Declaration of the Causes which Impel de State of Texas to Secede from the Federal Union," February 2, 1861; "A Declaration of the Immediate Causes which Induce and Justify the Secession of the State of Mississippi from the Union"; Georgia Secession, January 29, 1861, *The Avalon Project: Documents in Law, History and Diplomacy*, https://avalon.law.yale.edu/19th_century.

24. [Rhett], *Address of the People of South Carolina*, 4.

25. McCurry, *Confederate Reckoning*, chap. 2; Dew, *Apostles*, 71–73.

26. Neely, *Lincoln*, 235–74. Neely argues convincingly, against the grain, for the continuity

of democratic politics under a Confederacy which some have described as the product "not only a coup d'état but of a thoroughly reactionary one"; Neely, *Lincoln*, 263. I will argue that this continuity coexists with antidemocratic schemes and that the ensuing tensions and contradictions structure Confederate politics; DeRosa, "Rule of Law," 791.

27. Maier, *Ratification*, ix–xvi. Neely finds that the process of "deratifying" the constitution compares favorably with ratification, in that the depth of the ratification debates might have been, in the case of the small states, exaggerated, and that secession had been discussed for almost thirty years, "in effect creating a discourse that was much richer than the one on ratification"; Neely, *Lincoln*, 240–48, 260–63. Nonetheless, one could argue that, given that no state rejected the constitution or proposed possible amendments, the debates that preceded the ratification of the Confederate constitution seem rather perfunctory.

28. "A Declaration . . . Mississippi," *Avalon Project*, https://avalon.law.yale.edu/19th_century/csa_missec.asp.

29. Rable, *Confederate Republic*, 43, 66–67; Thomas, *Confederate Nation*, 44. Thomas R. Cobb, another member of the Georgia delegation, even described Stephens as "a man who had fought against our rights and liberty," and disparaged the assembly's "maudlin disposition to conciliate Union men"; Hull, "Making of the Confederate Constitution."

30. [George Fitzhugh], "What Is a Constitution?," *Debow's Review*, March 1861. Despite its growing influence during the war, this radical faction effected no changes in Confederate policy. See Bonner, "Proslavery Extremism."

31. "Speech Delivered to the Georgia Legislature," Milledgeville, December 11, 1862, in Hill, *Senator Benjamin H. Hill*, 251–72, 252–53. I am grateful to Greg Downs for his comments on this issue.

32. "The Two Constitutions," *Harper's Weekly*, March 30, 1861.

33. As Tulio Halperín Donghi has pointed out, the constitutional pacts of the 1850s and 1860s consolidated a legal framework for the continent's stability during the "neocolonial order" (1850–1930); Halperín Donghi, in *Contemporary History*, 115–207. For Argentina's 1853 constitution, see Botana, *La tradición republicana*. For Colombia's progressive experimentation with federalism (1853, 1858, 1863), see Ruiz Gutiérrez, *Federalismo y descentralización*. On Mexico's 1857 constitution, see Sinkin, *Mexican Reform*. On Ecuador's Catholic, centralizing republican constitutionalism (1861, 1869), see Buriano, *Navegando*. On Perú's 1854 civil war, which ended slavery, and its 1860 constitution, see Peralta Ruiz, "La guerra civil peruana."

34. Currie, "Through the Looking Glass," 1266, 1258, 1397. I am grateful to Gregory E. Dowd for his comments on the continuities of the Confederate constitution.

35. Constitution of the Confederate States, art. 5, sec. 1, *Avalon Project*, https://avalon.law.yale.edu/19th_century/csa_csa.asp.

36. Constitution of the Confederate States, art. 1, sec. 2, clause 5, *Avalon Project*, https://avalon.law.yale.edu/19th_century/csa_csa.asp.

37. "The Two Constitutions," *Harper's Weekly*, March 30, 1861; Marshall L. DeRosa argues that this is an emphatic assertion of state sovereignty and supremacy, and proof that they were parties to a compact, in which, as South Carolina's secession declaration stated, the "failure of one of the contracting parties to perform a material part of the agreement, entirely releases the obligation of the other." He describes the 1861 constitution as proof of Southerners' better comprehension of "the theory of our government. It is, indeed, a reactionary document, a reaction to inevitable changes . . . transforming the community of states into a national community of individuals"; DeRosa, *Confederate Constitution*, 45, 16–17, 38–56. The editor of Thomas Cobb's letters, while a delegate at Montgomery, describes the preamble as

holding "unmistakably" the sovereignty of the states, and "declared the Constitution a compact between them"; Hull, "Making of the Confederate Constitution," 292.

38. Thomas J. Withers, Benjamin H. Hill, February 28, 1861; William W. Boyce, Christopher Memminger, March 6, 1861; Hill, James Chesnut, March 7, 1861, in *Journal of the Congress of the Confederate States*, 1:859, 873, 876–77.

39. Constitution of the Confederate States, art. 3, sec. 1, *Avalon Project*, https://avalon.law.yale.edu/19th_century/csa_csa.asp.

40. Hamilton, "State Courts," 430, 426, 427.

41. Hamilton, "State Courts"; Neely, *Lincoln*, 319–33. Aaron R. Hall, who convincingly characterizes Confederate constitutionalism as modern, creative, centralizing, and statist, argues that the absence of a Supreme Court "necessarily [gave] the [Confederate] government amplified interpretive authority"; Hall, "Reframing," 262.

42. Hill, March 7, 1861, *Journal of the Congress of the Confederate States*, 1:876–77.

43. *Exposition and Protest*, 30.

44. Hull, "Making of the Confederate Constitution," 290.

45. Constitution of the Confederate States of America, art. 4, sec. 2, clause 3; sec. 3, clause 3; *Avalon Project*, https://avalon.law.yale.edu/19th_century/csa_csa.asp.

46. Smith, *Address to the Citizens of Alabama*, 19.

47. As we have seen in chapter 1, this was certainly the case for Mexican observers, who considered the clause proof of Anglo Americans' materialism and hypocrisy. See, for instance, José María Lafragua, foreign minister during the Mexican-American War, in Circular, November 27, 1846, *Algunos documentos*, 44.

48. Rable, *Confederate Republic*, 51–53.

49. Smith, *Address to the Citizens of Alabama*, 19.

50. Constitution of the Confederate States of America, art. 1, sec. 9, clauses 1 and 2, *Avalon Project*, https://avalon.law.yale.edu/19th_century/csa_csa.asp; Rable, *Confederate Republic*, 51–53.

51. Duncan F. Kenner, Robert B. Rhett, March 6, 1861, *Journal of the Congress of the Confederate*, 1:874.

52. Huston, *Calculating the Value*, 12–13, 2.

53. "Speech Delivered at Macon, Ga.," June 30, 1860; "Speech Delivered at Milledgeville, Ga.," November 15, 1860, in Hill, *Senator Benjamin H. Hill*, 229, 237–50, 243.

54. Constitution of the Confederate States of America, art. 1, sec. 8, clause 4, *Avalon Project*, https://avalon.law.yale.edu/19th_century/csa_csa.asp.

55. Constitution of the Confederate States of America, art. 1, sec. 8, clause 1, *Avalon Project*, https://avalon.law.yale.edu/19th_century/csa_csa.asp; Hall, "Reframing," 267–68.

56. Constitution of the Confederate States of America, March 11, 1861, art. 1, sec. 2, clause 3, *Avalon Project*, https://avalon.law.yale.edu/19th_century/csa_csa.asp.

57. Constitution of the Confederate States of America, art. 1, sec. 8, clauses 1, 3, and 7; sec. 7, clause 2; sec. 9, clause 9; art. 2, sec. 1, clause 1; sec. 2, clause 3, *Avalon Project*, https://avalon.law.yale.edu/19th_century/csa_csa.asp; "The Constitution of the Confederate States," *Debow's Review* 30, no. 1 (July 1861); Rable, *Confederate Republic*, 56–57.

58. Constitution of the Confederate States of America, art. 2, sec. 1, clause 1; sec. 2, clause 3, *Avalon Project*, https://avalon.law.yale.edu/19th_century/csa_csa.asp.

59. Hall and Ely, "South."

60. April 30, 1861, in Hull, "Making of the Confederate Constitution," 285.

61. Huston, *Calculating the Value*, 47.

62. Hall, "Reframing," 262.

63. "Documentos relativos," 1147, 1155.
64. Fowler, *Independent Mexico*, 188–245, 197, 242.
65. "Documentos relativos," 1162; On the political weight of the colonial legacy, see Pérez Vejo, "La difícil herencia" and "Las encrucijadas ideológicas."
66. See, for instance, Pesado, *Controversia pacífica*.
67. It is the case of the stern, erudite *La Cruz* (1855–58). See Gómez Aguado, "*La Cruz*."
68. Pesado, *Controversia pacífica*, 6–7.
69. "Discurso sobre la constitución de la Iglesia" (1857), in Couto, *Obras*, 1–75, 59–61, 66–74.
70. "Plan de Tacubaya," Mexico City, December 17, 1857, in *The Pronunciamiento in Independent Mexico, 1821–1876*, http://arts.st-andrews.ac.uk/pronunciamientos/dates.php?f=y&pid=1006&m=12&y=1857.
71. "Manifiesto del Gobierno Supremo de la República a los Mexicanos," January 28, 1858, in *Recopilación de leyes*, 17–24, 18–19.
72. "Modificación del Plan de Tacubaya," January 11, 1858, in *Recopilación de leyes*, 3–4.
73. "Decreto declarando nulas las disposiciones de la ley del 25 de junio de 1856," "Se deroga la ley de obvenciones parroquiales," "Empleados: Vuelvan a sus destinos aquellos que fueron separados por solo haberse negado a jurar la constitución," "Decreto restableciendo los fueros eclesiásticos y militar," January 28, 1858; "Registro civil. Derogación del decreto que lo estableció," March 30, 1858, in *Recopilación de leyes*, 25–28.
74. "Los llamados Estados se denominarán Departamentos," March 17, 1858, in *Recopilación de leyes*, 76.
75. The best overview of the war is Fowler, *La Guerra*.
76. "Días festivos: Recuerdo de las disposiciones de 9 de julio de 1853 en contra del abuso de algunos establecimientos . . . ," February 5, 1858, in *Recopilación de leyes*, 31–33. At Montgomery, Georgia's Thomas Cobb tried to include a similar disposition in the Confederate constitution. Cobb, March 6, 1861, *Journal of the Congress of the Confederate States*, 1:87.
77. "Territorio de Iturbide," March 12, 1858; "Erección territorio de Tlaxcala," May 8, 1858; "Separación de Nuevo León y Coahuila," October 7, 1858, in *Recopilación de leyes*, 68, 127–28, 277. "Departamento de Veracruz se divide en cuatro territorios," June 4, 1859; "División territorial del departamento de Toluca," June 4, 1859; "Departamento de Michoacán," June 11, 1859; "Departamento de Querétaro: Se divide en tres partidos judiciales," June 14, 1859; "División provisional del departamento de Guanajuato," "Tepic se erige en territorio," December 24, 1859, in *Recopilación de leyes* (1865), 257–59, 261–62, 280–82, 283–84, 379–81, 448.
78. "Se declaran traidores a la patria," April 1, 1859; "Decretos del llamado Gobierno constitucional: Protesta y reprobación," August 6, 1859; "Protesta del Supremo Gobierno contra el tratado ajustado por los rebeldes de Veracruz y Mr. McLane," in *Recopilación de leyes* (1865), 169, 450–55; "Miguel Miramón . . . a la Nación," Guadalajara, January 1, 1860, in *Recopilación de leyes* (1866), 3–7.
79. "Extranjeros: Se prohibe a autoridades civiles y jefes militares toda violencia," November 15, 1858; "Batallón de Guardia Nacional Victoria," February 4, 1858; "Batallón auxiliar del ejército," February 23, 1858; "Guardia civil: Su institución," July 19, 1858; "Contribución departamental para sostenimiento de las Compañías defensoras del orden y la propiedad," August 11, 1858; "Súbditos norteamericanos: No sean molestados en sus personas ni intereses," May 14, 1859, in *Recopilación de leyes* (1864), 319–20, 29–30, 40–41, 204–7, 214–17, 222–23.
80. Miguel María Echegaray to Félix Zuloaga, May 24, 1858, in Cruz Barney, *La República Central*, 2.

81. Cuevas served as a diplomat in Prussia and Great Britain and negotiated peace treaties with France (1838) and the United States (1847–48). He had been a senator and secretary of foreign relations. Cuevas, *Porvenir de México*, iv, vi, x, xii–xiii.

82. "Estatuto orgánico provisional de la República," Arts. 1, 34–45, 13, 14, 20, Mexico City, June 15, 1858, in Cruz Barney, *La República Central*, 125–39, 125, 133–38, 128, 130. It was not the first time that Conservatives tried to come up with an alternative system of representation that would give voice to society's wisest and most invested in maintaining order and promoting prosperity. For the 1846 Congress, elected by "classes," see Aguilar Rivera, "La convocatoria."

83. Cuevas himself rejected the US minister's proposal for a treaty in which, among other things, Mexico would sell Baja California to its northern neighbor, by arguing that such a momentous decision could not be made without the ratification of a representative legislative body. Luis Gonzaga Cuevas to John Forsyth, April 5, 1858, in "Crónica interior: Notas cambiadas," *La Sociedad*, April 29, 1859. Hanna Lerner has highlighted the difficulties of drafting constitutions in divided societies, to the point of making it practically impossible; Lerner, *Making Constitutions*.

84. Miranda, *Algunas reflexiones*, 7. Miranda drew copiously from the writings of Juan Donoso Cortés. The Spanish Conservative had seemed too radical—too mystical, even—to his Mexican colleagues in the early 1850s. By decade's end, his apocalyptic vision of a stark choice between a "dictatorship of the dagger" and that of the sword had become a staple of the rhetoric of Mexican Conservatives. See Nava Bonilla, "El Padre Miranda."

85. Óscar Cruz Barney found the manuscript of the statute and published it in 2009. Cruz Barney, *La República Central*.

86. Plan de Ayotla, December 20, 1858, Plan proclamado por el batallón de Celaya, acuartelado en San Agustín, por el que se modificó el de Ayotla [also known as the Plan de Navidad], December 25, 1858, in *The Pronunciamiento in Independent Mexico, 1821–1876*, https://arts.st-andrews.ac.uk/pronunciamientos/dates.php?f=y&pid=1340&m=12&y=1858, https://arts.st-andrews.ac.uk/pronunciamientos/dates.php?f=y&pid=1409&m=12&y=1858.

87. Proclama de Miramón, Guadalajara, January 1, 1859, in *The Pronunciamiento in Independent Mexico, 1821–1876*, https://arts.st-andrews.ac.uk/pronunciamientos/dates.php?f=y&pid=1515&m=1&y=1859.

88. "La hermosa reacción," in García Cantú, *El pensamiento*, 1:504–6.

89. The expression is from Fuentes Mares, *Y México se refugió*.

90. "Decreto sobre la formación de la Asamblea de Notables," in "Documentos relativos," 1130–36. The socioeconomic profile of Mexico's legislative elite has been studied by Noriega, "Elecciones y notables."

91. The most thorough analysis of church-state relations during this period is García Ugarte, *Poder político y religioso*. See also Pablo Mijangos's brilliant *Lawyer of the Church*.

92. "Documentos relativos," 1165–69.

93. "Documentos relativos," 1149–50.

94. "El progreso," *La Nación*, February 7, 1866.

95. *Discurso pronunciado en el palacio de Miramar*, 70–74, 73.

96. *Reglamento para los servicios*; "Proyecto de constitución, escrito por Carlota," August–September 1863, in Villavicencio Navarro, *Y mucho más libre*, 305–13. See also del Arenal, "El proyecto de constitución"; and Villavicencio Navarro, *Y mucho más libre*, 256–65.

97. Title III, arts. 25–31; Title IV, Arts. 32–44, in "Proyecto de constitución, escrito por Carlota."

98. Letter from Maximilian to José Ma. Esteva, Puebla, June 7, 1865, *El Diario del Imperio*, June 9, 1865. See the positive review of the statute in a liberal publication: "Obertura a toda Orquesta: Estatuto Orgánico," *La Orquesta*, April 5, 1865.

99. "Ley para las elecciones en los ayuntamientos," November 1, 1865, in *Boletín de las leyes del Imperio* (1865), 361–466.

100. López González, "Los proyectos constitucionales"; Pani, "Cuando la ley fundamental desbarata."

101. "Documentos relativos," 1158.

102. "Derechos del hombre bajo las monarquías," "El emperador y los partidos," *La Razón*, November 17 and October 19, 1864.

103. Letter from Juan José Caserta, Jesús López Portillo, Vicente Ortigosa, Antonio Álvarez del Castillo, and Rafael Jiménez Castro to Gen. José López Uraga, Guadalajara, June 4, 1864, in de Zamacois, *Historia de Méjico*, 17:353–56. These Guadalajara politicians felt they were "serving the Liberal cause" by asking General López Uraga to put down his arms against the French Intervention.

104. Ortigosa, *Cuatro memorias*, i–ii, 62. Ortigosa was a civil and chemical engineer, trained in France and Germany, who invented a tortilla-dough making machine. He was a member of the imperial Council of State. After 1867, he did not return to public life.

105. "Territorio del Imperio," February 8, 1865; "Atribuciones de los Comisarios Imperiales y Visitadores," October 11, 1865; "Ley orgánica de la administración departamental gubernativa," November 1, 1865, *Boletín de las leyes* (1863), 4:234–53, *Boletín de las leyes* (1865), 241–48, 346–59. "Idea de las divisiones territoriales en México, desde los tiempos de la dominación española hasta nuestros días," *El Mexicano*, June 14 and July 8, 1866.

106. Conflicts would be adjudicated in administrative courts in which the executive branch was both judge and party. "Ley sobre lo contencioso-administrativo," November 1, 1865, *Boletín de las leyes* (1865), 224–40.

107. Robles Pezuela, *Memoria*; Sánchez, "Los proyectos de colonización"; Gerali and Riguzzi, "Los veneros del emperador."

108. Ludlow, "La disputa financiera."

109. *Código civil del Imperio*, "Decreto adoptando el sistema métrico-decimal francés," October 27, 1865, "Ley de Instrucción Pública," December 27, 1866, *Colección . . . Imperio*, 5:45–47, 8:21–51.

110. The *actas* were compiled and mailed to Maximilian at Trieste, and many were published in the Conservative press. See, for instance, "Sección oficial: Texcoco," "Acajete," *La Sociedad*, July 17 and August 13, 1863. Pani, "Intervention and Empire."

111. Francisco Pimentel, large landowner and noted linguist, was a member of the commission, which he described as an "act of *liberalism*" that "solemnly" disproved those "superficial men of bad faith" who contended that "*monarchy* and *despotism* were synonymous." "Algunos apuntes sobre la Hacienda pública (art. 2°)," *La Sociedad*, October 28, 1864; italics in the original.

112. "Audiencias," January 1, 1865, in *Boletín de las leyes* (1865), 4:9–10. At issue were both broadening the population's access to authority and guaranteeing publicity. Ministers would hold hearings on designated days of the week but were not to be visited in their offices or speak privately of "official business."

113. Letter from Maximilian to Léopold I of Belgium, 1865, quoted in Conte Corti, *Maximiliano y Carlota*, 346.

114. The expression is by Francisco Pimentel, who in 1865 published his *Memoria sobre las*

causas; "Junta. Se instituye la denominada 'Protectora de Clases Menesterosas' con objeto de mejorar las condiciones de las clases desgraciadas," April 10, 1865, in *Boletín de las leyes* (1865), 4:374–75. The Junta Protectora is probably the imperial institution that has attracted the most scholarly attention. See González y González, "El indigenismo de Maximiliano"; Meyer, "La Junta Protectora"; del Arenal, "La protección del indio"; and Marino, "Ahora que Dios."

115. "Dictamen...," in "Documentos relativos," 1156.
116. Smith, *Address to the Citizens of Alabama*, 11, 14.

Chapter Four

1. Sumner, *Equal Rights of All*, 8.
2. "Convocatoria a elecciones y a plebiscito sobre reformas constitucionales," August 14, 1867, *Benito Juárez: Documentos*, 12:225, 1.
3. Campos Pérez, "1867"; "Cuestión del día," *El Siglo Diez y Nueve*, September 1, 1867, quoted on 1698.
4. Carmagnani, *Estado y mercado*.
5. Edwards, *Legal History*, 88, 90–119.
6. Quoted in Jones, *Blue and Gray Diplomacy*, 10.
7. The interim president's powers would be checked only by "respect for individual guarantees." "Plan de Ayutla reformado en Acapulco," art. 3, March 11, 1854, in *The Pronunciamiento in Independent Mexico, 1821–1876*, https://arts.st-andrews.ac.uk/pronunciamientos/getpdf.php?id=1559.
8. Santiago Vidaurri, governor of Nuevo León and Coahuila, defended the "independence" of his state and called for the return of its troops, for protection against "wild Indians." Most of Nuevo León's officers decided to remain under the orders of the Veracruz government. All claimed to abide by the "true will" of the pueblos. "Acta," Monterrey, September 25, 1859, in *Benito Juárez: Documentos*, 2:13, 21.
9. Laura Edwards has traced how, despite the Civil War's protagonists' constitutional devotion, the conflict "forever altered what they sought to preserve. At war's end, many of the legal system's foundational assumptions had been intentionally dismantled or unintentionally eviscerated"; Edwards, *Legal History*, 3.
10. Ackerman, *We the People*, 58.
11. Downs, *Second American Revolution*, 36. I closely follow the arguments in Downs, "Second American Republic," 11–54.
12. For two visions of the Republican Party's powerful motivations, see Gienapp, *Origins*; and Foner, *Free Soil*. For the Mexican radicals, see Blázquez, "Los liberales exiliados," 38–39.
13. Noriega, "Elecciones y notables." The best study of the 1856–57 Congress is Sinkin, *Mexican Reform*.
14. Freedom of worship was an especially unpopular initiative. *Puro* delegates nevertheless described its rejection by Congress as a betrayal of "the people" in favor of "the populace ... manipulated by scheming, meddlesome crones." Zarco, *Historia del Congreso*, 861–64.
15. Joaquín García Granados, Francisco Zarco, Ignacio Ramírez, September 26, 1856, in Zarco, *Historia del Congreso*, 510, 509, 519–25, 520–32.
16. "Bienes del clero regular y secular: Entran al dominio de la nación," June 12, 1859, in Arrillaga, *Recopilación de leyes*, 20:42–48, 47.
17. Decreto del Gobierno de la República, March 5, 1864, in Ávila, Martínez, and Morado, *Santiago Vidaurri*, 284–85.

18. Nevada became a state in 1864, Nebraska in 1867, and Colorado only in 1876. Garret Davis, William M. Stewart, April 4, 1866, *Congressional Globe*, 39th Cong., 1st sess., appendix, 185, 1755.

19. Samuel C. Pomeroy, *Congressional Globe*, 39th Cong., 1st sess., Senate, January 29, 1866, 708.

20. "Dictamen de la Comisión de Constitución," June 16, 1856, Ponciano Arriaga, June 23, 1856, in Zarco, *Historia del Congreso*, 306–29, 307, 391.

21. "Dictamen," June 16, 1856, in Zarco, *Historia del Congreso*, 312.

22. Dictamen," June 16, 1856, in Zarco, *Historia del Congreso*, 319.

23. Juan Antonio Gamboa, September 10, 1856. The single-chamber legislature was approved by a vote of 44 to 38; Zarco, *Historia del Congreso*, 839–40, 843.

24. Francisco Zarco, October 15, 1856; Ignacio Ramírez, November 22, 1856, in Zarco, *Historia del Congreso*, 947–48, 1048–49.

25. "Dictamen," June 16, 1856, in Zarco, *Historia del Congreso*, 318.

26. "Dictamen," June 16, 1856, in Zarco, *Historia del Congreso*, 313.

27. "Constitución federal de los Estados Unidos Mexicanos," Arts. 101–2, www.ordenjuridico.gob.mx/Constitucion/1857.pdf.

28. Sinkin, *Mexican Reform*.

29. "Constitución federal de los Estados Unidos Mexicanos," Art. 1, www.ordenjuridico.gob.mx/Constitucion/1857.pdf.

30. Anyone filing a suit, deed, claim, or contract would need the registry's certificate to do so. "Ley Orgánica del Registro Civil," Arts. 2, 3, 4, and 12, January 27, 1857, in Dublán and Lozano, *Legislación mexicana*, 8:3–20.

31. Plan de Ayutla, March 1, 1854, Arts. 6, 7, in *Plan de Ayutla*, 11–37. This speaks to the involvement of economic actors interested in free trade in the opposition to the Santa Anna government, including James Gadsden, the US minister to Mexico. Olliff, *Reforma Mexico*; Terrazas y Basante, "Miseria hacendaria." See chap. 7.

32. Rhi Sausi and Molina, *El mal necesario*; Rhi Sausi, "Breve historia."

33. Francisco Zarco, January 28–31, 1857, in Zarco, *Historia del Congreso*, 882–83.

34. Gregorio Payró, January 28–31, 1857, in Zarco, *Historia del Congreso*, 878–79; "Constitución federal de los Estados Unidos Mexicanos," Art. 124, www.ordenjuridico.gob.mx/Constitucion/1857.pdf; Zarco, *Historia del Congreso*, 886. Some form of tax on the circulation of good survived into the second half of the twentieth century. Aboites, "Alcabalas posporfirianas."

35. "El gobierno constitucional a la Nación," July 7, 1859, in Juárez et al., *Justificación de las Leyes*, 13–34. For many among the priests and laity, the government's will to reduce a sacrament to the "a simple transaction that is publicly convenient" meant "degrading and corrupting it"; de la Rosa, *El matrimonio civil*, 4.

36. "Baja del ejército permanente," December 27, 1860, https://archivos.juridicas.unam.mx/www/bjv/libros/6/2858/70.pdf.

37. The important and extensive literature on disentailment has recently been invigorated by innovative research on the diverse, protracted process of civil disentailment. For the classics, see Bazant, *Los bienes*; and Knowlton, *Church Property*. For recent contributions, see, among others, Kourí, *Pueblo Divided*; Marino, *Huixquilucan*; Escobar, Falcón, and Sánchez Rodríguez, *La desamortización*; and Pérez Montesinos, "Geografía, política y economía."

38. Lieber, *Amendments*, 6.

39. Vorenberg, *Emancipation Proclamation*, 18–22, 76–77, 237–38.

40. Lieber, *Amendments*, 35, 36–39.

41. Foner, *Second Founding*, 59.
42. Foner, *Fiery Trial*, 56–59, 182–89, 206–47. For the debates surrounding the Thirteenth Amendment, see Vorenberg, *Final Freedom*.
43. Oakes, *Freedom National*, 192–223.
44. Vorenberg, *Final Freedom*, 71–79, 167–75, 227–32.
45. Foner, *Second Founding*, 55.
46. The label is Charles Sumner's in *The One Man Power*, 11.
47. Foner, *Second Founding*, 71–72. See also John A. Bingham, *Congressional Globe*, 39th Cong., 1st sess., House, May 10, 1866, 2541–45.
48. Stewart, *Congressional Globe*, 39th Cong., 1st sess., Senate, April 4, 1866, 1755.
49. The most heated arguments targeted article 15 of the draft constitution, which denied state and federal legislators the authority to "prohibit or hamper the exercise of any form of religious worship." Proyecto de Constitución, in Zarco, *Historia del Congreso*, 331.
50. "Constitución federal de los Estados Unidos Mexicanos," Art. 30, www.ordenjuridico.gob.mx/Constitucion/1857.pdf. The intervention of foreign powers to protect their subjects proved destabilizing and irritating to governments throughout Latin America during the nineteenth century. Manuel de la Peña y Peña, who presided over Mexico's Supreme Court, devoted the third and final volume of his legal practice *Lessons* to foreigners, to decry the illegitimacy of extraterritoriality and to insist on their having to submit to the laws and courts of the country, without the intervention of their government. See de la Peña y Peña, *Lecciones de práctica forense*.
51. Peña y Ramírez, September 1, 1856, in Zarco, *Historia del Congreso*, 817. (Male) citizens were still required to maintain "an honest way of living" in order to vote, but this subjective condition had not been and did not become an instrument of disenfranchisement, as it would in the Jim Crow South.
52. "Constitución federal de los Estados Unidos Mexicanos," Art. 55, www.ordenjuridico.gob.mx/Constitucion/1857.pdf. Federal elections would be indirect in only one degree, so district electoral colleges would elect the president, members of Congress, and Supreme Court justices instead of voting, as they had before, for a second electoral college, presided by the state's governor. Medina Peña, *Invención del sistema político mexicano*, 108–11, 231–41.
53. Francisco Zarco, Ignacio Ramírez, September 18, 1856; José María Mata, November 25, 1856, *Historia del Congreso*, 861–64, 1057.
54. "Constitución federal de los Estados Unidos Mexicanos," Arts. 90–95, 79, www.ordenjuridico.gob.mx/Constitucion/1857.pdf.
55. Guillermo Langlois, August 18, 1856, *Historia del Congreso*, 737–40.
56. Ignacio L. Vallarta, August 19, 1856, *Historia del Congreso*, 741–50.
57. Session of November 27, 1857, *Historia del Congreso*, 1077.
58. Fausta Gantús and Alicia Salmerón have led a team of researchers that has thoroughly renovated our knowledge and understanding of nineteenth-century elections. See Gantús and Salmerón, *Prensa y elecciones* and *Cuando las armas hablan*; and Gantús, *Elecciones . . . Las fuentes* and *Elecciones . . . Las prácticas*.
59. Aguilar Rivera, "La redención democrática," 52–53.
60. "Constitución federal de los Estados Unidos Mexicanos," arts. 1–28, 101, www.ordenjuridico.gob.mx/Constitucion/1857.pdf. The amparo suit was perhaps less innovative than its sponsors argued, having deep roots in judicial practices during the viceregal period. Lira, *El amparo colonial*.
61. Eulogio Barrera, Ignacio Ramírez, October 28, 1856, Jesús Anaya Hermosillo, October 29, 1856, in Zarco, *Historia del Congreso*, 990–93.

62. "Dictamen de la comisión de Constitución," Prisciliano Díaz González, Juan Morales Ayala, Espiridión Moreno, June 16 and July 10, 18, 1856, in Zarco, *Historia del Congreso*, 313–14.

63. Vallarta, July 10, 1856, in Zarco, *Historia del Congreso*, 742. Vallarta, at twenty-five, was among the youngest members of the 1856 Congress. He would go on to become governor of the state of Jalisco (1861, 1862, 1871–75), minister of the interior (1868), minister of foreign relations (1876–78), and an influential chief justice (1877–82). He theorized enthusiastically about the amparo procedure in Vallarta, *El juicio de amparo*.

64. "Dictamen," in Zarco, *Historia del Congreso*, 324.

65. "Dictamen," Melchor Ocampo, October 20, 1856, in Zarco, *Historia del Congreso*, 324, 995.

66. "Dictamen," Ponciano Arriaga, October 28, 1856, in Zarco, *Historia del Congreso*, 324, 990–91. Paul de Flotte was a French naval officer, journalist, and politician who was elected to the Assemblée Nationale in 1850 as a socialist democrat. He died fighting with Garibaldi in Calabria in 1860 and penned *La Souveraineté du Peuple*.

67. Connecticut, Minnesota, Wisconsin, and Colorado had all voted against "impartial suffrage" that would not discriminate for reasons of color, race, or former status as an enslaved person. Van Alstyne, "Fourteenth Amendment," 70. The idea of colonizing Liberia with former slaves remained popular. See Burin, *Slavery and the Peculiar Solution*.

68. Andrew Johnson, "Veto Message," March 27, 1866, www.presidency.ucsb.edu/documents/veto-message-438.

69. Frederick Douglass at the 1869 meeting of the American Equal Rights Association, in Cady Stanton, Anthony, and Gage, *History of Woman Suffrage*, 2:382. See also Douglass, *What the Black Man Wants*; and Langston, "Citizenship and the Ballot."

70. Kendrick, "Journal," 264–91, 264; Foner, *Second Founding*, 60.

71. Lyman Trumbull, April 4, 1866, Senate, *Congressional Globe*, 39th Cong., 1st sess., 1765–67.

72. On March 2, 1867, Congress passed the act "to provide for the more efficient government of the Rebel States," and would pass three more laws organizing the military occupation of the former Confederate states—Tennessee excepted—in the following year; on April 9, 1866, it had passed, over Johnson's veto, an act "to protect all Persons in the United States in their Civil Rights." To provide first relief, then support in the transition to freedom, a Bureau of Refugees, Freedmen, and Abandoned Lands was established in March 1865, and Congress voted to renew its charter in 1866, but the bureau gradually received less funding and became inoperative in the early 1870s. Sumner, *Equal Rights of All*, 10.

73. *One Country, One Constitution*, 1, 4; italics in the original.

74. Reverdy Johnson; Edward Cowan, James Dixon, April 5, 1866, Senate, *Congressional Globe*, 39th Cong., 1st sess., 1777–78, 1782–83; 40th Cong., 3rd sess., 705; Davis, in appendix, 181–85.

75. Davis, in appendix, 184–84; National Union Executive Committee, *Negro Suffrage*, 4; Seaman, *What Miscegenation Is!*, 4. On "public rights," see Scott, "Discerning a Dignitary Offense."

76. "Dictamen," June 16, 1856, in *Historia del Congreso*, 319.

77. James L. Huston has shown that "slaveholding comprised far more national wealth than railroads and manufacturing . . . combined," and the South's cotton fed into the vanguard of global industrial capitalism. Huston, *Calculating the Value*, 27–29.

78. From the early years of independence, many politicians were convinced that the church's landed wealth was enormous and that it was stagnant, as were the lands held

communally by Indian pueblos. Disentailment was, then, to put into circulation enormous resources and solve many of the nation's problems. It was also a prerogative of the sovereign state. The Liberals' classic iteration of this position is [Mora], *Disertación sobre la naturaleza*. Similar arguments are taken up, to advocate for mid-century reforms, in Payno, *La reforma social*, and Pimentel, *La economía política*. Historians have found that Liberals' ideas of the church's landed wealth—always predominantly urban, and diminished after the decade-long independence war and the economic shakeup that followed—and their convictions that ecclesiastical institutions and peasant communities were, by definition, archaic and inefficient, were exaggerated. See Cervantes Bello, *De la impiedad y la usura* and "La propiedad eclesiástica."

79. Huston, *Calculating the Value*, 13.

80. Galusha A. Grow, February 20, 1862, House, *Congressional Globe*, 37th Cong., 2nd sess., 909–10. Advocates of homestead legislation blamed Southern Democrats for the congressional gridlock, but Gerald Wolff shows that, although voting on the bill in 1854 was strongly influenced by the stormy debate over the Kansas-Nebraska bill, it was not defeated by a "selfishly united slavocracy." Wolff, "Slavocracy," 111. In their 1860 party platform, Republicans included a demand for "the passage of the complete and satisfactory homestead measure" that had been approved by the House. Republican Party Platform of 1860, May 17, 1860, www.presidency.ucsb.edu/documents/republican-party-platform-1860.

81. Buchanan's Veto Message, June 23, 1860, in *Congressional Globe*, 36th Cong., 1st sess., 3263–64; [Grow], *Land for the Landless*, 1, 3–5; "Speech on the Homestead Bill," May 20, 1858, in *Speeches of Andrew Johnson*, 74, 33.

82. Buchanan's Veto Message, 3264; [Johnson], "Speech on the Homestead Bill," 13, 33–35, 74, 37; [Grow], *Land for the Landless*, 4. In a speech on the Senate floor in March 1858, the South Carolinian spoke of the "mudsills," a class which "in all social systems [had] to do the menial duties, to perform the drudgery of life . . . requiring but a low order of intellect and but little skill," but indispensable to the existence of "that other class which leads progress, civilization, and refinement." Cox Richardson, *To Make Men Free*, 15–16.

83. José María Castillo Velasco, June 16, 1856, in Zarco, *Historia del Congreso*, 364.

84. José María Castillo Velasco, June 16, 1856, in Zarco, *Historia del Congreso*, 364–65.

85. Ponciano Arriaga, June 23, 1856, in Zarco, *Historia del Congreso*, 387–404, 394, 396, 397, 402–3.

86. Payno, *La reforma social*, 65–66. Payno had been deeply involved in the—highly flawed—construction of Mexico's public finances during the first half of the nineteenth century. This pamphlet, published in May 1861, condemned the clergy for clinging to wealth that they managed but did not own, but also the state's overweening intervention in a process that should have stayed contained within civil society. See Córdoba, *Manuel Payno*.

87. Ley Lerdo, in Zarco, *Historia del Congreso*, 423–27.

88. Quoted in Covo, *Las ideas de la Reforma*, 110.

89. Francisco Zarco, June 28, 1856, in Zarco, *Historia del Congreso*, 431. The law was incorporated into the constitution by a vote of 76 to 3, accompanied by "visible signs of approval on the floor and in the galleries." January 24, 1857, in Zarco, *Historia del Congreso*, 1214.

90. "Alocución del papa Pío IX contra la constitución," Rome, December 15, 1856, in *The Pronunciamiento in Independent Mexico, 1821–1876*, https://arts.st-andrews.ac.uk/pronunciamientos/regions.php?r=116&pid=1533.

91. Edwards, *Legal History*, 36–38.

92. Galusha Grow, House, February 20, 1862, *Congressional Globe*, 37th Cong., 2nd sess., 909–10; Florer, "Major Issues," 459–68.

93. In some cases—such as the Union occupation of the South Carolina's Sea Islands—abandoned plantation land was allocated to the formerly enslaved. Ochiai, "Port Royal Experiment."

94. "Reglamento de la Ley de Nacionalización de los bienes del clero," Arts. 6–8, July 13, 1859, in Soberanes and Alejos Grau, *Las leyes de Reforma*, 213–21, 214–15.

95. Ludlow, "Las dinastías financieras."

96. Syrett, *Civil War*, 5.

97. Syrett, *Civil War*, 7–18.

98. Vorenberg, *Emancipation Proclamation*, introduction.

99. James Oakes has persuasively defended Republican antislavery convictions and actions. Oakes, "Reluctant to Emancipate?"; Oakes, *Freedom National*, 119–45. Their congruence and enthusiasm—perhaps less pervasive among the members of the congressional majority than Oakes supposes—was not influential enough to put emancipation at the center of legislative efforts and made their execution awkward. See also the searing Porter, "James Oakes' Treatment."

100. "The First Confiscation Act," August 6, 1861; "The Second Confiscation Act," July 17, 1862, in Syrett, *Civil War*, 191–92, 192–95. According to James McPherson, these statutes were so "confusing and poorly drawn" that they had little impact, although they were symbolically important; McPherson, *Battle Cry of Freedom*, 500–502. John Syrett adds to this Lincoln and Attorney General Edward Bates's rejection of punitive confiscation policies and the "inattention and declining interests" of congressional Republicans; Syrett, *Civil War*, 55–72, 120–36. For efforts to colonize freedmen outside of the United States, see Guyatt, "Future Empire."

101. Art. 3, sec. 3, of the US constitution establishes that "no attainder of treason shall work corruption of blood, or forfeiture except during the life of the person attainted," and Lincoln threatened to veto the Second Confiscation Act unless it was made clear that it was not retroactive, it would not affect lawmakers or judges who had not taken an oath to support the Confederate constitution and no punishment under the act would be "construed as to work forfeiture of the real estate of the offender beyond his natural life." Syrett, *Civil War*, 35–54, 185–89; "The Joint Resolution," July 17, 1862, in Syrett, *Civil War*, 195–96. Still, the First Confiscation Act "emancipated tens of thousands of slaves"; Oakes, "Reluctant to Emancipate?," 5–9.

102. Lieber, *Amendments*, 11–13, 36–39, 20–21, 15–18. In Lieber's words, "No one is sovereign within the policy of the United States [and in practical and legal terms] no one ought to be sovereign."

103. Quoted by Foner, *Second Founding*, 157. Foner asserts that "the Court's narrow reading of the constitutional amendments was a choice, not something predetermined by public opinion or historical context. . . . Overall, the late nineteenth-century decisions constitute a sad chapter in the history of race, citizenship and democracy in the United States." Foner, *Second Founding*, 130. Rebecca Scott has also argued for analyzing "historical context" as a field of contention, not a determining factor; Scott, "Derechos y honra públicos," 172–75. For the attrition of the amparo mechanism, see Rhi Sausi, "Derecho y garantías." Courts of law are the site where an individual's rights, when upheld, become a concrete reality, so it is not easy to think of an alternative in which federal authorities could have acted as more effective "guardians."

104. Bazant, *Los bienes*, 146–91; Knowlton, *Church Property*; Syrett, *Civil War*, 120–54; Cox, "Promise of Land."

105. Kantrowitz, "Not Quite Constitutionalized," 76; Kantrowitz, "Citizen's Clothing"; Genetin-Pilawa, "Ely S. Parker," 195; Berger, "Birthright Citizenship on Trial," 1191, 1258.

106. Gates, "Homestead Law."
107. Marino and Zuleta, "Una visión del campo," 470.

Chapter Five

1. John Alexander Macdonald, February 6, 1865, in *Parliamentary Debates*, 30–45.
2. I am grateful to Elisa Cárdenas for her thoughtful and exceptionally knowledgeable comments on these issues. I delved into the topic of religion and civil war more extensively in Pani, "Religión, república y guerra."
3. As Lincoln remarked in his Second Inaugural Address, March 4, 1865, www.nps.gov/linc/learn/historyculture/lincoln-second-inaugural.htm. On Lincoln's religious interpretation of the war, see Wilson, "Religion," 403–7; and Rable's splendid *God's Almost Chosen People*, 370–78.
4. Connaughton, *Iglesia, religión y leyes*, 15–38.
5. In the case of Mexico, where the political and religious community had overlapped since independence, contentious political issues could reflect, as Pamela Voekel has argued, different ecclesiological visions. Voekel, *For God and Liberty*.
6. [Sledd], *Sermon*, 3, 5, 21; "Manifiesto del Gral. Tomás Mejía," San Juan del Río, January 24, 1858, in *The Pronunciamiento in Independent Mexico, 1821–1876*, https://arts.st-andrews.ac.uk/pronunciamientos/getpdf.php?id=1262; Benito Juárez, "Manifiesto desde Guanajuato," January 19, 1858, www.memoriapoliticademexico.org/Textos/3Reforma/1858MBJ.html.
7. Swiss theologian Philip Schaff, quoted in Rable, *God's Almost Chosen People*, 11. See also Hatch, *Democratization*.
8. Pope Benedict XIV consecrated the Virgin of Guadalupe as Mexico's patron with a verse from Psalm 147:20: "Non fecit talliter omni nationi." The best study of this Marian devotion is Brading, *Mexican Phoenix*.
9. Rable, *God's Almost Chosen People*, 22–23; *El Partido Conservador*, 38.
10. "Dictamen acerca de la forma de gobierno que, para constituirse definitivamente, conviene adoptar en México; presentado por la Comisión especial que en la sesión del 8 de julio de 1863, fue nominada por la Asamblea de Notables reunida en cumplimiento del decreto de 16 de junio último," in "Documentos relativos," 1144–71.
11. Rable, *God's Almost Chosen People*, 69–89; "Proclama del General Echegaray," Puebla, January 1858, in *The Pronunciamiento in Independent Mexico, 1821–1876*, https://arts.st-andrews.ac.uk/pronunciamientos/participants.php?lw=E&lwo=&id=3123&pid=1256.
12. "Meditation on the Divine Will," September 1862, www.abrahamlincolnonline.org/lincoln/speeches/meditat.htm.
13. Rable, *God's Almost Chosen People*, 69, 73, 159; Circular from governor Manuel Zamora, Veracruz, July 12, 1857, Archivo General de la Nación (henceforth AGN), Justicia eclesiástica, vol. 180, no record number (1857); From Domingo Bureau to Minister of Justice, Manuel Ruiz, Veracruz, June 9, 1858, AGN, Justicia, vol. 614, record no. 31 (1858).
14. Constitution of the Confederate States of America, preamble, March 11, 1861, https://avalon.law.yale.edu/19th_century/csa_csa.asp.
15. Rable, *God's Almost Chosen People*, 69, 107–26, 95–106, 166–84.
16. "Sermon on the war, delivered in Saint Patrick's Cathedral," August 17, 1862, in [Hughes], *Complete Works*, 2:368–73, 373; Kurtz, *Excommunicated*, chap. 2.
17. Rubial, *La santidad controvertida*; Curiel, "San Felipe de Jesús."
18. Cárdenas, "El fin de una era."
19. [Sledd], *Sermon*, 7; Michelbacher, *Sermon*, 5.
20. Pedro, Bishop of San Luis, January 26, 1856; From the Commander General, Durango,

May 6, 1857; Government of Oaxaca, June 23, 1857; From Commander General of the State of Mexico to Minister of War, October 7, 1857; From Commander General, Guanajuato, AGN, Justicia Eclesiástica, vols. 179, 180, 182, and 174, no record number. Marta Eugenia García Ugarte has aptly described this a as a "rebellion," whose geography Pablo Mijangos has reconstructed; García Ugarte, *Poder político y religioso*, 1:581–720; Mijangos, *Entre Dios y la República*, 237–76.

21. "Manifiesto del general Mejía," January 22, 1858, in *The Pronunciamiento in Independent Mexico, 1821–1876*, https://arts.st-andrews.ac.uk/pronunciamientos/regions.php?r=34&pid=1261.

22. A group of guerrillas fell on the town of Nopalucan, Puebla, and stole "images of the saints," musical instruments, and "interesting documents," Secretaría de Estado y del Despacho de Gobernación, copy, June 21, 1859, AGN, Justicia eclesiástica, vol. 19 (1859). For the actions of the Lozadistas in Nayarit, who kidnapped the crucified Christ of Santiago Ixcuintla, see Lira, "De buenos mexicanos"; Van Osterhout, "Confraternities and Popular Conservatism"; and Brittsan, *Popular Politics*, 95–96. Edgar Mendoza analyzes the struggles of Oaxaca's Chocholteco pueblos over land, funds, the geography of local government, and the control of religious buildings and festivities, which often went beyond the turbulent years of reform and war; Mendoza, *Municipios, cofradías*, 274, 287–88, 348–59.

23. Connaughton, *La mancuerna discordante*, 165; Voekel, "Liberal Religion."

24. "Proclama del general Santos Degollado a los soldados constitucionalistas," November 18, 1859, in *Planes en la nación mexicana*, 6:104.

25. Valdés, *Memorial de la Guerra*, 87.

26. Manuel Eleuterio Gómez to Minister of Justice and Ecclesiastical Affairs, Mexico City, August 19, 1861, in AGN, Justicia, vol. 645, record no. 91.

27. Acta Constitutiva, Carta de Melchor Ocampo a Rafael Díaz Martínez, Veracruz, October 1859, in Kirk, "La formación," appendixes A and B; Voekel, "Liberal Religion," 84.

28. "El gobierno constitucional a la nación," Veracruz, July 7, 1859, in *Benito Juárez: Documentos*, 2:13, 1.

29. Juárez et al., *Justificación de las leyes*, 15–17.

30. *Manifestación que hacen al venerable clero*, 5–6.

31. *Manifestación que hacen al venerable clero*, 20–23.

32. *Manifestación que hacen al venerable clero*, 21.

33. García Ugarte, *Poder político y religioso*, 2:1148–65, 1204–26, 1277.

34. García Ugarte, *Poder político y religioso*; 2:1277–780; Mijangos, *Lawyer of the Church*, 189–230.

35. Antonio de la Luz Pérez, Santa María Molango, AGN, Fondo Justicia, vol. 452, record no. 74.

36. The expression is by Methodist minister William M. Leftwich, who complains about the Gospel being given a "modern, war interpretation." Leftwich, *Martyrdom in Missouri*, 2:38–40.

37. AGN, Fondo Miguel Rul, box 27, no record number; W. H. Elder to Edwin Stanton, Vidalia, July 30, 1864, in *Character Glimpses*, 53–57, 40. See also the case of St. Louis Presbyterian minister Samuel B. McPheeters, in MacArthur, "There Can Be No Neutral Ground."

38. W. H. Elder to President Lincoln, Natchez, April 7, 1864, in *Character Glimpses*, 48–49. Buffalo's bishop, John Timon, had not wanted the US flag to be flown over churches, so as not to alienate Southern sympathizers who might want to worship there. Riforgiato, "Bishop Timon," 74.

39. Testory, *El imperio y el clero*, 29; Arrillaga, *Algunas observaciones*, 8; Arrillaga, *Cuartas observaciones*, 3–4, 15, 9, 58–59.

40. Leftwich, *Martyrdom in Missouri*, 2:226, 26–27, 30.

41. Mijangos, *Entre Dios y la República*, 237–76.

42. Leftwich, *Martyrdom in Missouri*, 2:41.

43. Special Order no. 31, August 12, 1864, in *Character Glimpses*, 58–59.

44. Adame Goddard, "El juramento de la constitución," 36.

45. Cummings v. Missouri, 71 U.S. 277 (1867).

46. See LaCroix, *Interbellum Constitution*; and Salmerón and Gantús, *Un siglo de tensiones*.

47. James Madison, *Federalist Papers*, no. 45 (1788), https://avalon.law.yale.edu/18th_century/fed45.asp.

48. "Constitución federal de los Estados Unidos Mexicanos," sec. 1, Art. 29, February 5, 1857, www.ordenjuridico.gob.mx/Constitucion/1857.pdf. For the most thorough analysis of the history of emergency powers in nineteenth-century Mexico, see Aguilar Rivera, *El manto liberal*.

49. The expression "constitutionalization of politics" is Jack Rakove's, in "Thinking Like a Constitution," 22.

50. "An Act to provide for the collection of taxes," March 2, 1833, Pub. L. 22-, 4 Stat. 632.

51. As is it is described in Alfonso X's *Siete Partidas*, the influential thirteenth-century Castilian legal code, part 7, title 1, law 7; title 2, www.cervantesvirtual.com.

52. Rhenquist, *All the Laws but One*; Blair, *With Malice*, 13–35; Kettner, "Development of American Citizenship"; Mathisen, *Loyal Republic*; Fuentes Loza, *Los delitos políticos*; Ortelli, "Enemigos internos," 471–72.

53. Article 35 of the "Plan de la Monarquía Indígena," proclaimed in the small town of Chicontla, Puebla, read, "No one will be in any way disturbed for their previous political proceedings and opinions, but those opposing the accomplishment of this endeavor will be irremissibly put to death"; February 2, 1834, in *The Pronunciamiento in Independent Mexico, 1821–1876*, https://arts.st-andrews.ac.uk/pronunciamientos/search.php?searchString=monarquia&pid=869. Leaders of triumphant pronunciamientos would often issue "a broad and general amnesty for political acts or opinions." "Artículos propuestos por la guarnición de Querétaro al general José Antonio Mejía," Querétaro, June 25, 1833, in *The Pronunciamiento in Independent Mexico, 1821–1876*, https://arts.st-andrews.ac.uk/pronunciamientos/search.php?searchString=muerte&pid=1137. For treason cases against participants in tax rebellions, see Henderson, "Treason, Sedition."

54. Blair, *With Malice*, 15–30, 15. For the arbitrary, partisan use of law against internal enemies in the United States and Mexico during the first years of independence, see Pani, "Saving the Nation."

55. Rable, *Confederate Republic*, esp. 132–94, 236–54.

56. Coronado Guel, "Legislación expedida."

57. "Estatuto provisional del Imperio Mexicano," Art. 4, April 10, 1865, https://museodelasconstituciones.unam.mx/wp-content/uploads/2022/02/Estatuto-provisional-del-Imperio-Mexicano-1865-act.pdf.

58. For the Mexican case, the most persuasive treatise on this position is perhaps Munguía, *Del Derecho natural*, meant to serve as a textbook for would be lawyers. See Mijangos, *Lawyer of the Church*, 95–136.

59. Witt, *Lincoln's Code*, 50–65, 70, 66–78, 77.

60. Payno, *Carta que sobre los asuntos*, 4–5, 36.

61. Payno, *Carta que sobre los asuntos*, 36, 6.

62. The exchange followed the proclamation of the empire's "Black Decree" of October 1865, which outlawed republican resistance, ordered republicans' summary execution, and required the Imperial Cabinet to make an exception "for special reasons." Ortiz Monasterio, "Vicente Riva Palacio," 441–43.

63. González, "El sitio de Puebla." For more on the Puebla siege, see the articles in Aguilar Ochoa, *El sitio de Puebla*, 25–112. See also Loomans, *Huit mois de captivité*, 46–58. I am grateful to Samuel I. Magaña for the reference to Loomans's experience in Mexico.

64. Meketa, *Legacy of Honor*, 183–84. The law of nations exempted "whole categories of people . . . from the rigors of war": women, children, the old, and the sick. Witt, *Lincoln's Code*, 18.

65. The expression is George McClellan's. Letter to President Lincoln, Headquarters, Army of the Potomac, Camp near Harrison's Landing, Virginia, July 7, 1862, www.let.rug.nl/usa/documents/1851-1875/mcclellan-letter-to-lincoln-on-his-evacuation-from-the-penninsula-campaign-1862.php.

66. The wide circulation of descriptions of the "martyrdom" of civilians who assisted the wounded on the battlefield after Santos Degollado's defeat at Tacubaya in April 1859 is a case in point. Fowler, *La Guerra*, 270–80. Conversely, for recruitment of Indigenous forces, whose "cruelty" and "barbarism" allegedly spread to their companions-in-arms, see Brown, "Indianizing the Confederacy"; and García, "Indios nómadas."

67. Blair, *With Malice*, 77–79.

68. Eulalio Ortega and Jesús María Vásquez for defendant Maximilian von Hapsburg, Querétaro, June 13, 1867, in *Causa de Fernando Maximiliano de Habsburgo*, 334–35.

69. "Ley para castigar los delitos en contra de la nación," January 25, 1862, disp. 5542, in Dublán and Lozano, *Legislación mexicana*, 9:367–71.

70. Strobel, *Resistir es vencer*, 171–76, 225–62.

71. Lieber's *Guerrilla Parties* was a first step toward his influential code. For all of this paper's radical conclusions, and the fact that the War Department often favored summary executions, its impact was tempered by the concern of Union officers and cabinet members with human losses and retaliation, while Lincoln often commuted the death sentences of irregular forces. Witt, *Lincoln's Code*, 191–95.

72. "Reglamento para el servicio de las Fuerzas ligeras que con el nombre de guerrillas se forman para auxiliar las operaciones del ejército, en la presente invasión extranjera y para la pacificación del país." In *Colección . . . Supremo Gobierno*, 307–16. De Kérartry, "La contreguerrilla française."

73. For the origins, organization, and performance of popular guerrillas, see the important work of Monroy Casillas, "Los chinacos," "Un radical," and, on popular bands in Oaxaca and Porfirio Díaz's ambivalent feeling for untrained, audacious, but unreliable (because often "very drunk") *chinaco* fighters, "De la lucha," 104. For Conservative guerrillas, see Palomo González, "Gavillas de bandoleros."

74. McClellan to Lincoln, July 7, 1862, Series 1. General Correspondence, Abraham Lincoln Papers, Library of Congress, www.loc.gov/resource/mal.1685900/?st=pdf.

75. Witt, *Lincoln's Code*, 181–85, 4.

76. Witt, *Lincoln's Code*, 181–85, 4.

77. Hyman, *Era of the Oath*, iv.

78. McCurry, *Confederate Reckoning*, chap. 2.

79. Neely, *Fate of Liberty*, 100–127; Neely, *Southern Rights*, 80–98; Rehnquist, *All the Laws but One*, chap. 3; Neely, *Southern Rights*, 64–79. In contrast, William Blair has shown that

most military commissions did not deal with "frivolous cases" but only with "violent resistance to the government"; Blair, *With Malice*, 56, 311–19.

80. Richard E. Beringer, Herman Hattaway, Archer Jones, and William N. Still Jr. argue that it was the weakness of Confederate nationalism, not lack of men or resources, or poor logistics, that explain the South's defeat; Beringer et al., *Why the South Lost the Civil War*.

81. Rable, *Confederate Republic*, 111–73; McCurry, *Confederate Reckoning*.

82. McCurry, *Confederate Reckoning*, chap. 4.

83. McCurry, *Confederate Reckoning*; Faust, *Mothers of Invention*, 450–76.

84. McCurry, *Confederate Reckoning*, chaps. 4, 5.

85. McCurry, *Confederate Reckoning*, chap. 4.

86. McCurry, *Confederate Reckoning*, chaps. 4, 7.

87. McCurry, *Confederate Reckoning*, chap. 8.

88. *Message of the President*, November 7, 1864, 9–12.

89. Samuel Boykin in the *Macon Christian Index*, quoted in Dillard, "The Confederate Debate," 123. However, Philip Dillard shows that "common men and women" in Georgia were willing to sacrifice slavery to independence and arm the enslaved to fight in the Confederate armies.

90. US Constitution, Art. 1, sec. 5. In 1797, William Blount had been dismissed from the Senate for conspiring with Great Britain. Congressman George Santos was expelled from the House on December 1, 2024.

91. Senators James M. Mason and Robert M. T. Hunter of Virginia; Thomas Clingman and Thomas Bragg of North Carolina; James Chesnut of South Carolina; Alfred O. P. Nicholson of Tennessee; William K. Sebastian and Charles B. Mitchell of Arkansas; John Hemphill and Louis Wigfall of Texas; John C. Breckenridge of Kentucky; Trusten Polk and Waldo P. Johnson of Missouri; Jesse D. Bright of Indiana. Also expelled were House representatives John Bullock Clark, John William Reud, and Henry Cornelius Burnett. The Senate discussed at length if it should seat Benjamin Stark of Oregon and expel Lazarus Powell of Kentucky, but both were approved by a majority. Most of the senators who were disqualified had already left Washington to join the rebels; those remaining—most of them hailing from border states of the Ohio Valley—were chastised as treasonous "secret foes," plotting from within to obstruct the Union's war efforts. Waitman T. Wiley, Charles Sumner, February 2, 1862, June 5, 1862, *Congressional Globe*, 37th Cong., 2nd sess., 651–55, 2572.

92. Senators James A. Bayard, Jesse D. Bright, Lazarus W. Powell, and Garrett Davis, *Congressional Globe*, 37th Cong., 2nd sess., 391–98, 651–55, appendix, 71–85, 1208–16; Senator Sumner, quoted in Edwards, "Benjamin Stark," 334.

93. This was the case of the two Confiscation Acts—the second of which was titled "An Act to suppress Insurrection, to punish Treason and Rebellion, to seize and confiscate the property of Rebels, and for Other Purposes." Syrett, *Civil War*; McPherson, *Battle Cry of Freedom*; Blair, *With Malice*, 80–91, 130–33.

94. Future vice president Schulyer Colfax, quoted in Hyman, *Era of the Oath*, 21.

95. Hyman, *Era of the Oath*, 37, 41; Blair, *With Malice*, 137–47.

96. Hyman, *Era of the Oath*, 41.

97. Quoted in Hyman, *Era of the Oath*, 33.

98. Preliminary Emancipation Proclamation, September 22, 1862, www.archives.gov/exhibits/american_originals_iv/sections/transcript_preliminary_emancipation.html; Emancipation Proclamation, January 1, 1863, www.archives.gov/exhibits/featured-documents/emancipation-proclamation/transcript.html.

99. I first dealt with these issues in Pani, "Los 'castigos nacionales.'"

100. "Ley para castigar delitos contra la nación, contra el orden y la paz pública," December 6, 1856, "Ley para castigar los delitos en contra de la nación . . . ," January 25, 1862, in Dublán and Lozano, *Legislación mexicana*, disp. 4847, disp. 5542, 9:367–71; Disposiciones, November 3, 1858, July 25, 1860, in Dublán and Lozano, *Legislación mexicana*, disp. 5039, disps. 5103, 5104, 8:311–19, 658, 744–46; "Decreto del jefe político y militar del departamento de Zacatecas," in Zaldívar, *Recopilación*, 18–19; "Ley sobre conspiradores," *Diario oficial del Supremo Gobierno*, July 15, 1858. For a groundbreaking exploration of the French military courts, see Méndez Camacho, "Administración."

101. "Parte oficial," *El Diario del Imperio*, October 3, 1865.

102. "Decreto del general en jefe del ejército," December 27, 1860, in Dublán and Lozano, *Legislación mexicana*, disp. 5132, 8:781–82.

103. "Constitución federal de los Estados Unidos Mexicanos," Arts. 1–29, 23, February 5, 1857, www.ordenjuridico.gob.mx/Constitucion/1857.pdf.

104. The unwelcome diplomats were the Spanish and Guatemalan ministers and Luis Clementi, the papal delegate, who, the founders of the secular state insisted, lacked any "diplomatic representation." Circular de la Secretaría de Gobernación, January 25, 1861; Orden del Ministerio de Gobernación, January 17, 1861; Circular de la Secretaría de Relaciones Exteriores, January 25, 1861, in Dublán and Lozano, *Legislación mexicana*, disp. 5167, disp. 5155, disp. 5166, 9:20, 12, 18–20.

105. Representative I. M. Altamirano, June 27, 1861, in Buenrostro, *Historia del Segundo Congreso*, 1:219–20.

106. Circular del Ministerio de Hacienda, January 3, 1861; Circular Secretaría de Hacienda, August 15, 1861, "Abogados," February 8, 1861, in Dublán and Lozano, *Legislación mexicana*, disp. 5137, disp. 5425, disp. 5203, 9:4, 266, 64.

107. Representatives Vicente Riva Palacio, Pantaleón Tovar, Leandro Valle, Joaquín Escalante, Manuel M. Ortiz de Montellano, and José Linares, May 24, 25, 28, 1861, in Buenrostro, *Historia del Segundo Congreso*, 1:72–79.

108. Pradts, May 14, 1861, in Buenrostro, *Historia del Segundo Congreso*, 1:31–37.

109. Decreto del Congreso, June 4, 1861; December 2, 1861, in Dublán and Lozano, *Legislación mexicana*, disp. 5367, disp. 5479, 9:227, 330. Privates were meant to be paid between fifteen and seventeen dollars a month. Even in times of peace, they were rarely paid on time and in full. Ceja, *La fragilidad*, 75–76.

110. Manuel Payno before Congress acting as Grand Jury, July 22, 1861, in Buenrostro, *Historia del Segundo Congreso*, 1:198–202.

111. Altamirano, July 22, 1861, in Buenrostro, *Historia del Segundo Congreso*, 1:202–7.

112. Manuel Payno in Buenrostro, *Historia del Segundo Congreso*, 1:193–207.

113. "Averiguación sumaria contra Manuel Robles Pezuela," March 21, 1862; Ignacio de la Llave to Ignacio Zaragoza, General of the Army of the East, Jalapa, March 20, 1862, containing copies of secret draft invitations and proceedings for the pronunciamiento against the Juárez government, dated March 16, that had been discovered by the Veracruz government. Expediente administrativo del Extinto General de Brigada Manuel Robles Pezuela, vol. 3, Dirección General, Archivo e Historia, Secretaria de la Defensa Nacional (hereinafter AHSDN).

114. [Secretary of War] to Ignacio Zaragoza, Mexico City, March 22, 1862; Order of execution, Chalchicomula, March 22, 1862. Zaragoza, as the local military commander, did not enforce the 1862 law but opted instead for the 1856 law against conspirators. Despite its numerous gradations and more lenient content, the application of the earlier statute also called for execution. Expediente administrativo del Extinto General de Brigada Manuel Robles Pezuela, vol. 3, AHSDN. Robles Pezuela's declaration is in de Zamacois, *Historia de Méjico*, 16:91–92.

115. Maximilian to Minister to War, Mexico City, July 28, 1865, Expediente administrativo

del Extinto General de Brigada Manuel Robles Pezuela, vol. 3, AHSDN. A monthly pension of $100 was granted to his illegitimate daughter, Julieta.

116. Riva Palacio et al., *El Libro Rojo*; Quintero Machler, "De *Le livre rouge*."
117. Casanova, "La seducción de la tragedia," 159–74; Acevedo, "Las imágenes."
118. Hamnett, "La ejecución"; Villalpando, *Maximiliano*.
119. Stealy, "West Virginia's Constitutional Critique."
120. "Action of Tennessee Legislature."
121. "Proclamation by the Governor." I follow Phillips, *Rivers Ran Backward*, closely in this and what follows.
122. Phillips, *Rivers Ran Backward*, 83–168, 125, 139–40. Neely, *Lincoln*, 269.
123. Phillips, *Rivers Ran Backward*, 114–19.
124. Oakes, *Freedom National*, 145–91.
125. González Quiroga, *War and Peace*, 2.
126. Cerutti and González-Quiroga, "Guerra y comercio," 219–25.
127. García, "Indios nómadas," 170. Vidaurri governed Nuevo León—with a brief interlude—between 1855 and 1864 and annexed Coahuila in 1857.
128. García, "Indios nómadas," 175. Unlike the political elites of Saltillo, the state capital, merchants from Coahuila's northern *villas* did express their support for becoming part of Nuevo León; Valdés, *Fulguración y disolvencia*, 117–39.
129. Medina Peña, *Los bárbaros del Norte*, 298, 82; Valdés, *Fulguración y disolvencia*; Strobel, *El ejército liberal*, 312–23; Villarreal Lozano, *Cartas de Querétaro*.
130. García Sandoval, "Salazar Ilarregui."
131. Gantús, Alcalá Ferraéz, and Villanueva, *Campeche*.
132. Rugeley, *River People*, 217–73.
133. Lynch, "Southern California Chivalry," 163–67; Nelson, *Three-Cornered War*, 121, 139; Blyth, "Kit Carson," 55–56, 66–67.
134. Terrazas y Bastante et al., *Las relaciones*, 1:406. For the war's impact on the Rio Grande frontier, see González-Quiroga, *War and Peace*, 176–210, 182, 197; García, "Dominance in an Imagined Border," 51; and Cerutti and González-Quiroga, "Guerra y comercio," 252. By the late 1860s, the Matamoros region had returned to its precarious prewar economy and demography, as a result of the end of the civil war bonanza, political instability, and devastating natural disasters. Small but vibrant Bagdad, which a few years earlier had teemed with 4,000 inhabitants, and was left with a couple of hundred in 1867, tried to survive in the midst of flooding and landslides. The site would eventually be abandoned. Herrera Pérez, *Historia de una ciudad*, 188–90, 201–13.
135. Genetin-Pilawa, "Ely S. Parker."
136. Nayarit was Jalisco's quarrelsome seventh canton until it became a state in 1917. Its mid-nineteenth-century anti-Liberal alliance included many of the Indigenous Sierra towns embroiled in land disputes with neighboring haciendas, the British commercial house of Barron y Forbes and the Tepic governing elite, wary of Guadalajara's interventions in the port city of San Blas. Meyer, *Esperando a Lozada*; Brittsan, *Popular Politics*; Lira, "De buenos mexicanos," 1091.
137. Mallon, *Peasant and Nation*; Thomson and LaFrance, *Patriotism*; McNamara, *Sons of the Sierra*.
138. There is ample literature on the participation of immigrant groups—especially German and Irish—in the US Civil War: see, for example, Honeck, *We are the Revolutionists*; Keating, *Shades of Green*; and Ural, *Civil War Citizens*. For Mexico, see Taylor Hansen, "Voluntarios extranjeros."
139. Quigley, "Civil War Conscription," 388, 387.

140. Strobel, *Resistir es vencer*, 211–25; Flores Salinas, *Cartas desde México*; Eggers, *Memorias de México*; Haman, *Con Maximiliano*; Moyano Pahissa, *Los belgas de Carlota*; Niox, *Expédition*; Pitner, *Maximilian's Lieutenant*; Saavedra Casco, "Un episodio olvidado."

141. Máyer, *Campaña y Guarnición*; Salm Salm, *My Diary*; Doyle, *Cause of All Nations*; Kelly, "Lost Continent."

142. Pérez Tisserant, *Nuestra California*; Gonzales, *Política: Nuevomexicanos*, 358–63.

143. Órdenes Generales, no. 24, General Headquarters, Arizona District, Mesilla, December 2, 1862; in *Correspondencia de la Legación*, 3:253–54.

144. Jerry Thompson has written on the difficulties of accounting for the participation of Tejanos in the armies of the Civil War, since muster rolls in the frontier militias were lost, never compiled, or Spanish surnames were fumbled by non-Spanish speakers. He speaks of "as many as 4,000 Spanish-surnamed individuals" from Texas serving in the Civil War. Omar Valerio Jiménez writes that "an estimated 2,550 Mexican Texans joined Confederate troops and approximately 960 became Union soldiers." Thompson, *Tejanos in Gray*, xv; Valerio Jiménez, "Although We Are the Last Soldiers," 129. See also García, "Dominance," 43–59.

145. Gonzales, *Política: Nuevomexicanos*, 363–65.

146. Matías Romero to Minister of Foreign Affairs, Washington, February 26, 1863, in *Correspondencia de la Legación*, 3:252.

147. Santiago Tafolla, for instance, deserted in March 1864 from the Confederate troops that were patrolling the Eagle Pass area. He crossed the Rio Grande, shouted "¡Qué viva México!" and remained on the other side of the river for a year. Tafolla, *Life Crossing Borders*, chaps. 26 and 28; Pitt, *Decline of the Californios*, 229–48; Lynch, "Southern California Chivalry"; Hayes-Bautista, *El Cinco de Mayo*, 101–92; Thompson, *Tejano Tiger*, chap. 3; Thompson, *Tejanos in Gray*.

148. Thompson, *Tejano Tiger*, chap. 1.

149. Rafael Chacón to General Carleton, Fort Wingate, October 1, 1863, in Meketa, *Legacy of Honor*, 242; this appreciation of Benavides is by Charles Grimos Thorkell de Løcenskiold, who was sent by Texas governor Edward Clark to report on the situation at the border in the fall of 1861. Thompson, *Tejano Tiger*, chap. 3; *Sacramento Daily Union*, June 10, 1861, quoted in Lynch, "Southern California Chivalry," 149–60; *Mesilla Times*, March 30, 1861, quoted in Ganaway, "New Mexico," 65–66.

150. *La Voz de Méjico*, quoted in Hayes-Bautista, *El Cinco de Mayo*, 82, 64.

151. Hayes-Bautista, *El Cinco de Mayo*, 100–131, 101, 142; Miller, "Arms Across the Border," 16–37.

152. Meketa, *Legacy of Honor*, 172–73; Gonzáles, *Política*, 381–84.

153. Meketa, *Legacy of Honor*, 6–7, 127, 135–36; Rafael Chacón to General Carleton, Fort Wingate, October 1, 1863, in Meketa, *Legacy of Honor*, 242; Thompson, *Tejanos in Gray*, xiv–xv.

154. Meketa, *Legacy of Honor*, 173; Lynch, "Southern California Chivalry," 142–51, 194–95.

155. From Manuel Yturri to Elenita, camp near Candem, Arkansas, October 17, 1864, camp near Shreveport, Louisiana, February 28, 1865, Piedmont Springs, Texas, April 11, 1865, in Thompson, *Tejanos in Gray*, 59–60, 64–65.

156. Gonzales, *Política: Nuevomexicanos*, 379; Lynch, "Southern California Chivalry," 200–202; Nelson, *Three-Cornered War*, 99–114.

157. For the growing historiographical interest in the Western theater, see Arenson and Graybill, *Civil War Wests*.

158. Nelson, *Three-Cornered War*, 161–246, 236. In his memoir, Rafael Chacón was critical of Indian slavery and the creation of the Bosque Redondo reservation, which he deemed totally inadequate for agriculture.

159. I am very grateful to Juan Pedro Viqueira for his thoughtful comments on these issues.

There were no reliable national demographic statistics for the Mexican population until the end of the century. According to Rafael Durán, an army officer commissioned by the Mexican Society for Geography and Statistics to draw up a general census, "The movement of the Republic's population could not be determined," given the lack of comprehensive, systematic, thorough census data. He inferred that by 1862, Mexico's population had reached 8,629,982, of which over 2.5 million were "indigenous," while "castes" made up slightly over 4 million. Durán does not specify the criteria he used to define these "racial" groups. [Durán], "Memoria sobre el censo," 277.

160. Navarrete, "¿Qué significa ser indio?"; Briones, "Introducción."

161. Almada Bay, Contreras Tánori, and Reyes Gutiérrez, "Medidas ofensivas y defensivas"; Pimentel, *Memoria sobre las causas*.

162. Jean Meyer has argued that describing conflicts as "caste wars" was an "ideological argument to combat the enemy, [drawn upon] without Machiavellianism, but out of sincere fear." Meyer, *Esperando a Lozada*, 104. García Campos, "La invención." See also Rus, "Whose Caste War?"

163. Hämäläinen, *Comanche Empire*; Hämäläinen, *Lakota America*, 248–93; Ferrer Muñoz and Bono López, *Pueblos indígenas*, 546–75.

164. Lecaillon, *La question indienne*. For a political culture of negotiation and contingent political pacts between Sonora's Mayo, Opata, and Yaqui, see García Rivera and Grajeda Bustamante, "Cultura política."

165. Brittsan, *Popular Politics*, 82, 81–106.

166. Manuel Payno quoted in Meyer, *Esperando a Lozada*, 233; Manuel Lozada, San Luis, March 16, 1863, quoted in Meyer, *Esperando a Lozada*, 175; see also 171–96 and 235–56.

167. José Salazar Ilarregui, "Jefes y habitantes de Chan Santa Cruz," Mérida, November 1864, quoted in Blanco Cebada, "Actores sociales," esp. 92–94. The declaration was written in both Spanish and Maya.

168. Mallon, *Peasant and Nation*; Thomson and LaFrance, *Patriotism*; Thomson, "Memoirs and Memories"; McNamara, *Sons of the Sierra*; Patlán, *Tetela de Ocampo*.

169. Treaty of the Creek Nation, July 10, 1861, *Statutes at Large* (1861–62), 289–310, 289. Bernholz et al., "American Indian Civil War Treaties."

170. "Acts and Resolutions passed at the called Session of the General Council of the Choctaw nation," June 14, 1861, in Western History, Native American Manuscripts, Pitchlynn (1806–81), University of Oklahoma Libraries, Digital Collections, https://digital.libraries.ou.edu/cdm/singleitem/collection/pitchlynn/id/861/rec/3.

171. "Acts and Resolutions passed at the called Session of the General Council of the Choctaw nation," June 14, 1861; Treaty with Choctaws and Chickasaws, July 12, 1861, in *Statutes at Large* (1864), 311–31, 322.

172. Treaty with the Comanches of the Prairies and Staked Plains, August 12, 1831, *Statutes at Large* (1864), 354–62.

173. Treaty with the Osage, October 2, 1861; Treaty with Cherokees, October 7, 1861, *Statutes at Large* (1864), 363–73, 369; 394–411, 410. "Act ratifying the compact entered into between Creeks, Seminoles, Choctaws and Chickasaws at North Fork village," July 1, 1861, American Treaties Portal, http://treatiesportal.unl.edu/csaindiantreaties/csa_treaties.html.

174. Treaty with Choctaws and Chickasaws, July 12, 1862, *Statutes at Large* (1864), 311–31, 318.

175. Gral. Albert Pike, CSA, to [Choctaw Chief] George Hudson, Richmond, December 29, 1861, in Western History, Native American Manuscripts, Pitchlynn (1806–81), University of Oklahoma Libraries, Digital Collections, https://digital.libraries.ou.edu/cdm/singleitem/collection/pitchlynn/id/567/rec/2.

176. Representative Windom, February 28, 1863, *Congressional Globe*, 37th Cong., 3rd sess., appendix, 141–43. Nichols, "Other Civil War"; Chomsky, "United States Dakota War," 24.

177. Kelman, *Misplaced Massacre*, 145, 280; Blackhawk, *Rediscovery of America*, chap. 9.

178. Nichols, "Other Civil War," 5–7; Kelman, *Misplaced Massacre*, 14, 35.

179. Kelman, *Misplaced Massacre*, 15.

180. "Civilization" was considered a key element of Indian citizenship. Sweet, "Native Suffrage," 99.

181. Chomsky, "United States Dakota War," 90–91; Representative Windom, February 28, 1863, *Congressional Globe*, 37th Cong., 3rd sess., appendix, 143. As Zachary Brown has written, the almost absurd hypothesis that the Confederates had managed to orchestrate a barbarous alliance with Indigenous groups in the North was an effective rhetorical device "to rationalize the expulsion and mass annihilation of the Sioux" and other Native American nations. Brown, "Indianizing the Confederacy," 128.

182. Kelman, *Misplaced Massacre*, 280.

Chapter Six

I am very grateful for the generous, extraordinarily helpful comments Paolo Riguzzi and Héctor Strobel made on this chapter.

1. For the impact of new military technology, see Strobel, *Resistir es vencer*, 19–41. See also his description of the surprisingly successful, but woefully insufficient, revitalization of the armories around Mexico City in Strobel, "La artillería liberal."

2. As described by insurgent leader José María Morelos, art. 22, "Sentimientos de la Nación," Chilpancingo, September 14, 1813, www.ordenjuridico.gob.mx/Constitucion/1813.pdf; Pieper, "Contiendas imperiales"; Brownlee, *Federal Taxation*, 19–25; Wobeser, "La Consolidación de Vales Reales."

3. "Constitution of the United States," Art. 1, sec. 2; Art. 1, sec. 8, September 17, 1787, https://constitutioncenter.org/the-constitution/full-text; "Constitución federal de la República Mexicana," Art. 50, XVIII, XIX, XVI, October 4, 1824, www.ordenjuridico.gob.mx/Constitucion/1824B.pdf.

4. The US Constitution provided for Congress to call "forth the Militia, suppress Insurrections and repel Invasions" and allowed for the writ of habeas corpus to be suspended "in cases of rebellion or invasion," or if "public safety" required it, but did not establish procedures, responsibilities, or constraints. "Constitution of the United States," Art. 1, secs. 8–9, September 17, 1787, https://constitutioncenter.org/the-constitution/full-text.

5. Ortiz Escamilla, "La nacionalización"; Medina Peña, *Los bárbaros del Norte*, 264–72; Strobel, *El ejército liberal*, 35–75, 44, 71–74.

6. Serrano, *Igualdad, uniformidad*; Pollack, "De la contribución directa"; Brownlee, *Federal Taxation*, 23.

7. The independence war brought about a dramatic decentralization of economic and political power in New Spain: years of violence bolstered regional elites and broke down the sense of allegiance to the colonial government. For decades, loyalty would not be channeled toward the new, national, government. Serrano and Jauregui, introduction to *Hacienda y política*; Pérez Herrero, "'Crecimiento' colonial."

8. Serrano, *Igualdad, uniformidad*; Uhthoff, "La difícil concurrencia fiscal."

9. Edling, *Hercules in the Cradle*, 30–34, 34. The US Constitution, Art. 1, sec. 9, did restrict the scope of the power of direct taxation by tying it to state population and political representation. Brownlee, *Federal Taxation*, 34; Edling, *Hercules in the Cradle*, 40–41.

10. US Constitution, art. 1, secs. 9 and 2, "Constitution of the United States," September 17, 1787, https://constitutioncenter.org/the-constitution/full-text.

11. Brownlee, *Federal Taxation*, 33–39, 41, 37; Edling, *Hercules in the Cradle*, 30–49.

12. For liberalism's positive impact on the national economy, see Carmagnani, *Estado y mercado*; on the imposition of "order and economy" on public finances, see Quintanar Zárate, "Entre liberalismo y nacionalismo," 199–203.

13. Del Valle, "Los empréstitos"; Rodríguez O., "Los primeros empréstitos"; Nava, "Origen y monto," 93.

14. Hernández Jaimes, *La formación de la hacienda*; Tenenbaum, *México en la época*.

15. *Memoria presentada... por el C. Miguel Lerdo de Tejada*, 5–7. Olveda, "La disputa"; Marichal, "Las finanzas"; Serrano, "El humo"; Silva Riquer and López Martínez, "La organización fiscal."

16. Serrano, *Igualdad, uniformidad*, 147–60. On the resistance of non-Indigenous citizens to direct taxation, see Pollack, "De la contribución directa," 61–63. On the challenges of establishing and effective bureaucracy for the collection of direct taxes, see Jauregui, "La problemática administrativo-fiscal"; and Ibarra, "Catastro e impuestos directos."

17. Ibarra Bellon, *El comercio y el poder*.

18. Jeffersonian critics of Hamilton's program, in power after 1800, were "more hostile to debt," and in 1835 the federal government managed to completely liquidate its debt— domestic and foreign—"for the first and only time in U.S. history." Brownlee, *Federal Taxation*, 41–46; Aboites and Jáuregui, *Penuria sin fin*.

19. Brownlee, *Federal Taxation*, 44–46; Jáuregui, "Los ministros."

20. Edling, *Hercules in the Cradle*, 13.

21. Edling, *Hercules in the Cradle*, 81–107, 147.

22. MacMillan, *War*, 84–88, quote at 84.

23. McPherson, *Battle Cry of Freedom*, 429–30.

24. Guardino, *Dead March*, 31–70, 91–94. Conversely, MacMillan dates the symbolic birth of modern warfare to the day, September 20, 1792, when the French revolutionary forces defeated the Prussian army at Valmy. MacMillan, *War*, 84. For the recruitment methods of the Mexican Army, see Ceja, *La fragilidad*, 74–102.

25. Medina Peña, *Los bárbaros del Norte*; Strobel, *El ejército liberal*, 312–32; Guardino, *Dead March*, 101–22; Strobel, *El ejército liberal*, 35–75.

26. McPherson, *Battle Cry of Freedom*, 313–14.

27. McPherson, *Battle Cry of Freddom*, 313–14; Civil War Service by population, in www.battlefields.org/learn/articles/civil-war-casualties. In comparison, the Crimean War (1853–1856), which is also identified as a harbinger of modern warfare, lasted almost two and a half years and mobilized 1,562,900 men from five countries.

28. Nathan Adams, "Army: The Changes of the Army: Strategy, Size and Expenses," Sheridan at the Reins: Changing Perceptions of the Cavalry, Sheridan, and Native Americans During the Indian Wars, 1868–1877 (website), 2019, http://historyweb.digitalhistory.bsu.edu/ncadams/sheridanatthereins/army.html#.

29. Hernández López, "Militares conservadores," 281–303, 326–32; Strobel, *El ejército liberal*, 194–224, 339–40.

30. Hernández López, "Militares conservadores," 175–76.

31. As I mentioned in chapter 3, a group of Guadalajara Liberals encouraged López Uraga to put down his sword. He would join the empire shortly afterward. Juan José Caserta, Jesús López Portillo, Vicente Ortigosa, Antonio Álvarez del Castillo, and Rafael Jiménez Castro to

José López Uraga, Guadalajara, June 4, 1864, in de Zamacois, *Historia de Méjico*, 17:353–356; Hernández López, "Militares conservadores," 95–302.

32. Provisional agreement of September 8, 1857; [Juan Soto], *Memorias del Ministerio de Guerra y Marina, presentada al primer congreso constitucional de 1857, por el ministro del ramo*, in Hernández López, "Militares conservadores," 151.

33. Hernández López, "Militares conservadores," 201; Strobel, *El ejército liberal*, 260; Fowler, *La Guerra*, 261, 362.

34. Moloeznick, "Insurgencia y contraguerrilla"; Segura Muñoz, "La casa hecha cuartel."

35. Strobel, *El ejército liberal*, 333–46.

36. Hernández López, "Militares conservadores," 263–76.

37. Porfirio Díaz had taken Puebla, at the head of 6,000 men, in early April 1867, and would occupy Mexico City with 25,000 troops in June, after the capital had been left almost defenseless following the sound defeat of Leonardo Márquez's 1,200 men at San Lorenzo (April 15, 1867). Hernández López, "Militares conservadores," 340–43.

38. McPherson, *Battle Cry of Freedom*, 321–22.

39. Message from the President, March 28, 1862, *Journal of the Confederate Congress*, 5:156–57.

40. "An Act to further provide for the public defense," April 16, 1862; "An Act to amend an Act entitled 'An Act to provide further for the public defence,'" September 27, 1862; "An Act," 1864, *Statutes at Large* (1864).

41. McPherson, *Battle Cry of Freedom*, 322.

42. McPherson, *Battle Cry of Freedom*, 490–49, 600–602; Secs.1, 11, "An Act for enrolling and calling out the national Forces, and for other Purposes," March 3, 1863, *Congressional Record*, 37th Cong., 3rd sess., chaps. 74, 75.

43. "Speech Delivered to Georgia Legislative Assembly," Milledgeville, December 11, 1862, in Hill, *Senator Benjamin H. Hill*, 251–72, 258–59. For the detrimental effect of state governors' relying on patronage for the organization of troops, see McPherson, *Battle Cry of Freedom*, 326–27.

44. Shelden, "Measures." Only two Confederate senators voted against the Second Conscription Act; Rable, *Confederate Republic*, 155.

45. *Letter Addressed to Hon. Wm. C. Rives*.

46. Congressman Ancona (D-PA), February 28, 1863, *Congressional Globe*, 37th Cong., 3rd sess., appendix, 161–63.

47. *Record of Hon. C. L. Vallandigham*, 204.

48. Governor Joseph Brown to Jefferson Davis, Milledgeville, GA, May 9, 1862, in *Correspondence Between Governor Brown*, 9–15, 9.

49. Shelden, "Measures," 469–70.

50. Sec. 1, "An Act to further provide for the public defense," April 16, 1862, *Statutes at Large* (1864), 29–32.

51. McPherson, *Battle Cry of Freedom*, 490–91. For the effects of war fatigue and emancipation of recruitment, see Levine, "Draft Evasion," 821.

52. Sec. 2, "An Act for enrolling and calling out the national Forces, and for other Purposes," March 3, 1863, *Congressional Record*, 37th Cong., 3rd sess., chaps. 74, 75.

53. The words are Jefferson Davis's. "Message from the President," March 28, 1862, *Journal of the Confederate Congress*, 5:156–57.

54. McPherson, *Battle Cry of Freedom*, 430.

55. Rable, *Confederate Republic*, 155.

56. Immigrants made up about half of the enlisted as a result of the 1863 draft, but the

overwhelming majority did so voluntarily, having hired themselves out as substitutes. Abinder, "Which Poor Man's Fight?," 355.

57. In the July 1863 draft, 13.5 percent failed to report, as did 28.5 percent in the July 1864 draft. Levine, "Draft Evasion," 820–21.

58. Levine, "Draft Evasion," 819. Most of those who did not serve did so legally: over 569,000 were exempted—for medical or other reasons—paid for commutation or hired a substitute.

59. Rable, *Confederate Republic*, 249, 282.

60. Niox, *Expédition*, 328–30.

61. Hernández López, "Militares conservadores," 294–95, 298. Bazaine went as far as to have high-ranking officers surveilled, and charged some of the empire's earliest adherents— Generals Taboada, Zires, and Vicario—with conspiracy, despite lack of evidence; Hernández López, "Militares conservadores," 311–12.

62. Quoted by Hernández López, "Militares conservadores," 316.

63. Hernández López, "Militares conservadores," 294–95, 307–9.

64. "Ley orgánica del Ejército," January 26, 1865; "Organización de la Guardia Rural," July 7, 1865; "Ley sobre la organización de una legión de gendarmeria," January 8, 1865, in *Colección . . . Imperio*, 4:28–37, 133–37, 155–56. The Expeditionary Army's Gendarmerie was tasked with performing police work and training the Mexican Legión de Gendarmería. Haberbusch, "L'emploi de la gendarmerie."

65. "Circular sobre las atribuciones de los comandantes de las divisiones territoriales," October 22, 1865; "Reglamento sobre los uniformes del Ejército," November 1, 1865, in *Colección . . . Imperio*, 4:41–46, 107–30.

66. Hernández López, "Militares conservadores," 332–33.

67. "Orden del General en Jefe del Ejército Federal," January 5, 1861, in Dublán and Lozano, *Legislación mexicana*, disp. 5142, 9:6.

68. "Se prohiben las levas para el ejército," August 19, 1863, in *Boletín de las leyes* (1863), 1:234–35.

69. "Reglamento para la Guardia Nacional del Estado libre y soberano de Puebla," May 26, 1862, in *Colección . . . Imperio*, 97–116. Strobel, "El Ejército de Oriente."

70. All Mexican men aged eighteen to thirty-five would have to register. Those destined to service for seven years—or three years in the Rural Guard—would be drawn by lot. "Ley de sorteos para remplazo del ejército," November 1, 1865, in *Colección . . . Imperio*, 4:173–75.

71. "Decreto del Congreso," June 7, 1861, disp. 5369, in Dublán and Lozano, *Legislación mexicana*, 9:228–30. The constitution's article 5 read "no one can be compelled to furnish personal work without being fairly compensated and without his or her full consent." The decree also restricted freedom of speech and association, and the right to carry arms, for six months.

72. Representatives Suárez Navarro and Benítez, June 7, 1861, quoted in Strobel, *El ejército liberal*, 356. Forced impressment had not always been considered unlawful, and had been used repeatedly during the 1820s and 1830s. Ceja, *La fragilidad*, 83.

73. The battle of Camarón (April 1863), in Veracruz, and the fall of San Juan Bautista and Tabasco in February 1864, in which the Liberal forces were successful, are exceptions. Moloeznick, "Insurgencia y contraguerrilla"; Strobel, *Resistir es vencer*, 225–62; Monroy Casillas, "Tras la vida"; Segura Muñoz, "La casa hecha cuartel." For the terror provoked by bandits, see Báez Méndez, "Representaciones pictóricas," 105–9.

74. Jesús Terán to Minister of Foreign Affairs, Vienna, July 30, 1865, in Saldívar, *La misión confidencial*, 47–50.

75. "Parte Oficial. ¡Rendición de las fuerzas imperiales en Oaxaca!" *Boletín Oficial del*

Cuartel General de la Línea de Oriente, November 8, 1866, quoted in Monroy Casillas, "De la lucha," 106.

76. Niox, *Expédition*, 333–34.
77. Michel and Meyer, *Mascota*, 39.
78. McPherson, *For Cause and Comrades*, 4–13.
79. "Cuerpo del Ejército de Oriente: Prisioneros de Guerra," Zaragoza, May 18, 1863, in Carretero Madrid, "Prisionero de guerra," 134.
80. Troncoso, *Diario*, 279. Suárez Argüello, "Al servicio de la República." See also Ana Rosa Suárez Argüello's wonderful historical novel, *Un viaje a Nueva York*.
81. See Mallon, *Peasant and Nation*; Thomson and LaFrance, *Patriotism*; McNamara, *Sons of the Sierra*; and Pérez Ramírez, "Municipios de la Sierra Juárez," 33–58.
82. Meyer, *Esperando a Lozada*; Reed Torres, *El general Tomás*; Hamnett, "Mexican Conservatives"; Smith, *Roots of Conservatism*.
83. Kalyvas, *Logic of Violence*, 7–16, 12.
84. Fowler, *Grammar of Civil War*, 19–20.
85. Men from Tennessee, Virginia, Arkansas, Louisiana, North Carolina, Alabama, Texas, Florida, and Georgia; Current, *Lincoln's Loyalists*, 218. In his dissertation, which focuses on the "self-identified conservatives in Lincoln's cabinet," Mark A. Neely stresses the importance of ideological inclination and identity; Neely, "Lincoln's Conservatives."
86. Hernández López, "La 'reacción a sangre y fuego.'"
87. Strobel, *El ejército liberal*, 180–220.
88. Doyle, "Replacement Rebels," 9. See also Quigley, "Civil War Conscription."
89. Civil War Posters, 1861–1865, New York Historical Society, Museum and Library, https://digitalcollections.nyhistory.org/islandora/object/islandora%3A159313.
90. Benton, *Voting in the Field*, 4, 26–27, 306; Chandler, *Soldier's Right*, 5–6.
91. Chandler, *Soldier's Right*, 14–15. William Blair has shown how, in the 1864 elections, Republicans mobilized soldiers' vote to their favor, while Democrats bewailed the corruption of elections by soldiers' intimidating voters; Blair, *With Malice*, 191–233.
92. Quoted in McPherson, *For Cause and Comrades*, 128, 117–30, 119.
93. Doyle, "Replacement Rebels," 6–7, 22–23.
94. Altamirano, *Cuentos de invierno: Clemencia*; Mateos, *El Sol de Mayo* and *El Cerro de las Campanas*.
95. Primitivo Miranda, *Soldados de la Reforma en la Venta* (1858); Casimiro Castro, *Trajes mexicanos: Soldados del Sur* (1855). These depictions fit many of the descriptions made by French officers, who pitied the Mexican Indigenous soldiers, taken forcefully from their families, yet "sober, tireless when marching, knowing how to die well when it is needed." Niox, *Expédition*, 331–34. Compare with Agustín Arrieta, *El requiebro* (ca. 1850), *Escena militar* (n.d.), *Escena de mercado* (1850); and the images compiled by Ceja, *La fragilidad*, 138–310.
96. Díaz y de Ovando, "La vida mexicana"; Pani, "Cultura mexicana."
97. Brimmer, *Claiming Widowhood*.
98. Faust, *Mothers of Invention*; Chassen-López, *Mujer y poder*; Silber, *Daughters of the Union*, 41–86, 61–63. Silber contrasts the opening of opportunities for paid employment for women in wartime industries—over 100,000 factory, sewing, and arsenal jobs became available to Northern women during the war—and the increasingly difficult circumstances, in terms of low wages and crowded conditions, in which these women worked.
99. Gómez Tepexicuapan and Ratz, *Los viajes de Maximiliano*; Duncan, "Political Legitimation," 27–66.
100. Igler, *Carlota de México*; Galeana, "Carlota fue Roja."

101. Faust, "Altars of Sacrifice," 1200.
102. Silber, *Daughters of the Union*, 194–221, 207; Holder, "From Hand-Maiden"; Garrison, *With Courage and Delicacy*.
103. "La soldadera," *El Constitucional*, July 30, 1868, quoted in Ceja, *La fragilidad*, 305.
104. Ceja, *La fragilidad*, 301–62, 302; Strobel, *El ejército liberal*, 333–35; Strobel, *Resistir es vencer*, 32–36.
105. Gómez-Galvarriato Freer, *El pan nuestro*, 119–65, 119–25, 153–61.
106. Chowning, *Catholic Women*.
107. *Liberales ilustres*, 139; Kent, "Wearing Black." In Oaxaca, Juana Cata, a successful businesswoman, sold her goods in Liberal and Conservative camps, and gathered information for the Oaxacan Liberal commanders. Chassen-López, *Mujer y poder*.
108. Smith, "They Went to the Field." "Women-soldiers" also fought in Mexican armies, as they had in the independence wars and would during the Revolution, but they are almost impossible to account for. Ceja, *La fragilidad*, 309–11.
109. Blanton and Wike, *They Fought Like Demons*, chap. 2, "To Dress and Go as a Soldier: Means and Motivations."
110. Strobel, *Resistir es vencer*, 36.
111. E. M. de los Ríos, "Ignacia Reichy," in *Liberales ilustres*, 387–91, 391. Her last name is also spelled Riesch.
112. E. M. de los Ríos, "Margarita Maza de Juárez, 1826–1871"; Joaquín Trejo, "Soledad Solórzano de Régules, 1844–1884"; José Ferrel, "Agustina Ramírez," in *Liberales ilustres*, 131–44, 135; 429–38; 571–76.
113. American Battlefield Trust, "Civil War Casualties. The Cost of War: Killed, Wounded, Captured and Missing," last updated September 15, 2023, www.battlefields.org/learn/articles/civil-war-casualties.
114. Fowler, *La Guerra*, 22; Pérez Gallardo, *Martirologio*.
115. American Battlefield Trust, "Civil War Casualties"; Faust, *This Republic of Suffering*, 280–324, 325–42, 281, 330, 334–35. The important contributions made to these accounting and memorializing efforts by committed activists like Clara Barton, Walt Whitman, and William Fox should nevertheless not be underestimated.
116. Faust, *This Republic of Suffering*, 334, 311–24; Pérez Gallardo, *Martirologio*.
117. Machiavelli, *The Prince*, chap. 17.
118. Brownlee, *Federal Taxation*, 60–61.
119. Brownlee, *Federal Taxation*, 61.
120. Razaghian, "Financing," 12–13; *Tariff of the Confederate States* 3–4.
121. Edling, *Hercules in the Cradle*, 38–40.
122. The tax would also be levied on cotton transported on ships flying the flag of nations that did not recognize the CSA. Crawford, *Anglo-American Crisis*, 97; *A Bill to be entitled An Act to provide and export duty on cotton*; Davis, *Civil War Taxes*, chap. 7.
123. See, for example, "Extención de doble alcabala en el Distrito Federal a los efectos que se expresa," May 5, 1861, in Dublán and Lozano, *Legislación mexicana*, disp. 5616, 9:441. Pani, "Novia de republicanos," 165–67.
124. Sexton, *Debtor Diplomacy*, 82.
125. *Memoria presentada . . . por el C. Miguel Lerdo de Tejada*, 6.
126. Jan Bazant examines the three forced loans imposed by the Conservative government on "stingy capitalists" in the summer of 1858. Bazant, *Los bienes*, 158–70.
127. Strobel, "La artillería liberal"; Bazant, *Los bienes*, 158.
128. Strobel, *El ejército*, 265, 301, 330.

129. Payno, *México y sus cuestiones*, 246–99, 257.
130. Payno, *México y sus cuestiones*, 102–7.
131. Márquez, *Manifiestos*, 14–16.
132. Payno, *México y sus cuestiones*, 107, 337–42.
133. Razaghian, "Financing," 13.
134. Edling, *Hercules in the Cradle*, 186.
135. Edling, *Hercules in the Cradle*, fig. 6.1, 183.
136. Burdekin and Langdana, "War Finance," 353–55; Razaghian, "Financing."
137. Edling, *Hercules in the Cradle*, 178; Brownlee, *Federal Taxation*, 59, 291.
138. Sexton, *Debtor Diplomacy*, 79.
139. Razaghian, "Financing," 13. D'Erlanger was married to the daughter of John Slidell, Confederate representative in France, who had served as Polk's minister to Mexico. The Confederate government initially placed 3 million pounds worth of bonds, for which it received an income of 90 percent of their face value. The firm bought half of the bonds back, for the Confederate agents to resell them, carefully managing the operations in order to support the price. The bonds yielded a "not unreasonable" 12 percent interest a year. The loan's performance compares favorably to the US experience in 1812 and that of other countries throughout the first half of the nineteenth century, and the Union's bond issues. Gentry, "Confederate Success," 161, 187, 186. See also Sexton, *Debtor Diplomacy*, 155–74; Slidell at 163.
140. Edling, *Hercules in the Cradle*, 187. In San Francisco, General Sánchez Ochoa, for instance, offered the products of the customshouses on the Pacific as guarantee for 10 million in bonds, which the republican government declared null and void, and the tried to sell them in New York through John C. Fremont, who was to get 6 of the 10 million. Romero, *Responsabilidades contraidas*, 8–9.
141. Payno, *Cuentas, gastos*, nos. 17–18, 909–10; Gille, "Los capitales franceses," 138, 144; Topik, "Controversia crediticia"; Ludlow, "La disputa financiera."
142. Jay Sexton noted in his analysis of Confederate financial policies abroad, these operations were not only financial but also political and diplomatic. Sexton, *Debtor Diplomacy*, 165. For the fascinating mix between modern finances, Saint-Simonian aspirations, and imperialism that propelled France's intervention in Mexico, see Glaser, "Age of Regeneration."
143. Edling, *Hercules in the Cradle*, 187; Cox Richardson, *To Make Men Free*, 25–28; Raghazian, "Financing," 12–13. Jay Sexton describes how the weight and influence of British bondholders on the US financial markets were controversial and unpopular, and underpinned the "rhetorical power of Anglophobia." Sexton, *Debtor Diplomacy*, 82–189.
144. In 1860 dollars. Goldin and Lewis, "Economic Cost," 303, 305, 308.
145. Payno, *Cuentas, gastos*, 738, 741–42, 926. Throughout this period the US dollar and the Mexican peso were, conveniently, on par.
146. The phrase is by José María Mata, Juárez's secretary of the treasury, as he explained how the hopes that nationalization would underpin healthier public finances had "vanished." Mata, *Memoria de Hacienda*, 4. *Guía de Memorias de Hacienda de México, 1822–1910*, 2012, http://memoriasdehacienda.colmex.mx.
147. Serrano, *Igualdad, uniformidad*, 32–40, 46–70; Mata, *Memoria de Hacienda*, 10.
148. Mata, *Memoria de Hacienda*, 13.
149. "Cesación del cobro de alcabalas, derecho de traslación de dominio, Efectos que quedan libres de alcabala y derecho municipal"; "Sobre Contribución Predial, Derechos de hipoteca, Derechos de patente Contribuciones de Profesiones," February 4, 1861; "Se suprime impuesto de peajes y se establece impuesto sobre fincas rústicas," April 25, 1861, in Dublán and Lozano, *Legislación mexicana*, disps. 5165, 5194, 5317, 9:18, 38, 172.
150. Mata, *Memoria de Hacienda*, 8–9.

151. "Se establece en el Distrito una contribución de 1% sobre capitales," August 21, 1861; "Se establece una contribución de 1% sobre todo capital que pase de $1000," January 30, 1863; "Se impone una contribución de 1% sobre todo capital que exceda de $500," July 31, 1863; "Impone una contribución sobre capitales de $5000 en adelante," August 2, 1864; "Circular sobre el establecimiento de la contribución federal," December 16, 1861; "Se establece un impuesto extraordinario," June 27, 1862; "Ordena que se cobren dobles los derechos que se recaudan," April 29, 1862; "Se establece el derecho de Timbre," February 9, 1861; "Derecho que debe pagar el algodón," July 28, 1863, all in Dublán and Lozano, *Legislación mexicana*, disps. 5431, 5808, 5900, 5963, 5491, 5667, 5605, 5813, 5899, 9:254, 579, 647, 690, 481, 436, 337, 583.

152. Mata, *Memoria de Hacienda*, 1, 7–8.

153. Tratado de Miramar, April 1, 1864, arts. 9, 10, 7, 10, 11, www.inehrm.gob.mx/work/models/inehrm/Resource/576/1/images/documento_tratadosmiramar1.pdf. The treaty specifies money amounts in French francs. For consistency, I have converted them into pesos (five francs per peso, *per* Payno).

154. Becerril Hernández, *Hacienda pública*, 135–40.

155. Becerril Hernández, *Hacienda pública*, 202–10, 161–98.

156. Landowners were to pay half a *real* for every 35,112 square meters. "Informe con que el director de los negocios de Hacienda dio cuenta . . . ," "Reglamento," "Legislación," in *El Diario del Imperio*, May 28, June 13, August 2, 1866.

157. *Exposición dirigida a S.M.*, 5, 11–14.

158. Tomás Morán y Crivelli, "Discurso que en apoyo del dictamen de la mayoría de la sección primera sobre no ser admisible el proyecto de la contribución predial presentado por la comisión francesa pronunció . . . , vecino de Puebla y representante de Tlaxcala," in AGN, *Segundo Imperio*, vol. 13, Consejo de Estado, Proyectos.

159. Becerril Hernández, *Hacienda pública*, 202–94.

160. Edling, *Hercules in the Cradle*, 205; Brownlee, *Federal Taxation*, 62–63; Cox Richardson, *To Make Men Free*, 26.

161. Edling, *Hercules in the Cradle*, 190–92. See also Cox Richardson, *To Make Men Free*, 28–29.

162. Ransom, "Economics of the Civil War."

163. Morrill quoted in Edling, *Hercules in the Cradle*, 205; Brownlee, *Federal Taxation*, 62–66.

164. Razaghian, "Financing," 14.

165. Davis, *Civil War Taxes*, chap. 7.

166. Razaghian, "Financing," 13; Burdekin and Langdana, "War and Finance."

167. Razaghian, "Financing," 21–22; Ransom, "Economics."

168. McPherson, *Battle Cry of Freedom*, 850.

Chapter Seven

1. Matías Romero to Minister of Foreign Relations, Washington, April 4, 1865, in de la Luz Topete, *Labor diplomática*, 298–99.

2. "Puntos que deberán tratarse en las conferencias con el Comisionado de Estados Unidos," August 24, 1847, in Castillo Nájera, *El tratado de Guadalupe*, 53–55.

3. Gutiérrez Ardila, "Un sistema."

4. The best analyses of US-Mexico relations during this period are Terrazas y Basante, *Inversiones, especulación*, and "Miseria hacendaria." For the dispute between companies over the Tehuantepec concession, and the US and Mexican stakeholders involved, see Suárez Argüello, *El camino de Tehuantepec*, 17–114.

5. Terrazas y Basante et al., *Las relaciones*, 1:373–89.

6. See Olliff, *Reforma Mexico*.

7. Terrazas y Basante, "Miseria hacendaria," 91.

8. This is how José María Mata, Mexico's minister in Washington in 1858–60, described it. Mata to Benito Juárez, Washington, July 2, 1858, in *Benito Juárez: Documentos*, 2:9, 17. See also Riguzzi, *¿Reciprocidad imposible?*, 61–87; Galeana, *El tratado McLane–Ocampo*; Terrazas y Basante, *Los intereses norteamericanos*. I rehearsed some of these arguments in Pani, "La crisis como oportunidad."

9. James Buchanan, Second Annual Message to Congress on the State of the Union, December 6, 1858, www.presidency.ucsb.edu/documents/second-annual-message-congress-the-state-the-union. Buchanan recommended establishing a "temporary protectorate" over the border states of Chihuahua and Sonora in 1858 and "employing military force to enter Mexico" in 1859. At the end of October 1861, representatives of the British, French, and Spanish governments agreed to engage in "common action" against Mexican authorities for their "arbitrary and degrading conduct." La Convención de Londres, October 31, 1861, www.memoriapoliticademexico.org/Textos/4IntFrancesa/1861LCL.html.

10. Forsyth talked up the fact that the Gulf of California and the Yaqui River would become "natural borders" between neighboring nations. Minister of Foreign Affairs, Luis Gonzaga Cuevas, to John Forsyth, "Crónica interior: Notas cambiadas," *La Sociedad*, April 29, 1859. Cuevas was one of the three Mexican negotiators of the Treaty of Guadalupe Hidalgo.

11. James Buchanan, Third Annual Message to Congress on the State of the Union, December 19, 1858, www.presidency.ucsb.edu/documents/third-annual-message-congress-the-state-the-union.

12. McLane, *Reminiscences*, 143.

13. Riguzzi, *¿Reciprocidad imposible?*, 70–72.

14. McLane, *Reminiscences*, 143.

15. Ponce, "As Dead," 346; Suárez Argüello, "Contra el execrable," 1871.

16. Octaviano Muñoz Ledo, Minister of Foreign Relations, to Lewis Cass, Mexico City, December 17, 1859; and Miguel Miramón, "Manifiesto a la nación," Guadalajara, January 1, 1860, both quoted in Suárez Argüello, "Contra el *execrable*," 1874–75.

17. The citizens and municipal governments of Cuatitlán and Tepeaca to the Ministry of the Interior, quoted in Suárez Argüello, "Contra el execrable," 1884.

18. Ponce, "As Dead," 348–56.

19. Ponce, "As Dead," 378.

20. Judge McCabed, quoted in Bulnes, *Juárez y las Revoluciones*, 489. For a critical assessment of this "inadmissible and inappropriate" verdict, see Iglesias Calderón, *Las supuestas traiciones*, 474–75.

21. The Ministry of War's memorandum of February 25, 1860, in Iglesias Calderón, *Las supuestas traiciones*, 280. The historiographical debate surrounding the McLane–Ocampo Treaty has been heated and ideological, see Suárez Argüello, "Contra el execrable," 1858–1860.

22. Matías Romero to Minister of Foreign Relations, November 9, 1860, in Schoonover, *Mexican View*, 30; William Seward to Matías Romero, Washington, April 5, 1861, quoted in Terrazas y Basante, *Los intereses norteamericanos*, 46.

23. For the South's influence on antebellum US foreign policy, see Karp, *This Vast Southern Empire*.

24. Thomas Corwin to William Seward, Mexico City, June 26, 1861, in Terrazas y Basante, *Los intereses norteamericanos*, 49.

25. Terrazas y Basante, *Los intereses norteamericanos*, 9–10.

26. Corwin to Seward, Mexico City, March 28, 1862, in *Papers Relating to Foreign Affairs . . . Third Session*, doc. 585, https://history.state.gov/historicaldocuments/frus1862/d585.

27. Gurza, "Against Slave Power?"

28. Terrazas y Basante et al., *Las relaciones*, 1:421–22.

29. William H. Seward to Thomas Corwin, Washington, May 28, 1862, in *Papers Relating to Foreign Affairs . . . Third Session*, doc. 588, https://history.state.gov/historicaldocuments/frus1862/d588.

30. These include the Wyke–Zamacona treaty (November 1861), rejected by the Mexican Congress for giving up control of the nation's customshouses, and the increasingly accommodating Wyke–Doblado (also known as the Puebla Convention) and Zarco–Saligny agreements (April 1862). Nava, "Origen y monto," 97; Villegas Revueltas, "Charles Wyke."

31. Thomas Corwin to William H. Seward, Mexico City, March 24, 1862, in *Papers Relating to Foreign Affairs . . . Third Session*, doc. 588, https://history.state.gov/historicaldocuments/frus1862/d588.

32. Terrazas y Basante, *Los intereses norteamericanos*, 83–85. Gerardo Gurza identifies the continuities in the apparently innovative American colonization projects of the Civil War. Gurza, "Matías Romero."

33. Jones, *Blue and Gray Diplomacy*; Terrazas y Basante, "¿Dónde quedó?"

34. Jones, *Blue and Gray Diplomacy*, 2; Sexton, *Debtor Diplomacy*, 7–15; Black, *Napoleon III*, 23–40; Terrazas y Basante et al., *Las relaciones*, 1:399; Shawcross, *France, Mexico*.

35. Doyle, *Age of Reconstruction*, 74–75.

36. *Correspondencia . . . naciones beligerantes*, iii; Schoonover, *Dollars over Dominion*; Doyle, "Reconstruction and Anti-Imperialism."

37. William H. Seward to all ministers of the United States , Department of State, Washington, March 9, 1861, in *Papers Relating to Foreign Affairs . . . Second Session*, doc. 3, https://history.state.gov/historicaldocuments/frus1861/d3.

38. Senator Thomas R. R. Cobb, quoted in Jones, *Blue and Gray Diplomacy*, 9. Confederate attitudes, and the political, sometimes haphazard, character of their foreign policy was, according to Howard Jones, "a classic example of overconfidence breeding naïveté"; Jones, *Blue and Gray Diplomacy*, 13–17, 20.

39. The best study of imperial foreign policy is still Blumberg, "Diplomacy of the Mexican Empire." See also Olvera, *Al servicio diplomático*; Palacios, "De imperios y repúblicas." On Mexican relations with the CSA, see Gurza, *Una vecindad efímera*.

40. De Vattel, *Law of Nations*, vi, lx–lxi.

41. Belissa, "Le cosmopolitisme," 725, 729–30.

42. Witt, *Lincoln's Code*, 2–3.

43. Which is how they were described by one of Mexico's most influential *iusnaturalistas*, Bishop Clemente de Jesús Munguía; Munguía, *Del Derecho natural*, 4:6.

44. Witt, *Lincoln's Code*, 142–56; Lyons quoted at 144. See also Blair, *With Malice*, 68–79; Jones, *Blue and Gray Diplomacy*; and Neff, *Justice in Blue and Gray*.

45. Jones, *Blue and Gray Diplomacy*, 40; Chadwick, "Back to the Future." The Union's economic warfare would, eventually, be more effective, given the North's significantly greater demographic and economic muscle.

46. See Jones, *Union in Peril*, 38–56, 80–99.

47. Sainlaude, *France and the American Civil War*; Jones, *Blue and Gray Diplomacy*, 3. The staunch Bonapartist senator Michel Chevalier published *La France*, 20–21.

48. Jones, *Blue and Gray Diplomacy*, 27; Doyle, *Age of Reconstruction*, 74–75. For a different view of Seward as a man who, throughout his life, "had maintained a strong aversion to war

and a disposition to discuss, conciliate, and negotiate, rather than to bluster, boast, confront, and combat," see Ferris, "Lincoln and Seward," 36.

49. William H. Seward to William L. Dayton, Washington, April 7, 1864, in *Papers Relating to Foreign Affairs . . . First Session*, part 3, doc. 336, https://history.state.gov/historicaldocuments/frus1865p3/d336.

50. William H. Seward to John Bigelow, Washington, March 13, 1865, in *Papers Relating to Foreign Affairs . . . First Session*, part 3, doc. 355, https://history.state.gov/historicaldocuments/frus1865p3/d355; Bigelow to Seward, Paris, March 15, 1865, in *Papers Relating to Foreign Affairs . . . First Session*, part 2, doc. 377, https://history.state.gov/historicaldocuments/frus1865p2/d377; Seward to Bigelow, Washington, December 16, 1865, in *Papers Relating to Foreign Affairs . . . First Session*, part 3, doc. 423, https://history.state.gov/historicaldocuments/frus1865p3/d423.

51. See, for instance, Thomas Corwin to William H. Seward, Mexico City, June 28, 1862, doc. 593, https://history.state.gov/historicaldocuments/frus1862/d593; Corwin to Seward, Mexico City, July 28, 1862, doc. 596, https://history.state.gov/historicaldocuments/frus1862/d596; and Corwin to Seward, Mexico City, March 24, 1862, doc. 584, https://history.state.gov/historicaldocuments/frus1862/d584, all in *Papers Relating to Foreign Affairs . . . Third Session*; and Gurza, *Una vecindad efímera*; Fuentes Mares, "La misión."

52. As Howard Jones explains, "equal treatment" was "virtually impossible," since actions that benefited one belligerent were necessarily detrimental to the other. Jones, *Blue and Gray Diplomacy*, 5–6.

53. William H. Seward to Matías Romero, December 15, 1862, in *Correspondencia . . . naciones beligerantes*, 30.

54. Seward to Romero, December 15, 1862, in *Correspondencia . . . naciones beligerantes*, 31; Matías Romero to Ministry of Foreign Affairs, Washington, July 22, 1865, in de la Luz Topete, *Labor diplomática*, 302.

55. Matías Romero to Minister of Foreign Affairs, Washington, November 22, 1862, in *Correspondencia . . . naciones beligerantes*, 12–13; Matías Romero to Minister of Foreign Affairs, Washington, September 18, 1862; February 20, 1862; March 24, 1864, in de la Luz Topete, *Labor diplomática*, 241–44, 227, 278–80.

56. Romero to Minister of Foreign Affairs, Washington, June, 9, 1866, in Schoonover, *Mexican View*, 213.

57. Jesús Terán to Minister of Foreign Affairs, Vienna, July 30, 1865, in Saldívar, *La misión confidencial*, 47–50, 47.

58. Matías Romero to Minister of Foreign Relations, Washington, April 4, 1865, in de la Luz Topete, *Labor diplomática*, 298–99. See Paolo Riguzzi's remarkable *Diplomacia de supervivencia*.

59. Riguzzi, "Escribe sin cesar"; Sexton, *Monroe Doctrine*, 152–53; Doyle, *Age of Reconstruction*, 49, 68, 82–95; Schoonover, *Mexican Lobby*, ix–xviii. Thomas Schoonover finds that this "prodigious worker" was Seward's third-most-active correspondent among foreign representatives in Washington, writing 2,850 items a year—300 of them for the State Department: over 4,000 manuscript pages; Schoonover, *Mexican View*, 15–16.

60. Romero to Minister of Foreign Relations, Washington, March 18, 1864, in Schoonover, *Mexican View*, 159–60; "Conferencia con el general Grant," Washington, May 8, 1865, in *Correspondencia*, 5:297. Schoonover has identified this document as the only one in which the published version waters down Romero's statement, for it changes Mexicans' "desire" for the presence of US soldiers into their not finding the idea "disagreeable." Schoonover, *Mexican Lobby*, xiv–xv.

61. Sexton, *Monroe Doctrine*, 123–58; Terrazas y Basante, "¿Dónde quedó?"; Riguzzi, "Mexico and the Monroe Doctrines."
62. Sexton, *Monroe Doctrine*, 123–24.
63. At the Cooper Union in January 1866, quoted in Doyle, *Age of Reconstruction*, 4.
64. William H. Seward to Matías Romero, Washington, August 7, 1865, in *Correspondencia ... naciones beligerantes*, 73–74. The blessings of republicanism, added Seward, were "the reward of ... popular virtues." No nation, no matter how "benevolent," could secure them for another.
65. Matías Romero to Minister of Foreign Relations, January 19, 1865, in de la Luz Topete, *Labor diplomática*, 96.
66. John Bigelow to William H. Seward, Paris, June 1, 1865, in *Papers Relating to Foreign Affairs ... First Session*, part 2, doc. 420, https://history.state.gov/historicaldocuments/frus1865p2/d420; [Blair], *Monroe Doctrine*, 5.
67. *Mexico and the Monroe Doctrine*, 13, 5–6; [Blair], *Monroe Doctrine*, 5.
68. [Blair], *Monroe Doctrine*, 7.
69. Matías Romero to Minister of Foreign Relations, August 28, 1862, in *Correspondencia ... naciones beligerantes*, 3–7.
70. *Monroe Doctrine ... De Jarnette of Virginia*.
71. [Jay], *Mr. Jay's Letter*, 1.
72. Leavitt, *Monroe Doctrine*, 14, 12, 47. See also [Jay], *Mr. Jay's Letter*; Sexton, *Monroe Doctrine*, 152–53; and Doyle, "Reconstruction and Anti-Imperialism," 47–48.
73. García Martínez, "El espacio," 19.
74. Jorge Cañizares-Esguerra has pointed out, in his critique of "entangled histories" that "describe interactions at the margins, not at the core," that we might have given borderlands history some flashy "new clothes" that do not necessarily enhance our understanding of the historical process. I hope this book shows that parallel processes, mutual—if varying and uneven—influence, as well as contact, make for entanglement at different levels, but a long, porous international border and a very diverse cast of actors certainly offer greater potential for unstable combinations of conflict and cooperation. Cañizares-Esguerra, "Entangled Histories."
75. García, "Dominance," 47–51, 45.
76. P. H. Sheridan, New Orleans, telegram received in cipher at Washington, June 30, 1865, enclosed in William H. Seward to John Bigelow, Washington, July 6, 1865, in *Papers Relating to Foreign Affairs ... First Session*, part 3, doc. 379, https://history.state.gov/historicaldocuments/frus1865p3/d379; Thompson, *Cortina*, pos. 2319/4927; 2304/4927; 2328–2376/4927; Herrera Pérez, *Historia de una ciudad*, 193–95.
77. Cruz García, "Aires de guerra"; Thompson, *Cortina*, chap. 6.
78. "Actualidades," *La Sociedad*, January 27, 1866.
79. González Quiroga, *War and Peace*, 231.
80. González Quiroga, *War and Peace*, 184.
81. González Quiroga, *War and Peace*, 184, 196–97. See also Tyler, "Santiago Vidaurri."
82. Thompson, *Cortina*, chaps. 2, 5.
83. Miller, "Arms Across the Border," 51–52.
84. Tovar Mota, "José María Carvajal," 21–24.
85. Edwards, *Shelby's Expedition*, 8, 7.
86. Miller, "Arms Across the Border," 43.
87. Sheridan, *Personal Memoirs*, 2:208; P. H. Sheridan to Gral. John Rawlins, Telegram received in cipher at Washington, July 8, 1865, enclosed in William H. Seward to John Bigelow,

Washington, July 10, 1865, in *Papers Relating to Foreign Affairs . . . First Session*, part 3, doc. 380, https://history.state.gov/historicaldocuments/frus1865p3/d380.

88. Sheridan, *Personal Memoirs*, 2:227–28, 210; Doyle, *Age of Reconstruction*, 84–85.

89. Van Hoy, "Mexican Exiles," 58, 51.

90. Miller, "Arms Across the Border," 37–41, 41–47, 47–52, 53–59.

91. Sheridan mentions at least 30,000 muskets from the Baton Rouge arsenal. Sheridan, *Personal Memoirs*, 2:213–24; Doyle, *Age of Reconstruction*, 96–103.

92. Miller, "Arms Across the Border," 44, 46–47, 15; Doyle, *Age of Reconstruction*, 85–88.

93. Miller, "Arms Across the Border," 54–56.

94. Miller, "Arms Across the Border," 60, 46.

95. Sheridan, *Personal Memoirs*, 2:227–28.

96. Sexton, *Monroe Doctrine*, 157. "North America's egoism" during the French Intervention was a trope in Mexican political discourse well into the first decade of the twentieth century. See Iglesias Calderón, *El egoísmo norteamericano*; and Pani and Riguzzi, "Mexico and the American Civil War."

97. Riguzzi, "Mexico and the Monroe Doctrines," 786.

98. Sebastián Lerdo de Tejada to Matías Romero, Chihuahua, December 10, 1864, quoted in Sexton, *Monroe Doctrine*, 135–36.

99. Vicuña Mackenna, *Diez meses*, 420.

100. Maier, "Consigning the Twentieth Century." Mexico's border with Guatemala would remain a contentious issue until 1882. Toussaint and Vázquez Olivera, *Territorio, nación y soberanía*.

101. See Evans, *Our Sister Republic*, which chronicles William Seward's visit to the neighboring nation.

102. William H. Seward to Thomas Corwin, Washington, April 6, 1861, in *Papers Relating to Foreign Affairs . . . Second Session*, doc. 36, https://history.state.gov/historicaldocuments/frus1861/d36.

103. Terrazas y Basante et al., *Las relaciones*, 1:386–97, 2:68–69.

104. Leavitt, *Monroe Doctrine*, 47, 12–13.

105. Terán commended foreign powers for not entering into an analysis of the regime's "legitimacy" but considered that they were wrong in recognizing one of two de facto governments. He spoke of British precedents, referenced jurist Vittorio de Rossi, and circuitously asserted that this was the "uniform position" of law of nations authors. Jesús Terán to Lord John Russell, Foreign Secretary, July 22, 1864, in *Benito Juárez: Documentos*, 9:125, 1.

106. Matías Romero to Minister of Foreign Relations, Washington, September 23, 1865, in Schoonover, *Mexican View*, 204.

107. In the face of Seward's criticism of Maximilian's execution, which he argued did not dissociate "the Republic from terrorism," Romero insisted—with some dissimulation—that the Juárez government's actions were in accordance with "what the U.S. had done with the South's insurgents"; Matías Romero to Minister of Foreign Relations, July 4 and 15, 1867, in de la Luz Topete, *Labor diplomática*, 372–73, 401.

108. Jesús Terán to Minister of Foreign Relations, Florence, April 20, 1865, in Saldívar, *La mission confidencial*, 42.

109. Torres Caicedo, *Unión Latino-Americana*, 6.

110. "Las dos Américas," *El Correo de Ultramar*, February 15, 1857, quoted in Marichal, "El nacimiento," 709.

111. Torres Caicedo, *Unión Latino-Americana*, 72; Calvo, *Derecho internacional*, 1:72, i.

112. Calvo, *Derecho internacional*, 1:iii.

113. For the development and relevance of Latin American internationalism, see Marichal, "El nacimiento." For the twentieth century, see Scarfi, *Hidden History*.
114. Long and Schulz, "Republican Internationalism," 647–49.
115. Torres Caicedo, *Unión Latino-Americana*, 68.
116. Calvo, *Derecho internacional*, 1:142–43.

Epilogue

1. Downs, *After Appomattox*.
2. Nicoletti, *Secession on Trial*, 11–13, 99–102, 313–25.
3. "Ley para castigar los delitos en contra de la nación . . . ," January 25, 1862, in Dublán and Lozano, *Legislación mexicana*, disp. 5891, disp. 5542, 9:367–71.
4. Próspero C. Vega for defendant Tomás Mejía, Querétaro, June 12, 1867, and Eulalio Ortega and Jesús María Vásquez for defendant Maximilian von Hapsburg, Querétaro, June 13, 1867, in *Causa de Fernando Maximiliano*, 19, 334–35. Jefferson Davis was then awaiting trial in prison. Eulalio María Ortega, Próspero Vega, and Mariano Riva Palacio were distinguished jurists. Riva Palacio was also an important politician, former governor of the State of Mexico, and the father of one of the heroes of the war: officer, man of letters, and lawmaker Vicente Riva Palacio.
5. Manuel Azpiroz, prosecutor, Querétaro, June 13, 1867, in *Causa de Fernando Maximiliano*, 371.
6. The most articulate defense of the June 1867 judicial process is the passionate *Manifiesto justificativo*, mistakenly attributed to Juárez: *Manifiesto justificativo*, 64–65. For an excellent analysis of this pamphlet, see García de León Melo, "De historias contestatarias," 42–50.
7. *Manifiesto justificativo*, 65.
8. [Altamirano], *La nota de Campbell*, 6.
9. *Manifiesto justificativo*, 64–65. While rejecting following the US example in the case against Jefferson Davis, this pamphlet calls for observing the same principles that led to the execution of "Booth's accomplices, who included a woman."
10. "Amnistía a los culpables de infidencia a la patria y otros delitos de orden político," in Dublán and Lozano, *Legislación mexicana*, disp. 6827, 9:184–85; "Indultos de la pena capital," in Zaldívar, *Diccionario*, 418–19.
11. Nicoletti, *Secession on Trial*, 8, 2–17, 172–79, 204.
12. Nicoletti, *Secession on Trial*, 313–26.
13. The Prize Cases; Texas v. White, Nicoletti, *Secession on Trial*, 245, 319.
14. Fowler, *Grammar of Civil War*, 177–212; Weeks, *Juarez Myth*; Villalobos, *El culto a Juárez*; Cox, *Dixie's Daughters*; Davis, *Cause Lost*; Blight, *Race and Reunion*.
15. For the transformations and adjustments, throughout the continent, of this "Republican moment," see Campos Pérez, "1867"; Sabato, *La política en las calles*; Capdevila, *Une guerre totale*; Izecksohn, *Dos guerras*; McEvoy, *La utopía republicana*; and Ferrer, *Insurgent Cuba*.
16. Spanish republican Emilio Castelar described what he was trying to build, for stability and efficacy's sake, as a "república posible." For his influence on late nineteenth-century Mexican liberalism, see Hale, "Emilio Castelar," 50, 52–54. The period constitutes what US historiography has labeled the "Gilded Age" and what Tulio Halperín Donghi describes as the "neocolonial order," in *Contemporary History*, 115–207. Sandra Kuntz calls it the "era of liberal capitalism," in *El comercio exterior*; and Mauricio Tenorio refers to it as the "pragmatic purgatory" of the relatively peaceful transatlantic order that followed 1876, in *La paz*, 133.
17. Kloppenberg, *Toward Democracy*, 1.

BIBLIOGRAPHY

Primary Sources

ARCHIVES

Archivo General de la Nación (Mexico City)
Dirección General, Archivo e Historia, Secretaria de la Defensa Nacional (Mexico City)

PERIODICALS

El Correo de Ultramar (Mexico City)
La Cruz: Periódico exclusivamente religioso, establecido ex-profeso para difundir las doctrinas y vindicarlas de los errores dominantes (Mexico City)
De Bow's Review (New Orleans)
El Diario del Imperio (Mexico City)
Diario Oficial del Supremo Gobierno (Mexico City)
Doña Clara: Periódico político, católico, lírico y poético, con caricaturas y pretensiones de arreglar el mundo (Mexico City)
Harper's Weekly: A Journal of Civilization (New York)
The Liberator (Boston)
Mesilla (AZ) Times
El Mexicano: Periódico bisemanal, dedicado al pueblo (Mexico City)
El Monitor Republicano (Mexico City)
La Nación: Periódico político, científico y literario (Mexico City)
New York Herald
Niles National Register (Baltimore)
La Orquesta: Periódico omniscio, de buen humor y con caricaturas (Mexico City)
La Razón de México: Periódico político y literario (Mexico City)
Sacramento Daily Union
Saint Louis Republican
El Siglo Diez y Nueve (Mexico City)
La Sociedad: Periódico político y literario (Mexico City)
El Universal: Periódico independiente (Mexico City)
La Voz de México: Diario político, religioso, científico y literario (Mexico City)

BOOKS, PAMPHLETS, AND GOVERNMENT PUBLICATIONS

Actas oficiales y minutario de decretos del Congreso Extraordinario Constituyente de 1856–1857. Mexico City: El Colegio de México, 1957 [1857].
"Action of Tennessee Legislature." Nashville, May 6, 1861.
An Act to punish offences against State Property, passed by the legislative assembly of the territory of Kansas. Shawnee, KS: John T. Brady, 1855.
The Address of the People of South Carolina, assembled in Convention, to the People of the Slaveholding States of the United States. Charleston: Evans and Cogswell, 1860.
Aguilar y Marocho, Ignacio. La Batalla de Jueves Santo: Poema dedicado a Ignacio Comonfort y Juan José Bas. n.p., 1857.

Alamán, Lucas. *Examen imparcial de la administración del general vicepresidente D. Anastasio Bustamante*. Mexico City: Consejo Nacional para la Cultura y las Artes, 2008 [1834].

Algunos documentos sobre el Tratado de Guadalupe y la situación de México durante la invasión americana. Mexico City: Secretaría de Relaciones Exteriores, 1930.

[Altamirano, Ignacio Manuel]. *La nota de Campbell (Observaciones sobre ella por ...)*. Mexico City: Tipografía del Instituto Literario, 1867.

Altamirano, Ignacio Manuel. *Cuentos de invierno: Clemencia*. Mexico City: F. Díaz de León y Santiago White, 1869.

Arrillaga, Basilio José. *Algunas observaciones sobre el opúsculo intitulado "El imperio y el clero mexicano," del señor abate Testory*. Mexico City: M. Murgía, 1865.

———. *Cuartas observaciones sobre el opúsculo intitulado "El imperio y el clero mexicano," del señor abate Testory, capellán mayor del ejército francés por ... sacerdote mexicano*. Mexico City: Murgía, 1865.

———. *Recopilación de leyes, decretos, bandos, reglamentos, circulares y providencias de los supremos poderes y otras autoridades de la República Mexicana. Obra útil a toda clase de personas y necesaria a muchos individuos, como funcionarios públicos, curiales y empleados de oficinas, formada por orden del Supremo gobierno por el Lic. . . ..* 26 vols. Mexico City: Vicente García Torres, 1828–1864.

Benjamin, Judah P. *Speech of Hon. J. P. Benjamin of Louisiana, on the Right of Secession. Delivered in the Senate of the United States, December 31, 1860*. Washington, DC: Lemuel Towers, 1860.

A Bill to be entitled An Act to provide and export duty on cotton and tobacco exported from the Confederate states to the ports or in ships of any foreign country which has not recognized the independence of the Confederate states. Richmond, VA: n.p., 1863.

[Blair, Montgomery]. *The Monroe Doctrine: Speech of Hon. Montgomery Blair, at Hagerstown, Md., on 12th July, 1865, exposing the alliance of the American secretary of state with Louis Napoleon to overthrow the Monroe doctrine and establish a despotism on this continent*. n.p.: n.p., 1865.

Boletín de las leyes del Imperio Mexicano: Comprende las Leyes, Decretos y Reglamentos Generales, nos del 1 al 176, expedidos por el Emperador Maximiliano desde 1 de julio hasta el 31 de diciembre de 1865. Mexico City: Andrade y Escalante, 1866.

Boletín de las leyes del Imperio Mexicano, o sea código de la restauración. Colección completa de las leyes y demás disposiciones dictadas por la Intervención francesa, por el supremo poder ejecutivo provisional y por el Imperio mexicano, con un apéndice de los documentos más notables y curiosos de la época, publicados por José Sebastián Segura. 4 vols. Mexico City: Imprenta Literaria, 1863.

Buenrostro, Felipe. *Historia del Segundo Congreso Constitucional de la República Mexicana que funcionó en los años de 1861, 1862 y 1863*. 2 vols. Mexico City: Suprema Corte de Justicia, 2005 [1874].

Bulnes, Francisco. *Juárez y las Revoluciones de Ayutla y Reforma*. Mexico City: Instituto de Investigaciones Dr. José María Luis Mora, 2011 [1905].

Cady Stanton, Elizabeth, Susan B. Anthony, and Matilda Joslyn Gage, eds. *History of Woman Suffrage*. 3 vols. New York: E. O. Jenkins, 1866.

Calvo, Carlos. *Derecho internacional teórico y práctico de Europa y América*. 2 vols. Paris: Librarie Diplomatique, Durand et Pedoné-Lauriel Libraires, 1868.

Causa de Fernando Maximiliano de Habsburgo que se ha titulado emperador de México, y sus llamados generales Miguel Miramón y Tomás Mejía, sus cómplices: Por delitos contra

la independencia y seguridad de la nación, el orden y la paz pública, el derecho de gentes y las garantías individuales. Mexico City: T. F. Neve, 1868.
Chandler, William B. *The Soldier's Right to Vote: Who Opposes It? Who Favors It? Or the Record of the McClellan Copperheads, Against Allowing the Soldier who fights, the Right to Vote while Fighting.* Washington, DC: Lemuel Towers, 1864.
Character Glimpses of Most Reverend William Henry Elder, D. D. New York: Frederick Pustet, 1911.
Chevalier, Michel. *La France, le Mexique et les États Confédérés.* Paris: E. Dentu, 1863.
Código civil del Imperio Mexicano. Mexico City: M. Villanueva, 1866.
Colección de leyes, decretos y circulares expedidos por el Supremo Gobierno y del Estado en la época del llamado Imperio. Mexico City: Mariano L. López, 1867.
Colección de leyes, decretos y reglamentos que interinamente forman el sistema político, administrativo y judicial del Imperio. 8 vols. Mexico City: Andrade y Escalante, 1865–66.
The Congressional Globe. 46 vols. Washington, DC: Blair and Rives, 1834–73.
Correspondence Between Governor Brown and President Davis of the Constitutionality of the Conscription Act. Atlanta: Atlanta Intelligence, 1862.
Correspondencia de la Legación Mexicana en Washington durante la Intervención extranjera, 1860–1868: colección de documentos para formar la historia de la Intervención en México. 9 vols. Mexico City: Imprenta de Palacio, 1871.
Correspondencia entre la Legación de la República Mexicana en Washington, el Departamento de Estado de los Estados Unidos de América y el Gobierno Mexicano con relación a la exportación de armas y municiones de guerra de los Estados Unidos para puertos de naciones beligerantes. New York: n.p., 1866.
Couto, José Bernardo. *Obras del Dr. José Bernardo Couto.* Vol. 1, *Opúsculos varios.* Mexico City: V. Agüeros, 1858.
The Crittenden Compromise: A Surrender; Speech of Henry Wilson, delivered in the Senate, February 21st, 1861, on the resolutions of Mr. Crittenden. Washington, DC: n.p., 1861.
Crittenden, John J. *Speech of John J. Crittenden, of Kentucky, on his resolutions, delivered in the Senate of the United States, January 7, 1861.* Washington, DC: n.p., 1861.
Cuevas, Luis G. *Porvenir de México ó juicio sobre su estado político en 1821 y 1851.* Mexico City: Ignacio Cumplido, 1851.
Davis, Jefferson. *Speech of the Hon. Jefferson Davis of Mississippi, delivered in the US Senate, on the 10th day of January 1861, upon the message of the President of the United States on the Condition of Things in South Carolina.* Baltimore: John Murphy, 1861.
———. *Speech of the Honorable Jefferson Davis of Mississippi on the Measures of Compromise, delivered in the Senate of the United States, June 28, 1850.* Washington, DC: Towers, 1850.
de Flotte, Paul. *La Souveraineté du Peuple: Essais sur l'esprit de la Révolution.* Paris: Pagnerre, 1851.
de Kérartry, Émile. "La contre-guerrilla française au Mexique: Souvenirs des Terres Chaudes." *Revue des Deux Mondes* 59 (1865): 692–737.
de la Peña y Peña, Manuel. *Lecciones de práctica forense mejicana, escritas a beneficio de la Academia Nacional de Derecho Público y Privado de Méjico.* 3 vols. Mexico City: Juan Ojeda, 1835.
de la Rosa, Agustín. *El matrimonio civil, considerado en sus relaciones con la religión, la familia y la sociedad.* Guadalajara: Rodríguez, 1859.
de Vattel, Emer. *The Law of Nations; or, Principles of the Law of Nature, Applied to the Conduct and Affairs of Nations and Sovereigns, with Three Early Essays on the Origin and Nature of Natural Law and on Luxury.* Indianapolis: Liberty Fund, 2008 [1797].

Discurso pronunciado en el palacio de Miramar el 3 de Octubre de 1863 por D. J. M. Gutiérrez de Estrada . . . y contestación de S.A.I. y R. el Archiduque. Paris: Ad. Laine y J. Havard, 1863.

"Documentos relativos a la misión política encomendada a la Asamblea General de Notables, que dio resultado la adopción del sistema monárquico en México y la elección para emperador de S.A.R.I.Y.R. el archiduque Fernando Maximiliano de Austria." [1864]. In *México: Una forma republicana de gobierno*, edited by Alejandro Morales Becerra. *La forma de gobierno en los Congresos Constituyentes de México*, 2:1144–72. Mexico City: Universidad Nacional Autónoma de México, 2016.

Douglas, Stephen A. "First Joint Debate at Ottawa, August 21, 1858: Mr. Douglas's Speech." In *Political Debates Between Abraham Lincoln and Stephen A. Douglas*. Cleveland, OH: Burrows Bros., 1907.

Douglass, Frederick. *The Constitution of the United States: Is It Pro-Slavery or Anti-Slavery?* Halifax, Nova Scotia: T. and W. Birtwhistle, 1860.

———. *What the Black Man Wants: Speech at the Annual Meeting of the Massachusetts Anti-Slavery Society in Boston*. Boston: Geo. C. Rand & Avery, 1865.

Dublán, Manuel, and José María Lozano. *Legislación mexicana; ó, Colección completa de las disposiciones legislativas expedidas desde la independencia de la República, ordenada por los licenciados . . .* 35 vols. Mexico City, 1876. www.biblioweb.tic.unam.mx/dublanylozano/.

[Durán, Rafael]. "Memoria sobre el censo de la República Mexicana escrita por el socio de número de la Sociedad Mexicana de Geografía y Estadística D. Rafael Durán y leída en la sesión del 15 de enero de 1863." *Boletín de la Sociedad de Geografía y Estadística* 9 (1862): 263–78.

Edwards, John N. *Shelby's Expedition to Mexico: An Unwritten Leaf of the War*. Kansas City: Kansas City Times Steam Book and Job Printing House, 1872.

Evans, Albert S. *Our Sister Republic: A Gala Trip Through Tropical Mexico in 1869–1870*. Hartford, CT: Columbian, 1870.

Exposición dirigida a S.M. el emperador por algunos propietarios de fincas rústicas y urbanas en los departamentos de Zacatecas, Aguascalientes y Fresnillo, con motivo de las leyes dictadas el 26 de mayo próximo pasado. Mexico City: Ignacio Cumplido, 1866.

Exposition and Protest, reported by the Special Committee of the House of Representatives on the Tariff, read and ordered to be printed. December 19, 1828. Columbia, SC: D. W. Sims, State Printer, 1829.

[Grow, G. A.]. *Land for the Landless. Speech of the Hon. . . . of Pennsylvania, in the House of Representatives, February 29, 1860*. New York: Office of the New York Tribune, 1860.

Hall, William A. *The Historic Significance of the Southern Revolution: A Lecture Delivered by Invitation in Petersburg, Va., March 14 and April 29, 1864, and in Richmond, Va., April 7 and April 29, 1864*. Petersburg, VA: A. F. Crutchfield, 1864.

Hill, Benjamin H. *Senator Benjamin H. Hill of Georgia: His Life, Speeches, and Writings*. Atlanta: H. C. Hudgins, 1891.

[Hughes, John]. *The Complete Works of the Most Rev. . . . , Archbishop of New York: Comprising His Sermons, Letters, Lectures, Speeches, Carefully Compiled from the Best Sources, and Edited by Lawrence Kehoe*. 2 vols. New York: Lawrence Kehoe, 1866.

Hugo, Victor. *Actes et paroles*. Paris: J. Hetzel, 1888–1926.

Iglesias Calderón, Fernando. *El egoísmo norteamericano durante la Intervención francesa*. Mexico City: Económica, 1905.

———. *Las supuestas traiciones de Juárez*. Mexico City: Fondo de Cultura Económica, 1972 [1907].

[Jay, John]. *Mr. Jay's Letter on the Recent Relinquishment of the Monroe Doctrine.* Washington, DC: H. Polkinhorn & Sons, 1865.
Journal of the Confederate Congress, 1861–1865. 7 vols. Washington, DC: Government Printing Office, 1904–5.
Juárez, Benito, Melchor Ocampo, Manuel Ruiz, and Miguel Lerdo de Tejada. *Justificación de las Leyes de Reforma.* Mexico City: Instituto Nacional de Estudios Históricos de las Revoluciones de México, 2020 [1859].
Kansas: The Lecompton Constitution. Speech of Hon. John J. Crittenden of Kentucky in the Senate of the United States, March 17, 1858. Washington, DC: C. W. Fenton, 1858.
Labastida y Dávalos, Pelagio Antonio. *Carta pastoral del Ilustrísimo Sr. Dr. Don . . . por gracia de Dios y de la Santa Sede Obispo de Puebla de los Ángeles dirige a todos sus diocesanos con motivo de la nueva Constitución publicada en la Capital de su diócesis el 12 del último abril.* Rome: Civiltà Cattolica, 1857.
Langston, John Mercer. "Citizenship and the Ballot: The Relations of the Colored American to the Government and Its Duty to Him. A Colored Man the First Hero of the Revolutionary War." In *Freedom and Citizenship: Selected Lectures and Addresses of Hon. John Mercer Langston LL.D., United States Minister Resident in Haiti, with an Introductory Sketch by Rev. J. E. Rankin, D.D., of Washington,* 99–122. Washington, DC: Rufus H. Darby, 1883.
Leavitt, Joshua. *The Monroe Doctrine.* New York: Sinclair Tousey, 1863.
Leftwich, William M. *Martyrdom in Missouri: A History of Religious Proscription, the Seizure of Churches and the Persecution of Ministries of the Gospel, in the State of Missouri, during the Late Civil War and Under the "Test-Oath" of the New Constitution.* 2 vols. St. Louis, MO: SW Book, 1870.
Letter Addressed to Hon. Wm. C. Rives, by John H. Gilmer, on the Existing Status of the Revolution. n.p., 1864.
Lettre de Victor Hugo à Juarez, président de la République Mexicaine. Brussels: J. H. Briard, 1867.
Liberales ilustres mexicanos de la Reforma y la Intervención. Mexico City: Hijo del Ahuizote, 1890.
Lieber, Francis. *Amendments of the Constitution, Submitted to the Consideration of the American People.* New York: Loyal Publication Society, 1865.
———. *Guerrilla Parties: Considered with reference to the laws and usages of war.* New York: D. Van Nostrand, 1862.
———. *What Is Our Constitution: League, Pact or Government? Two Lectures on the Constitution of the United States concluding a course on the Modern State, delivered in the Law School of Columbia College, during the Winter of 1860 and 1861, for which is appended an address on Secession written in the year 1851.* New York: Baker & Goodwin, 1861.
Loomans, Charles. *Huit mois de captivité chez les Indiens au Mexique, 1865 (après Tacambaro).* Brussels: Davely, 1873.
Manifestación que hacen al venerable clero y fieles de sus respectivas Diócesis y a todo el mundo católico los Ilustrísimos Señores Arzobispo de México y Obispos de Michoacán, Linares, Guadalajara y el Potosí y el Sr. Dr. D. Francisco Serrano, representante de la Mitra de Puebla en defensa del clero y de la doctrina católica con ocasión del manifiesto y los decretos expedidos por el Sr. Lic. D. Benito Juárez en la ciudad de Veracruz los días 7, 12, 13 y 23 de junio de 1859. Mexico City: Andrade y Escalante, 1859.
Manifiesto justificativo de los castigos nacionales en Querétaro: El fusilamiento de Maximiliano de Habsburgo. Edited by Isaí Hidekel Tejada Vallejo. Mexico City: Cámara de Diputados, LXI Legislatura, 2010 [1867].

Márquez, Leonado. *Manifiestos: El Imperio y los imperialistas, por... Lugarteniente del Imperio. Rectificaciones de Ángel Pola*. Mexico City: F. Vázquez, 1904.

Mata, José María. *Memoria de Hacienda del Sr. Diputado D.... presentó al presidente de la República el 5 de mayo de 1861 al separarse del Ministerio de Hacienda para entrar al Congreso*. n.p., n.d.

Mateos, Juan A. *El Cerro de las Campanas (Memorias de un Guerrillero): Novela histórica*. Mexico City: Ignacio Cumplido, 1868.

———. *El sol de mayo (memorias de la Intervención): Novela histórica*. Mexico City: Ignacio Cumplido, 1869.

Mayer, Edelmiro. *Campaña y Guarnición: Memorias de un militar argentino en el ejército republicano de Benito Juárez*. Buenos Aires: Centro de Estudios Unión para la Nueva Mayoría, 1998 [1892].

McLane, Robert M. *Reminiscences, 1827–1897*. n.p.: n.p., 1903.

Memoria presentada al Excmo. Señor Presidente Sustituto de la República por el C. Miguel Lerdo de Tejada... de la marcha que han seguido los negocios de la Hacienda Pública, en el tiempo que estuvo a su cargo la Secretaría del Ramo. Mexico City: Vicente García Torres, 1857.

Message of the President to the Senate and House of Representatives of the Confederate States of America. November 7, 1864. n.p., n.d.

Mexico and the Monroe Doctrine. n.p., n.d.

Michel, Agustín, and Jean Meyer. *Mascota en la Gran Década Nacional, 1857–1867*. Guadalajara: Universidad de Guadalajara, 1994.

Michelbacher, Maximilian J. *A Sermon delivered on the Day of Prayer, Recommended by the President of the Confederate States of America, the 27th of March, 1863, at the German Hebrew Synagogue "Bayth Ahabah."* Richmond, VA: McFarlane and Ferguson, 1863.

Miranda, Francisco Javier. *Algunas reflexiones sobre la cuestión de la paz*. Mexico City: Andrade y Escalante, 1860.

The Monroe Doctrine. Speech of Hon. D. C. De Jarnette of Virginia, in the Confederate House of Representatives, January 30, 1865. Richmond, VA: Confederate House of Representatives, 1865.

[Mora, José María Luis]. *Disertación sobre la naturaleza y aplicación de las rentas y bienes eclesiásticos, sobre la autoridad a que se hallan sujetos en cuanto a su creación, aumento, subsistencia o supresión. Su autor, Un ciudadano de Zacatecas*. Mexico City: Galván, 1833.

Munguía, Clemente de Jesús. *Del Derecho natural en sus principios comunes y en sus diversas ramificaciones: o sea, curso elemental de derecho natural y de gentes, público, político y constitucional, y principios de legislación*. 4 vols. Mexico City: La Voz de la Religión, 1849.

———. *Opúsculo escrito por el Ilmo. Sr. Obispo de Michoacán Lic.... en defensa de la soberanía, derechos y libertades de la Iglesia, atacadas en la Constitución civil de 1857 y en otros decretos expedidos por el actual Supremo Gobierno de la Nación*. Morelia: Arango, 1857.

National Union Executive Committee. *Negro Suffrage and Social Equality*. n.p., 1866.

The Nebraska Question; comprising Speeches in the United States Senate by Messrs. Douglas, Chase; Smith, Everett, Wade, Badger, Seward, Sumner, together with the history of the Missouri Compromise, Daniel Webster's Memorial in Regard to it. History of the Annexation of Texas. Organization of Oregon Territory. Compromise of 1850. New York: Redfield, 1854.

New Mexico: Convention of Delegates. Journal and Proceedings of a convention of delegates elected by the people of New Mexico, held at Santa Fe on the 24th of September, 1849, presenting a plan for a civil government of said territory of New Mexico, and asking the action of Congress thereon. February 25, 1850. Referred to the Committee on Territories, and ordered to be printed. Washington, DC: n.p., 1850.

Niox, Gustave Léon. *Expédition au Mexique, 1861–1867, récit politique et militaire*. Paris: Librairie Militaire J. Dumaine, 1874.

Official Proceedings of the Democratic National Convention, held in 1860 at Charleston and Baltimore. Proceedings at Charleston, April 23–May 3, prepared and published under the direction of John G. Parkhurst, Recording Secretary. Cleveland: Nevin's Print, Plain Dealer Job Office, 1860.

One Country, One Constitution and One People. Speech of Hon. John A. Bingham of Ohio, in the House of Representatives, February 28, 1866. In support of the proposed amendment to enforce the Bill of Rights. n.p., 1866.

Opening Argument of Mr. Whipple in the Supreme Court of the United States, in the case of MARTIN LUTHER, against LUTHER M. BORDEN, and others, in behalf of the defendants. n.p., 1848.

Ortigosa, Vicente. *Cuatro memorias sobre puntos de administración*. Mexico City: Ignacio Cumplido, 1866.

Palmer, B. M. *The South: Her Peril and Her Duty. A Discourse, delivered in the First Presbyterian Church, New Orleans, on Thursday, November 29, 1860*. New Orleans: Office of the True Witness and Sentinel, 1860.

Papers Relating to Foreign Affairs, Accompanying the Annual Message of the President to the Two Houses of Congress at the Commencement of the First Session of the Thirty-Ninth Congress. Parts 2 and 3. Washington, DC: Government Printing Office, 1865.

Papers Relating to Foreign Affairs, Accompanying the Annual Message of the President to the Two Houses of Congress at the Commencement of the Second Session of the Thirty-Seventh Congress. Vol. 1. Washington, DC: Government Printing Office, 1861.

Papers Relating to Foreign Affairs, Accompanying the Annual Message of the President to the Two Houses of Congress at the Commencement of the Third Session of the Thirty-Seventh Congress. Vol. 1. Washington, DC: Government Printing Office, 1862.

Parliamentary Debates on the Subject of the Confederation of the British North American Provinces, 3rd Session, 8th Provincial Parliament of Canada. Quebec City: Hunter, Rose, 1865.

El Partido Conservador en México. Mexico City: J. M. Andrade y F. Escalante, 1855.

Payno, Manuel. *Carta que sobre los asuntos de México dirige al Sr. Gral. Forey, comandante en jefe de las tropas francesas, el ciudadano . . .* Mexico City: Vicente García Torres, 1862.

———. *Cuentas, gastos, acreedores y otros asuntos del tiempo de la Intervención francesa y el Imperio. Obra escrita y publicada por orden del Gobierno de la República por . . . , de 1861 a 1867*. Mexico City: Ignacio Cumplido, 1868.

———. "Memoria sobre la revolución de diciembre de 1857 y enero 1858" [1861]. In *Opúsculos de Payno, 1850–1867*, 11–82. Mexico City: Bibliófilos Mexicanos, 1960.

———. *México y sus cuestiones financieras con la Inglaterra, la España y la Francia. Memoria que por orden del supremo Gobierno Constitucional de la República escribe el C . . .* Mexico City: Ignacio Cumplido, 1862.

———. *La reforma social en España y México: Apuntes históricos y principales leyes sobre desamortización de bienes eclesiásticos*. Mexico City: Universitaria, 1958 [1861].

Pérez Gallardo, Basilio. *Martirologio de los defensores de la independencia, 1863–1867.* Mexico City: Imprenta del Gobierno en Palacio, 1875.
Pesado, José Joaquín. *Controversia pacífica sobre la nueva constitución Mexicana.* Morelia: I. Arango, 1857.
Pimentel, Francisco. *La economía política aplicada a la propiedad territorial en México.* Mexico City: Ignacio Cumplido, 1866.
———. *Memoria sobre las causas que han originado la situación actual de la raza indígena de México y medios de remediarla.* Mexico City: Andrade y Escalante, 1864.
Plan de Ayutla. Mexico City: Instituto Nacional de Estudios Históricos de las Revoluciones de México, 2015 [1854].
Planes en la nación mexicana. Vol. 6, *1857–1910.* Mexico City: El Colegio de México, Senado de la República, 1987.
Prieto, Guillermo. *Viajes de orden suprema: Años de 1853, 1854 y 1855.* Mexico City: Vicente García Torres, 1857.
"Proclamation by the Governor." Frankfort, KY, May 20, 1861. https://scholarworks.uni.edu/cgi/viewcontent.cgi?article=1005&context=nhomefront.
Ramírez, José Fernando. *México durante su guerra con los Estados Unidos.* Mexico City: Librería de la Viuda de Charles Bouret, 1905.
Ramsay, David. *A Dissertation on the Manner of Acquiring the Character and Privileges of a Citizen of the United States.* n.p., 1789.
The Record of Hon. C. L. Vallandigham on Abolition, the Union and the Civil War. 9th ed. Columbus: J. Walter, 1863.
Reglamento para los servicios de honor y ceremonial de la Corte. Mexico City: J. M. Lara, 1866.
Report of the Debates of the Convention of California on the Formation of the State Constitution, in September and October 1849. Washington, DC: John T. Towers, 1850.
Report on the Trial of Thomas Wilson Dorr for treason against the State of Rhode Island, containing the argument of counsel and the charge of the Chief Justice Durfee. Boston: Tappan & Dennet, 1844.
[Rhett, Robert]. *The Address of the People of South Carolina, assembled in Convention, the People of the Slaveholding States of the United States,* December 25, 1860. Charleston: Evans & Cogswell, 1860.
The Rhode Island Question: Mr. Webster's Argument in the Supreme Court of the United States, in the case of Martin Luther vs. Luther M. Borden and Others. Washington, DC: J. and G. S. Gideon, 1848.
The Rights of the People to Establish Forms of Government: Mr. Hallet's Argument in the Rhode Island Causes Before the Supreme Court of the United States. Boston: Beals & Greene, 1848.
Riva Palacio, Vicente, Manuel Payno, Juan A. Mateos, and Rafael Martínez de la Torre. *El Libro Rojo de México.* 2 vols. Mexico City: A. Pola, 1906.
Roa Bárcena, José María. *La quinta modelo.* Mexico City: Universidad Nacional Autónoma de México, 2022 [1857]. https://lanovelacorta.com/novelas-en-transito/la-quinta-modelo.pdf.
Robbins, James J. *Report of the Trial of Castner Hanway for Treason, in the Resistance of the Execution of the Fugitive Slave Law of September, 1850.* Philadelphia: King and Baird, 1852.
Robles Pezuela, Luis. *Memoria presentada a S.M. el Emperador por el ministro de fomento Luis Robles Pezuela de los trabajos ejecutados en su ramo el año de 1865.* Mexico City: Ministerio de Fomento, 1865.

Romero, Matías. *Responsabilidades contraídas por el gobierno nacional de México con los Estados-Unidos, en virtud de los contratos celebrados por sus agentes, 1864–1867.* Mexico City: Imprenta del Gobierno, 1867.
Salm Salm, Felix. *My Diary in Mexico in 1867: Including the Last Days of the Emperor Maximilian; with Leaves from the Diary of Princess Salm-Salm.* 2 vols. London: R. Bentley, 1868.
Seaman, L. *What Miscegenation Is! And what we are to expect Now that Mr. Lincoln is Re-elected.* New York: Waller & Willetts, 1865.
Sheridan, Philip Henry. *Personal Memoirs of . . . , General in the United States Army: New and Enlarged Edition with an Account of His Life from 1871 to His Death in 1888 by Brigadier General Michael V. Sheridan.* 2 vols. Boston: D. Appleton, 1902.
Sierra O'Reilly, Justo. *Diario de nuestro viaje a los Estados Unidos (la pretendida anexión de Yucatán).* Mexico City: Porrúa e Hijos, 1938 [1848].
[Sledd, Robert N.]. *A Sermon Delivered in the Market Street, M.E. Church, Petersburg, Va.: Before the Confederate Cadets, on the Occasion of Their Departure for the Seat of War. Sunday 22nd, 1861.* Petersburg: A. F. Crutchfield, 1861.
Smith, Robert H. *An Address to the Citizens of Alabama on the Constitution and the Laws of the Confederate States of America.* Mobile: Mobile Daily Register Print, 1861.
Speeches of Andrew Johnson, president of the United States. With a biographical introduction by Frank Moore. Boston: Little, Brown, 1865.
The Statutes at Large of the Confederate States of America, Passed at the First Session of the Second Congress; 1864. Carefully Collated with the Originals at Richmond. Public Laws of the Confederate States of America, Passed at the First Session of the Second Congress. Richmond, VA: R. M. Smith, Printer to Congress, 1864. https://docsouth.unc.edu/imls/24conf/24conf.html.
The Statutes at Large of the Provisional Government of the Confederate States of America, from the Institution of Government, February 8, 1861, to its termination, February 8, 1862 Inclusive. Arranged in Chronological Order. Together with the Constitution of the Provisional Government, the Permanent Constitution of the Confederate States and Treaties Concluded by the Confederate States with Indian Tribes. Edited by James M. Matthews. Richmond, VA: R. M. Smith, Printer to Congress, 1864.
Stevens, Thaddeus. *Speech of Mr. Thaddeus Stevens of Pennsylvania, in the House of Representatives, in Reference to the President's Annual Message Made in Committee of the Whole, February 20, 1850.* Washington, DC: Buell & Blanchard, 1850.
Suárez Iriarte, Francisco. *Defensa pronunciada ante el gran jurado el 21 de marzo de 1850, por Francisco Suárez Iriarte, acusado en 8 de agosto de 1848 por el Secretario de Relaciones en aquella fecha de los crímenes de sedición contra el Gobierno de Querétaro en infidencia contra la patria en sus actos como presidente de la Asamblea municipal de la Ciudad y Distrito de México.* Mexico City: R. Rafael, 1850.
Sumner, Charles. *The Equal Rights of All: The Great Guarantee and Present Necessity for the Sake of Security and to Maintain a Republican Government. Speech of . . . of Massachusetts in the United States Senate, February 6 and 7, 1866.* Washington, DC: Congressional Globe Office, 1866.
———. *"The One Man Power vs. Congress!": Address of the Honorable Charles Sumner at the Music Hall, Boston, October 2, 1866.* Boston: Wright & Porter, 1866.
Tariff of the Confederate States of America, approved by Congress, May 21, 1861, To Be of Force from and after August 31, 1861. Charleston, SC: Evans & Cogswell, 1861.
Testory, Louis. *El imperio y el clero mexicano.* Mexico City: Comercio, 1865.

Torres Caicedo, José María. *Unión Latino-Americana. Pensamiento de Bolívar para formar una liga americana: su origen y sus desarrollos y estudio sobre la gran cuestión que tanto interesa a los estados débiles, a saber: ¿Un gobierno legítimo es responsable por los daños y perjuicios ocasionados a los extranjeros por las facciones?* Paris: Rosa y Bouret, 1865.

Troncoso, Francisco P. *Diario de las operaciones militares del sitio de Puebla en 1863, escrito por el teniente coronel... durante el asedio de la plaza.* Mexico City: Secretaría de Guerra y Marina, 1909.

Valdés, Manuel. *Memorial de la Guerra de Reforma. Diario del Coronel...* Mexico City: Imprenta y Fototipia de la Secretaría de Fomento, 1913.

Vallarta, Ignacio L. *El juicio de amparo y el writ of Habeas Corpus: ensayo crítico-comparativo sobre estos recursos constitucionales.* Mexico City: Francisco Díaz de León, 1881.

Vicuña Mackenna, Benjamín. *Diez meses de misión a los Estados Unidos de Norteamérica como agente confidencial de Chile.* Santiago: Libertad, 1867.

Zaldívar, Luis G. *Recopilación de leyes, decretos, bandos, circulares y providencias de los Supremos Poderes y otras autoridades.* Mexico City: A. Boix, 1866.

———. *Diccionario de la legislación mexicana, que comprende las leyes, bandos, reglamentos, circulares y providencias del supremo gobierno y otras autoridades del Supremo Gobierno y otras autoridades de la Nación.* Mexico City: Imprenta de la "Constitución Social," 1868.

Zarco, Francisco. *Historia del Congreso Constituyente del 1857.* Mexico City: Instituto Nacional de Estudios Históricos de las Revoluciones de México, 2009 [1857].

Secondary Sources

Abinder, Tyler. "Which Poor Man's Fight? Immigrants and the Federal Conscription of 1863." *Civil War History* 52, no. 4 (2006): 344–72.

Aboites, Luis. "Alcabalas posporfirianas: Modernización tributaria y gobierno estatal." *Historia Mexicana* 51, no. 2 (2001): 363–93.

Aboites, Luis, and Luis Jáuregui, eds. *Penuria sin fin: Historia de los impuestos en México, siglos XVIII–XX.* Mexico City: Instituto de Investigaciones Dr. José Luis Mora, 2005.

Acevedo, Esther. "Las imágenes del último Maximiliano: Pasión, muerte y resurrección de Maximiliano." *Letras Libres*, June 2017. https://letraslibres.com/revista/las-imagenes-del-ultimo-maximiliano-pasion-muerte-y-resurreccion-de-maximiliano/.

———. *Testimonios artísticos de un episodio fugaz, 1864–1867.* Mexico City: Museo Nacional de Arte, 1995.

Ackerman, Bruce. *We the People: Foundations.* Cambridge, MA: Belknap, 1991.

Adame Goddard, Jorge. "El juramento de la constitución de 1857." *Anuario mexicano de historia del derecho* 10 (1998): 21–37.

Aghulon, Maurice. *La République au village: Les populations du Var de la Révolution à la Seconde République.* Paris: Plon, 1970.

Aguilar Ochoa, Arturo, ed. *El sitio de Puebla: 150 aniversario.* Mexico City: Instituto Nacional de Estudios Históricos de las Revoluciones de México, Secretaría de Educación Pública; Puebla: Benemérita Universidad Autónoma de Puebla, 2012.

Aguilar Rivera, José Antonio. *Elecciones y gobierno representativo en México, 1810–1910.* Mexico City: Fondo de Cultura Económica, 2021.

———. *El manto liberal: Los poderes de emergencia en México, 1821–1876.* Mexico City: Universidad Nacional Autónoma de México, 2001.

———. *El sonido y la furia: La persuasión multicultural en México y Estados Unidos.* Mexico City: Taurus, 2004.

———. "La convocatoria, las elecciones y el congreso extraordinario de 1846." *Historia Mexicana* 61, no. 2 (2011): 531–88.

———. "La redención democrática: México, 1821–1861." *Historia Mexicana* 69, no. 1 (2019): 7–56.

Aguilar Rivera, José Antonio, and Rafael Rojas, eds. *El republicanismo en Hispanoamérica: Ensayos de historia intelectual y política.* Mexico City: Centro de Investigación y Docencia Económicas, Fondo de Cultura Económica, 2002.

Alcántara Machuca, Edwin. "La elección de Lucas Alamán y los conservadores como diputados al Congreso de 1849: *El Universal* frente a los procesos y conflictos electorales." In *Prensa y elecciones: Formas de hacer política en el México del siglo XIX*, edited by Fausta Gantús and Alicia Salmerón, 27–54. Mexico City: Instituto de Investigaciones Dr. José María Luis Mora, 2014.

Almada Bay, Ignacio, David Contreras Tánori, and Amparo Reyes Gutiérrez. "Medidas ofensivas y defensivas de los vecinos de Sonora en respuesta a las incursiones apaches, 1854–1890: El despliegue de una autodefensa limitada." *Historia Mexicana* 65, no. 3 (2016): 1193–269.

Altschuler, Glenn C., and Stuart M. Blumin. *Rude Republic: Americans and Their Politics in the Nineteenth Century.* Princeton, NJ: Princeton University Press, 2001.

Anderson, Benedict. *Imagined Communities: Reflections on the Origin and Spread of Nationalism.* London: Verso, 1991.

Andrews, Catherine. "Discusiones en torno de la reforma de la Constitución Federal de 1824 durante el primer gobierno de Anastasio Bustamante (1830–1832)." *Historia Mexicana* 56, no. 1 (2006): 71–116.

———, ed. *De Cádiz a Querétaro: Historiografía y bibliografía del constitucionalismo mexicano.* Mexico City: Fondo de Cultura Económica, Centro de Investigación y Docencia Económicas, 2017.

Archer, Christon I. "The Militarization of Politics or the Politization of the Military? The Novohispano and Mexican Officer Corps, 1810–1860." *Estudios Ibero-Americanos* 36, no. 2 (2010): 208–41.

Arenson, Adam, and Andrew R. Graybill, eds. *Civil War Wests: Testing the Limits of the United States.* Berkeley: University of California Press, 2015.

Arroyo, Israel. *Juárez y sus gabinetes: Republicanismo y división de poderes.* Mexico City: Cámara de Diputados, LXV Legislatura, 2021.

———. *La arquitectura del Estado mexicano: Formas de gobierno, representación política y ciudadanía, 1821–1857.* Mexico City: Instituto de Investigaciones Dr. José María Luis Mora; Puebla: Benemérita Universidad Autónoma de Puebla, 2011.

———. "Monarquismo y republicanismo: Las primeras regencias de España y México." *Espacio, tiempo y forma* 22 (2010): 107–50.

Ávila, Alfredo. *Para la libertad: Los republicanos en tiempos del imperio, 1821–1823.* Mexico City: Universidad Nacional Autónoma de México, 2005.

Ávila, Alfredo, and Alicia Salmerón. *Partidos, facciones y otras calamidades: Debates y propuestas acerca de los partidos políticos en México, siglo XIX.* Mexico City: Consejo Nacional para la Cultura y las Artes, Fondo de Cultura Económica, Universidad Nacional Autónoma de México, 2012.

Ávila, Jesús, Leticia Martínez, and César Morado. *Santiago Vidaurri: La formación de un liderazgo regional desde Monterrey, 1809–1867.* Monterrey: Universidad Autónoma de Nuevo León, 2012.

Azuela, Alicia. *Diego Rivera en Detroit*. Mexico City: Universidad Nacional Autónoma de México, 1985.

Báez Méndez, Andrea Saraí. "Representaciones pictóricas y escritas del asalto a la diligencia o cómo era viajar ante el peligro de bandidos: Puebla sobre el camino real México-Veracruz, 1833–1869." MA thesis, Benemérita Universidad Autónoma de Puebla, 2022.

Bailyn, Bernard. *The Ideological Origins of the American Revolution*. Cambridge, MA: Belknap, 1992.

Baumgartner, Alice L. *South to Freedom: Runaway Slaves to Mexico and the Road to Civil War*. New York: Basic Books, 2020.

Bazant, Jan. *Los bienes de la Iglesia en México, 1856–1875: Aspectos económicos y sociales de la revolución liberal*. Mexico City: El Colegio de México, 1977.

Beard, Charles A., and Mary A. Beard. *The Rise of American Civilization*. 2 vols. New York: Macmillan, 1927.

Becerril Hernández, Carlos. *Hacienda pública y administración fiscal: La legislación tributaria del Segundo Imperio mexicano (Antecedentes y desarrollo)*. Mexico City: CONACYT, Instituto de Investigaciones Dr. José María Luis Mora, 2015.

Beckert, Sven. *Empire of Cotton: A Global History*. New York: Alfred A. Knopf, 2014.

Belissa, Marc. "Le cosmopolitisme du Droit de Gens (1713–1795): Fraternité universelle et intérêt national au siècle des Lumières et pendant la Révolution Française." *Annales historiques de la Révolution Française* 306 (1996): 723–33.

Benavides, José Luis. "Californios! Whom Do You Support? *El Clamor Público*'s Contradictory Role in the Racial Formation Process in Early California." *California History* 84, no. 2 (2006/2007): 56–66.

Bender, Thomas. *A Nation Among Nations: America's Place in World History*. New York: Hill and Wang, 2006.

Benito Juárez: Documentos, discursos y correspondencia. Edited by Jorge L. Tamayo, digital edition by Héctor Cuauhtémoc Hernández Silva. Mexico City: Universidad Autónoma Metropolitana Azcapotzalco, 2006. Compact disc.

Bensel, Richard F. *Yankee Leviathan: The Origins of Central State Authority in America, 1859–1877*. Cambridge: Cambridge University Press, 1991.

Benton, Josiah H. *Voting in the Field: A Forgotten Chapter of the Civil War*. Norwood, MA: Plimpton, 1915.

Berge, Dennis E. "A Mexican Dilemma: The Mexico City Ayuntamiento and the Question of Loyalty, 1846–1848." *Hispanic American Historical Review* 50, no. 2 (1970): 229–56.

Berger, Bethany B. "Birthright Citizenship on Trial: *Elk v. Wilkins* and *United States v. Wong Kim Ark*." *Cardozo Law Review* 37 (2016): 1185–258.

Beringer, Richard E., Herman Hattaway, Archer Jones, and William N. Still Jr. *Why the South Lost the Civil War*. Athens: University of Georgia Press, 1991.

Bernholz, Charles D., Laura K. Weakly, Brian L. Pytlik Zillig, and Karin Dalziel. "American Indian Civil War Treaties: The Instruments Formed by the Confederate States of America in Indian Territory." *Library Collections, Acquisitions, and Technical Services* 35 (2011): 29–31.

Bestor, Arthur. "The American Civil War as a Constitutional Crisis." *American Historical Review* 69, no. 2 (1964): 327–52.

Black, Shirley J. *Napoleon III and Mexican Silver*. Silverton, CO: Ferrell, 2000.

Blackhawk, Ned. *The Rediscovery of America: Native Peoples and the Unmaking of U.S. History*. New Haven, CT: Yale University Press, 2023. Kindle.

Blair, William A. *With Malice Toward Some: Treason and Loyalty in the Civil War Era*. Chapel Hill: University of North Carolina Press, 2014.

Blanco Cebada, Luis Antonio. "Actores sociales y cultura política del noroeste yucateco durante el Segundo Imperio mexicano (1863–1867)." *Temas Antropológicos: Revista Científica de Investigaciones Regionales* 40, no. 1 (2017–18): 79–108.

Blanton, DeeAnn, and Lauren Cook Wike. *They Fought Like Demons: Women Soldiers and the American Civil War*. Baton Rouge: Louisiana State University Press, 2002.

Blázquez, Carmen. "Los liberales exiliados y la Junta Revolucionaria de Brownsville, 1853–1855." *La Palabra y el Hombre*, 1981, 37–49.

Blight, David W. *Race and Reunion: The Civil War in American Memory*. Cambridge, MA: Belknap, 2002.

Blumberg, Arnold. "The Diplomacy of the Mexican Empire, 1863–1867." *Transactions of the American Philosophical Society* 61, no. 8 (1971): 1–152.

Blyth, Lance R. "Kit Carson and the War for the Southwest: Separation and Survival Along the Río Grande, 1862–1868." In *Civil War Wests: Testing the Limits of the United States*, edited by Adam Arenson and Andrew R. Gray, 53–69. Berkeley: University of California Press, 2015.

Bonner, Robert E. "Proslavery Extremism Goes to War: The Counterrevolutionary Confederacy and Reactionary Militarism." *Modern Intellectual History* 6, no. 1 (2009): 261–85.

Botana, Natalio. *La tradición republicana: Alberdi, Sarmiento y las ideas políticas de su tiempo*. Buenos Aires: Sudamericana, 1997.

Bowman, Matthew. *The Mormon People: The Making of an American Faith*. New York: Random House, 2012. Kindle.

Brading, David A. *Los orígenes del nacionalismo mexicano*. Mexico City: Secretaría de Educación Pública, 1973.

———. *Mexican Phoenix: Our Lady of Guadalupe; Image and Tradition across Five Centuries*. Cambridge: Cambridge University Press, 2001.

Brimmer, Brandi Clay. *Claiming Widowhood: Race, Respectability, and Poverty in the Post-Emancipation South*. Durham, NC: Duke University Press, 2020.

Briones, Claudia. "Introducción: Madejas de alteridades, entramados de Estados-nación. Diseños y telares de ayer y hoy en América Latina." In *Nación y alteridad: Mestizos, indígenas y extranjeros en el proceso de formación nacional*, edited by Daniela Gleizer and Paula López Caballero, 17–65. Mexico City: UAM–Cuajimalpa, Ediciones EyC, 2015.

Brittsan, Zachary. *Popular Politics and Rebellion in Mexico: Manuel Lozada and La Reforma, 1855–1876*. Nashville: Vanderbilt University Press, 2015.

Brown, Zachary. "'Indianizing the Confederacy': Understanding of War Cruelty During the American Civil War and the Sioux Uprising of 1862." *Penn History Review* 23, no. 2 (2016): 115–36.

Brownlee, W. Elliott. *Federal Taxation in America: A History*. New York: Cambridge University Press, 2016. Kindle.

Burdekin, Richard C. K., and Farrokh Langdana. "War Finance in the Southern Confederacy, 1861–1865." *Explorations in Economic History* 30 (1993): 353–76.

Buriano, Ana. *Navegando en la borrasca: Construir la nación de la fe en el mundo de la impiedad, Ecuador, 1860–1875*. Mexico City: Instituto Mora, 2008.

Burin, Eric. *Slavery and the Peculiar Solution: The American Colonization Society*. Gainesville: University Press of Florida, 2008.

Campos García, Melchor. "La invención de la Guerra de Castas en Yucatán, 1847–1927." *Tzinzun: Revista de Estudios Históricos* 77 (2023): 153–84.

Campos Pérez, Lara. "1867: ¿Momento republicano?" *Historia Mexicana* 71, no. 1 (2022): 1683–721.

———. "Ensayo bibliométrico sobre el republicanismo y la idea republicana en México de la restauración de la República y la caída de Porfirio Díaz." *Ariadna Histórica: Lenguajes, Conceptos, Metáforas* 10 (2021): 313–44.

Canal, Jordi. "Guerras civiles en Europa en el siglo XIX o guerra civil europea." In *Guerras civiles: Una clave para entender la Europa de los siglos XIX y XX*, edited by Jordi Canal and Eduardo González Calleja, 25–38. Madrid: Casa de Velázquez, 2012.

Cancio, Raúl C. *España y la Guerra Civil Americana, o la globalización del contrarrevolucionismo*. Alcalá, Spain: Universidad de Alcalá, 2015.

Cañizares-Esguerra, Jorge. "Entangled Histories: Borderlands Historiographies in New Clothes?" *American Historical Review* 112, no. 3 (2007): 787–99.

Capdevila, Luc. *Une guerre totale: Paraguay, 1864–1870; Essai d'histoire du temps présent*. Rennes, France: Presses Universitaires de Rennes, 2007.

Cárdenas, Elisa. "El fin de una era: Pío IX y el *Syllabus*." *Historia Mexicana* 65, no. 2 (2015): 719–46.

Careaga, Lorena. *De llaves y cerrojos: Yucatán, Texas y Estados Unidos a mediados del siglo XIX*. Mexico City: Instituto Mora, 2000.

———. *Hierofanía combatiente: Lucha, simbolismo y religiosidad en la Guerra de Castas*. Chetumal: Universidad de Quintana Roo, 1998.

Carmagnani, Marcello. *Estado y mercado: La economía política del liberalismo mexicano, 1850–1911*. Mexico City: El Colegio de México, Fondo de Cultura Económica, 1994.

Carmagnani, Marcello, and Alicia Hernández Chávez. "La ciudadanía orgánica mexicana, 1850–1910." In *Ciudadanía política y formación de las naciones: Perspectivas históricas de América Latina*, edited by Hilda Sabato, 371–404. Mexico City: El Colegio de México, Fondo de Cultura Económica, 1999.

Carretero Madrid, Jorge. "Prisionero de guerra del Imperio francés: Diario del Teniente Coronel Cosme Varela. Episodio histórico ocurrido durante la Intervención." In *El sitio de Puebla: 150 aniversario*, edited by Arturo Aguilar Ochoa, 113–46. Mexico City: Instituto Nacional de Estudios Históricos de las Revoluciones de México, Secretaría de Educación Pública; Puebla: Benemérita Universidad Autónoma de Puebla, 2012.

Casanova, Rosa. "La seducción de la tragedia: Fotografías de Maximiliano de Habsburgo." *Cristal Bruñido: Fotografía Histórica* 26, no. 77 (2019): 155–74.

Castillo Nájera, Francisco. *El tratado de Guadalupe: Ponencia al Congreso Mexicano de Historia, VIII reunión (Durango, septiembre 17–26 de 1947)*. Mexico City: Talleres Gráficos de la Nación, 1947.

Ceballos, Manuel, ed. *Encuentro en la frontera: Mexicanos y norteamericanos en un espacio común*. Mexico City: El Colegio de México; Ciudad Victoria: Colegio de la Frontera Norte, Universidad Autónoma de Tamaulipas, 2001.

———. "Los dos Laredos: Historia compartida y experiencia de la frontera." In *Encuentro en la frontera: Mexicanos y norteamericanos en un espacio común*, edited by Manuel Ceballos, 233–57. Mexico City: Colegio de México, Ciudad Victoria: El Colegio de la Frontera Norte, Universidad Autónoma de Tamaulipas, 2001.

Ceja, Claudia. *La fragilidad de las armas: Reclutamiento, control y vida social en el ejército en la Ciudad de México durante la primera mitad del siglo XIX*. Mexico City: El Colegio de México, 2022.

Cerutti, Mario, and Miguel Ángel González-Quiroga. "Guerra y comercio en torno al Río Bravo (1855–1867): Línea fronteriza, espacio económico común." *Historia Mexicana* 40, no. 2 (1991): 217–97.

Cervantes Bello, Francisco Javier. *De la impiedad y la usura: Los capitales eclesiásticos y el crédito en Puebla, 1825–1863*. Mexico City: El Colegio de México, 1993.

———. "La propiedad eclesiástica en Puebla en la primera mitad del siglo XIX: La formación de la opinión pública en favor de la desamortización." In *La Iglesia y sus bienes: De la amortización a la desamortización*, edited by Pilar Martínez López-Cano, Elisa Speckman, and Gisela von Wobeser, 275–91. Mexico City: Universidad Nacional Autónoma de México, 2004.

Chadwick, Elizabeth. "Back to the Future: Three Civil Wars and the Law of Neutrality." *Journal of Conflict and Security Law* 1, no. 1 (1996): 1–31.

Chassen-López, Francie. *Mujer y poder en el siglo XIX: La vida extraordinaria de Juana Catarina Romero, Cacica de Tehuantepec.* Mexico City: Penguin Random and Taurus, 2020.

Childers, Christopher. "Interpreting Popular Sovereignty: A Historiographical Essay." *Civil War History* 58 (2011): 48–70.

Chomsky, Carol. "The United States Dakota War Trials: A Study in Military Injustice." *Stanford Law Review* 43, no. 1 (1990): 13–98.

Chowning, Margaret. *Catholic Women and Mexican Politics, 1750–1940.* Princeton, NJ: Princeton University Press, 2023.

Connaughton, Brian. *Entre la voz de Dios y el llamado de la patria: Religión, identidad y ciudadanía en México, siglo XIX.* Mexico City: Fondo de Cultura Económica, 2010.

———. *Iglesia, religión y leyes de Reforma.* 2 vols. Xalapa: Universidad Veracruzana, 2011.

———. *La mancuerna discordante: La república católica liberal en México hasta la Reforma.* Mexico City: Gedisa, Universidad Autónoma Metropolitana Iztapalapa, 2019.

Conte Corti, Egon César. *Maximiliano y Carlota.* Mexico City: Fondo de Cultura Económica, 1983.

Córdoba, Irina. *Manuel Payno: Los derroteros de un liberal moderado.* Zamora: El Colegio de Michoacán, 2006.

Coronado Guel, L. E. "Legislación expedida por los poderes federales en San Luis Potosí en 1862, 1863 y 1867: Fuente para el entendimiento de la Guerra de Intervención francesa." *Revista de El Colegio de San Luis* 5, no. 9 (2015): 138–58.

Cosío Villegas, Daniel. "México y Estados Unidos." In *Los extremos de América*, 43–74. Mexico City: Fondo de Cultura Económica, 2004.

Costeloe, Michael. "Mariano Arista and the 1850 Presidential Election in Mexico." *Bulletin of Latin American Research* 18, no. 1 (1999): 5–70.

Coudart, Laurence. "La regulación de la libertad de prensa (1863–1867)." *Historia Mexicana* 65, no. 2 (2015): 269–687.

Covo, Jacqueline. *Las ideas de la Reforma en México (1855–1861).* Mexico City: Universidad Nacional Autónoma de México, 1983.

Cox, Karen L. *Dixie's Daughters: The United Daughters of the Confederacy and the Preservation of Confederate Culture.* Gainesville: University Press of Florida, 2003.

Cox, LaWanda. "The Promise of Land for Freedmen." *Mississippi Valley Historical Review* 45, no. 3 (1958): 413–40.

Cox Richardson, Heather. *To Make Men Free: A History of the Republican Party.* New York: Basic Books, 2014.

Crawford, Martin. *The Anglo-American Crisis of the Mid-Nineteenth Century: The Times and America, 1850–1862.* Athens: University of Georgia Press, 1987.

Crespo, María Victoria. *Del rey al presidente: Poder ejecutivo, formación del Estado y soberanía en la Hispanoamérica revolucionaria, 1810–1826.* Mexico City: El Colegio de México, 2013.

Crutchfield, James A. *Revolt at Taos: The New Mexican and Indian Insurrection of 1847.* Lanham, MD: Republic of Texas Press, 1995.

Cruz Barney, Óscar. *La República Central de Félix Zuloaga y el Estatuto Orgánico provisional de la República de 1858.* Mexico City: Universidad Nacional Autónoma de México, 2009.

Cruz García, Ricardo. "Aires de guerra: La invasión al puerto de Bagdad en enero de 1866. El epicentro de un decisivo conflicto entre potencias." *Relatos e Historias de México* 139 (2020): 40–49.

Cunningham, Michele. *Mexico and the Foreign Policy of Napoleon III.* London: Palgrave, 2001.

Curiel, Gustavo. "San Felipe de Jesús: Figura y culto (1629–1862)." In *Historia, leyendas y mitos de México: Su expresión en el arte. XI Coloquio Internacional de Historia del Arte*, 71–98. Mexico City: Universidad Nacional Autónoma de México, 1988.

Current, Richard N. *Lincoln's Loyalists: Union Soldiers from the Confederacy.* Boston: Northeastern University, 1992.

Currie, David P. "Through the Looking Glass: The Confederate Constitution in Congress, 1861–1865." *Virginia Law Review* 90, no. 5 (2004): 1257–399.

Davis, John Martin, Jr. *Civil War Taxes: A Documentary History, 1861–1900.* Jefferson, NC: McFarland, 2019.

Davis, William C. *The Cause Lost: Myths and Realities of the Confederacy.* Lawrence: University Press of Kansas, 1996.

"Débats: Transnationalizing North American History." *Nuevo Mundo / Mundos Nuevos*, April 2010. http://journals.openedition.org/nuevomundo/59492.

de la Luz Topete, María, ed. *Labor diplomática de Matías Romero en Washington, 1861–1867.* Mexico City: Secretaría de Relaciones Exteriores, 1976.

del Arenal, Jaime. "El proyecto de constitución del Segundo Imperio mexicano: Notas sobre el manuscrito de la archiduquesa Carlota." In *Más nuevas del imperio: Estudios interdisciplinarios acerca de Carlota de México*, edited by Susanne Igler and Roland Spiller, 41–54. Madrid: Iberoamericana; Frankfurt am Main: Vervuet, 2001.

———. "La protección del indio en el Segundo Imperio mexicano: La Junta protectora de las clases menesterosas." *Ars Iuris* 6 (1991): 1–35.

DeLay, Brian. *War of a Thousand Deserts: Indian Raids and the U.S.-Mexican War.* New Haven, CT: Yale University, 2008.

de León, Arnoldo. *They Called Them Greasers: Anglo Attitudes toward Mexicans in Texas, 1821–1900.* Austin: University of Texas Press, 1983.

del Valle, Guillermina. "Los empréstitos de fines de la Colonia y su permanencia en el gobierno de Iturbide." In *Hacienda y política: Las finanzas públicas y los grupos de poder en la Primera República Federal mexicana*, edited by José Antonio Serrano and Luis Jauregui, 49–78. Mexico City: Instituto de Investigaciones Dr. José María Luis Mora; Zamora: El Colegio de Michoacán, 1998.

Demers, Maurice, and Catherine Vézina, eds. *Historias conectadas de América del Norte.* Mexico City: Centro de Investigación y Docencia Económicas, 2021.

DeRosa, Marshall L. *The Confederate Constitution of 1861: An Inquiry into American Constitutionalism.* Kindle. Columbia: University of Missouri Press, 1991.

———. "The Rule of Law v. the Misrule of Ideology: The Confederacy and Constitutional Interpretation." *Texas Law Review* 77, no. 789 (1999): 790–806.

Dew, Charles B. *Apostles of Disunion: Southern Secession Commissioners and the Causes of the Civil War.* Kindle. Charlottesville: University of Virginia Press, 2001.

de Zamacois, Niceto. *Historia de Méjico desde sus tiempos más remotos hasta nuestros días.* 18 vols. Barcelona: J. F. Parres, 1877–82.

Díaz y de Ovando, Clementina. "La vida mexicana al filo de la sátira: La Intervención francesa y el Segundo Imperio." *Anales del Instituto de Investigaciones Estéticas* 45 (1976): 13–17.
Dillard, Philip D. "The Confederate Debate over Arming Slaves: Views from Macon and Augusta Newspapers." *Georgia Historical Quarterly* 79, no. 1 (1995): 117–46.
Downs, Gregory P. *After Appomattox: Military Occupation and the Ends of War.* Cambridge, MA: Harvard University Press, 2015.
———. "The Mexicanization of American Politics: The United States' Transnational Path from Civil War to Stabilization." *American Historical Review* 117, no. 2 (2012): 387–409.
———. *The Second American Revolution: The Civil War–Era Struggle over Cuba and the Rebirth of the American Republic.* Chapel Hill: University of North Carolina Press, 2019.
Doyle, Don H. *The Age of Reconstruction: How Lincoln's New Birth of Freedom Remade the World.* Princeton, NJ: Princeton University Press, 2024.
———. *The Cause of All Nations: An International History of the Civil War.* New York: Basic Books, 2014.
———. "Reconstruction and Anti-Imperialism: The United States and Mexico." In *Reconstruction Across the Americas*, edited by William A. Link, 47–80. Gainesville: University Press of Florida, 2019.
Doyle, Patrick J. "Replacement Rebels: Confederate Substitution and the Issue of Citizenship." *Journal of the Civil War Era* 8, no. 1 (2018): 3–31.
Du Bois, W. E. B. *Black Reconstruction in America: An Essay Toward a History of the Part Which Black Folk Played in the Attempt to Reconstruct Democracy in America, 1860–1880.* New York: Oxford University Press, 2007 [1935].
Dumond, Don E. *The Machete and the Cross: Campesino Rebellion in Yucatan.* Lincoln: University of Nebraska Press, 1997.
Duncan, Robert H. "Embracing a Suitable Past: Independence Celebrations Under Mexico's Second Empire." *Journal of Latin American Studies* 30, no. 2 (1998): 249–77.
———. "Political Legitimation and Maximilian's Second Empire in Mexico, 1864–1867." *Mexican Studies / Estudios Mexicanos* 12 (1996): 27–66.
Edling, Max M. *A Hercules in the Cradle: War, Money and the American State, 1783–1867.* Chicago: Chicago University Press, 2014.
Edwards, G. Thomas. "Benjamin Stark, the US Senate, and 1862 Membership Issues." *Oregon Historical Quarterly* 72, no. 4 (1971): 315–38.
Edwards, Laura F. *A Legal History of the Civil War and Reconstruction: A Nation of Rights.* Cambridge: Cambridge University Press, 2015. Kindle.
Eggers, Henrik. *Memorias de México.* Edited by Walter Astié-Burgos. Mexico City: Miguel Ángel Porrúa, 2005.
Egnal, Marc. "Rethinking Secession in the Lower South: The Clash of Two Groups." *Civil War History* 9 (2004): 261–90.
Eissa-Barroso, Francisco. "Mirando hacia Filadelfia desde Anáhuac: La Constitución estadounidense en el Congreso Constituyente mexicano de 1823–1824." *Política y Gobierno* 17, no. 1 (2010): 97–125.
Entin, Gabriel. "Catholic Republicanism: The Creation of the Spanish American Republics During Revolution." *Journal of the History of Ideas* 79, no. 1 (2018): 105–23.
Escobar, Antonio, Romana Falcón, and Martín Sánchez Rodríguez, eds. *La desamortización civil desde perspectivas plurales.* Mexico City: CIESAS, El Colegio de México; Zamora: El Colegio de Michoacán, 2017.
Etcheson, Nicole. *Bleeding Kansas: Contested Liberty in the Civil War Era.* Lawrence: University Press of Kansas, 2004.

Falcón, Romana. "En medio del asedio bélico: Defensas institucionales, resistencias y rebeliones de los pueblos del centro y sur del país, 1846–1856." In *El México profundo en la gran década de la desesperanza (1846–1856)*, edited by Raymond Buve and Romana Falcón, 143–70. Puebla: Benemérita Universidad Autónoma de Puebla, EyC, 2016.

Farber, Daniel. *Lincoln's Constitution*. Chicago: University of Chicago Press, 2003.

Faust, Drew Gilpin. "Altars of Sacrifice: Confederate Women and the Narratives of War." *Journal of American History* 76, no. 4 (1990): 1200–228.

———. *The Creation of Confederate Nationalism: Ideology and Identity in the Civil War South*. Baton Rouge: Louisiana State University, 1982.

———. *Mothers of Invention: Women of the Slaveholding South in the American Civil War*. Chapel Hill: University of North Carolina Press, 2004.

———. *This Republic of Suffering: Death and the American Civil War*. New York: Knopf, 2008.

Fehrenbacher, Don E. *The Dred Scott Case: Its Significance in American Law and Politics*. Oxford: Oxford University Press, 1978.

Ferrer, Ada. *Insurgent Cuba: Race, Nation, and Revolution, 1868–1898*. Chapel Hill: University of North Carolina Press, 1999.

Ferrer Muñoz, Manuel, and María Bono López. *Pueblos indígenas y Estado nacional en el siglo XIX*. Mexico City: Universidad Nacional Autónoma de México, 1998.

Ferris, Norman B. "Lincoln and Seward in Civil War Diplomacy: Their Relationship at the Outset Reexamined." *Journal of the Abraham Lincoln Association* 12, no. 1 (1991): 21–42.

Finkelman, Paul. *Slavery and the Founders: Race and Liberty in the Age of Jefferson*. London: Routledge, 1996.

———. "States' Rights North and South in Antebellum America." In *An Uncertain Tradition: Constitutionalism and the History of the South*, edited by Kermit L. Hall and James W. Ely, 125–58. Athens: University of Georgia Press, 1989.

Fioravanti, Maurizio, *Constitución: De la Antigüedad a nuestros días*. Madrid: Trotta, 2001.

Fleche, Andre M. *The Revolution of 1861: The American Civil War in an Age of Nationalist Conflict*. Chapel Hill: University of North Carolina Press, 2012.

Florer, John H. "Major Issues in the Congressional Debate of the Morrill Act of 1862." *History of Education Quarterly* 8, no. 4 (1968): 459–68.

Florescano, Enrique. *Imágenes de la patria a través de los siglos*. Mexico City: Taurus, 2005.

Flores Escalante, Justo Miguel. *Soberanía y excepcionalidad: La integración de Yucatán al Estado mexicano, 1821–1848*. Mexico City: El Colegio de México, 2017.

Flores Salinas, Berta. *Cartas desde México: Dos fuentes militares para el estudio de la Intervención francesa, 1862–1867*. Mexico City: Miguel Ángel Porrúa, 2001.

Foner, Eric. *The Fiery Trial: Abraham Lincoln and American Slavery*. New York: W. W. Norton, 2010.

———. *Free Soil, Free Labor, Free Men: The Ideology of the Republican Party before the Civil War*. New York: Oxford University Press, 1970.

———. *The Second Founding: How the Civil War and Reconstruction Remade the Constitution*. New York: W. W. Norton, 2019.

———. "The Wilmot Proviso Revisited." *Journal of American History* 56, no. 2 (1969): 269–79.

Fowler, Will. "El pronunciamiento mexicano del siglo XIX: Hacia una nueva tipología." *Estudios de Historia Moderna y Contemporánea de México* 38 (2009): 2–34.

———. *The Grammar of Civil War: A Mexican Case Study, 1857–1861*. Lincoln: University of Nebraska Press, 2022.

———. *Independent Mexico: The Pronunciamiento in the Age of Santa Anna, 1821–1858.* Lincoln: University of Nebraska Press, 2016.
———. *La Guerra de Tres Años, 1857–1861: El conflicto del que nació el Estado laico mexicano.* Mexico City: Crítica, 2020.
———. *Santa Anna of Mexico.* Lincoln, NE: Bison, 2009.
———. "The Sierra Gorda Pronunciamientos of 1848–1849 and the Origins of Popular Conservatism in Mexico." In *Mexico, 1848–1853: Los años olvidados,* edited by Pedro Santoni and Will Fowler, 115–40. New York: Routledge, 2019.
Fowler, Will, and Pedro Santoni. "Setting the Scene: The History and Historiography of Post-War Mexico, 1848–1853." In *Mexico, 1848–1853: Los años olvidados,* edited by Pedro Santoni and Will Fowler, 1–33. New York: Routledge, 2019.
Franklin, John Hope. *George Washington Williams: A Biography.* Chicago: University of Chicago Press, 1985.
Freeman, Joanne. *The Field of Blood: Violence in Congress and the Road to the Civil War.* New York: Farrar, Straus and Giroux, 2018.
Fuentes Loza, Alicia. *Los delitos políticos (1808–1936).* Salamanca, Spain: Gráficas Cervantes, 1994.
Fuentes Mares, José. "La misión de Mr. Pickett." *Historia Mexicana* 11, no. 4 (1962): 487–518.
———. *Y México se refugió en el desierto: Luis Terrazas; Historia y destino.* Mexico City: Jus, 1954.
Furet, François. *Penser la Révolution française.* Paris: Gallimard, 1983.
Galeana, Patricia. "Carlota fue Roja." In *Más nuevas del Imperio: Estudios interdisciplinarios acerca de Carlota de Méjico,* edited by Susanne Igler and Roland Spiller, 55–67. Frankfurt am Main: Iberoamericana Vervuet, 2001.
———. *El tratado McLane–Ocampo: La comunicación interoceánica y el libre comercio.* Mexico City: Porrúa, Universidad Nacional Autónoma de México, 2006.
Ganaway, Loomis M. "New Mexico and the Sectional Controversy, 1846–1861: IV (concl.)." *New Mexico Historical Review* 19 no. 1 (1944), 55–79.
Gantús, Fausta. *Elecciones en el México del siglo XIX: Las fuentes.* Mexico City: Instituto Mora, CONACYT, 2015.
———. *Elecciones en el México del siglo XIX: Las prácticas.* 2 vols. Mexico City: Instituto de Investigaciones Dr. José María Luis Mora, 2016.
Gantús, Fausta, and Alicia Salmerón, eds. *Contribución a un diálogo abierto: Cinco ensayos de historia electoral latinoamericana.* Mexico City: Instituto de Investigaciones Dr. José María Luis Mora, CONACYT, 2016.
———. *Cuando las armas hablan, los impresos luchan, la exclusión agrede... Violencia electoral, México, 1812–1912.* Mexico City: Instituto de Investigaciones Dr. José María Luis Mora, 2016.
———. *Prensa y elecciones: Formas de hacer política en el México del siglo XIX.* Mexico City: Instituto de Investigaciones Dr. José María Luis Mora, 2014.
———. *Un siglo de tensiones: Gobiernos federales y fuerzas regionales. Dinámicas políticas en el México del siglo XIX.* 2 vols. Mexico City: Instituto Mora, CONAHCYT; Campeche: Universidad Autónoma de Campeche, 2024.
Gantús, Fausta, Carlos Alcalá Ferraéz, and Laura Villanueva. *Campeche: Historia breve.* Mexico City: Fondo de Cultura Económica, 2011.
García, Luis Alberto. "Dominance in an Imagined Border: Santos Benavides' and Santiago Vidaurri's Policing of the Río Grande." In *Border Policing: A History of Enforcement and Evasion in North America,* edited by Holly M. Karibo and Geoge T. Díaz, 43–59. Austin: University of Texas Press, 2020.

———. "Indios nómadas y conservadores: La guerra y la construcción del enemigo en Nuevo León, 1855–1867." In *Violencia, representaciones y estrategias: La guerra y sus efectos en México, Colombia y Guatemala, siglos XVI–XX*, edited by Sergio Alejandro Cañedo Gamboa and Juan Ortiz Escamilla, 159–88. Zamora: El Colegio de Michoacán; San Luis Potosí: El Colegio de San Luis, Archivo Histórico del Estado; Xalapa: Universidad Veracruzana, 2021.

García Cantú, Gastón, ed. *El pensamiento de la reacción mexicana: Historia documental (1810–1962)*. Mexico City: Empresas Editoriales, 1965.

García de León Melo, Oliva. "De historias contestatarias: El Sitio de Querétaro y el fusilamiento de Maximiliano de Habsburgo a través de los escritos mexicanos y europeos de 1867 a 1869." BA thesis, Universidad Nacional Autónoma de México, 2006.

García González, David. "Vencidos pero no convencidos: Los conservadores y su lucha por México durante la República Restaurada, 1867–1876." MA thesis, Universidad Autónoma Metropolitana, 2018.

García Martínez, Bernardo. "El espacio del (des)encuentro." In *Encuentro en la frontera: Mexicanos y norteamericanos en un espacio común*, edited by Manuel Ceballos, 19–54. Mexico City: El Colegio de México; Nuevo Laredo: El Colegio de la Frontera Norte; Ciudad Victoria: Universidad Autónoma de Tamaulipas, 2001.

———. "En busca de la geografía histórica." In *Cincuenta años de investigación histórica en México*, edited by Gisela von Wobeser, 127–42. Guanajuato: Universidad de Guanajuato; Mexico City: Universidad Nacional Autónoma de México, 1998.

García Rivera, Edna Lucía, and Aarón Aurelio Grajeda Bustamante. "Cultura política y prácticas étnicas de negociación en Sonora: Dos ejemplos de la primera mitad del siglo XIX." *Culturales* 8 (2020): 1–32.

García Sandoval, Ivett. "Salazar Ilarregui y los proyectos imperiales para Yucatán, 1864–1865." In *Un siglo de tensiones: Gobiernos generales y fuerzas regionales. Dinámicas políticas en el México del siglo XIX*, edited by Fausta Gantús and Alicia Salmerón, 1:51–84. 2 vols. Mexico City: CONAHCYT, Instituto Mora; Campeche: Universidad Autónoma de Campeche, 2024.

García Ugarte, Marta Eugenia. *Poder político y religioso: México, siglo XIX*. 2 vols. Mexico City: Universidad Nacional Autónoma de México, Miguel Ángel Porrúa, 2010.

Garriga, Carlos, ed. *Historia y constitución: Trayectos del constitucionalismo hispano*. Mexico City: Centro de Investigaciones y Docencia Económicas, El Colegio de México, Escuela Libre de Derecho; Zamora: El Colegio de Michoacán; Madrid: HICOES, Universidad Autónoma de Madrid, 2010.

Garrison, Nancy Scripture. *With Courage and Delicacy: Civil War on the Peninsula. Women and the U.S. Sanitary Commission*. Boston: Da Capo, 2003.

Gates, Paul W. "The Homestead Law in an Incongruous Land System." *American Historical Review* 41, no. 4 (1936): 652–81.

Genetin-Pilawa, C. Joseph. "Ely S. Parker and the Paradox of Reconstruction Politics in Indian Country." In *Civil War Wests: Testing the Limits of the United States*, edited by Adam Arenson and Andrew Graybill, 183–205. Berkeley: University of California Press, 2015.

Gentry, Judith Fenner. "A Confederate Success in Europe: The Erlanger Loan." *Journal of Southern History* 36, no. 2 (1970): 157–88.

Gerali, Francesco, and Paolo Riguzzi. "Los veneros del emperador: Impulso petrolero global, intereses y política del petróleo en México durante el Segundo Imperio, 1863–1867." *Historia Mexicana* 65, no. 2 (2015): 747–808.

Gettleman, Marvin E. *The Dorr Rebellion: A Study in American Radicalism, 1833–1849*. New York: Random House, 1973.
Gienapp, William E. *The Origins of the Republican Party, 1852–1856*. New York: Oxford University Press, 1987.
Gille, Geneviève. "Los capitales franceses y la expedición a México." In *Un siglo de deuda pública en México*, edited by Leonor Ludlow and Carlos Marichal, 125–51. Mexico City: El Colegio de México, 1998.
Glaser, Noah. "The Age of Regeneration: Capitalism and the French Intervention in Mexico (1861–1867)." PhD diss., University of Illinois at Chicago, 2022.
Glymph, Thavolia. *Out of the House of Bondage: The Transformation of the Plantation Household*. Cambridge: Cambridge University Press, 2008.
Gobat, Michel. "The Invention of Latin America: A Transnational History of Anti-Imperialism, Democracy, and Race." *American Historical Review* 118, no. 5 (2013): 1345–75.
Goldfield, David. *America Aflame: How the Civil War Created a Nation*. London: Bloomsbury, 2011.
Goldin, Claudia D., and Frank D. Lewis. "The Economic Cost of the American Civil War: Estimates and Implications." *Journal of Economic History* 35, no. 2 (1970): 299–326.
Gómez Aguado, Guadalupe. "*La Cruz*: Periódico exclusivamente religioso o de cómo plantear un proyecto de nación a través de la prensa." *Decires* 15, no. 18 (2015): 63–86.
Gómez-Galvarriato Freer, Aurora. *El pan nuestro de cada día: Una historia de la tortilla de maíz*. Mexico City: El Colegio de México, 2024.
Gómez Tepexicuapan, Amparo, and Konrad Ratz. *Los viajes de Maximiliano en México (1864–1867)*. Mexico City: Consejo Nacional para la Cultura y las Artes, 2013.
Gonzales, Philip B. "Mexican Party, American Party, Democratic Party: Establishing the American Political Party in New Mexico, 1848–1853." *New Mexico Historical Review* 88, no. 3 (2013): 253–85.
———. *Política: Nuevomexicanos and American Political Incorporation, 1821–1910*. Lincoln: University of Nebraska Press, 2016.
González, María del Refugio. "El sitio de Puebla, 16 de marzo al 17 de Mayo de 1863." In *Historia y Constitución: Homenaje a José Luis Soberanes Fernández*, edited by Miguel Carbonell Sánchez and Óscar Cruz Barney, 2:191–207. 2 vols. Mexico City: Universidad Nacional Autónoma de México, 2015.
González de la Vara, Martín. "El traslado de familias al norte de Chihuahua y la conformación de una región fronteriza, 1848–1854." *Frontera Norte* 6, no. 11 (2017): 9–21.
González Navarro, Moisés. *Anatomía del poder en México, 1848–1853*. Mexico City: El Colegio de México, 1977.
———. *Raza y tierra: La Guerra de Castas y el henequén*. Mexico City: El Colegio de México, 1970.
González Quiroga, Miguel Ángel. *War and Peace on the Rio Grande Frontier, 1830–1880*. Norman: University of Oklahoma Press, 2020.
González y González, Luis. "El indigenismo de Maximiliano." In *La Intervención francesa y el imperio de Maximiliano cien años después*, edited by Arturo Arnaiz y Freg and Claude Bataillon, 103–10. Mexico City: Asociación Mexicana de Historiadores e Instituto Francés de América Latina, 1965.
Granados, Luis Fernando. *Sueñan las piedras: Alzamiento ocurrido en la Ciudad de México, 14, 15 y 16 de septiembre de 1847*. Mexico City: Consejo Nacional para la Cultura y las Artes, Editorial Era, Instituto Nacional de Antropología e Historia, 2003.

Greenberg, Amy S. *A Wicked War: Polk, Clay, Lincoln and the 1846 U.S. Invasion of Mexico.* New York: Alfred Knopf, 2012.

Griswold del Castillo, Richard. *The Treaty of Guadalupe Hidalgo: A Legacy of Conflict.* Norman: University of Oklahoma Press, 1992.

Guardino, Peter. *The Dead March: A History of the Mexican American War.* Cambridge, MA: Harvard University Press, 2018.

———. *The Time of Liberty: Popular Political Culture in Oaxaca, 1750–1850.* Durham, NC: Duke University Press, 2005.

Guelzo, Allen C. "Houses Divided: Lincoln, Douglas, and the Political Landscape of 1858." *Journal of American History* 94 no. 2 (2007): 391–417.

Güemez Pineda, Arturo. *Mayas, gobierno y tierras frente a la acometida liberal en Yucatán, 1812–1847.* Zamora: El Colegio de Michoacán; Mérida: Universidad Autónoma de Yucatán, 2005.

Guerra, François-Xavier. "El pronunciamiento en México: Prácticas e imaginarios." *Trace: Procesos mexicanos y centroamericanos* 37 (2000): 15–26.

Gurza, Gerardo. "Against Slave Power? Slavery and Runaway Slaves in Mexico United States Relations, 1821–1857." *Mexican Studies / Estudios Mexicanos* 35, no. 2 (2019): 143–70.

———. "Matías Romero, la Doctrina Monroe y los proyectos de colonización estadunidense en México, 1864–1867." In *La construcción de un vínculo: Matías Romero entre México y Estados Unidos, 1860–1898*, edited by Gerardo Gurza, 59–92. Mexico City: Instituto de Investigaciones Dr. José María Luis Mora, CONAHCYT; Zamora: El Colegio de Michoacán, 2023.

———. *Una vecindad efímera: Los Estados Confederados de América y su política exterior hacia México, 1861–1865.* Mexico City: Instituto de Investigaciones Dr. José María Luis Mora, 2001.

Gurza, Gerardo, and Andrew Torget, eds. *These Ragged Edges: Histories of Violence Along the U.S.-Mexico Border.* Chapel Hill: University of North Carolina Press, 2022.

Gutiérrez Ardila, Daniel. "Un sistema para la América independiente." In *Las declaraciones de independencia: Los textos fundamentales de las independencias americanas*, edited by Alfredo Ávila, Jordana Dym, and Erika Pani, 441–78. Mexico City: El Colegio de México, Universidad Nacional Autónoma de México, 2013.

Guyatt, Nicholas. "'The Future Empire of Our Freedmen': Republican Colonization Schemes in Texas and Mexico, 1861–1865." In *Civil War Wests: Testing the Limits of the United States*, edited by Adam Arenson and Andrew Graybill, 95–117. Berkeley: University of California Press, 2015.

Haberbusch, Benoît. "L'emploi de la gendarmerie au Mexique (1861–1867), force prévôtale ou force de sécurité intérieure?" *Revue historique des armées* 258 (2010): 1–12.

Hahn, Steven. *A Nation Under Our Feet: Black Political Struggles in the Rural South from Slavery to the Great Migration.* Cambridge, MA: Belknap, 2005.

———. *A Nation Without Borders: The United States and Its World in an Age of Civil Wars, 1830–1910.* New York: Viking, 2016.

———. *The Political Worlds of Slavery and Freedom.* Cambridge, MA: Harvard University Press, 2009.

Hale, Charles A. "Emilio Castelar y México." *Letras Libres*, December 1999, 50–55.

———. "Los mitos políticos de la nación mexicana: El liberalismo y la Revolución." *Historia Mexicana* 46, no. 4 (1997): 821–37.

Hall, Aaron R. "Reframing the Fathers' Constitution: The Centralized State and the

Centrality of Slavery in the Confederate Constitutional Order." *Journal of Southern History* 83, no. 2 (2017): 255–96.
Hall, Kermit L., and James W. Ely Jr. "The South and the American Constitution." In *An Uncertain Tradition: Constitutionalism and the History of the South*, edited by Kermit L. Hall and James W. Ely Jr., 3–16. Athens: University of Georgia Press, 1989.
Halperín Donghi, Tulio. *The Contemporary History of Latin America*. Durham, NC: Duke University Press, 1993.
Hämäläinen, Pekka. *The Comanche Empire*. New Haven, CT: Yale University Press, 2008.
———. *Lakota America: A New History of Indigenous Power*. New Haven, CT: Yale University Press, 2023.
Haman, Brigitte. *Con Maximiliano en México: Del diario del príncipe Carl Khevenhüller, 1864–1867*. Mexico City: Fondo de Cultura Económica, 1989.
Hamilton, J. G. de Roulhac. "The State Courts and the Confederate Constitution." *Journal of Southern History* 4, no. 4 (1938): 425–48.
Hamnett, Brian. "La ejecución del emperador Maximiliano de Habsburgo y el republicanismo mexicano." In *Historia y nación (actas del Congreso en homenaje a Josefina Zoraida Vázquez)*, vol. 2, *Política y diplomacia en el siglo XIX mexicano*, edited by Luis Jáuregui and José Antonio Serrano, 227–44. Mexico City: El Colegio de México, 1998.
———. "Mexican Conservatives, Clericals, and Soldiers: The 'Traitor' Tomás Mejía Through Reform and Empire, 1855–1867." *Bulletin of Latin American Research* 20, no. 2 (2001): 187–209.
Hanna, Alfred Jackson, and Kathryn Abbey Hanna. *Napoleon III and Mexico: American Triumph over Monarchy*. Chapel Hill: University of North Carolina Press, 1971.
Harz, Louis. *The Liberal Tradition in America: An Interpretation of American Political Thought since the Revolution*. San Diego: Harcourt Brace, 1955.
Hatch, Nathan O. *The Democratization of American Christianity*. New Haven, CT: Yale University Press, 1991.
Hayes-Bautista, David E. *El Cinco de Mayo: An American Tradition*. Berkeley: University of California Press, 2012. Kindle.
Henderson, Dwight F. "Treason, Sedition and Fries' Rebellion." *American Journal of Legal History* 14, no. 4 (1970): 308–18.
Hernández, José Ángel. *Mexican American Colonization During the Nineteenth Century: A History of the U.S.-Mexico Borderlands*. Cambridge: Cambridge University Press, 2012.
Hernández Jaimes, Jesús. "La estrategia de los caciques y la lucha por el poder en el Sur, 1845–1846." In *Mecánica política: Para una relectura del siglo XIX mexicano. Antología de correspondencia política*, edited by Beatriz Rojas, 183–214. Mexico City: Instituto de Investigaciones Dr. José María Luis Mora; Guadalajara: Universidad de Guadalajara, 2006.
———. *La formación de la hacienda pública mexicana y las tensiones centro-periferia, 1821–1835*. Mexico City: El Colegio de México, 2013.
Hernández López, Conrado. "La 'reacción a sangre y fuego': Los conservadores en 1855–1867." In *Conservadurismos y derechas en la historia de México*, edited by Erika Pani, 1:266–99. 2 vols. Mexico City: Consejo Nacional para la Cultura y las Artes, Fondo de Cultura Económica, 2009.
———. "Militares conservadores en la Reforma y el Segundo Imperio (1857–1867)." PhD diss., El Colegio de México, 2001.
Herrera Pérez, Octavio. *Historia de una ciudad heróica, leal e invicta en la frontera y*

noreste de México. Matamoros: Ayuntamiento de la Heróica Matamoros, 2016–18; Quintanilla, 2018.

Hietala, Thomas R. *Manifest Design: American Exceptionalism and Empire*. Rev. ed. Ithaca, NY: Cornell University Press, 2003.

Hofstadter, Richard. *The Idea of a Party System: The Rise of Legitimate Opposition in the United States, 1780–1840*. Berkeley: University of California Press, 1969.

Hogan, Michael. *The Irish Soldiers of Mexico*. Guadalajara: Fondo Editorial Universitario, 1997.

Holder, Victoria L. "From Hand Maiden to Right Hand: The Civil War." *AORN Journal* 78, no. 3 (2003): 448–64.

Holt, Michael F. *The Fate of Their Country: Politicians, Slavery Extension, and the Coming of the Civil War*. New York: Hill and Wang, 2005.

———. *The Political Crisis of the 1850s*. New York: John Wiley & Sons, 1978.

———. *The Rise and Fall of the American Whig Party: Jacksonian Politics and the Onset of the Civil War*. Oxford: Oxford University Press, 1999.

Holzer, Harold. *Lincoln and the Power of the Press: The War for Public Opinion*. New York: Simon & Schuster, 2014.

Honeck, Mischa. *We Are the Revolutionists: German-Speaking Immigrants and American Abolitionists After 1848*. Athens: University of Georgia Press, 2011.

Hull, A. L., ed. "The Making of the Confederate Constitution." *Publications of the Southern History Association* 9, no. 5 (1905): 272–92.

Huston, James L. *Calculating the Value of the Union: Slavery, Property Rights and the Economic Origins of the Civil War*. Chapel Hill: University of North Carolina Press, 2004.

Hyman, Harold Melvyn. *Era of the Oath: Northern Loyalty Tests During the Civil War and Reconstruction*. Philadelphia: University of Pennsylvania Press, 1954.

Ibarra, Antonio. "Catastro e impuestos directos: Una reforma liberal fallida en la primera república federal mexicana, 1824–1834." *Boletín de Historia Económica* 3 no. 4 (2006): 15–25.

Ibarra Bellon, Araceli. *El comercio y el poder en México, 1821–1864: La lucha por las fuentes financieras entre el Estado central y las regiones*. Mexico City: Fondo de Cultura Económica; Guadalajara: Universidad de Guadalajara, 1998.

Igler, Susanne. *Carlota de México*. Mexico City: Planeta, 2005.

Izecksohn, Vitor. *Dos guerras en las Américas: Raza, ciudadanía y construcción del Estado en los Estados Unidos y en el Brasil, 1861–1870*. Buenos Aires: Prometeo, 2024.

Jauregui, Luis. "La problemática administrativo-fiscal de un país naciente: México, 1821–1824." *Estudios de Historia Moderna y Contemporánea* 59 (2020): 33–69.

———. "Los ministros, las memorias de Hacienda y el presupuesto en México, 1825–1855: Una visión desde el gasto público." *Estudios de Historia Moderna y Contemporánea* 48 (2014): 3–38.

Johansson, Frédéric. "El imposible pluralismo político: Del exclusivismo y otros vicios de los partidos políticos en el México de la Reforma." In *Partidos, facciones y otras calamidades: Debates y propuestas acerca de los partidos políticos en México, siglo XIX*, edited by Alfredo Ávila and Alicia Salmerón, 106–39. Mexico City: Consejo Nacional para la Cultura y las Artes, Fondo de Cultura Económica, Universidad Nacional Autónoma de México, 2012.

Jonas, Raymond. *Hapsburgs on the Rio Grande: The Rise and Fall of the Second Mexican Empire*. Cambridge: Cambridge University Press, 2024.

Jones, Howard. *Blue and Gray Diplomacy: A History of Union and Confederate Foreign Relations*. Chapel Hill: University of North Carolina Press, 2010.

———. *Union in Peril: The Crisis over British Intervention in the Civil War*. Chapel Hill: University of North Carolina Press, 2012.
Kalyvas, Stathis N. *The Logic of Violence in Civil War*. Cambridge: Cambridge University Press, 2006.
Kantrowitz, Stephen. "Citizen's Clothing: Reconstruction, Ho-Chunk Persistence and the Politics of Dress." In *Civil War Wests: Testing the Limits of the United States*, edited by Adam Arenson and Andrew Graybill, 242–63. Berkeley: University of California Press, 2015.
———. "Not Quite Constitutionalized: The Meanings of 'Civilization' and the Limits of Native American Citizenship." In *The World of the Civil War Made*, edited by Gregory P. Downs and Kate Masur, 75–104. Chapel Hill: University of North Carolina Press, 2015.
Karp, Matthew. *This Vast Southern Empire: Slaveholders at the Helm of American Foreign Policy*. Cambridge, MA: Harvard University Press, 2016.
Keating, Ryan W. *Shades of Green: Irish Regiments, American Soldiers, and Local Communities in the Civil War Era*. New York: Fordham University Press, 2017.
Kelly, Brian. "Slave Self-Activity and the Bourgeois Revolution in the United States: Jubilee and the Limits of Black Freedom." *Historical Materialism: Research in Critical Marxist Theory* 27, no. 3 (2019): 31–76.
Kelly, Patrick. "The Lost Continent of Abraham Lincoln." *Journal of the Civil War Era* 9, no. 2 (2019): 223–48.
Kelman, Ari. *A Misplaced Massacre: Struggling over the Memory of Sand Creek*. Cambridge, MA: Harvard University Press, 2013.
Kendrick, Benjamin B. "The Journal of the Joint Committee of Fifteen on Reconstruction." PhD diss., Columbia University, 1914.
Kent, Holly. "Wearing Black, Wearing Bows: Union Women and the Politics of Dress in the US Fashion Press, 1861–1865." *Women's History Review* 26, no. 4 (2016): 555–67.
Kettner, James H. "The Development of American Citizenship in the Revolutionary Era: The Idea of Volitional Allegiance." *American Journal of Legal History* 18, no. 3 (1974): 208–42.
Kirk, Daniel. "La formación de una Iglesia nacional mexicana, 1859–1872." MA thesis, Universidad Nacional Autónoma de México, 2001.
Kloppenberg, James. "From Hartz to Tocqueville: Shifting the Focus from Liberalism to Democracy in America." In *The Democratic Experiment: New Directions in American Political History*, edited by Meg Jacobs, William J. Novak, and Julian E. Zelizer, 350–80. Princeton, NJ: Princeton University Press, 2003.
———. *Toward Democracy: The Struggle for Self-Rule in European and American Thought*. Oxford: Oxford University Press, 2016.
Knowlton, Robert J. *Church Property and the Mexican Reform, 1856–1910*. DeKalb: Northern Illinois University Press, 1976.
Kourí, Emilio. *A Pueblo Divided: Business, Property, and Community in Papantla, Mexico*. Stanford, CA: Stanford University Press, 2004.
Kuntz, Sandra. *El comercio exterior de México en la era del capitalismo liberal, 1870–1929*. Mexico City: El Colegio de México, 2007.
Kurtz, William B. *Excommunicated from the Union: How the Civil War Created a Catholic America*. New York: Fordham University Press, 2016. Kindle.
LaCroix, Alison. *The Interbellum Constitution: Constitution, Union, Commerce and Slavery in the Age of Federalism*. New Haven, CT: Yale University Press, 2024. Kindle.
Lear, John. "Diego Rivera Paints the Proletariat." In *Diego Rivera's America*, edited by James Oles, 184–89. San Francisco: SFMOMA in association with University of California Press, 2022.

Lecaillon, Jean-François. *La question indienne sous le règne de Maximilien: Illusions de l'indigénisme et comportement des communautés de Michoacan*. Paris: Centre National de Recherche Scientifique, 1987.

———. *Napoléon III et le Mexique: Les illusions d'un grand dessein*. Paris: L'Harmattan, 1994.

Lempérière, Annick. *Entre Dios y el rey: La república. La Ciudad de México de los siglos XVI al XIX*. Mexico City: Fondo de Cultura Económica, 2013.

León Garduño, Ángela. *Entre tradición y modernidad: La conformación de beneficencia durante el Segundo Imperio mexicano*. Mexico City: Instituto Nacional de Estudios Históricos de las Revoluciones de México, 2024.

Lerner, Hanna. *Making Constitutions in Deeply Divided Societies*. Cambridge: Cambridge University Press, 2011.

Levine, Peter. "Draft Evasion in the North During the Civil War, 1863–1865." *Journal of American History* 67, no. 4 (1981): 816–34.

Lira, Andrés. *El amparo colonial y el juicio de amparo mexicano (Antecedentes novohispanos del juicio de amparo)*. Mexico City: Fondo de Cultura Económica, 1972.

———. "Patrimonios hereditarios bajo el orden constitucional de 1824, tres casos: 1826, 1828 y 1830." In *De Cádiz al siglo XXI: Doscientos años de constitucionalismo en México e Hispanoamérica*, edited by Adriana Luna, Pablo Mijangos, and Rafael Rojas, 153–62. Mexico City: Centro de Investigación y Docencia Económica, Taurus, 2012.

Lira, Regina. "De buenos mexicanos, cristianos, soldados y valientes: Pueblos coras y huicholes en la Sierra de Nayar, 1840 a 1880." *Historia Mexicana* 69, no. 3 (2020): 1091–142.

Litwack, Leon F. *Been in the Storm So Long: The Aftermath of Slavery*. New York: Knopf Doubleday, 1980.

Long, Tom, and Carsten-Andreas Schulz. "Republican Internationalism: The Nineteenth-Century Roots of Latin American Contributions to International Order." *Cambridge Review of International Affairs* 35, no. 5 (2022): 639–61.

López González, Georgina. "Los proyectos constitucionales conservadores, 1857–1865." In *La tradición constitucional en México (1808–1940)*, edited by Catherine Andrews, 1:137–58. 2 vols. Mexico City: Archivo General de la Nación, Centro de Investigación y Docencia Económicas, Secretaría de Relaciones Exteriores, 2017.

Ludlow, Leonor. "La disputa financiera por el imperio de Maximiliano y los proyectos de fundación de instituciones de crédito (1863–1867)." *Historia Mexicana* 47, no. 4 (1998): 765–805.

———. "Las dinastías financieras en la Ciudad de México: De la libertad comercial a la reforma liberal." PhD diss., El Colegio de Michoacán, 1995.

Luna, Adriana, Pablo Mijangos, and Rafael Rojas, eds. *De Cádiz al siglo XXI: Doscientos años de constitucionalismo en México e Hispanoamérica (1812–2012)*. Mexico City: Taurus, 2012.

Luna Argudín, María. *El Congreso y la política mexicana (1875–1911)*. Mexico City: El Colegio de México, Fondo de Cultura Económica, 2006.

Lynch, Daniel B. "Southern California Chivalry: The Convergence of Southerners and Californios in the Far Southwest, 1846–1866." PhD diss., University of California, Los Angeles, 2015.

MacArthur, Marcus J. "There Can Be No Neutral Ground: Samuel B. McPheeters and the Collision of Church and State in St. Louis, 1860–1864." *Journal of Presbyterian History* 89, no. 1 (2011): 16–26.

Machiavelli, Niccolò. *The Prince*. Translated by W. K. Marriott. Project Gutenberg eBook, 1998. https://www.gutenberg.org/cache/epub/1232/pg1232-images.html.
MacMillan, Margaret. *War: How Conflict Shaped Us*. New York: Random House, 2020.
Madeley, John T. S. "America's Secular State and the Unsecular State of Europe." In *Religion, State and Society: Jefferson's Wall of Separation in Comparative Perspective*, edited by Robert Fatton Jr. and R. K. Ramazani, 109–36. New York: Palgrave MacMillan, 2009.
Maier, Charles S. "Consigning the Twentieth Century to History: Alternative Narratives for the Modern Era." *American Historical Review* 105, no. 3 (2000): 807–31.
Maier, Pauline. *Ratification: The People Debate the Constitution, 1787–1788*. New York: Simon and Schuster, 2010.
Maizlish, Stephen E. *A Strife of Tongues: The Compromise of 1850 and the Ideological Foundations of the American Civil War*. Charlottesville: University of Virginia Press, 2018.
Mallon, Florencia. *Peasant and Nation: The Making of Postcolonial Mexico and Peru*. Berkeley: University of California Press, 1995.
Marichal, Carlos. "El nacimiento de los estudios internacionales sobre América Latina: Comentarios a las obras de José María Torres Caicedo y Carlos Calvo, a mediados del siglo XIX." *Foro Internacional* 40, no. 221 (2015): 707–36.
———. "Las finanzas del Estado de México en la temprana república: Federalismo y centralismo." In *Hacienda y política: Las finanzas públicas y los grupos de poder en la Primera República Federal mexicana*, edited by José Antonio Serrano and Luis Jauregui, 175–202. Mexico City: Instituto Mora; Zamora: El Colegio de Michoacán, 1998.
Marino, Daniela. "Ahora que Dios nos ha dado padre: El Segundo Imperio y la cultura jurídico-política campesina en el centro de México." *Historia Mexicana* 55, no. 4 (2006): 1353–410.
———. *Huixquilucan: Ley y justicia en la modernización del espacio rural mexiquense, 1856–1910*. Madrid: Tierra Nueva, 2016.
Marino, Daniela, and María Cecilia Zuleta. "Una visión del campo: Tierra, propiedad y tendencias de la producción, 1850–1930." In *Historia económica general de México: De la Colonia hasta nuestros días*, edited by Sandra Kuntz, 437–72. Mexico City: El Colegio de México, Secretaría de Economía, 2010.
Martínez, Oscar J. "El Paso y Ciudad Juárez." In *Encuentro en la frontera: Mexicanos y norteamericanos en un espacio común*, edited by Manuel Ceballos, 217–31. Mexico City: El Colegio de México; Ciudad Victoria: El Colegio de la Frontera Norte, Universidad Autónoma de Tamaulipas, 2001.
Mathisen, Erik. *The Loyal Republic: Traitors, Slaves, and the Remaking of Citizenship in Civil War America*. Chapel Hill: University of North Carolina Press, 2018.
———. "The Second Slavery, Capitalism and Emancipation in Civil War America." *Journal of the Civil War Era* 8, no. 4 (2018): 677–99.
McCormick, Richard P. *The Second American Party System: Party Formation in the Jacksonian Era*. New York: W. W. Norton, 1973.
McCurry, Stephanie. *Confederate Reckoning: Power and Politics in the Civil War South*. Kindle. Cambridge, MA: Harvard University Press, 2010.
McEvoy, Carmen. *La utopía republicana: Ideales y realidades en la formación de la cultura política peruana (1871–1919)*. Lima: Pontificia Universidad Católica del Perú, 1997.
McNamara, Patrick J. *Sons of the Sierra: Juárez, Díaz, and the People of Ixtlán, Oaxaca, 1855–1920*. Chapel Hill: University of North Carolina Press, 2012.
McNierney, Michael, ed. *Taos 1847: The Revolt in Contemporary Accounts*. Boulder, CO: Johnson, 1980.

McPherson, James M. *Abraham Lincoln and the Second American Revolution.* New York: Oxford University Press, 1992.

——. *Battle Cry of Freedom: The Civil War Era.* New York: Ballantine, 1988.

——. *For Cause and Comrades: Why Men Fought in the Civil War.* New York: Oxford University Press, 1997.

Medina Peña, Luis. *Invención del sistema político mexicano: Forma de gobierno y gobernabilidad en México en el siglo XIX.* Mexico City: Fondo de Cultura Económica, 2007.

——. *Los bárbaros del Norte: Guardia Nacional y política en Nuevo León, siglo XIX.* Mexico City: Fondo de Cultura Económica, 2014.

Meketa, Jacqueline Dorgan, ed. *Legacy of Honor: The Life of Rafael Chacón, a Nineteenth-Century New Mexican.* Albuquerque: University of New Mexico Press, 1986.

Méndez Camacho, Erik Ricardo. "Administración de justicia militar y la corte marcial del Valle de México durante la Regencia Imperial y el Segundo Imperio mexicano." MA thesis, Universidad Autónoma Metropolitana Iztapalapa, 2023.

Mendoza, Edgar. *Municipios, cofradías y tierras comunales: Los pueblos chocholtecos de Oaxaca en el siglo XIX.* Oaxaca: Universidad Autónoma Benito Juárez de Oaxaca, 2011.

Meyer, Jean. *Esperando a Lozada.* Zamora: El Colegio de Michoacán, 1984.

——. "La Junta Protectora de Clases Menesterosas: Indigenismo y agrarismo en el Segundo Imperio mexicano." In *Indio, nación y comunidad en el México del siglo XIX,* edited by Antonio Escobar, 329–64. Mexico City: Centro de Estudios Mexicanos y Centroamericanos, Centro de Investigaciones y Estudios Superiores en Antropología Social, 1993.

Mijangos, Pablo. *Entre Dios y la República: La separación Iglesia-Estado en México, siglo XIX.* Mexico City: Tirant lo Blanch, 2018.

——. "Guerra civil y Estado Nación en Norteamérica." In *El poder y la sangre: Guerra, Estado y nación de la década de 1860,* edited by Guillermo Palacios and Erika Pani, 43–62. Mexico City: El Colegio de México, 2014.

——. *The Lawyer of the Church: Bishop Clemente de Jesús Munguía and the Clerical Response to the Mexican Liberal Reforma.* Lincoln: University of Nebraska Press, 2015.

Miller, Robert Ryal. "Arms Across the Border: United States Aid to Juárez During the French Intervention in Mexico." *Transactions of the American Philosophical Society* 63, no. 6 (1973): 1–68.

——. *Shamrock and Sword: The Saint Patrick's Battalion in the US Mexican War.* Norman: University of Oklahoma Press, 1989.

Miller, William L. *Arguing About Slavery: John Quincy Adams and the Great Battle in the United States Congress.* New York: Vintage, 1998.

Moloeznick, Marcos Pablo. "Insurgencia y contraguerrilla durante la Guerra de Intervención francesa en México (enseñanzas para la doctrina de guerra mexicana)." *Revista del CESLA* 11 (2008): 119–33.

Monroy Casillas, Ilihutsy. "De la lucha de los chinacos en Miahuatlan, Oaxaca, 1864–1867." In *El Segundo Imperio y la resistencia republicana en el Sur-Sureste de México: Centésimo quincuagésimo aniversario del triunfo de la República,* edited by Alfonso Millán López and Emilio Rodríguez Herrera, 79–110. Mexico City: Centro de Estudios de Derecho e Investigaciones Parlamentarias, 2018.

——. "Los chinacos en la batalla del 5 de mayo y el sitio de Puebla: Aproximación al surgimiento de las guerrillas populares durante la Intervención francesa en México." In *¡Heroica Puebla de Zaragoza! 150 años del sitio de 1863, estudios y documentos,* edited by Alberto Enríquez Perea, 151–80. Puebla: Benmérita Universidad Autónoma de Puebla, 2013.

———. "Tras la vida de un guerrillero decimonónico: Huellas históricas del chinaco Catarino Fragoso a través de distintos archivos." In *Apéndice: Memorias del 1er Congreso de Historia Militar a través de los archivos históricos*, 181–95. Mexico City: Secretaría de la Defensa Nacional, 2015.

———. "Un radical en el Occidente de México. El aparente secuestro a dos diplomáticos por Antonio Rojas, 1859–1861." *Seminario de Historia Mexicana* 9, no. 1 (2009): 9–24.

Montejano, David. *Anglos and Mexicans in the Making of Texas, 1836–1986*. Austin: University of Texas Press, 1987.

Morgan, Edmund S. *Inventing the People: The Rise of Popular Sovereignty in England and America*. New York: W. W. Norton, 1988.

Morse, Richard M. *Prospero's Mirror: A Study in New World Dialectic*. Redwood City, CA: Stanford University Press, 1981.

Moyano Pahissa, Ángela. *Los belgas de Carlota: La expedición belga al Imperio de Maximiliano*. Mexico City: Pearson Educación, 2011.

Myers, Jorge. *Orden y virtud: El discurso republicano en el régimen rosista*. Quilmes, Argentina: Universidad Nacional de Quilmes, 1995.

Nava, Guadalupe. "Origen y monto de la deuda pública en 1861." In *Un siglo de deuda pública en México*, edited by Leonor Ludlow and Carlos Marichal, 53–80. Mexico City: El Colegio de México, 1998.

Nava Bonilla, Norberto. "El Padre Miranda: Un conservador radical." In *Derecho, Guerra de Reforma, Intervención francesa y Segundo Imperio*, edited by José Luis Soberanes, Serafín Ortiz Ortiz, Emmanuel Rodríguez Baca, and Sebastián Daniel Ojeda Bravo, 71–89. Mexico City: Universidad Nacional Autónoma de México; Tlaxcala: Universidad Autónoma de Tlaxcala, 2022.

Navarrete, Federico. "¿Qué significa ser indio en el siglo XIX?" In *Los indígenas en la Independencia y en la Revolución Mexicana*, edited by Miguel León Portilla and Alicia Mayer, 171–90. Mexico City: Instituto Nacional de Antropología e Historia, Universidad Nacional Autónoma de México, 2010.

Neels, Mark A. "Lincoln's Conservatives: Conservative Unionism and Political Tradition in the Civil War Era." PhD diss., Southern Illinois University, 2015.

Neely, Mark E., Jr. *The Fate of Liberty: Abraham Lincoln and Civil Liberties*. New York: Oxford University Press, 1991.

———. *Lincoln and the Triumph of the Nation: Constitutional Conflict in the American Civil War*. Chapel Hill: University of North Carolina Press, 2011.

———. *Southern Rights: Political Prisoners and the Myth of Confederate Constitutionalism*. Charlottesville: University Press of Virginia, 1999.

Neff, Stephen C. *Justice in Blue and Gray: A Legal History of the Civil War*. Cambridge, MA: Harvard University Press, 2010.

Nelson, Megan Kate. *The Three-Cornered War: The Union, the Confederacy, and Native Peoples in the Fight for the West*. New York: Scribner, 2020.

Nichols, David A. "The Other Civil War: Lincoln and the Indians." *Minnesota History*, Spring 1974, 3–15.

Nicoletti, Cynthia. *Secession on Trial: The Treason and Prosecution of Jefferson Davis*. Cambridge: Cambridge University Press, 2017.

Nimtz, August H. "Marx and Engels on the US Civil War: The 'Materialist Conception of History' in Action." *Historical Materialism* 19, no. 4 (2011): 169–92.

Noriega, Cecilia. "Elecciones y notables: Una expresión del poder regional." In *Mecánica política: Para una relectura del siglo XIX mexicano. Antología de correspondencia política*, edited by Beatriz Rojas, 125–82. Mexico City: Instituto de Investigaciones Dr. José María Luis Mora; Guadalajara: Universidad de Guadalajara, 2006.

———. "Los grupos parlamentarios en los congresos mexicanos, 1810–1857." In *El poder y el dinero: Grupos y regiones mexicanos en el siglo XIX*, edited by Beatriz Rojas, 120–58. Mexico City: Instituto de Investigaciones Dr. José María Luis Mora, 1994.

Oakes, James. *Freedom National: The Destruction of Slavery in the United States, 1861–1865*. New York: Norton, 2013.

———. "Reluctant to Emancipate? Another Look at the First Confiscation Act." *Journal of the Civil War Era* 3, no. 4 (2013): 458–66.

Ochiai, Akiko. "The Port Royal Experiment Revisited: Northern Visions of Reconstruction and the Land Question." *New England Quarterly* 74, no. 1 (2001): 94–117.

O'Gorman, Edmundo. "Do the Americas Have a Common History?" In *Do the Americas Have a Common History? A Critique of the Bolton Theory*, edited by Lewis Hanke, 103–40. New York: Knopf, 1962.

———. *México, el trauma de su historia*. Mexico City: Universidad Nacional Autónoma de México, 1977.

———. "Precedentes y sentido de la Revolución de Ayutla." In *Plan de Ayutla*, 29–74. Mexico City: Instituto Nacional de Estudios Históricos de las Revoluciones de México, 2015.

Olliff, Donathon C. *Reforma Mexico and the United States: A Search for Alternatives to Annexation, 1854–1861*. Tuscaloosa: University of Alabama Press, 1981.

Olveda, Jaime. "La abolición de la esclavitud en México, 1810–1917." *Signos históricos*, 15, no. 29 (2013): 8–34.

———. "La disputa por el control de los impuestos en los primeros años independientes." In *Hacienda y política: Las finanzas públicas y los grupos de poder en la Primera República Federal mexicana*, edited by José Antonio Serrano and Luis Jauregui, 115–32. Mexico City: Instituto Mora; Zamora: El Colegio de Michoacán, 1998.

Olvera, David. *Al servicio diplomático del imperio: Correspondencia inédita de Alonso Peón de Regil, ministro de México en Italia durante el Segundo Imperio mexicano*. Mexico City: Cuadernos del Cronista *in ilo tempore*, 2023.

Onuf, Peter. "Thomas Jefferson's Christian Nation." In *Religion, State and Society: Jefferson's Wall of Separation in Comparative Perspective*, edited by Robert Fatton Jr. and R. K. Ramazani, 17–36. New York: Palgrave MacMillan, 2009.

Ortelli, Sara. "Enemigos internos y súbditos desleales: La infidencia en Nueva Vizcaya en tiempos de los Borbones." *Anuario de Estudios Americanos* 61, no. 2 (2004): 467–89.

Ortiz Escamilla, Juan. "La nacionalización de las fuerzas armadas en México." In *Las armas de la nación: Independencia y ciudadanía en Hispanoamérica, 1750–1850*, edited by Manuel Chust and Juan Marchena, 291–324. Seville: Universidad Pablo de Olavide; Valencia: Universitat Jaume I, 2007.

Ortiz Monasterio, José. "Vicente Riva Palacio y los derechos del hombre." In *La génesis de los derechos humanos en México*, edited by Margarita Moreno-Bonett and María del Refugio González, 439–49. Mexico City: Universidad Nacional Autónoma de México, 2006.

Osterhammel, Jürgen. *The Transformation of the World: A Global History of the Nineteenth Century*. Princeton, NJ: Princeton University Press, 2014.

Palacios, Guillermo. "De imperios y repúblicas: Los cortejos entre México y Brasil, 1822–1867." *Historia Mexicana* 51, no. 3 (2002): 559–618.

Palomo González, Gerardo. "Gavillas de bandoleros, 'bandas conservadoras' y Guerra de Intervención en México (1863)." *Estudios de Historia Moderna y Contemporánea* 25 (2003): 71–113.

Palti, Elías. *El tiempo de la política: El siglo XIX reconsiderado*. Buenos Aires: Siglo XXI, 2007.
———. *La política del disenso: La "polémica en torno al monarquismo" (México, 1848–1850) . . . y las aporías del liberalismo*. Mexico City: Fondo de Cultura Económica, 1998.
Pani, Erika. "Aquellos hermanos nuestros . . . Ciudadanía y exclusión en los territorios conquistados." *Historia Mexicana* 70, no. 3 (2021): 1095–136.
———. "Cuando la ley fundamental desbarata: Los conservadores y la constitución de 1857." *Jahrbuch für Geschichte Lateinamerikas / Anuario de Historia de América Latina* 55 (2018): 108–26.
———. "Cultura mexicana, canon español." In *España y el Imperio de Maximiliano*, edited by Clara E. Lida, 215–60. Mexico City: El Colegio de México, 1999.
———. "El proyecto de Estado de Maximiliano a través de la vida cortesana y del ceremonial público." *Historia Mexicana* 45, no. 2 (1995): 423–60.
———. *El Segundo Imperio: Pasado de usos múltiples*. Mexico City: Centro de Investigación y Docencia Económicas, Fondo de Cultura Económica, 2004.
———. "Intervention and Empire: Politics as Usual?" In *Malcontents, Rebels, and Pronunciados: The Politics of Insurrection in Nineteenth-Century Mexico*, edited by Will Fowler, 236–54. Lincoln: University of Nebraska Press, 2012.
———. "La crisis como oportunidad: John Forsyth Jr., Robert M. McLane y Thomas Corwin." In *Embajadores de Estados Unidos en México: Diplomacia de crisis y oportunidades*, edited by Roberta Lajous, Erika Pani, Paolo Riguzzi, and María Celia Toro, 95–110. Mexico City: El Colegio de México, Secretaría de Relaciones Exteriores, 2021.
———. "La innombrable: Monarquismo y cultura política en el México decimonónico." In *Prácticas populares, cultura política y poder en México, siglo XIX*, edited by Brian Connaughton, 369–94. Mexico City: Universidad Autónoma Metropolitana I, Casa Juan Pablos, 2008.
———. "Los 'castigos nacionales': Justicia y política en tiempos de guerra." In *El Imperio napoleónico y la monarquía en México*, edited by Patricia Galeana, 565–88. Mexico City: Siglo XXI, Senado de la República, 2012.
———. "Novia de republicanos, franceses y emperadores: La Ciudad de México durante la Intervención francesa." *Relaciones: Estudios de Historia y Sociedad* 21, no. 3 (2000): 133–73.
———. "Religión, república y guerra: Las guerras civiles norteamericanas, 1858–1867." In *Batallas entre religión y modernidad en México, siglo XIX*, edited by Madallena Burelli and David Carbajal, 115–40. Mexico City: Miguel Ángel Porrúa, 2023.
———. "Saving the Nation Through Exclusion: Alien Laws in the Early Republic in the United States and Mexico." *The Americas* 65, no. 2 (2008): 17–246.
Pani, Erika, ed. *Estado, nación y constitución, 1821–1908*. Mexico City: Centro de Investigación y Docencia Económicas, Fondo de Cultura Económica, 2010.
Pani, Erika, and Paolo Riguzzi. "Mexico and the American Civil War in the Long Term: Impact, Influence and the Shadows of History." In *Echoes of the American Civil War Abroad*, edited by Ivan Kurilla and Victoria Zhuravleva. Lanham, MD: Lexington, forthcoming.
Patlán, Venancio. *Tetela de Ocampo durante la Guerra de Intervención francesa*. Puebla: Comité Nacional Conmemorativo del 150 Aniversario de la Batalla de Puebla, Consejo Estatal para la Cultura y las Artes de Puebla, 2012.
Peralta Ruiz, Víctor. "La guerra civil peruana de 1854: Los entresijos de una revolución." *Anuario de Estudios Americanos* 70, no. 1 (2013): 195–219.

Pérez Herrero, Pedro. "'Crecimiento' colonial versus 'crisis' nacional: Consideraciones sobre un modelo explicativo." In *Cincuenta años de historia en México*, edited by Alicia Hernández Chávez and Manuel Miño Grijalva, 1:241–72. 2 vols. Mexico City: El Colegio de México, 1991.

Pérez Montesinos, Fernando. "Geografía, política y economía del reparto liberal en la meseta purépecha, 1851–1914." *Historia Mexicana* 66, no. 4 (2017): 2073–149.

Pérez Ramírez, Tatiana. "Municipios de la Sierra Juárez: Configuración espacial, participación armada y organización política, 1855–1939." PhD diss., El Colegio de México, 2017.

Pérez Tisserant, Emmanuelle. *Nuestra California: Une histoire politique de la Californie mexicaine. De Zorro à la ruée vers l'or*. Rennes: Presses Universitaires de Rennes, 2023.

Pérez Vejo, Tomás. "La difícil herencia: Hispanofobia e hispanofilia en el proceso de construcción nacional mexicano." In *Los caminos de la ciudadanía: México y España en perspectiva comparada*, edited by Manuel Suárez Cortina and Tomás Pérez Vejo, 219–30. Santander, Spain: Universidad de Cantabria, 2010.

———. "Las encrucijadas ideológicas del monarquismo mexicano en la primera mitad del siglo XIX." In *Experiencias republicanas y monárquicas en México, América Latina y España, siglos XIX y XX*, edited by Marco Antonio Landavazo and Agustín Sánchez Andrés, 327–48. Morelia: Universidad Michoacana de San Nicolás de Hidalgo, 2008.

Phillips, Christopher. *The Rivers Ran Backward: The Civil War and the Remaking of the American Middle Border*. New York: Oxford University Press, 2016.

Pieper, Renate. "Contiendas imperiales y política fiscal: España y Gran Bretaña en el siglo XVIII." In *Finanzas y política en el mundo iberoamericano: Del Antiguo Régimen a las naciones independientes, 1754–1850*, edited by Luis Jauregui and Ernest Sánchez Santiró, 63–76. Mexico City: Instituto Mora, Universidad Nacional Autónoma de México; Toluca: Universidad Autónoma del Estado de México, 2001.

Pinheiro, Holly A., Jr. *The Families' Civil War: Black Soldiers and the Fight for Racial Justice*. Athens: University of Georgia Press, 2022.

Piqueras, José Antonio. *El federalismo: La libertad protegida, la convivencia pactada*. Madrid: Cátedra, 2014.

Pi Suñer, Antonia. *El general Prim y la cuestión de México*. Mexico City: Universidad Nacional Autónoma de México, 1996.

Pitner, Ernst. *Maximilian's Lieutenant: A Personal History of the Mexican Campaign, 1864–67*, edited and translated by Gordon Etherington-Smith. Albuquerque: University of New Mexico Press, 1993.

Pitt, Leonard. *The Decline of the Californios: A Social History of the Spanish-Speaking Californians, 1846–1890*. Berkeley: University of California Press, 1966.

Pocock, J. G. A. *The Machiavellian Moment: Florentine Political Thought and the Atlantic Republican Tradition*. Princeton, NJ: Princeton University Press, 2003.

Pollack, Aaron. "De la contribución directa proporcional a la capitación en la Hispanoamérica republicana: Los límites impuestos por la constitución fiscal." *Araucaria: Revista Iberoamericana de Filosofía, Política y Humanidades* 18, no. 36 (2016): 59–86.

Ponce, Pearl T. "As Dead as Julius Ceasar: The Rejection of the McLane–Ocampo Treaty." *Civil War History* 53, no. 4 (2007): 342–78.

Porter, Angi. "James Oakes' Treatment of the First Confiscation Act in *Freedom National: The Destruction of Slavery in the United States, 1861–1865*." *Howard Law Journal* 57, no. 137 (2023): 138–62.

Potter, David M., and Don E. Fehrenbacher. *The Impending Crisis, 1848–1861*. New York: Harper Collins, 1976.

Quigley, Paul. "Civil War Conscription and the International Boundaries of Citizenship." *Journal of the Civil War Era* 4, no. 3 (2014): 373–97.
———. "Independence Day Dilemmas in the American South, 1848–1865." *Journal of Southern History* 75, no. 2 (2009): 235–66.
Quijada, Mónica. "Sobre el origen y difusión del nombre 'América Latina' (o una variación heterodoxa en torno al tema de la construcción social de la verdad)." *Revista de Indias* 58, no. 214 (1998): 595–616.
Quintanar Zárate, Iliana. "Entre liberalismo y nacionalismo en México: El pensamiento económico de José Yves Limantour (1892–1911)." *Economía* 38, no. 76 (2015): 189–212.
Quintero Machler, Alejandro. "De *Le livre rouge* a *El libro rojo*: La mexicanización de un proyecto literario francés." *Literatura Mexicana* 32, no. 2 (2021): 11–41.
Rable, George C. *The Confederate Republic: A Revolution Against Politics*. Chapel Hill: University of North Carolina Press, 1994.
———. *God's Almost Chosen People: A Religious History of the Civil War*. Chapel Hill: University of North Carolina Press, 2010.
Rakove, Jack N. "Thinking Like a Constitution." *Journal of the Early Republic* 24, no. 1 (2004): 1–26.
Ransom, Roger L. "Economics of the Civil War." EH.Net Encyclopedia, edited by Robert Whaples. August 24, 2001. http://eh.net/encyclopedia/the-economics-of-the-civil-war.
Razaghian, Rose. "Financing the Civil War: The Confederacy's Financial Strategy." Yale ICF Working Paper no. 04–45, January 2005, 1–47.
Reed, Nelson. *The Caste War of Yucatan*. Stanford, CA: Stanford University Press, 1964.
Reed Torres, Luis. *El general Tomás Mejía frente a la doctrina Monroe: La Guerra de Reforma, la Intervención y el Imperio a través del archivo inédito del caudillo conservador queretano*. Mexico City: Porrúa, 1989.
Rehnquist, William H. *All the Laws but One: Civil Liberties in Wartime*. New York: Alfred Knopf, 2001. Kindle.
Reséndez, Andrés. *Changing National Identities at the Frontier: Texas and New Mexico, 1800–1850*. Cambridge: Cambridge University Press, 2004.
———, ed. *A Texas Patriot on Trial in Mexico: José Antonio Navarro and the Texan Santa Fe Expedition*. Dallas: DeGolyer Library, Clements Center for Southwest Studies, 2005.
Reyes Heroles, Jesús. *El liberalismo mexicano*. 3 vols. Mexico City: Universidad Nacional Autónoma de México, 1957–58.
Rhi Sausi, María José. "Breve historia de un longevo impuesto: El dilema de las alcabalas en México, 1821–1896." MA thesis, Instituto de Investigaciones Dr. José María Luis Mora, 2017.
———. "Derecho y garantías: El juicio de amparo y la modernización jurídica liberal." In *Constitución, Nación y Reforma*, edited by Erika Pani, 120–62. Mexico City: Centro de Investigación y Docencia Económicas, Fondo de Cultura Económica, 2010.
Rhi Sausi, María José, and María del Ángel Molina. *El mal necesario: Gobierno y contribuyentes ante el dilema de las alcabalas, siglos XIX y XX*. Mexico City: Universidad Nacional Autónoma de México, 2014.
Riding, Alan. *Distant Neighbors: A Portrait of the Mexicans*. New York: Alfred A. Knopf, 1985.
Riforgiato, Leonard R. "Bishop Timon, Buffalo and the U.S. Civil War." *Catholic Historical Review* 73, no. 1 (1987): 62–80.
Riguzzi, Paolo. *Diplomacia de supervivencia, información y comunicación estratégica: La defensa de la República mexicana en Estados Unidos, 1861–1867*. Mexico City: El Colegio de México, forthcoming.

———. "Escribe sin cesar: La diplomacia de la información de Matías Romero entre México y Estados Unidos, 1863–1898." In *Itinerarios e intercambios en la historia intelectual de México*, edited by Miruna Achim and Aimer Granados, 127–63. Mexico City: Universidad Autónoma Metropolitana Cuajimalpa, Consejo Nacional para la Cultura y las Artes, 2011.

———. "Mexico and the Monroe Doctrines, 1863–1920: From Appropriation to Rejection." *Diplomatic History* 47, no. 5 (2023): 781–801.

———. *¿Reciprocidad imposible? La política del comercio entre México y Estados Unidos, 1857–1938*. Mexico City: Instituto de Investigaciones Dr. José María Luis Mora; Zinacantepec: El Colegio Mexiquense, 2003.

Rivera, Diego. *Portrait of America, by Diego Rivera, with an Explanatory Text by Bertram D. Wolf*. New York: Covici, Friede, 1934.

Roberts, Tim. "The United States and the European Revolutions of 1848." In *The European Revolutions and the Americas*, edited by Guy P. C. Thomson, 76–99. London: Institute of Latin American Studies, 2002.

Rodgers, Daniel T. *Contested Truths: Keywords in American Politics Since Independence*. New York: Basic Books, 1987.

Rodó, José Enrique. *Ariel*. Montevideo, 1900.

Rodriguez, Sarah K. "The Greatest Nation on Earth: Politics and Patriotismo of the First Anglo American Immigrants to Mexican Texas, 1820–1824." *Pacific Historical Review* 86, no. 1 (2017): 50–83.

Rodríguez O., Jaime E. "Los primeros empréstitos mexicanos, 1824–1825." In *Un siglo de deuda pública en México*, edited by Leonor Ludlow and Carlos Marichal, 81–124. Mexico City: El Colegio de México, 1998.

Rojas, Beatriz. "Constitución histórica: 'No la hallareis escrita como comedia por escenas.'" *Historias* 76 (2010): 89–106.

———, ed. *Mecánica política: Para una relectura del siglo XIX mexicano. Antología de correspondencia política*. Mexico City: Instituto de Investigaciones Dr. José María Luis Mora; Guadalajara: Universidad de Guadalajara, 2006.

Rojas, Rafael. *Las repúblicas de aire: Utopía y desencanto en la revolución de Hispanoamérica*. Mexico City: Taurus, 2009.

Rosanvallon, Pierre. "Para una historia conceptual de los políticos (nota de trabajo)." *Prismas: Revista de historia intelectual* 6 (2006): 123–33.

Rothera, Evan C. *Civil Wars and Reconstructions in the Americas: The United States, Mexico, and Argentina, 1860–1880*. Baton Rouge: Louisiana State University Press, 2022.

Rubial, Antonio. *La santidad controvertida: Hagiografía y conciencia criolla alrededor de los venerables no canonizados de Nueva España*. Mexico City: Fondo de Cultura Económica, 1999.

Rubin, Anne Sarah. *A Shattered Nation: The Rise and Fall of the Confederacy, 1861–1868*. Chapel Hill: University of North Carolina Press, 2005.

Rueda, Salvador. *El diablo de Semana Santa: El discurso político y el orden social en la Ciudad de México en 1850*. Mexico City: Instituto Nacional de Antropolgía e Historia, 1991.

Rugeley, Terry. *Maya Wars: Ethnographic Accounts from Nineteenth-Century Yucatan*. Norman: University of Oklahoma Press, 2001.

———. *Rebellion Now and Forever: Mayas, Hispanics and Caste War Violence in Yucatán, 1800–1880*. Stanford, CA: Stanford University Press, 2009.

———. *The River People in Flood Time: The Civil Wars in Tabasco, Spoiler of Empires*. Stanford, CA: Stanford University Press, 2014.

Ruiz Gutiérrez, Paola. *Federalismo y descentralización en la Nueva Granada: Autonomía local y poder municipal en la constitución del Estado, 1848–1863*. Bogotá: Uniandes, 2021.

Rus, Jan. "Whose Caste War? Indians, Ladinos and the Chiapas 'Caste War' of 1869." In *Spaniards and Indians in Southeastern Mesoamerica: Essays on the History of Ethnic Relations*, edited by Murdo J. MacLeod and Robert Wasserstorm, 127–68. Lincoln: University of Nebraska Press, 1983.

Saavedra Casco, Arturo. "Un episodio olvidado de la historia de México: El batallón sudanés en la Guerra de Intervención y el Segundo Imperio (1862–1867)." *Estudios de Asia y África* 46, no. 3 (2011): 709–35.

Sabato, Hilda. *La política en las calles: Entre el voto y la movilización. Buenos Aires, 1862–1880*. Buenos Aires: Sudamericana, 1998.

———. *Las repúblicas del Nuevo Mundo: El experimento político latinoamericano del siglo XIX*. Buenos Aires: Penguin Random House, 2021.

Sabato, Hilda, and Alberto Lettieri. *La vida política en la Argentina del siglo XIX: Armas, votos y voces*. Buenos Aires: Fondo de Cultura Económica, 2003.

Sainlaude, Stève. *France and the American Civil War: A Diplomatic History*. Chapel Hill: University of North Carolina Press, 2019.

Saldívar, Gabriel, ed. *La misión confidencial de Jesús Terán en Europa, 1863–1866*. Mexico City: Secretaría de Relaciones Exteriores, 1974.

Sánchez, Evelyne. "Los proyectos de colonización bajo el Segundo Imperio y el fortalecimiento del Estado mexicano." *Historia Mexicana* 63, no. 2 (2013): 689–743.

Sánchez de Tagle, Esteban. "Un protectorado americano para la Ciudad de México." *Relaciones: Estudios de historia y sociedad* 22, no. 86 (2001): 210–48.

Sanders, James E. *The Vanguard of the Atlantic World: Creating Modernity, Nation and Democracy in Nineteenth-Century Latin America*. Durham, NC: Duke University Press, 2014.

Santoni, Pedro. *Mexicans at Arms: Puro Federalists and the Politics of War, 1845–1848*. Fort Worth: Texas Christian University Press, 1996.

———. "'Where Did the Other Heroes Go?' Exalting the *Polko* National Guard Battalions in Nineteenth-Century Mexico." *Journal of Latin American Studies* 34, no. 4 (2002): 807–44.

Scarfi, Juan Pablo. *The Hidden History of International Law in the Americas: Empire and Legal Networks*. Oxford: Oxford University Press, 2017.

Schlereth, Eric S. "Privileges of Locomotion: Expatriation and the Politics of Southwestern Border Crossing." *Journal of American History* 100, no. 4 (2014): 995–1020.

———. "Voluntary Mexicans: Allegiance and the Origins of the Texas Revolution." In *Contested Empire: Rethinking the Texas Revolution*, edited by Sam W. Haynes and Gerald D. Saxon, 13–41. College Station: Texas A&M University Press, 2015.

Schoen, Brian, Jewel L. Spangler, and Frank Towers, eds. *Continent in Crisis: The U.S. Civil War in North America*. New York: Fordham University Press, 2023.

Schoonover, Thomas. *Dollars over Dominion: The Triumph of Liberalism in Mexican–United States Relations, 1861–1867*. Baton Rouge: Louisiana State University, 1978.

———, ed. *A Mexican View of America in the 1860s: A Foreign Diplomat Describes Civil War and Reconstruction*. Plainsboro, NJ: Dickinson University Press, Associated University Press, 1991.

———, ed. and trans. *Mexican Lobby: Matías Romero in Washington, 1861–1867*. Lexington: University Press of Kentucky, 1986.

Scott, Rebecca J. "Derechos y honra públicos: Louis Martinent, Plessy contra Ferguson y el acceso a la ley en Luisiana, 1888–1917." *Debate y perspectivas* 4 (2004): 171–97.

———. "Discerning a Dignitary Offense: The Concept of Equal 'Public Rights' During Reconstruction." *Law and History Review* 38, no. 3 (2020): 519–53.

Segura Muñoz, Iván. "La casa hecha cuartel: La transformación socio-espacial de la Ciudad de México y Guadalajara a causa de la ocupación militar durante la Intervención francesa (1862–1867)." PhD diss., Universidad de Guadalajara, forthcoming.

Serrano, José Antonio. "El humo en discordia: Los gobiernos estatales, el gobierno nacional y el estanco del tabaco (1824–1836)." In *Hacienda y política: Las finanzas públicas y los grupos de poder en la Primera República Federal mexicana*, edited by José Antonio Serrano and Luis Jauregui, 203–27. Mexico City: Instituto de Investigaciones Dr. José María Luis Mora; Zamora: El Colegio de Michoacán, 1998.

———. *Igualdad, uniformidad y proporcionalidad: Contribuciones directas y reformas fiscales en México, 1810–1846*. Zamora: El Colegio de Michoacán; Mexico City: Instituto de Investigaciones Dr. José María Luis Mora, 2007.

Serrano, José Antonio, and Luis Jauregui. Introduction to *Hacienda y política: Las finanzas públicas y los grupos de poder en la Primera República Federal mexicana*, edited by José Antonio Serrano and Luis Jauregui, 9–20. Mexico City: Instituto de Investigaciones Dr. José María Luis Mora; Zamora: El Colegio de Michoacán, 1998.

Serrano, Sol. *¿Qué hacer con Dios en la República? Política y secularización en Chile (1845–1885)*. Santiago: Fondo de Cultura Económica, 2008.

Sexton, Jay. *Debtor Diplomacy: Finance and American Foreign Relations in the Civil War Era, 1837–1873*. Oxford, UK: Clarendon, 2014.

———. *The Monroe Doctrine: Empire and Nation in Nineteenth-Century America*. New York: Hill and Wang, 2015.

Shawcross, Edward. *France, Mexico and Informal Empire in Latin America, 1820–1867: Equilibrium in the New World*. Cambridge: Cambridge University Press, 2018.

Shelden, Rachel A. "Measures for a Speedy Conclusion: A Reexamination of Conscription and Civil War Federalism." *Civil War History* 55, no. 4 (2009): 469–98.

Shelden, Rachel A., and Erik B. Alexander. "Dismantling the Party System: Party Fluidity and the Mechanisms of Nineteenth Century U.S. Politics." *Journal of American History* 110, no. 3 (2023): 419–48.

Silber, Nina. *Daughters of the Union: Northern Women Fight the Civil War*. Cambridge, MA: Harvard University Press, 2005.

Silva Riquer, Jorge, and Jesús López Martínez. "La organización fiscal alcabalatoria de la Ciudad de México, 1824–1835." In *Hacienda y política: Las finanzas públicas y los grupos de poder en la Primera República Federal mexicana*, edited by José Antonio Serrano and Luis Jauregui, 265–90. Mexico City: Instituto de Investigaciones Dr. José María Luis Mora; Zamora: El Colegio de Michoacán, 1998.

Sinkin, Richard. *The Mexican Reform, 1855–1876: A Study in Liberal Nation-Building*. Austin: University of Texas Press, 1979.

Sisneros, Manuel. "Los Emigrantes Nuevomexicanos: The 1849 Repatriation to Guadalupe and San Ignacio, Chihuahua, Mexico." MA thesis, University of Texas at El Paso, 2001.

Smith, Adam I. P. *The Stormy Present: Conservatism and the Problem of Slavery in Northern Politics, 1846–1865*. Chapel Hill: University of North Carolina Press, 2017.

Smith, Benjamin T. *The Roots of Conservatism in Mexico: Catholicism, Society, and Politics in the Mixteca Baja, 1750–1962*. Albuquerque: New Mexico University Press, 2012.

Smith, Emmaline. "They Went to the Field and Were Forgotten: Female Civil War Soldiers in Public Memory." MA thesis, University of South Carolina, 2016.

Smith, Ralph A. "El contrabando en la guerra con Estados Unidos." *Historia Mexicana* 11, no. 3 (1962): 361–81.
Soberanes, José Luis, and Carmen-José Alejos Grau. *Las leyes de Reforma y su aplicación en México*. Mexico City: Universidad Nacional Autónoma de México, 2021.
Sommer, Doris. *Foundational Fictions: The National Romances of Latin America*. Berkeley: University of California Press, 1993.
Sordo Cedeño, Reynaldo. *El Congreso en la Primera República Centralista*. Mexico City: El Colegio de México, 1993.
———. "El Congreso y la guerra con Estados Unidos, 1846–1848." In *México al tiempo de su guerra con Estados Unidos (1846–1848)*, edited by Josefina Z. Vázquez, 47–103. Mexico City: El Colegio de México, Fondo de Cultura Económica, Secretaría de Relaciones Exteriores, 1998.
Soto, Miguel. *La conspiración monárquica en México, 1845–1846*. Mexico City: EOSA, 1988.
Spangler, Jewel L., and Frank Towers, eds. *Remaking North American Sovereignty: State Transformation in the 1860s*. New York: Fordham University Press, 2021.
Sperber, Jonathan. *The European Revolutions, 1848–1851*. Cambridge: Cambridge University Press, 2005.
Stealy, John Edmund, III. "West Virginia's Constitutional Critique of Virginia: The Revolution of 1861–1863." *Civil War History* 58, no. 1 (2011): 9–47.
St. John, Rachel. *Line in the Sand: A History of the Western U.S.-Mexico Border*. Princeton, NJ: Princeton University Press, 2011.
———. "The Unpredictable America of William Gwin: Expansion, Secession, and the Unstable Borders of Nineteenth-Century North America." *Journal of the Civil War Era* 6, no. 1 (2016): 56–84.
Strobel, Héctor. "El Ejército de Oriente y los límites de patriotismo, 1861–1863." *Secuencia: Revista de Historia y Ciencias Sociales* 114 (2022): 1–34.
———. *El ejército liberal en la Reforma: Guardia nacional, fuerzas militares y movilización popular, 1854–1861*. Mexico City: Fondo de Cultura Económica, forthcoming.
———. "La artillería liberal en la Reforma, o de fundir campanas para fabricar cañones." *Tzintzun: Revista de Estudios Históricos* 77 (2023): 97–122.
———. *Resistir es vencer: Historia militar de la Intervención francesa en México, 1862–1867*. Mexico City: Universidad Nacional Autónoma de México, Grano de Sal, 2024.
Suárez Argüello, Ana Rosa. "Al servicio de la República: Los exiliados liberales mexicanos en Nueva York y su relación con Matías Romero." In *La construcción de un vínculo: Matías Romero entre México y Estados Unidos, 1860–1898*, edited by Gerardo Gurza, 93–127. Mexico City: CONAHCYT, Instituto de Investigaciones Dr. José María Luis Mora; Zamora: El Colegio de Michoacán, 2023.
———. "Contra el execrable e ignominioso Tratado McLane–Ocampo: La reacción conservadora frente a las relaciones entre Estados Unidos y el gobierno liberal." *Historia Mexicana* 72, no. 4 (2023): 1857–97.
———. "De los esclavos fugitivos a los santuarios: Los límites entre el poder federal y el estatal." In *Descifrando a Trump desde la historia*, edited by Ana Rosa Suárez Argüello, 127–54. Mexico City: Instituto de Investigaciones Dr. José María Luis Mora, CONACYT, 2020.
———. *El camino de Tehuantepec: De la visión a la quiebra (1854–1861)*. Mexico City: Instituto de Investigaciones Dr. José María Luis Mora, 2013.
———. *Un viaje a Nueva York en tiempos de guerra*. Mexico City: Malix, 2023.
Suárez de la Torre, Laura, and Miguel Ángel Castro, eds. *Empresa y cultura en tinta y papel*

(1800–1860). Mexico City: Instituto de Investigaciones Dr. José María Luis Mora, Universidad Nacional Autónoma de México, 2001.

Sutton, Robert K. *Stark Mad Abolitionists: Lawrence, Kansas, and the Battle over Slavery in the Civil War Era*. New York: Skyhorse, 2017.

Sweeney, Lean. "Sobre su cadáver: Diplomacia entre México y Estados Unidos y la ejecución de Maximiliano de Habsburgo en México, 19 de junio de 1867." *Historia Mexicana* 68, no. 4 (2019): 1639–1696.

Sweet, Jameson. "Native Suffrage: Race, Citizenship, and Dakota Indians in the Upper Midwest." *Journal of the Early Republic* 39 (2019): 99–109.

Syrett, John. *The Civil War Confiscation Acts: Failing to Reconstruct the South*. New York: Fordham University, 2005.

Tafolla, Santiago. *A Life Crossing Borders: Memoir of a Mexican American Confederate / Las memorias de un mexicanoamericano en la Confederación*, edited by Carmen and Laura Tafolla. Houston: Arte Público, 2010. Kindle.

Taibo, Paco Ignacio, II. *Patria*. 3 vols. Mexico City: Planeta, 2017.

Tapia, Regina. "Competencia electoral: Honor y prensa. México en 1857." In *Prensa y elecciones: Formas de hacer política en el México del siglo XIX*, edited by Fausta Gantús and Alicia Salmerón, 55–77. Mexico City: Instituto de Investigaciones Dr. José María Luis Mora, 2014.

Taracena, Arturo. *De héroes olvidados: Santiago Imán, los huites y los antecedentes bélicos de la Guerra de Castas*. Mexico City: Universidad Nacional Autónoma de México, 2015.

Taylor, Alan. *American Civil Wars: A Continental History, 1850–1873*. New York: W. W. Norton, 2024.

Taylor Hansen, Lawrence Douglas. "Voluntarios extranjeros en los ejércitos liberales mexicanos, 1854–1867." *Historia Mexicana* 37, no. 2 (1987): 205–37.

Tenenbaum, Barbara A. *México en la época de los agiotistas, 1821–1857*. Mexico City: Fondo de Cultura Económica, 1985.

Tenorio, Mauricio. *Artilugio de la nación moderna: México en las exposiciones universales, 1880–1930*. Mexico City: Fondo de Cultura Económica, 1999.

———. *Latin America: The Allure and Power of an Idea*. Chicago: University of Chicago Press, 2017.

———. *La paz, 1876*. Mexico City: Fondo de Cultura Económica, 2018.

———. "On the Limits of Historical Imagination: North America as a Historical Essay." *International Journal* 61, no. 3 (2006): 567–87.

———. "The Riddle of a Common History: The United States in Mexican Textbook Controversies." *Journal of Educational Media, Memory and Society* 1, no. 1 (2009): 93–116.

Terrazas y Basante, Marcela. "¿Dónde quedó la doctrina Monroe? Estados Unidos ante la Intervención francesa en México." In *El poder y la sangre: Guerra, estado y nación en la década de 1860*, edited by Guillermo Palacios and Erika Pani, 367–94. Mexico City: El Colegio de México, 2014.

———. *Inversiones, especulación y diplomacia: Las relaciones entre México y los Estados Unidos durante la dictadura santannista*. Mexico City: Universidad Nacional Autónoma de México, 2000.

———. *Los intereses norteamericanos en el noroeste de México: La gestión diplomática de Thomas Corwin, 1861–1864*. Mexico City: Universidad Nacional Autónoma de México, 1990.

———. "Miseria hacendaria y crisis revolucionaria: Espacios para una 'diplomacia de la anexión.' La gestión de James Gadsen en México." In *Embajadores de Estados Unidos*

en México: Diplomacia de crisis y oportunidades, edited by Roberta Lajous, Erika Pani, Paolo Riguzzi, and María Celia Toro, 69–94. Mexico City: El Colegio de México, Secretaría de Relaciones Exteriores, 2021.
Terrazas y Basante, Marcela, Gerardo Gurza Lavalle, Paolo Riguzzi, and Patricia de los Ríos. *Las relaciones México–Estados Unidos, 1756–2010*. 2 vols. Mexico City: Universidad Nacional Autónoma de México, Secretaría de Relaciones Exteriores, 2012.
Thibaud, Clément. "Para una historia policéntrica de los republicanismos atlánticos (1770–1880)." *Prismas: Revista de Historia Intelectual* 23 (2019): 145–62.
Thomas, Emory M. *The Confederate Nation: 1861–1865*. New York: Harper Torch, 1979.
Thompson, E. P. *Whigs and Hunters: The Origin of the Black Act*. New York: Pantheon, 1975.
Thompson, Jerry D. *Cortina: Defending the Mexican Name in Texas*. College Station: Texas A&M University Press, 2007. Kindle.
———. *Tejano Tiger: José de los Santos Benavides and the Texas-Mexico Borderlands, 1823–1891*. Fort Worth: Texas Christian University Press, 2017. Kindle.
———. *Vaqueros in Blue and Gray*. College Station: Texas A&M University Press, McWhiney Foundation, 2000.
Thompson, Jerry D., ed. *Tejanos in Gray: Civil War Letters of Captains Joseph Rafael de la Garza and Manuel Yturri*. College Station: Texas A&M University Press, 2011.
Thomson, Guy P. C. "Memoirs and Memories of the European Intervention in the Sierra de Puebla, 1868– 1991." In *Mexican Soundings: Essays in Honour of David A. Brading*, edited by Eric Van Young and Susan Deans-Smith, 169–92. London: Institute of Latin American Studies, 2007.
Thomson, Guy P. C., ed. *The European Revolutions and the Americas*. London: Institute of Latin American Studies, 2002.
Thomson, Guy P. C. with David G. LaFrance. *Patriotism, Politics, and Popular Liberalism in Nineteenth-Century Mexico: Juan Francisco Lucas and the Puebla Sierra*. Lanham, MD: Rowman and Littlefield, 2001.
Timmons, Joe T. "The Referendum in Texas on the Ordinance of Secession, February 23, 1861: The Vote." *East Texas Historical Journal* 11, no. 2 (1973): 12–28.
Tinker Salas, Miguel. *In the Shadow of the Eagles: Sonora and the Transformation of the Border During the Porfiriato*. Berkeley: University of California Press, 1997.
———. "Los dos Nogales." In *Encuentro en la frontera: Mexicanos y norteamericanos en un espacio común*, edited by Manuel Ceballos, 259–79. Mexico City: El Colegio de México; Ciudad Victoria: El Colegio de la Frontera Norte, Universidad Autónoma de Tamaulipas, 2001.
Topik, Steven C. "Controversia crediticia: Los 'azulitos' del periodo de Maximiliano." In *Los negocios y las ganancias, de la Colonia al México moderno*, edited by Leonor Ludlow and Jorge Silva-Riquer, 445–70. Mexico City: Instituto de Investigaciones Dr. José María Luis Mora, Universidad Nacional Autónoma de México, 1993.
Torget, Andrew J. *Seeds of Empire: Cotton, Slavery, and the Transformation of the Texas Borderlands, 1800–1850*. Chapel Hill: University of North Carolina Press, 2018.
Toussaint, Mónica, and Mario Vázquez Olivera. *Territorio, nación y soberanía: Matías Romero ante el conflicto de límites entre México y Guatemala*. Mexico City: Secretaría de Relaciones Exteriores, 2012.
Tovar Mota, Valentina. "José María Carvajal y la construcción del Estado nacional en la frontera norestense, 1859." *Estudios de Historia Moderna y Contemporánea de México* 63 (2023): 5–33.

Towers, Frank. "Partisans, New History, and Modernization: The Historiography of the Civil War's Causes, 1861–2011." *Journal of the Civil War Era* 1, no. 2 (2011): 237–64.

Tracy, Joshua T. "The 'Mexicanization' of the United States: Mexico in U.S. Public Discourse, 1862–1880." MA thesis, Texas Tech University, 2014.

Trejo, Zulema. *Redes, facciones y liberalismo: Sonora, 1850–1876*. Hermosillo: El Colegio de Sonora; Zamora: El Colegio de Michoacán, 2012.

Truett, Samuel. *Fugitive Landscapes: The Forgotten History of the U.S.-Mexico Borderlands*. New Haven, CT: Yale University Press, 2006.

Truett, Samuel, and Elliott Young, eds. *Continental Crossroads: Remapping U.S.-Mexico Borderlands History*. Durham, NC: Duke University Press, 2004.

Tyler, R. Curtis. "Santiago Vidaurri and the Confederacy." *The Americas* 26, no. 1 (1969): 66–76.

Ugalde, Alejandro. "*Maintenant c'est la bataille!* Diego Rivera y el muralismo mexicano en Nueva York, 1933–1934." *Nierika: Revista de Arte Ibero* 4 (2013): 8–22.

Uhthoff, Luz María. "La difícil concurrencia fiscal y la contribución federal, 1861–1924: Notas preliminares." *Historia Mexicana* 54, no. 1 (2004): 129–78.

Ural, Susannah J. *Civil War Citizens: Race, Ethnicity and Identity in America's Bloodiest Conflicts*. New York: New York University Press, 2010.

Valdés, Hugo. *Fulguración y disolvencia de Santiago Vidaurri*. Mexico City: Instituto Nacional de Estudios Históricos de las Revoluciones de México, 2017.

Valerio Jiménez, Omar S. "Although We Are the Last Soldiers: Citizenship, Ideology and Tejano Unionism." In *Lone Star Unionism, Dissent, and Resistance: Other Sides of Civil War Texas*, edited by Jesús F. de la Teja, 123–45. Norman: University of Oklahoma Press, 2016.

———. *Remembering Conquest: Mexican Americans, Memory and Citizenship*. Chapel Hill: University of North Carolina Press, 2024.

———. *River of Hope: Forging Identity and Nation in the Río Grande Borderlands*. Durham, NC: Duke University Press, 2013.

Valéry, Paul. *Les fruits amers de la démocratie*. Paris: Espaces et Signes, 2017.

Van Alstyne, William W. "The Fourteenth Amendment, the 'Right' to Vote and the Understanding of the Thirty-Ninth Congress." *Supreme Court Review*, 1965, 33–86.

Van Hoy, Teresa. "Mexican Exiles and the Monroe Doctrine, New York and the Borderlands." *Camino Real* 7, no. 10 (2015): 39–60.

Van Osterhout, K. Aaron. "Confraternities and Popular Conservatism on the Frontier: Mexico's Sierra del Nayarit in the Nineteenth Century." *The Americas* 71, no. 1 (2014): 101–30.

———. "Popular Conservatism in Mexico: Religion, Land and Popular Politics in Nayarit and Querétaro, 1750–1873." PhD diss., Michigan State University, 2014.

Varon, Elizabeth. *Disunion! The Coming of the American Civil War, 1789–1859*. Chapel Hill: University of North Carolina Press, 2008.

Vázquez, Josefina Z. "Los primeros tropiezos." In *Historia general de México*, 525–82. Mexico City: El Colegio de México, 2000.

———. *Nacionalismo y educación en México*. Mexico City: El Colegio de México, 1975.

Vázquez Mantecón, Carmen. *Santa Anna y la encrucijada del Estado: La dictadura (1853–1855)*. Mexico City: Fondo de Cultura Económica, 1986.

Veliz, Claudio. *The New World of the Gothic Fox: Culture and Economy in English and Spanish America*. Berkeley: University of California Press, 1994.

Villalobos, Rebeca. *El culto a Juárez: La construcción retórica del héroe (1872–1976)*. Mexico City: Universidad Nacional Autónoma de México, Grano de Sal, 2020.

Villalpando, José Manuel. *Maximiliano frente sus jueces*. Mexico City: Escuela Libre de Derecho, 1993.
Villarreal Lozano, Javier. *Cartas de Querétaro: Saltillenses en la caída del Imperio*. Saltillo: H. Ayuntamiento de Saltillo, Archivo Municipal de Saltillo, Instituto Municipal de Cultura, 2005.
Villavicencio Navarro, Víctor. *"Y mucho más libre y feliz que una república": El monarquismo mexicano decimonónico. Momentos, proyectos, personajes*. Mexico City: Instituto Tecnológico Autónomo de México, Instituto Nacional de Estudios Históricos de las Revoluciones de México, 2023.
Villegas Revueltas, Silvestre. "Charles Wyke y su misión en el México juarista." *Estudios de Historia Moderna y Contemporánea* 32 (2006): 6–33.
———. *El liberalismo moderado en México, 1852–1864*. Mexico City: Universidad Nacional Autónoma de México, 1997.
Voekel, Pamela. *For God and Liberty: Catholicism and Democracy in the Atlantic World in the Age of Revolution*. Oxford: Oxford University Press, 2022.
———. "Liberal Religion: The Schism of 1861." In *Religious Culture in Modern Mexico*, edited by Martin A. Nesvig, 78–105. Lanham, MD: Rowman and Littlefield, 2007.
Vorenberg, Michael. *The Emancipation Proclamation: A Brief History with Documents*. Boston: Bedford / St. Martin's, 2010. Ebook.
———. *Final Freedom: The Civil War, the Abolition of Slavery, and the Thirteenth Amendment*. Cambridge: Cambridge University Press, 2001.
Waldstreicher, David. *In the Midst of Perpetual Fetes: The Making of American Nationalism, 1776–1820*. Chapel Hill: University of North Carolina Press, 1997.
Weeks, Charles A. *The Juarez Myth in Mexico*. Tuscaloosa: University of Alabama Press, 1987.
Werner, Michael, and Bénédicte Zimmermann. "Penser l'histoire croisée: Entre empirie et réflexivité." *Annales: Histoire, Sciences Sociales* 58, no. 1 (2003): 7–36.
Wilentz, Sean. *No Property in Man: Slavery and Antislavery at the Nation's Founding*. Cambridge, MA: Harvard University Press, 2018.
Wilson, Charles Reagan. "Religion and the American Civil War in Comparative Perspective." In *Religion and the American Civil War*, edited by Randall M. Miller, Harry S. Stout, and Charles Reagan Wilson, 385–407. New York: Oxford University Press, 1998.
Winders, Richard Bruce. *Mr. Polk's Army: The American Military Experience in the Mexican War, 1846–1848*. College Station: Texas A&M University Press, 1997.
Witt, John Fabian. *Lincoln's Code: The Laws of War in American History*. New York: Free Press, 2012.
Wobeser, Gisela von. "La Consolidación de Vales Reales como factor determinante de la lucha de independencia en México, 1804–1808." *Historia Mexicana* 56, no. 2 (2006): 373–425.
Wolff, Gerald. "The Slavocracy and the Homestead Problem of 1854." *Agricultural History* 40, no. 2 (1966): 101–12.
Woods, Michael E. "What Twenty-First-Century Historians Have Said About the Causes of Disunion: A Civil War Sesquicentennial Review of the Recent Literature." *Journal of American History* 99, no. 2 (2012): 415–39.
Zeltsman, Corinna. *Ink Under the Fingernails: Printing Politics in Nineteenth-Century Mexico*. Berkeley: University of California Press, 2021.

INDEX

Alabama, 29, 82, 85
Alamán, Lucas, 56, 62, 175
Altamirano, Ignacio Manuel, 153, 188
Appomattox, Battle of, 103, 203, 231
Arista, Mariano, 47, 61
Arizona, 162–63
Arkansas, 82, 169
Armijo, Manuel, 32, 245n75
Arriaga, Ponciano, 113, 123–24
Arrieta, José Agustín, 188–89
Arrillaga, Basilio, 139
Arteaga, José María, 154
Austria, 19, 136
Ayutla (*pronunciamiento*, revolution of), 63, 91, 105, 109, 116

Bagdad, Tamaulipas, 158, 222, 271n134
Baja California, 208–13, 257n83
Baltimore, MD, 55
Barton, Clara, 190
Baz, Juan José, 64, 70
Bell, John, 56
Benavides, Santos, 161–62, 221, 272n149
Bent, Charles, 33
Bigelow, John, 220
Bingham, John A., 118
bonds, 20, 31, 126, 195-198, 224, 234
Brown, John, 1–3, 54
Brown, Joseph E., 182
Brownsville, TX, 159, 222
Buchanan, James, 27, 122, 212
Burns, Anthony, 54

Cahuenga Treaty (1847), 33
Calhoun, John C., 23, 28, 40, 65, 86, 141, 248n33
California, 22–23, 32–36, 51–53, 65–66, 158, 160–63, 208
Calpulalpan, Battle of, 111, 144, 152
Calvo, Carlos, 229, 287, 290

Campbell, Lewis, 233
Campeche, 38, 157
Canada, 4–5, 132, 218, 226, 237, 251n112
Carlota (empress of Mexico), 96, 160, 189
Carvajal, José María, 197
Cass, Lewis, 243
Caste War (1848–1903), 38–43; Chan Santa Cruz (rebel capital), 38, 165
Castillo Velasco, José María, 123–24
Castro, Casimiro, 188
Central America, Federal Republic of, 48
Cerro de las Campanas, Querétaro, 231
Chacón, Rafael, 144, 162–63
Chalchicomula, Puebla, 154
Charles I (king of Spain). *See* Charles V (Holy Roman emperor)
Charles V (Holy Roman emperor), 96, 165
Charleston, SC, 13, 55, 289
Chase, Samuel P., 50, 196–98
Chesnut, James, 86
Chevalier, Michel, 291
Chi, Cecilio, 39
Chihuahua, 23
Chile, 215, 219
Chivington, John, 167–68
Christiana, PA, 251
Churubusco, Battle of, 30
Cincinnati platform (1856), 55
Clay, Henry, 11, 53
Clementi, Luis 137
Coahuila, 23, 92; annexed to Nuevo León, 157
Colorado, 107, 167–68
Comonfort, Ignacio, 63, 70–72, 75, 91, 139, 153, 178, 193, 209
Conservative Party (Mexico): defeats of, 16, 63–64, 233–34; ideas of, 46, 57–60; and political regimes, 12–13, 61–63, 75–80, 89–98, 211–13; at war, 70–71, 133–35, 151–54, 159, 178–79, 182–86, 195–96

constitution, 139–45; constitutionalism in political culture, 5–8, 15, 46–50, 69, 172–76, 184, 210, 215–17, 232–34; 1836 constitution (Mexico), 30, 116, 141, 173; 1857 constitution (Mexico), 12–14, 59–64, 75–76, 107–11, 261n49, 263n89; implementation of, 5, 45, 65, 172–73; interpretation of, 24, 28–29, 35–36, 51–52, 67–69; and reform, 60–64, 70–72, 80–101, 111–13, 114–21, 122–28, 134–40, 149–51; state constitutions, 41–43, 67, 187–88
Cooke, Jay, 198
Corona, Ramón, 169
Cortina, Juan N., 222–23
Corwin, Thomas, 212–14
Crittenden, John J., 71
Cuba, 3, 212
Cuevas, Luis G., 92–93, 282n10

Davis, Jefferson, 52–53, 71, 83, 145–49, 179, 222, 228, 232–35, 246
debt, 176, 193–201, 195–98, 226–28; in Mexico, 13, 76, 92, 110, 174–76, 200, 213–14, 279n126; in the United States, 88, 113, 118, 126, 174–75, 216, 280n139. *See also* bonds
Degollado, Santos, 94, 135, 152, 154, 178, 196, 268n66
DeJarnette, Daniel C., 220
Democratic Party (United States): dissention within, 28, 50–56, 67–68; on issues of expansion and territorial governance, 160–62, 168, 188, 212, 263n80; resistance to Reconstruction, 233; on the soldiers' vote, 278n91; on violence, 249n54
d'Erlanger, Émile, 197
Díaz, Porfirio, 185, 231
Díaz de Bonilla, Manuel, 249
Dix, Dorothea, 190
Dixon, James, 262
Doblado, Manuel, 138, 213–14
Dominican Republic, 215
Dorr, Thomas, 42–43
Douglas, Stephen E., 50–56, 66–68, 211
Douglass, Frederick, 65, 69
Drouyn de Lhuys, Édouard, 216
Dupin, Charles-Louis, 145–46
Durango, 23–24

Echeagaray, Miguel María, 92, 133
Elder, William H., 138
Escobedo, Mariano, 179
Europe, 27, 37, 58, 84, 214–15, 220, 229

Flagg, Azariah C., 50
Flotte, Paul de, 117
Forey, Élie, 183, 186
Forsyth, John, 209
France, 19, 37, 40, 84, 98, 160, 186, 225, 228, 252
Fries, John, 174

Gadsden, James, 208
Galicia Chimalpopoca, Faustino, 100
Garza, Joseph Rafael de la, 163
Georgia, 71, 82, 147, 182, 253, 269n89, 278n85
Glorieta Pass, Battle of, 162
Gómez, Manuel Eleuterio, 136
Gómez Farías, Valentín, 142
González Ortega, Jesús, 106, 111, 144, 152, 179
Gran Colombia, 48
Grant, Ulysses S., 11, 103, 159, 203, 219, 223, 227, 231
Great Britain, 41, 87, 197, 228, 249; British Honduras, 38–40; British North America (*see* Canada)
Great Salt Lake, 66
Guadalajara, Jalisco, 61, 159, 165, 179, 191–92
Guadalupe Hidalgo, Treaty of, 19, 23–27, 32, 34–36, 51–53, 158
Guanajuato, Guanajuato, 154
Guaymas (port), 210
Guerra, Pablo de la, 35–36
Guerrero, 62

Hale, John P., 27, 29, 52
Hall, William A., 77
Halleck, Henry, 145
Hammond, James H., 122
Harris, Isham, 155
Hilliard, Henry, 29
Holmes, Oliver W., 72
Houston, Sam, 40–41, 82
Howe, Julia, 187
Hugo, Victor, 3

Indigenous peoples, 24–28, 53, 131, 156–160, 163–70, 208, 268n66
— in Mexico, 62, 92, 177, 271n136, 273n159; Liberal visions of, 123–24; Maximilian's vision of, 79, 100–101; and the war, 135, 144, 154
— in the United States, 32–36, 128, 166–69, 244n68, 274n180, 274n181, 278n95; Dakota War (1862), 167–68; Sand Creek Massacre, 167–68
Iturbide, Agustín, 13, 80, 92

Jalisco, 164, 169
Jecker, Juan Bautista, 195
Jefferson, Thomas, 108, 117
Johnson, Andrew, 107, 112, 118, 222, 233
Jomini, Antoine-Henri de, 176
Juárez, Benito, 3; during the French Intervention, 76, 143; policies of, 99, 104–6, 111, 125, 137, 152–53, 198–200, 228, 232; during the Reform War, 12, 75, 95, 193; and the United States, 210–14, 218–21, 223–25

Kansas, 66–67, 107, 249, 251, 289; Lecompton constitution, 67
Kearny, Stephen, 32–33
Kentucky, 56, 82, 155

Labastida y Dávalos, Pelagio A., 95, 233
La Carbonera, Battle of, 185
La Mesa, Battle of, 33
La Mesilla Treaty, 208
Laredo, TX, 16
law of nations: importance of, to Latin American republics, 229–30; to legitimize social hierarchies, 77, 91 120, 150; as part of political culture 14, 26, 32, 38, 53; in war, 143–47, 195, 215–18, 221, 224;
Leavitt, Joshua, 220, 228
Lee, Robert E., 22, 32, 39, 197, 203, 205, 231
Leftwich, William M., 139
Lerdo de Tejada, Miguel, 60, 124–26, 174
Lerdo de Tejada, Sebastián, 226
Liberal Party (Mexico), 2–3, 31, 50; and the 1857 constitution, 12, 45, 70, 75–76, 90–91, 104–11, 115–18, 121–28, 165, 199–200; and the empire, 98, 101; identified as "republican," 99, 180, 192, 199, 228–30, 233, 238; and partisan rhetoric, 56–63, 191–93; *puros*, 25–28, 31, 63, 106, 115, 259n14, 243n43; and the United States, 212–13, 224, 217–26; and the war, 94–95, 133–38, 144–46, 151–55, 157–59, 167–68, 177–79, 183–86, 196, 233–34
Lieber, Francis, 65, 71, 112, 127, 145, 162, 228
Lincoln, Abraham, 1, 3, 103, 118, 231; election of, 56, 82, 132–34; and Mexico, 212; and slavery, 118, 126, 198; and the war, 75, 167, 179–81, 217–20
Livermore, Mary, 190
London, 174, 198, 216
López de Santa Anna, Antonio, 20, 62–64, 105, 141, 157, 178, 187
López Uraga, José, 178
Lorencez, Charles de, 183
Louisiana, 29, 71, 82, 85, 138
Louis-Philippe (king of France), 19
loyalty, 5, 14, 21, 31–32, 52, 82, 101, 126, 132, 139–40, 144–50, 157–60. *See also* oath
Lozada, Manuel, 159, 165, 169

MacDougall, James A., 219
Machiavelli, Niccolò, 193
Madison, James, 7
Madrid, 210
Manet, Édouard, 13
Marcy, William L., 33, 50
Márquez, Leonardo, 145, 196
Marx, Karl, 2–3, 9
Mascota, Jalisco, 186
Mata, José María, 199,
Mateos, Juan A., 188
Maximilian (emperor of Mexico), 13; execution of, 103, 232–33, 236; and foreign policy and debt, 187–98, 200, 227–28; visions of state and nation, 79, 95–102, 143, 152, 165, 188; and the war, 184, 220
Mayer, Edelmiro, 160
Maza de Juárez, Margarita, 191
Mazatlán, Sinaloa, 210
McLane, Robert M., 210–12
Meglia, Pedro Francisco, 138
Mejía, Tomás, 103, 135, 154, 159, 169, 183, 232

Méndez, Ramón, 155
Mérida, Yucatán, 38, 157, 165
Mexico City: as contested capital, 10, 12, 58–59, 76, 91, 131, 152, 157, 174–75, 199, 231; during the Mexican War, 20–23, 28, 31
Michoacán, 136, 144, 165, 294
Minnesota, 167–68
Miramón, Miguel, 75–77, 103, 143, 178
Miranda, Francisco J., 94–95
Miranda, Primitivo, 188
Mississippi, 71, 83
Missouri, 82, 156
Monroe, James, 40–41, 220–26
Monterrey, Nuevo León, 159, 222
Montgomery, AL, 83–86, 102, 194
Montoya, Pablo, 33
Moore, Isaac, 29
Moreno, Espiridión, 116
Morny, Charles Auguste Louis Joseph de, 195
Morrill, Justin, 201

Napoléon III (emperor of the French), 104; and the French Intervention in Mexico, 183–86, 207–8, 216–18; interest in the New World, 13, 76, 96–98, 220
Natchez, 138
Navarro, José Ángel, 163
Nayarit, 159, 165, 186
Nebraska, 66, 107
Nevada, 107, 162
New Mexico, 23, 32, 33, 35, 36, 158, 162–63, 208
New Orleans, LA, 194, 212
New York, 50, 215
Nogales, Sonora, 210
North America, 21, 238; and diplomacy, 212–15, 228–30; republican crisis, 10–12, 48, 61, 77; and war, 160, 165, 177, 193–97
North Carolina, 82
Nuevo León, 106, 157

oath, 31–33, 70, 91, 113, 139–40, 150, 174, 203, 234, 264n101. *See also* loyalty
Oaxaca, 49, 75, 159, 165, 186
Ocampo, Melchor, 99, 152–54, 210
Ohio, 40, 213

O'Horan, Tomás, 155
Ortega, Eulalio, 268n68
Otero, Mariano, 24, 245n75

Paris, 198, 220, 229
Parker, Ely S., 159
Paso del Norte, 10, 76
Pat, Jacinto, 39
Payno, Manuel, 124, 144, 153, 196–98, 229
Pérez Gallardo, Basilio, 192–93
Philadelphia, PA, 83, 87, 175
Pico, Andrés, 33, 162
Piedras Negras, Coahuila, 157
Pike, Albert, 166–67
Pimentel, Francisco, 164
Pitchlynn, Peter, 166
Pius IX (pope), 125
Polk, James K., 11, 19–24, 27–28, 40
Pomeroy, Samuel, 119
Pope, John, 168
Price, Sterling, 33
pronunciamiento, 48, 62, 72, 90, 105, 110, 117, 151, 153, 183
Puebla, 76, 144, 154, 159, 165, 186, 192
Puebla, Battle of, 3

Querétaro, 13, 43, 103, 164, 179, 186, 231–32
Quintana Roo, 38
Quintero, Agustín, 222–23

Ramírez, Agustina, 192
Ramírez, Ignacio, 124
recruitment, military, 19, 27, 30, 45, 106, 148, 172–79, 185–88, 268n66; draft laws, 92, 140, 159–61, 180–87, 224, 276n56, 277n57; forced impressment, 86, 148–49, 177, 184–86, 277n72
Régules, Nicolás, 192
Reichy, Ignacia, 191–92
religion, 31, 76–80, 132–35, 138–40; defense of, 12, 21, 24, 90–94, 125, 135–38, 177, 186–87; importance of, 60–62, 99, 266n22; and Liberal policies, 109, 115; in the United States, 54, 78, 140
Republican Party (United States), 134, 212, 259n12; on the constitution, 52–56, 68, 107, 111, 113, 118–19; 1860 presidential

election, 71–72, 81; and Mexico, 218–20; on slavery, 126–28, 264nn99–100; and the war, 149, 194, 278n9
Rhode Island, 21, 37, 41–43, 66
Richmond, VA, 10, 131, 194–95, 220
Rio Bravo (Rio Grande), 4; as border, 23–25, 28, 210, 224–25; as borderlands, 156–60, 194–96
Riva Palacios, Vicente, 144
Rivera, Diego, 1–2, 237
Robles Pezuela, Manuel, 154
Rome, 136–38
Romero, Matías, 197, 212, 214, 219, 225, 228, 237
Root, Joseph M., 40
Rosa, Luis de la, 37
Rousseau, Jean Jacques, 5

Salazar, Carlos, 154
Salazar Ilarregui, José, 157, 165
Salm-Salm, Felix de, 100
San Antonio, TX, 168
Sánchez Ochoa, Gaspar, 162
San Gabriel, Battle of, 33
San Luis Potosí, 143, 196
San Pascual, Battle of, 33
San Patricios, 30–31
Santa Barbara, CA, 35
Schofield, John, 224
Scott, Dred, 65, 67–68. See also *Scott v. Sanford*
Scott, Winfield, 20, 22–23, 31
Scott v. Sanford (1857), 12, 51, 55, 65–67, 141. See also Scott, Dred
Seward, William H., 45, 52, 56, 71, 159, 212–16, 226
Shelby, Joseph O., 223
Sheridan, Philip H., 223
Sherman, William T.,
Sierra del Nayar, 164
Sierra Gorda, 41–43, 164, 186
Sierra O'Reilly, Justo, 39
Slidell, John, 197
Sonoma, CA, 162
Sonora, 23, 49, 159, 165, 208
South Carolina, 57, 65, 71, 82–83
Spain, 3, 36, 38, 62, 84
Stephens, Alexander H., 77, 83, 252

Stevens, Thaddeus, 118–19
Stiles, William, 37
Suárez Iriarte, Francisco, 31
Suchiate River, 4
Sumner, Charles, 54, 119
Supreme Court: in Mexico, 25, 91–92, 97, 106–8, 115–16; in United States, 12, 41–43, 46, 51, 55, 65–69, 85–86, 119, 127, 140

Tabasco, 158
Tacámbaro, Michoacán, 144
Tamaulipas, 23
Taney, Roger, 43, 67–69
Tanori, Refugio, 159, 169
Taos, NM, 33
tariffs, 174–75, 193–94, 210, 222; in Mexico, 38, 57, 156–57, 198–200; in the United States, 52, 88, 141, 202. See also taxes
Taxco, Guerrero, 136
taxes, 35, 121, 141–42, 171–76, 193–95, 198, 203; in Mexico, 39, 57, 94, 99, 110, 123–24, 151, 174, 187, 199–201, 209, 213; in the United States, 20, 147–48, 201–3. See also tariffs
Taylor, Zachary, 22
Tehuantepec Isthmus, 208, 212–14
Tennessee, 56, 82, 155
Tepic, Nayarit, 165
Terán, Jesús, 218, 228
Testory, Louis, 139
Texas, 11, 21, 23, 30, 37, 66, 71, 82, 159, 156, 160, 162, 163
Thouvenel, Édouard, 216
Tocqueville, Alexis de, 117
Torres Caicedo, José María, 229
Trist, Nicholas, 23
Trumbull, Lyman, 119
Tyler, John, 71

Valdés, Manuel, 136
Vallandigham, Clement C. L., 180
Vallarta, Ignacio L, 116, 264n63
Valle, Leandro, 152–54
Vallejo, Mariano Guadalupe, 162
Valverde, Battle of, 162
Vance, Zebulon, 182,
Vattel, Emer de, 26, 215
Vega, Plácido, 162

Veracruz: as contested capital, 10, 75, 111, 131, 136, 179, 192–96, 200, 212; as an important port, 28, 76, 154, 183, 185, 210
Vicario, Juan, 183
Victoria, Guadalupe, 47–48
Vicuña Mackenna, Benjamín, 219, 226
Vidaurri, Santiago, 106, 154–57, 222
Vigil, Donaciano, 33
Vigil, Juan Bautista, 20, 32, 245n75
Virginia, 82, 155, 180

Wakeman, Thaddeus B., 127
Washington, DC, 10, 21–25, 67, 107, 131, 147–49, 155, 162, 166, 174–75, 195–97, 203, 210, 212, 216–20, 227–28, 233
Wheeling, WV, 155
Whig Party (United States), 11, 28, 40–42, 50–56
Williams, George Washington, 160
Wisconsin, 67
women, 109, 133, 144, 147–48, 168, 186–92, 222

Yancey, William L., 85
Yturri y Castillo, Manuel, 163
Yucatán, 30, 37–43, 66, 157, 164–65

Zamacona, Manuel María, 213
Zarco, Francisco, 59
Zuloaga, Félix, 91–95, 143, 153, 193–95

www.ingramcontent.com/pod-product-compliance
Lightning Source LLC
Chambersburg PA
CBHW030000240426
43672CB00007B/763